Set Fair for Roanoke

SIR WALTER RALEGH
From the Portrait in the National Gallery of Ireland, Dublin

DAVID BEERS QUINN

Set Fair for Roanoke
Voyages and Colonies, 1584-1606

Published for
America's Four Hundredth Anniversary Committee by
the University of North Carolina Press
Chapel Hill and London

© 1985 The University of North Carolina Press

Manufactured in the United States of America

First printing, January 1985
Second printing, February 1986

Library of Congress Cataloging in Publication Data

Quinn, David B.
Set fair for Roanoke.

Bibliography: p.
Includes index.
1. Raleigh's Roanoke colonies, 1584–1590. I. Title.
F229.Q56 1984   973.1   84-2345
ISBN 0-8078-1606-X
ISBN 0-8078-4123-4 pbk.

To the shade of Thomas Harriot

CONTENTS

I L L U S T R A T I O N S & M A P S

NOTE ON EDITING

It should be noted that dates used by Englishmen
are according to the Julian calendar,
which was ten days ahead of the Gregorian calendar,
adopted by Catholic Europe in 1582.
Where confusion might arise, double dating is given.
The year-date is always that of the calendar year.

Spelling and punctuation are modernized throughout.

PREFACE

This book intends to be a plain and relatively full story of the English voyages of exploration and colonization to North America between 1584 and 1590. Their central feature is the attempt to establish a colony of settlement on Roanoke Island, inside the Outer Banks of North Carolina and, later, on Chesapeake Bay. Roanoke Island stands very much at the center of the story, however. The colonizing activities, which provide the principal focus for the narrative, were combined with the exploration of a substantial part of the coastal region of North Carolina and extended into southern Virginia. It is possible to follow the explorers in detail while they mapped the region and described its natural resources. They also gave us for the first time a detailed view of the inhabitants, the Native Americans, Indians as for so long we have called them, and so enable us to discern something of their attitudes toward these people.

It is fortunate that the contemporary published documents are so full and so good as they are. They, themselves, make up the bulk of the narrative, but an attempt has been made to add other sources to them, to put them in the context of the England of their time, and to make clear what were the objectives of the period in attempting to colonize North America. Complete as the surviving documents are in some respects, they do not tell us everything we would like to know, or indeed need to know, in order to understand what was done and what was attempted. A writer faced with this problem has three choices. At one extreme, he can restrict himself to what is exactly, or more or less exactly, known; at the other, he can let his fancy ride free from the documents and fill the gaps with whatever theories may cross his mind in order to make a good story (that is, enter the field of historical fiction). The third alternative is more difficult; it is to stick as closely to the documents as they will permit, but to point out carefully their limitations, ambiguities, and omissions, and then attempt, cautiously, to fill them, or suggest ways of filling them, by indicating probable or possible solutions to the gaps and contradictions in the narratives. A danger here is that of stating a hypothesis and then going on to treat it as an established fact, so that further hypotheses can be built on it. In dealing with such tenuous materials as we have on the Lost Colony, this practice may not have been wholly avoided, however strenuous the attempts to do so have been. One way in which the historian can maintain his perspective is to rely on the program of archaeological research on Roanoke Island and on the Indian sites that the colonists are known, or thought, to have visited. This is still very much an ongoing study and may ultimately add more to our knowledge than can be included in this book. Apart from the chances of new material emerging (which is slight on the documentary side), any set of hypotheses may be replaced by newer and better ones as new minds and new insights emerge. Historical interpretation, like archaeology, is also an ongoing study. So this cannot, in the nature of the topic, be regarded as anything more than a conscientious interim report, but, it is hoped, not altogether an uninteresting one.

The drawings of John White form a unique graphic source of which extensive use has been made: they too will reveal more when they are closely integrated with the result of the long-term archaeological program. The most speculative section deals with the Lost Colonists, the men, women, and children from the British Isles who were never seen again after August 1587. The attempt to knit together the scraps of hard information, vague tales, and carefully judged speculation has not been an easy task, but it has been an interesting and exciting one. It remains open to subsequent writers to produce convincing alternatives. All this is not to say that the book is concerned only with problems. It has an interesting, important, and at times thrilling tale. It is not for the most part a new tale, but it is hoped that, told in the way it is told here, it may be a little fuller and somewhat different from earlier attempts to tell the story, and even a degree more challenging. The historian's capacity to relate the story of the past and to explain it as far as possible varies from one individual to another and from one decade to another. This does not pretend to be the last word; it cannot be.

The book may be found idiosyncratic in some of its features. It gives no references to the basic documents, as they are all printed in *The First Colonists*, edited by D. B. and A. M. Quinn (Raleigh: Department of Cultural Resources, 1982), and frequently elsewhere (see p. 443 below). They ought to be read in full by all those who wish to understand both what happened and what were the rewards and limitations of these sources, preserved for us by Richard Hakluyt, the younger. The name of the chief entrepreneur of the enterprises is spelled Ralegh (as he did from 1587 to 1618), not Raleigh as is usual in North Carolina and elsewhere. The name of Simão Fernandes has been anglicized as Simon Fernandes, rather than Simon Fernandez, to indicate his Portuguese origin. Some Indian names are treated eclectically, as spellings in English are a matter of opinion, for example, Pomeioc instead of Pomeiooc, which has rather better authority. There may be other slight variations from common practice, but so far as possible neither too great departures from rigorous scholarship nor concessions to popular taste have been made.

To put this book into perspective, some account of an autobiographical character may prove useful. I have been interested in early English colonial expansion ever since I graduated B.A. from the Queen's University of Belfast in 1931, and though I wrote on early Tudor Ireland for my graduate dissertation in the University of London, I did so under the supervision of a colonial historian, A. P. Newton of King's College, London, who fostered my interest, first stirred by J. E. Todd in Belfast, in those men who attempted to found colonies in the early modern period either in Ireland or America or both. I taught British colonial history at Southampton for six years, and by the end of that period I had collected the documents on and sketched the life of Sir Humphrey Gilbert, Ralegh's half brother, who was the pioneer in English colonial ventures in North America after the experience that he gained in Ireland. The Hakluyt Society published this material in 1940.

I moved to Belfast in 1939 and at my old university developed there some specialist teaching on the earliest colonizing efforts of Tudor England in both Ireland and America. During 1943 I was for a time working in London and was invited by A. L. Rowse to contribute a small volume to a new series called "Teach Yourself History" on Sir Walter Ralegh and the British Empire. I was fortunate while

I was considering this to see the original John White drawings of Algonquian Indians at the British Museum. Archibald MacLeish, at the time assistant secretary of state, wished to consider the publication of the drawings to commemorate the early cultural links between the United Kingdom and America. For his sake the drawings were brought from their wartime security home, but were soon returned there for several years when the project fell through. I had fallen in love with them, however, and decided that the popular book on Ralegh would give me a chance to work on them.

The Ralegh book did not finally come out until 1947 (1949 in New York); in the meantime I had moved to the University College of Swansea (a campus of the University of Wales) and had been spending all the time I could on the background of the Roanoke voyages and other early American ventures. By the summer of 1948, having written two articles on the Roanoke voyages, one on the preparations for the 1585 expedition and another on the reasons why I thought the ventures failed, I was fortunate enough to obtain from the Leverhulme Fellowships Committee enough dollars (very scarce in England at that time) to enable me to spend three months in the United States. My plan at that time was to lay foundations for the documentation of all the English expeditions and colonies down to 1620, without realizing the size of this task.

I worked in the New York Public Library and in a few New England institutions, but made little progress with the Roanoke material, which I aimed to annotate fully, until I came to the Institute of Early American History and Culture at Williamsburg, with whose director, Carl Bridenbaugh, I had already been closely in touch. His interest in my project led him to arrange with John Gordon, then a graduate student at the institute, the sponsorship of the Coast Guard for a visit to the Carolina Outer Banks. The three of us sailed from Elizabeth City to Ocracoke Island and so obtained some idea of the great extent of the sounds. The hospitality of the Coast Guard enabled us to work our way north to Kitty Hawk by stages and to see the beaches from jeeps, then the only form of transport. The view of the numerous wrecks then lining the shore gave me an enduring impression of the dangers of the coast (even if many wrecks were the work of German enemies, not the weather). We were also able to coast by sea from Oregon Inlet almost to Cape Henry and so see the land as the early explorers had viewed it. A brief visit to the fort site at Roanoke Island followed. The National Park Service had begun its excavation program, but the site still contained unsightly reconstructed log cabins.

Raleigh was the next stop. The State Library was a useful starting point, but I got the most help on the natural history side from Harry T. Davis, at the Museum of Natural History, and from Christopher Crittenden, at the Department of Archives and History. My real education, though, began in Chapel Hill. Mary Thornton in the North Carolina Collection gave me a thorough grounding on what North Carolinians had done on the subject of my researches, and Charles Rush, then university librarian, was most helpful with introductions. W. C. Coker and H. R. Totten, famous names now, took me through the botanical identifications needed to understand Thomas Harriot's work. Moreover, Rush took me to Davidson to meet W. P. Cumming, already a leading authority on maps of the Southeast, beginning a long-lasting friendship and occasional collaboration.

Before I returned to England, I had also sampled the Library of Congress's exceptional collection of Spanish materials on North America and I had the good fortune to work briefly with James A. Geary of Catholic University, the leading authority on Algonquian languages, who was to provide invaluable material for my work. I was also in correspondence with J. C. Harrington and, through his kindness, was later able to summarize the archaeological data acquired by him at Fort Raleigh down to the end of 1953.

Back in Wales I returned to work on microfilm and photostats of Spanish materials so that I was able to publish a paper on Spanish reactions to the Roanoke voyages, a subject hitherto unresearched, in 1951. The collection of materials on the Roanoke voyages was greatly helped by R. A. Skelton, superintendent of the Map Room of the British Museum and secretary-editor for the Hakluyt Society. The two-volume work The Roanoke Voyages, 1584–1590 eventually emerged in the Hakluyt Society series in 1955, causing some surprise that it ran to just over 1,000 pages. It included extensive indexes by Alison Quinn, whose help in other ways made the completion of the task possible. She had been working with me on Spanish paleography and in 1955 we were able to spend time in Spain, working at the Museo Naval and the Biblioteca Nacional, both in Madrid, in the

Archivo General at Simancas, and in the Archivo General de Indias at
Seville. We made some interesting discoveries but only one or two
that referred to the Roanoke voyages.

Before the publication of The Roanoke Voyages I had made contacts
which were to be of great value later. One was through the arrival of
Paul Hulton in the Department of Prints and Drawings in the British
Museum. I had begun to collect and list the drawings of John White,
with whatever identification and texts I could, and included this
material in my collection, but only with the active cooperation of
Paul Hulton. The other contact was with William C. Sturtevant of the
Smithsonian Institution, who was to make it possible to annotate the
White drawings with effective ethnographic and ethnological identi-
fications. This inspired us to begin work on a definitive edition of The
American Drawings of John White, which was to be a major preoccupation
of both of us for nearly a decade.

Visits to the United States in 1957 and 1959 helped me forward
my work on the White drawings and to extend the range of my
knowledge, especially at the Folger Library, of the English literature of expansion. I was able to discuss problems of comparative
colonial expansion at the Lisbon Conference (the five hundredth
anniversary of Prince Henry the Navigator) in 1960 and read a paper
on Simon Fernandes, which was afterward published. The long ordeal of preparing and seeing the White drawings through the press
effectively employed Hulton and Quinn in the years following. In
1964 we had the satisfaction of seeing the drawings appear in two
fine volumes, published jointly by the British Museum and the University of North Carolina Press. A sabbatical year working in the John
Carter Brown, Folger, and Huntington libraries in 1963–64 enabled
Alison and myself to accompany Sir Frank Francis to the White
House in March 1964 when a specially bound copy was presented to
Ladybird Johnson, who showed that she had some real appreciation
of the value of the drawings. During this period we both developed
our knowledge of European expansion in the Americas, but the only
book that came out of it was sponsored by the Folger on The Elizabe-
thans and the Irish (1966), which was not entirely irrelevant to the
American colonizing ventures.

R. A. Skelton and I had already formed the project of publishing
in facsimile the neglected first edition of Hakluyt's Principall naviga-

tions (1589), which contained the first accounts of the Roanoke volumes and contained two documents, on White's 1588 voyage and the agreement of 1589 by a syndicate formed to assist the 1587 colony, which were not afterward reprinted. We undertook to provide a substantial introduction, while Alison prepared an extensive index of names and subjects which has proved invaluable for later comparative study of Elizabethan enterprises. This appeared in two volumes in 1965 under the auspices of the Hakluyt Society. Following this Nico Isreal, the Dutch publisher, invited me to introduce facsimiles of Hakluyt's earliest work, *Divers voyages touching the discoverie of America* (1582) and *A journal of several voyages into New France* (1580), which Hakluyt had earlier induced Florio to translate. These were important steps toward the launching of the Roanoke voyages. They appeared in 1967, along with a separately bound volume by me, *Richard Hakluyt, Editor.*

In the late 1960s I was able to make a few minor discoveries, namely that Thomas Harriot had helped Ralegh prepare an abortive expedition in search of the Lost Colonists in 1602 and that there were "Virginians," Indians perhaps from the Chesapeake, in London in 1603. These were published in 1970 while I was Harrison Visiting Professor at the College of William and Mary. By that time I had been asked by Harper and Row to contribute a volume on the early voyages and colonies in North America for the New American Nation series. I warned them that it would be some time before I could complete this, and it did not in fact come out until 1977. In the meantime a collection of my papers and studies had been published by Alfred Knopf, *England and the Discovery of America, 1481–1620* (1974). This contained reprints of earlier papers on the Roanoke voyages together with a new study of the exiguous materials on the Lost Colony. Another project that was brought to completion, after the death of R. A. Skelton in a car accident in 1970, was *The Hakluyt Handbook* (2 vols., 1974), which was primarily a bibliographical guide but which contained a study of what Hakluyt had done and not done with regard to the Roanoke voyages that I contributed myself. Skelton had planned with W. P. Cumming a fine illustrated book *The Discovery of North America*, which I helped to complete after his death, and which includes excellent examples of John White's work. Over the years 1971–74 it found a wide market in North America, Europe (in French and German), and England. It was the best publicity the White drawings and the Roanoke voyages could have had. This volume was followed by a further volume, masterminded by W. P. Cumming, on the exploration of North America, 1634–1776, but the North Carolina element was provided by W. P. Cumming and my contribution was a general introduction only.

Alison Quinn and I were asked to contribute a volume, *Virginia Voyages from Hakluyt* (effectively, the voyages to Roanoke Island), to the Oxford University Press Series of Memoirs and Travels. This appeared in 1973 and was the basis for *The First Colonists*, already referred to. My *Raleigh and the British Empire* had been revised several times (London, 1960; New York, 1962) and last appeared, as *Ralegh and the British Empire*, in Penguin Books in 1973. By this time I was near retirement from Liverpool, but completed my textbook for Harper and Row before I did so. *North America from Earliest Discovery to First Settlements* appeared in 1977 and has been invaluable to me in teaching the early colonial period at St. Mary's College of Maryland and at the University of Michigan at Ann Arbor during subsequent postretirement visits to the United States, as there the Roanoke voyages have been placed fully in the general pattern of European activity in North America down to 1612.

In the late 1960s a Thomas Harriot seminar was instituted at Oxford by the efforts of Rosalind Tanner and A. C. Crombie. Through the efforts of John W. Shirley this was held at the University of Delaware in 1971, out of which emerged Shirley's edition of the papers read there, *Thomas Harriot, Renaissance Scientist*, which included a new survey by me of Harriot's influence in America. His great store of unpublished papers, almost wholly scientific, has been the focus of subsequent annual seminars at Oxford and at Durham University. New materials on his navigation and astronomy have relevance to North Carolina, but unfortunately only a few scraps have any direct reference to America; his major studies on the Indians of North Carolina were lost, some apparently in the Fire of London in 1666. One survival is his so-called "Secret Language"; this now proves to be a phonetic scheme worked out to record the sounds of the Algonquian language, but was used by him only to experiment with its use and to sign a few surviving documents and maps.

From 1973 onward, Alison Quinn, Susan Hillier (a former graduate student at Liverpool), and I were engaged on the mammoth project of compiling a documentary history of North America to 1612. This eventually appeared as *New American World* in five volumes, in 1979. It included two new documents on the Roanoke voyages, one recording something of a conversation with Ralph Lane after his return in 1586 and the other narrating (not too accurately) voyages from 1584 to 1587 in which Richard Butler, then a prisoner in Spain, had taken part. The relevant maps and a generous selection of other Roanoke voyage documents were also included, together with the first full collection of the colonizing plans made by the Elizabethans for America.

Since the planning for the four hundredth anniversary of the Roanoke voyages and colonies began in 1980, my wife and I have both been frequently in North Carolina, discussing plans for pamphlets and books with the four hundredth anniversary committee, under the early chairmanship of H. G. Jones and later with the editor in chief, William S. Powell. We have also been brought to Fort Raleigh to consult with others about possible lines of archaeological research on Roanoke Island, where Phillip Evans has been the guiding spirit. It was a very pleasant surprise, in the middle of this, to be awarded an honorary degree of LL.D. by the University of North Carolina in 1981, and especially to be presented for it by Gillian T. Cell, a former student of mine at Liverpool, then a professor of history at Chapel Hill and subsequently chairman of the Department of History there. She herself is a distinguished writer on early English expansion, specializing on Newfoundland. In the later discussions on publications for the anniversary it became evident that a narrative by me and a further edition of the John White drawings by Paul Hulton would be desirable. America's Four Hundredth Anniversary Committee eventually commissioned us to write those books. This, of mine, was aided by the award of a fellowship at the National Humanities Center for the second semester of the year 1982–83. Kent Mullikin, the associate director (with the new director, Charles Blitzer); Alan W. Tuttle, librarian; Rebecca Sutton, assistant librarian; Margaret Bocting, Karen Carroll, Madeline Moyer, and Ineke Hutchison, manuscript typing staff; together with my fellow Fellows, have made this a most enjoyable and profitable experience and enabled me to complete the writing in six months.

Alison and I would like to think we have made all the contributions we can to the study of the Roanoke voyages (they include a pamphlet on the Lost Colonists). We would like to see the pioneer work of William S. Powell, done in 1956 in London using mainly printed sources, on the elusive origins and identification of the colonists of 1585 and 1587 continued by him. This work so far has yielded only a few positive and a number of very tentative identifications. We ourselves feel we have one more task to complete, namely a facsimile edition, with a full commentary, of Hakluyt's "Particuler discourse" (known as the *Discourse on Western Planting*). This is the key document on the background to the Roanoke voyages, even if it failed in 1584, when it was presented as a confidential report to the Queen (it was not published until 1877), to induce her to take direct responsibility for American colonies. Its advice can be traced as dominant in Ralegh's concern with the colonial ventures of subsequent years.

Very many recognitions for help are necessary, though some will be found in the notes and bibliography and credits for the illustrations. H. G. Jones and William S. Powell have been our standbys in Chapel Hill. The help of Thomas L. Hartman and Phillip Evans at Fort Raleigh, and David S. Phelps at East Carolina University has proven invaluable. J. C. Harrington too has remained a helpful friend throughout, as has William C. Sturtevant. The advice of Professor J. Frederick Fausz at St. Mary's College of Maryland has been most valuable throughout. In England, Helen Wallis and Paul Hulton have been our main supports. Many others have answered queries and offered advice; we thank them all for making this task easier. Alison Quinn has borne with the typing and checking, as well as acting as my severest critic throughout, and it is she who has made the index. I am deeply indebted to the University of North Carolina Press for its courtesy and help—to the director, the editor, and the copyeditor—and to America's Four Hundredth Anniversary Committee and the National Humanities Center for enabling me to write it.

David B. Quinn
March 1984

PART 1

Voyages and Colonies, 1584–1586

Ralegh's Involvement in the North American Enterprise

Master Water Rawley is in very high favour with the Queen's Majesty; neither my Lord of Leicester nor master Vice-Chamberlain [Sir Francis Knollys] in so short time ever was in the like, which special favour hath been within this two months [March 1583]. I have heard it credibly reported that Master Rawley hath spent within this half year above 3000 pounds. He is very sumptuous in his apparel, and I take it he hath his diet out of the Privy Kitchen, but all the vessels with which he is served at his table, is silver with his own arms on the same. He hath attending on him at least thirty men whose liveries are chargeable, of which number half be gentlemen, very brave fellows, divers having chains of gold. The whole Court doth follow him. . . . His lodging is very bravely furnished with arras, the chamber wherein himself doth lie hath a field bed all covered with green velvet, laid with broad silver lace, and upon every corner and on the top set with plumes of white feathers with spangles. He hath all other delights and pleasure abundantly and above all he behaveth himself to the good liking of every man.[1]

This word picture of Queen Elizabeth I's newly risen favorite was given us at the beginning of May 1583 by a young Londoner who had recently encountered him. Ralegh is the man who was to be associated most closely with the Roanoke colonies; even though he never visited North America, his power, influence, and ideas dominate any consideration of what happened there from 1584 to 1590 and after.

Walter Ralegh was a younger son of a family of minor gentry in south Devon.[2] His mother had been married before to a somewhat

3

richer gentleman, Otho Gilbert of Greenway and Compton. With him she had given birth to three boys who would be of some importance in later life: John Gilbert, who succeeded to his father's estates in 1547 and became vice-admiral of Devon; Humphrey Gilbert, who was to live a varied life in and out of the Queen's Court and who really initiated the planning of English colonies in North America into which he drew his half brother Walter; and Adrian Gilbert, who planned voyages himself, practiced medicine, and received patronage in high quarters. Walter's own elder brother, Carew Ralegh, who was to outlive him, eventually married an heiress and became a prominent figure in Wiltshire. Walter Ralegh, senior, made money from piracy and privateering and settled in Exeter in the 1560s.

About 1568, Walter accompanied a band of Devonshire men who went as volunteers to fight on the Huguenot side in the French religious wars. He saw some heavy fighting and learned the trade of a soldier. He returned, we suspect, with some spoil, which enabled him to pursue his education as a gentleman. He is next found at Oxford University, where he was a member of Oriel College between 1572 and 1574, though perhaps he did not stay there continuously, and he left, as most of his contemporaries did, without taking a degree. He migrated to London to follow the traditional course of learning a little law and the rules of social intercourse and personal advancement at Lyons Inn, one of the Inns of Chancery, in 1575 and at the prestigious Middle Temple in 1576. By 1578 he was in attendance at Court, introduced there, we suspect, by Sir Humphrey Gilbert, who had been knighted for military service in Ireland, but we do not know precisely how he supported himself.

In the Middle Temple he would have come to know Richard Hakluyt, the elder, a lawyer whose primary interest was in the economics of the new geography and who had both a growing correspondence with Spanish Mexico and Portuguese India and consulted with merchants about the chances of English overseas voyaging as a new area of speculative investment. By 1578 he was coming around to the view that North America was the most promising field for English intervention, because by the reports he had read it was fertile, occupied by people who might accept European trade, and empty of European settlements and so could provide land for English occupation. Sir Humphrey Gilbert had also reached the same conclusion.

Gilbert, indeed, had become fanatical about it.[3] In Ireland in the 1560s he had come to the conclusion that England itself offered too little scope for enterprise, especially for the younger sons of the gentry, and that there was neither land to be had nor economic activity to be engaged in which would offer them occupation, riches, and, ultimately, power. Events, and the Queen's policies, ruled out Ireland for the time being as a field for English colonization, but North America was open for experiment. He had some influence at Court, and somehow he persuaded the Queen to give him a blank check to engage in an imperial venture in land and commerce in the West. We suspect, though we do not know, that Sir Francis Walsingham, the Queen's secretary of state, may have persuaded her, as he and Gilbert thought alike that Spain's empire should be emulated as well as humbled.

Gilbert's patent of 11 June 1578 was extraordinarily vague. He was to explore lands not actually possessed by any Christian prince or people, and occupy them in the Queen's name. He might take Englishmen with him to settle who would remain under the Queen's allegiance, but would have extensive rights to govern any settlements he might create, though the settlers would retain all their rights under English law and custom. He could resist challenges to his authority (we can presume challenges by the inhabitants of the lands as well as European contestants). For all these things he would owe the Queen only one-fifth of all the gold and silver ore that might be found. Although no limits were set, Gilbert construed the grant to give him monopoly rights extending from Spanish Florida to the Arctic, perhaps including even the Northwest Passage if it should be found. For a private individual this was an incredible opportunity, but could an individual, particularly a man who had wide experience but little money, do anything about it?

Yet Gilbert had struck at the right time. He appealed to many of the courtiers, to the West Country gentlemen, and, above all, to the piratical sea captains who had surreptitiously been carrying on a sea war against Spain, and stealing other ships as well. By early November he had mobilized ten ships at Plymouth, heavily armed and containing no less than 520 men. This was sufficient to carry through a major raid on the Spanish Caribbean before making any attempt to reconnoiter the shores of North America. The expedition split, however, when Henry Knollys, son of the Queen's vice-chamberlain, Sir

Francis Knollys, refused to acknowledge Gilbert's authority. Knollys then sailed off with three ships, intending only to carry out piratical attacks off the coasts of western Europe. Gilbert's seven ships included the tiny *Squirrel* of only eight tons, to which he was deeply attached. He set out on 19 November 1578.

Gilbert had deeply involved Walter Ralegh in his venture. He chartered from William Hawkins, the great Plymouth merchant, the ship *Falcon*, formerly an old royal vessel and said to have been newly repaired for Ralegh's first sea venture. She was of 80 tons burden, and her pilot under Captain Walter Ralegh was the Portuguese, Simon Fernandes. The ship began to leak off the Scilly Isles and held Gilbert back so that his vessels were caught in a storm and driven to take shelter in Cork Harbour. From there only the *Falcon* and one other vessel appear to have been able to get away; Gilbert returned with the rest to Plymouth. The *Falcon* ran down the Atlantic coast to the Canaries, by which time supplies of water and wine were used up. Some supplies were obtained, and the ship may have sailed as far south as the Cape Verdes before turning back, as she was becoming increasingly unseaworthy. Fernandes was making for Puerto Rico, where he evidently hoped to refit the ship, but instead she was back in England by May. Gilbert then went off on Irish service for the Queen to recoup a little of his costs. In 1580, however, he took proceedings against William Hawkins in the Court of Chancery alleging the *Falcon* was ill-found for the voyage and demanding damages.[4] Fernandes gave valuable evidence about the ship, and Ralegh, who knew the Hawkins family well, also appeared, though he was cautious about the defects of the ship and did not greatly help Gilbert's case. By this time he was described (3 February 1580) as "one of the extraordinary Esquires of the Body of the Queen's Majesty," showing that he had acquired at least a nominal office on the fringe of the Court among the young men who made up the circle of attendants of Elizabeth I.

At Court, Ralegh soon got a reputation as a proud, hot-tempered, and imperious man, but one whose personality commended itself to statesmen like the earl of Leicester and Sir Francis Walsingham, as well, apparently, as the Queen. To cool his hot blood and give him experience he was sent to Ireland in 1580 as captain of a company of soldiers engaged in quenching the embers of a rising in Munster. He also took part in the siege and capture of Smerwick, where a force of Continental mercenaries sent by the Pope and supported by Philip II had arrived too late to help the Munster insurgents. Entrusted with a substantial amount of responsibility by Lord Grey of Wilton, the lord deputy, he made himself something of an authority on Irish affairs, not hesitating to criticize Grey in letters to the Queen. Returning late in 1581, he quickly caught the personal attention of Queen Elizabeth, who received him into her inner circle and heaped rewards on him.

His preoccupations were not all with wealth and show and attendance on the Queen. Soon after his return from Ireland, he was involved once more with Sir Humphrey Gilbert, who had returned from Ireland in 1580 and begun a new campaign for an American venture. This time he was selling outright lands and commercial privileges in North America, which he had never seen, though Fernandes had made a rapid visit to what we presume to have been Norumbega (modern New England) in 1580. His focus in 1578 had been the southeastern part of North America, we think, but now it was the temperate shores of Norumbega, specifically Verrazzano's "Refugio," Narragansett Bay, last seen, unless Fernandes found it again, in 1524, but appearing on many maps. Courtiers, idealists like Sir Philip Sidney, gentlemen mainly from the southwest, a few London merchants and the citizens of the declining port of Southampton, and, especially, Catholic gentlemen, threatened by increasing fines for nonconformity (an act raising fines to penal proportions came into force in 1581), were all gradually drawn into his net in 1582.

Of several expeditions planned in that year, though none set sail, one was Gilbert's own. He spent the summer of 1582 putting it together in Southampton, but was unable to sail. Among the vessels brought together, the largest and finest was a new ship bought by Walter Ralegh from the Southampton merchant Henry Oughtred. This vessel of 200 tons, renamed the *Bark Ralegh*, was equipped at a total cost of some £2,000, a large sum for that period and proof that Ralegh now had money. Poor organization and contrary winds forced Gilbert to hold back until the end of the year, when he was unable to leave the English Channel. Poorer but determined, he eventually set sail on 11 June 1583. The Queen would not permit Ralegh to go and did not wish Gilbert to sail himself either, but to leave the reconnaissance to others. The *Bark Ralegh* was commanded by Michael Butler, formerly Ralegh's lieutenant in Ireland; after two days she turned back and deserted Gilbert, fatally weakening his expedition. Gilbert was to blame the men as cowards, but there is some evidence there was sickness on board and also that food supplies were considered inadequate for the Atlantic crossing. Ralegh thus had no share in Gilbert's last and fatal enterprise.

Gilbert's annexation of Newfoundland in a ceremony at St. John's Harbour was a symbolic act of possession, with just the possibility of raising rents and taxes on fish from the hundreds of vessels that visited the island's shores in summer. His main purpose was to work down the mainland coast to allocate lands for himself and for some of the many subscribers who had bought about twenty million acres from him, sight unseen. But the wrecking of the *Delight* on Sable Island left him with only two vessels. One of these was the ubiquitous *Squirrel*, and in her he was lost at sea off the Azores. Edward Hayes returned alone in the *Golden Hind* on 22 September, full of the advantages of holding Newfoundland. One of Gilbert's Catholic supporters, Sir George Peckham, made a final attempt to arouse support for a venture of his own, but early in 1584 he had to admit defeat.

During the years 1582–83 the first pamphlets advocating colonization in North America had appeared, including Richard Hakluyt, the younger's *Divers voyages touching the discoverie of America* in 1582,[5] a collection of what was then known in England; a commendatory poem on Gilbert by the Hungarian Stephen Parmenius, who was lost on the voyage;[6] a tract by Christopher Carleill, Walsingham's stepson, which went into several editions;[7] and Peckham's *True reporte* which came out at the end of 1583.[8] For the first time North America had received extensive publicity in England. On that Walter Ralegh was to attempt to capitalize fully in 1584.

Ralegh must have made his fateful decision to follow up the Gilbert ventures very shortly after Sir George Peckham had abandoned in January 1584 his own hopes of succeeding where Gilbert had failed. Christopher Carleill was still in the field, however. His pamphlet, which in one edition was titled *A breef and sommarie discourse upon the entended voyage to the hethermoste partes of America*, proposed a commercial colony near the mouth of the St. Lawrence. The pamphlet had first appeared as early as April 1583, but he was still collecting, or trying to collect, subscriptions from corporate towns for his project between February and April 1584. There was clearly a tacit agreement that his venture would not compete with that of Gilbert, or with those of Ralegh in 1584. He eventually left England in July, but appears to have had setbacks at sea, and he was back in Ireland by early August. He next brought his vessels into the service of the Irish government and spent the greater part of the next nine years in military service there, though he was to visit the Roanoke colony very briefly in June 1586 when he was serving on Sir Francis Drake's West Indian voyage.

Other things also had to be got out of the way before Ralegh could act. Humphrey Gilbert had assigned his rights north of 50 degrees to Dr. John Dee, but Dee had given up all plans for northern voyages when he left for an extended visit to the continent in September, passing on his rights to Adrian Gilbert, Ralegh's half brother. Adrian had these rights confirmed by patent on 6 February 1584, though it was left to the London merchant William Sanderson and others to finance the voyages made by John Davis under this patent between 1585 and 1587. The rights, too, of Sir John Gilbert, as Sir Humphrey's heir, had to be safeguarded, or at least the fishing interests assured so that a fresh attempt would not be made to control them. We do not know which reason operated to exclude Ralegh from any concern with Newfoundland. It may have been because it was already regarded as part of the Queen's dominions in consequence of its annexation by Humphrey Gilbert in August 1583. When these things had been settled, the way was clear for the drafting of a patent for Ralegh, dated 16 March 1584, which was formally issued on 25 March 1584 and was to last for seven years only if he had not established a settled colony within that period.

The patent was, apart from exclusions indicated already, identical to that which Humphrey Gilbert had received in June 1578.[9] Once again it was wholly vague as to what areas of the globe it covered— "remote heathen and barbarous lands, countries and territories not actually possessed of any Christian prince and inhabited by Christian people." Ralegh was empowered to take with him any of the Queen's subjects "to travel thitherward or to inhabit there with him." He was to have power to impress ships and seamen (the permission was later limited to the counties of Devon and Cornwall and the city of

Bristol) to transport his settlers. Once there he was to enjoy the widest possible powers of government under the Queen and to hold the lands forever, subject only to the payment (as in Gilbert's case) of one-fifth of all gold and silver ore to the Queen. He was authorized to expel all those who resisted him or who attempted to settle without his license, and this was to extend to six hundred miles north and south of the area where his settlements were located. All such lands once occupied "shall be of the allegiance of us our heirs and successors," that is, the colonists and their colonies were to remain parts of the dominions of the English crown and enjoy the privileges of this association in the same manner as residents in other territories. Ralegh could impose laws and administer them, but with the provision that "the said laws and ordinances may be as near as conveniently they may be to the form of the laws, statutes, government or policy of England." Moreover, they must not be "against the true Christian faith or religion now professed in the Church of England, nor in any way withdraw any of the subjects or people of those lands or places from the allegiance of us, our heirs and successors, as their immediate sovereigns under God."

This extensive constitution for the first colonies to be actually established in North America is of great interest. It set out the rights of the proprietor in some detail, but qualified them by insisting that the colonies should be governed according to English law and religion and that the settlers should enjoy the full privileges they had as the subjects of the Queen. There was much left unsaid. Were the settlers to have the right to return if they did not wish to stay? Did they have any local rights of representation in lawmaking? There was nothing to determine whether these and many other considerations would be kept in mind. The patent did not, however, embody any of the plans that Humphrey Gilbert had set down on paper in 1582 for an elaborate feudal hierarchy and for the allocation of lands and rights according to the rates of subscription made to the venture. Nor was there any separate provision made for estates to be laid out for Ralegh's personal or family use.

Gilbert had set great store on such archaic rights and privileges. Ralegh was more pragmatic. We know of no commitments he made during the years 1584–90 that tied his colonists to a particular form of proceeding. He was free to make very different arrangements with

1. Sir Walter Ralegh and His Son Wat.
Courtesy of the National Portrait Gallery, London.

different groups. He was prepared to experiment and see what experiments would produce. Yet, in theory, according to his patent, he had supreme power under the Queen to organize and rule the colonies as he saw fit. If a single individual, and not the state, was to have the authority to create and govern colonies across the ocean, the patent of 1584 and the way that Ralegh subsequently acted under it offered a sensible and practical basis for the initiation of a colonizing venture, if indeed it could be done by private interests. Much depended, of course, on the quality of the agents who would carry out his plans, as his commitments at Court and in office would not allow him to stay in his colonies himself. It depended on the wise choice of colonists and their behavior in the new lands. Above all, it demanded the continued attention to his colonies by Ralegh himself. If he were diverted by too many other commitments, they would suffer, and indeed were to do so.

All these arrangements were made on the apparent assumption that the English would be free to act in their colonies, to seize and occupy land, and to create new societies of their own as though the land were unoccupied. The non-Christian inhabitants were ignored, their rights to lands implicitly denied, their own organization of their societies not even considered to be worth mention. The legal framework affected English subjects alone: the native inhabitants were left to the colonists' mercy, good or bad, even though in practice policies had to be evolved to meet the actual circumstances of a land already occupied for millennia by peoples who had very different societies of their own and to whom Europeans were not only strange but were inevitably regarded as intruders, with whom it might or might not prove possible to live.

Behind the Roanoke colonies, though they were the first to be attempted in North America, there lay a long period of English overseas enterprise.[10] Englishmen may have sighted Newfoundland as early as the 1480s, and John Cabot clearly delineated eastern Newfoundland, which he thought was Asia, in 1497. His successors did sufficient exploration to become convinced that this great landmass stood between them and Asia; Sebastian Cabot's attempt in 1508–9 to get around it by a northwesterly route to reach Asia failed, but this was confirmation of the continental character of the landmass. Apart from beginning the cod fishery at Newfoundland in 1502, in which the English were followed by other European nations, they left much of the exploration of southeastern North America to the Spanish. In 1527 an English ship sailed along the coast from Labrador to Florida and the West Indies, but nothing followed. North America was a disappointment. Few Indians were seen, and they did not impress, as they had no golden ornaments or precious stones to exhibit.

It was left to the French to penetrate the interior by way of the St. Lawrence, but they expected too much and were disappointed. When the French developed an interest in "Florida" in the 1560s, the English did plan a colony in what is now South Carolina in 1563 but did not proceed with it, and English ships called at the St. Johns River in 1565 to see how French settlers were doing there, shortly before the Spanish killed off all the colonists and declared that their sphere of influence extended up the whole eastern coast of North America. In 1566 a Spanish expedition formally annexed the Outer Banks, and thereby North Carolina, to Spain; in 1570 another attempted to found a mission on Chesapeake Bay, but their ships returned only to kill the Powhatan Indians, who had themselves massacred the Spanish missionaries.

From mid-century onward the English were more interested in trying to colonize parts of Ireland, in order to bring that country more fully under English control, than in planning colonies in America. Soldier colonists were introduced and some garrisons established, but little civilian settlement developed, even after Sir Thomas Smith in 1571 planned a great city, Elizabetha, not far from modern Belfast and published propaganda about how attractive Ireland was for settlement. (Promotion literature directed in the 1580s toward North American settlement would take much the same line.) Even in the 1580s, when the Roanoke voyages were taking place, the major English colonizing enterprise, involving thousands of people, was that being undertaken in Munster. In one area of America only did the English intervene spectacularly, the far northwest.

The revival of the concept of a Northwest Passage led to an expedition under Martin Frobisher in 1576 which showed some prospect, though it was ill-founded, of a passage. Samples of minerals brought back giving promise of gold led to two great follow-up expeditions in 1577 and 1578 to bring hundreds of tons of rock from

Baffin Island, but in the end the ore was found to contain no precious metals. Although it was the occasion for the first wave of major publicity for English overseas enterprises, this failure led to some disillusionment about the chances of exploiting any part of the Americas not preempted, as Florida had been in 1565, by the Spanish. It was at this point that Sir Humphrey Gilbert turned from dreams of gold to visions of free land and embarked on the course that led to his death at sea and the passage of his projects and rights to Walter Ralegh.

England at this time was in many ways a small and weak country. She had control of only parts, and fluctuating parts at that, of Ireland, of which Elizabeth I was also queen. Scotland was a separate kingdom, still subject to French influence, even though the English had invested much diplomacy and money to keep that country friendly. Relations with France fluctuated widely: when the French felt especially threatened by Philip II of Spain, they tended to draw nearer England, and England, when it felt threatened by Spain, responded. The French Protestants, Huguenot Calvinists, had been pro-English, but they had been greatly weakened by a Catholic massacre in 1572. Queen Elizabeth, whose sister Mary had been married to Philip while she was Queen of England, was careful after her accession to assert her continued friendship toward Spain. If Philip deeply resented her failure to maintain the Roman Catholic worship, reinstituted by Mary, and her creation of a somewhat ambiguously Protestant church in England, he was not free to interfere there. He was having trouble with the rich Netherlands provinces over his attempted supression of their Protestant minority and their traditional rights of autonomous rule because Philip could conceive of no satisfactory system of government that was not both authoritarian and Catholic. Massacres and coercion of the Netherlands by Philip's armies in the late 1560s alarmed England and her Queen, because they considered that if the Netherlands were finally subdued, England's turn would come.

By 1572, Queen Elizabeth was allowing her subjects to volunteer to fight for the Protestant Netherlanders and protecting their warships, so that she became involved to some extent in the struggles in the Low Countries. Moreover, her own subjects were beginning to infiltrate the territories and waters in the western ocean that Spain regarded as its own. John Hawkins's attempt at trading in slaves and merchandise between 1562 and 1568 in the Caribbean brought about fighting, Spanish repression, English reprisals, and a state close to war. After some years of tension, however, Philip and Elizabeth concluded that their mutual commercial interests and Spain's desire to keep the English out of the Netherlands wars were a primary consideration. This led to a truce in 1573 and a formal treaty of peace between them in 1574, which lasted, nominally, though increasingly in name only, until 1585. Well before that time the northern provinces of the Netherlands had joined together as the United Provinces against Spain and were creating a new state dominated by the province of Holland. Meanwhile, Philip was gradually mastering by diplomacy as well as force the provinces that make up modern Belgium by killing off or expelling many Protestants and giving a small amount of autonomy to the Catholics. Against this background of unrest in the Low Countries, Englishmen were making an ever more vigorous display of aggression and antagonism against Spanish and Portuguese domination of the oceanic world outside European waters, Portugal and its African and Oriental empire, together with Brazil, having been absorbed by Spain in 1580.

Francis Drake disappeared on an overseas voyage in 1577 and reappeared in 1580 with a vast treasure stolen from the Spanish on the Pacific coast of South America. He had also in rather light-hearted fashion formally annexed Upper California to England, as New Albion, and made the first direct contacts with the Portuguese-dominated Spice Islands before completing the second circumnavigation of the globe. Earlier, Drake had been one of a number of English pirates who had raided and robbed Central America and the Caribbean Islands, and such actions were continuing at the time the first Roanoke venture was launched under Ralegh's auspices in 1584.

Philip II had been amazingly tolerant of English intrusions—though of course he killed as many English and French pirates as his naval officers could catch. His preoccupation with the Netherlands and repeated hopes of a successful plot to assassinate Elizabeth, of which he supported several, in hope that she might then be succeeded by the Catholic Mary Queen of Scots (a prisoner of Elizabeth's since 1568) and so draw England into the Spanish camp, held him back. Just a year after the first voyage of reconnaissance to eastern North America under Ralegh's auspices, however, Philip broke with the English, seized English ships found trading in Spanish ports, and began a commercial struggle. The English responded by releasing a flock of some two hundred privateers, licensed to attack Spanish and Portuguese vessels and plunder them, to pay, at least in theory, for Spanish injuries done to the merchants and shipowners or their associates. This unofficial sea war was to increase in intensity in 1585–86 when Sir Francis Drake, as he now was, invaded the Caribbean and damaged Spanish pride and commercial enterprise in a major raid on a number of their towns. A final plot against the Queen led her to agree to the execution of Mary Queen of Scots in 1587. From that time on open war with Spain was clearly joined, even if no declaration of war was ever made.

Spain hoped to relieve pressure in the Netherlands, to which Elizabeth had sent an army to aid the United Provinces, by a great maritime demonstration, which might not conquer England for Spain but at least would terrorize it into abandoning the Dutch and also giving up the privateering war against Spain. The threat of the Great Armada hung over England from 1586 to 1588, absorbing most of its ships, men, and money. The dispersal of the Spanish fleet when it came was a turning point in Elizabethan England. It was followed in 1589 by a formidable attempt to free Portugal from Spain, which failed. During these years all thought of colonizing North America faded into the background. By 1590 both sides were settling down for a long sea war. The English raiders were as active and successful as ever, even if they always failed to capture the main convoy of American silver coming to Spain. For its part, Spain prepared ever newer and larger invasion fleets against England, which achieved nothing, though it did take partially effective measures to protect its own fleets and its colonial towns from English attack.

This is the external background to the Roanoke voyages, which must be kept in mind throughout any study of the Roanoke enterprises for the limitations it imposed on the attempts at colonization from 1585 onward. The internal situation, too, should not be neglected. England was a small and relatively sparsely populated country. Its population was rising in the years of relative peace after 1558, a peace that had been rare in the early years of the sixteenth century. With a population approaching four million during the last twenty years of the century, the country was beginning to stretch its wings. The rise in the number of people in a preindustrial society aroused fears of overpopulation. England had no spectacular external trade successes to record, but its basic trade in unfinished woolen cloth was maintained, in spite of major disruptions caused by the Netherlands revolt, as a major earner of foreign exchange and a means of importing a wide variety of products of which it was short at home. The country was also dyeing a certain amount of its heavier woolen cloths for sale in colder climates, while French and Low Countries refugees who found safety in Protestant England introduced the weaving of finer woolen cloth and also of silk, which added variety to English exports and cut down the need for imports. Foundries for cast iron multiplied; the most successful of them produced excellent cast iron cannon that were soon in much demand abroad, as well as essential to defense at home. Iron pots and other utensils and nails and suchlike small wares were emerging in quantity from many small workshops, especially in the English Midlands. The rise of small industries outside the towns and the expansion of the internal market were significant. The heavier metal industries, and such new ones as sugar refining, which was made possible by privateering seizures of Brazilian sugar, centered around London, which was spreading down both sides of the Thames and inland in all directions. Northern and western England and Wales were still mainly pastoral, but agriculture in the east and southeast was flourishing; more wheat and other food supplies for an ever-growing London were being produced almost every year, while very many of the expanding population found homes and occupations in or near London, which had risen in size from some 50,000 in 1500 to some 215,000 a century later.

There had been much successful speculation in land, largely maintained by sales of royal lands from the time of the suppression of the monasteries onward, and merchant investment in land and development of agriculture and of mineral rights by landowners (copper mining was engaged in extensively, as was the exploitation of coal). If many parts of the country remained very poor and the general standard of living of the common people was rising, very slowly, if at all, men of the middling rank were prospering in commerce and industry and in the expanding professions and techniques of law, medicine, instrument making, land surveying, and many others. A number of the gentlemen and some of the nobility found themselves with money to spend which they were willing to invest in overseas speculation. Although there was some interest in colonization, the main impetus for the discovery and exploitation of new markets came from London merchants, who sought both new markets for cloth and the newer products of English industry as well as new products as imports. The increased demand for naval stores and supplies, hemp and flax, tar and timber, brought English vessels to the Baltic in increasing numbers, while furs and wax, along with similar naval stores, led the Muscovy or Russia Company from 1555 onward into active trade to northeastern Europe. At the same time, English ships were building a trade in southern Europe, first with the western and then with the eastern Mediterranean. In the former they could sell woolens and Newfoundland fish and get wines, olive oil, and alum (necessary for cloth and leather making); in the latter they could find wine and currants and take a share in the reviving overland spice trade, which the Portuguese were increasingly unable to check, in return for cloth and metals. They were penetrating, too, into Morocco, selling cloth for materials to make gunpowder, and down the West African coast, where they might pick up gold, ivory, and malagueta pepper in return for metals, metal trinkets, and a little cloth.

The established trade in parts of western Europe was becoming increasingly uncertain. The Netherlands ceased to be the greatest market and source of supply for England, though trade with the United Provinces picked up as they established themselves economically. France was weakened by civil war, and trade with her declined. Trade with Spain for wines, fruits, and fine quality iron ores and leather goods, as well as exotic products of the western Indies, was first hampered by friction and then stopped, though it was eventually partly replaced by seizures by privateers.

The economic picture of England at this time is thus a mixed one. Many men had been displaced by changes in industry and agriculture, and others were unemployed because jobs could not wholly keep pace with a growing population; so there were men and women willing to migrate. At the same time, maritime industries were expanding, many more smallish ships were being built for more distant commerce (many for the Newfoundland fishery), and the Queen subsidized the construction of larger merchant vessels, which might be called on for naval service when required. By the 1580s she, herself, was building a small but highly effective navy of her own, whose galleons were to show fighting qualities that out-shone all but the finest of Spanish warships.[11] It was within this context that Walter Ralegh and the colonial theorizers were to move from speculation to action.

Preliminaries of the 1584 Voyage

Although we have little detail of the preparations Ralegh made to avoid the mistakes and, ultimately, fatal consequences of Sir Humphrey Gilbert's voyage and to select and prepare his vessels for an exploratory expedition, we do know that he took a long view of the preliminary steps that should be taken. There was a strong feeling, which Drake shared, that English navigation lagged behind that of Spain and Portugal in that there were no training institutions for pilots and masters. We know, however, that individual tutors were being employed to teach young men interested in taking part in sea voyages, and that private schools were being created in London to instruct men in practical mathematics. At some time in 1583, either before or after the fiasco leading to the return of the *Bark Ralegh*, Ralegh employed Thomas Harriot to remedy this state of affairs. Harriot, a young Oxford graduate, had since 1580 been devoting himself to the applications of mathematics to navigation at sea. He taught Ralegh himself something about navigation, but his chief task was to ensure that the men who commanded and navigated the vessels Ralegh intended to send to sea should not only have experience at sea but also be equipped with the knowledge they could now acquire on land. Harriot held classes for such men, using his textbook, the *Arcticon*, which he refers to later but which has not survived. The problems with which he was concerned then, and was to be involved in for many years later, imply, in the words of the most recent authoritative study,

> knowing exactly where on the face of the earth the lands being sought were located (hence his interest in charts, maps and the exact determination of latitude and longitude), how to go from where they were to where they wanted to be (which called for

the location of the ship on the open sea through exact knowledge of the mathematics of the spheres of the earth and heavens) with the greatest efficiency in the use of time, ships and men (which led to careful analysis of the navigational tools available and the improvement of their accuracy).[1]

The more abstruse aspects of these studies were to occupy much of Harriot's later life but it is clear that by 1584 he had equipped Ralegh's pilots, masters, and, to some extent at least, his captains (who were not necessarily sailors) with enough knowledge of navigational techniques, through the use of instruments and exact observation, to give them the best chances he could of arriving at and returning safely from North America. It would be wrong to assume that practical experience at sea was not of great importance—it was usually vital—or that even with the best use of the instruction given success was assured, because instruments were inaccurate or inadequate (as yet, no clock could be made that was accurate enough to enable longitude to be calculated at sea) and empirical methods were very unreliable. But the use of such means of preparing his men shows Ralegh's seriousness and intelligence. It is likely, but by no means certain, that Harriot accompanied the 1584 venturers to see how his methods worked. If he did he was also to be employed in linguistic studies so that Englishmen could understand and be understood by the native peoples they encountered.[2]

The two men who led the first expedition to reconnoiter a site for a North American colony and who located, with some help from their pilot, the Outer Banks of North Carolina in 1584, are not known in any great detail. Philip Amadas was a member of a well-known Plymouth merchant family which had bought lands in Cornwall and which ranked as gentry. He had evidently had some experience at sea and may also have served in the army, as he apparently knew something of fortification. He entered Ralegh's household sometime before 1584 and may well have been one of those who was tutored in instrumental navigation by Thomas Harriot at Ralegh's expense. Small in stature—he was referred to jokingly in 1585 as "little Amadas"—he seems to have been a man of hot temper. Early in 1585, after returning from his first voyage, he was at the helm of a double wherry, a substantial four-oared river boat belonging to Ralegh, coming from Deptford to London. On his way he

steered his boat into another river boat and incurred the impreca-
tions and threats of the boatman, whereupon he tried to attack his
opponent and removed the helm staff to do so. In defense, the
waterman took up a stretcher to throw back but missed Amadas and
struck one of the rowers instead. Amadas swore vengeance on him
but did not carry it out.[3] For his services on the 1584 voyage, Ralegh
nominated him Admiral of Virginia, when the place had been named
in 1585, and sent him out as a prominent member of the first colony.
He was both resourceful and effective, but little is known about him
after his return to England in 1586.

Arthur Barlowe had probably entered Ralegh's service earlier. He
was one of his subordinates in the company that Ralegh commanded
in the Irish wars in 1580–81. We know nothing whatever about his
seagoing experience except that he had made a voyage to the eastern
Mediterranean and so had some. He was single-minded and competent and brought his ship home rapidly and effectively. His journal,
too, which was the basis for the document that gives an account of
the voyage and is a classic of its kind, demonstrates, however much it
was rewritten by Ralegh or Harriot, that his powers of observation
were remarkably good and that he had a sensibility to the atmosphere of an alien society that was exceptional among Englishmen. It
is to Arthur Barlowe and his journal that we owe the happy effect of
the first voyage and the brilliant light he throws on the first contacts
in this area between Englishmen and Native Americans.

In the first voyage to North America in 1578–79 Simon Fernandes
(Simão Fernandes in his native Portuguese) had served as master
under Ralegh in the *Falcon*.[4] An experienced pilot, he had been in
England for some years, become a Protestant, and narrowly escaped
being executed as a pirate. He rehabilitated himself and became a
dependent of Sir Francis Walsingham, the secretary of state. Ralegh
said he had behaved well on the voyage of 1578–79, but he was not
always to do so. His chief asset to the English was his claim to have
been in the Spanish service and to have explored the coast of North
America, in particular the area we know as the Outer Banks of North
Carolina. His pilotage did not bring him so far in 1579 because the
Falcon proved unseaworthy after she left the Canaries and was sailed
home. We have no information on which Spanish voyage between
1561 and 1572, if on any, he had been present. It may be suspected

that he was the Domingo Fernandes who piloted a Spanish ship into an opening in the Outer Banks in 1566 and annexed the land as San Bartolomé.[5] Domingo Fernandes was a native of Simon's home island of Terceira, and if he was not the same man under a different forename, is likely (despite the commonness of the name) to have been a relative. Or was Simon's knowledge not gained from direct experience but from a chart brought back by Domingo? Although a pirate by inclination and a dangerous enemy, Simon had shown intrepid leadership by sailing Gilbert's small frigate, the Squirrel, to Norumbega and back in 1580. He had not been on Gilbert's last voyage in 1583 as he had been elsewhere employed, but he was a necessary choice as pilot in the reconnaissance to be led by Amadas and Barlowe in 1584, and he justified his claim to be familiar with the coast by guiding them to Hatarask Inlet, which for a time was named Port Ferdinando in his honor.

John White, who was later to be Harriot's partner in the 1585 colony, and whose claim by 1590 to have made five voyages to America would indicate that he was on this one, was a member of a Cornish family from Truro. He had come to London and become a painter and possibly a land surveyor as well.[6] He may have been apprenticed to one of the sergeant painters who did decorative painting for the Court and houses of the nobility and also tried their hand at portraits. The name of John White is on the 1580 list of the members of the Painter Stainers' Company, which was one of the minor City of London guilds, and it is probably he. The interest aroused by the solitary Eskimo brought to London by Martin Frobisher's first Northwest Passage voyage in 1576—he was painted there before his death—led, we think, to White's being chosen to go on the second voyage to Baffin Island in 1577 to draw sketches from life of these unusual people, whose Asiatic appearance indicated that they could provide a clue to the long-sought route to China by the northwest. We have a version of a lively scene drawn by White of Eskimo encountering Frobisher's men that shows their kayaks. White was able to make closer studies of the Eskimo man first captured by Frobisher and then of the women and child taken later. These showed remarkable fidelity to life. Indeed, his drawings may have been engraved in a little book, now lost, as they were soon known on the Continent.

These studies, with little doubt, led Ralegh to employ White as an artist on the North American voyages. We have no specific evidence, besides his own statement, that he was with the 1584 expedition, and no pictures directly associated with the voyage have been identified. But later he and Harriot were to collaborate in a close study of the land and its inhabitants and together to make maps of the area now covered by parts of North Carolina and Virginia. Thus it is permissible to regard White's presence, with that of Harriot, as necessary for a preliminary reconnaissance of the area, so that they could later carry out the extensive project of 1585–86 with careful preparation and with full knowledge of what was involved in it.

We know little of the other men who were listed in Barlowe's narrative of the voyage.[7] William Greeneville was almost certainly a relative of Sir Richard Grenville, who was to lead the 1585 expedition, but the degree of relationship has not been established. John Wood has been identified by William S. Powell with a prominent resident of Sandwich, who was afterward knighted, but the name was a common one and it would be unsafe to accept it without reservation. James Browewich could have been the Master Bremige of the 1585 expedition, but this is little more than a guess. Benjamin Wood is, however, clearly identifiable as the sea captain who was to command a vessel bound for the East Indies in 1591 but who was lost at sea after visiting the Malay Peninsula. Nicholas Petman and John Hughes (the latter with a Welsh name) are unknown. Besides these there would have been some thirty others at least, possibly more. The only other individual we know by name was Richard Butler, an Irishman, who had been in Ralegh's service for some time. He was, very much later, captured in Spain by the Spanish and interrogated about 1596 as a spy.[8] He provided some information on the expedition that we do not otherwise have, but his memory was not always reliable, or perhaps he did not always tell the exact truth; nevertheless, he must be considered as one of our sources for the voyage.

We do not know the names of the two ships that sailed westward in 1584. Described in the narrative as barks, the implication is that they were small vessels. But one was larger than the other. The "Admiral," as the flagship of an expedition was called at this time, may have been of 50 or 60 tons, probably not more, and was captained by

Amadas who commanded the expedition and had Simon Fernandes with him as pilot. The other vessel was a pinnace, which we might guess was about 30 tons, though she may have been a little larger. She was commanded by Arthur Barlowe and, if they were present, had Harriot and White on board. Although we have no record of what equipment and stores they carried, a deposition by Fernandes[9] on the supplies of the *Falcon*—an 80-ton vessel that carried seventy men—in 1578 may give us some idea of what the equipment of the 1584 barks amounted to, always remembering that Fernandes considered the *Falcon's* equipment inadequate for a long voyage. We can assume the vessels were armed and indeed, by implication, we know that Amadas's ship must have been fairly heavily so. But they were unlikely to have had between them as many as the fifteen cast iron pieces and some sixteen other guns the *Falcon* carried. On the other hand, we must double some of the items we have for 1578 because there were two vessels; however, the partial inventory can help us to fit out the two ships in 1584.

Each ship would carry at least one spare suit of sails or sailcloth to make them. The *Falcon* had twelve bolts of poldavys (a type of sail canvas) sufficient for a mainsail, a foresail and a mizzen, and a main topsail. It is likely that each bark would have required much the same amount, the pinnace perhaps a little less. Spare anchors and cables would be essential for both vessels and we do not hear of the vessels having any difficulty in maintaining their position in the treacherous waters off and inside the Outer Banks of North Carolina. They would need chain pumps and oakum, as the *Falcon* had, to stanch leaks. The *Falcon* had ample spare rope including five coils of small rope, weighing about five hundredweight, twine, ratlines, marline, "deesye" lines (deep sea or dipsy lines), and latchet lines (for tying the bonnets of the topsail). There were plenty of nails—ordinary nails, spikes, and scoop nails. Basic equipment would also consist of two sounding lines each, one for deep water (probably one hundred fathoms long), with lead to sink them. Each vessel would have at least three compasses and six half-hour running glasses to help estimate speed and reckon time. There would also be more sophisticated navigating instruments, including probably some of the more complex types with which Harriot was experimenting, that would be in the captain's custody, as well as the standard astrolabes, quadrants, and cross staffs that the master would require. They would also carry charts of western European waters and copies of older Spanish charts of eastern North America, of which we know Fernandes had at least one in 1580.

They would be laden with food and supplies for a six months' voyage. Two kettles and two peasepots, with wood billets (Norway billets on the *Falcon*), would be a minimum provision for cooking, and a platter and can for each man, with a few trays. There would also be a plentiful supply of candles. The officers and gentlemen would have their own equipment. The basic food supply would be biscuits and flour—the *Falcon* carried 3,000 biscuits and enough flour to bake 8,000 more. Then came fish—for the *Falcon* 3,000 salt cod and some dried cod, ling, and conger eel. Meat in barrels came next, followed by beef and pork, beans and peas, and some vinegar. For liquid there was primarily water, enough tuns and barricos (containers of varying size) to last as long as seemed practicable, and a substantial amount of beer. Canary and Gascon wine might be reserved for the officers, though they would also have private stores.

The armament would consist of a number of relatively heavy cast pieces and some smaller guns such as fowlers and bases, together with round shot, crossbars, and gunpowder. Small arms would include calivers, bows and sheaves of arrows, bills, pikes, targets (small round shields), morions, and other protective headpieces. Some of the gentlemen would carry headpieces and body armor of their own. Boats would be essential—one large ship's boat of perhaps two tons, and a smaller skiff or two, especially if close inspection was to be made of unknown shoals and anchorages.

The vessels themselves would be rather small, stout ships, the "Admiral" with a broad beam and, apparently, a shallow draft. The pinnace would be shorter, with a narrower beam. On each the foremast and mainmast, with two courses, would carry square sails, and the mizen a triangular lateen. These would be supplemented by smaller subsidiary sails for use when winds were favorable. The main cabin in each ship would be in the stern, above the rudder and its housing; there the officers and gentlemen would live in a number of small compartments. The crew's quarters would center on the forecastle, though, for the most part, they would have to sleep on deck or between decks. It is probable that below the main deck there was a gun deck, and, amidships, an extensive hold. Such vessels would normally be used for cargo-carrying to and from cross-channel and western European ports, but would be specially sheathed with timber for passage through tropical waters. Both were evidently good sailers, well handled, as they kept company all the way out. They were sailed on a long voyage with exemplary skill.

The Initial Contact

At the end of April the 1584 expedition of Amadas and Barlowe found sailing conditions reasonably good as the vessels made their way south off western Europe and, at the Canaries, which they reached on 10 May, encountered the trade winds and current that would bring them rapidly across the Atlantic, a passage achieved by 10 June. It seems likely that the men put ashore on the south coast of Puerto Rico, obtaining fresh water, and elsewhere in the Caribbean, some fresh food. Some of the men fell ill and they removed themselves as rapidly as possible after a twelve-days' stay. We know they sailed rather too far to the southeast, miscalculating the strength of the Gulf current, so that perhaps they sailed between Puerto Rico and Española and came up on the Florida current, which was less strong than they expected. They coasted Florida under the pilotage of Simon Fernandes and sounded close to shore on 2 July, when they smelled the land breezes. Two days later they saw land, coasting some 120 miles along the barrier islands from Cape Fear northward. It is probable that from time to time they sent boats ashore to sound and to look for an entry. Richard Butler says they put in at Wococon (roughly modern Ocracoke), but Arthur Barlowe clearly states that the first entry found was that at the north tip of the island of Hatarask (part of modern Bodie Island). This had a depth at high tide of only twelve feet so that it is not strange they had some difficulty in entering. That they did so at all indicates that the vessels were small and of relatively shallow draft.

Barlowe's narrative then records the significant event of taking possession of the land. They went ashore a few hundred yards on the port side to "take possession of the same in the right of the queen's most excellent Majesty, as rightful queen and princess of the same, and after delivered the same over to your [Ralegh's] use according to her Majesty's grant and letters patents, under her Highness' Great Seal." They performed ceremonies appropriate to such an occasion, Philip Amadas presumably having delivered to him a rod and a turf of the soil, as Sir Humphrey Gilbert had in Newfoundland in 1583. Barlowe notes that they also erected some sort of post, with the Queen's arms on it or attached to it. Then follows his famous passage:

> We viewed the land about us, being whereas we first landed, very sandy and low towards the water side, but so full of grapes as the very beating and surge of the sea overflowed them, of which we found such plenty, as well here as in all places else, both on the sand and on the green soil on the hills, as in the plains, as well on every little shrub, as also climbing towards the tops of the high cedars, that I think in all the world the like abundance is not to be found: and myself, having seen those parts of Europe that most abound, find such difference as were incredible to be written.

Now this would not be possible anywhere near where they landed—not far from the unstable Oregon Inlet—but then the Outer Banks were on average perhaps a mile wider and the vegetation much more luxurious. The sweet summer grape was ripe and close to the water because it would have been a spring tide, which facilitated their entry into the inlet. The white and red cedar forests have gone but a remnant survives on Colington Island farther north on the inner shores of the Outer Banks and in the Nags Head Woods. Hatarask Island then extended southward to the inlet the Indians called Chacandepeco, just north of modern Cape Hatteras. Amadas, Barlowe, and their men walked inland to the sound side of the island and to Barlowe its flora and fauna were fabulously rich:

> Under the bank or hill whereon we stood we beheld the valleys replenished with goodly cedar trees, and having discharged our harquebusshot [they were carrying calivers], such a flock of cranes (the most part white) [probably herons] arose under us, with such a cry redoubled by many echoes as if an army of men had shouted all together.

2. "The arrival of the Englishemen in Virginia," 1584.
Theodor de Bry. *America*. Part 1. Frankfurt am Main, 1590, plate 2.

> This island hath many goodly woods and full of deer, conies hares, and fowl [birds in general], even in the midst of summer, in incredible abundance. The woods are ... the highest and reddest cedars of the world ... pines [several species], cypress, sassafras, the lentisk or the tree that beareth the mastic [sweet gum], the tree that beareth the rind of black cinnamon [possibly dogwood] ... and many other of excellent smell and quality.

Now, stripped by wave and storm, and eroded to narrow strips in places, this island is a bare shadow of what it was, but roots exposed by waves show Barlowe was right. The simple eloquence of Barlowe's language, no doubt heightened in places by Ralegh's hand after the explorers' return, did much to sell the idea that this area was a very Eden, even if its fragile beauty and its lack of major agricultural resources were in the end to prove deceptive. In some respects this ideal picture helped to create too favorable an impression of the land in England, and may be thought to have contributed to the long-term failure of the 1584–90 enterprises.

The Indians of nearby Roanoke Island may have exercised a vague and not undisputed hegemony over the other Indian groups around the great expanse of water on which the English looked to the west on 4 July 1584. Their chief, Wingina (afterward he renamed himself Pemisapan, though we will keep the original name), had been wounded in the wars, possibly with the people of Secotan. Neighboring groups lived in rapidly alternating conditions of friendship and conflict. The cultural basis of the life of these people was maritime as much as agricultural. They frequently lived during the summer in temporary camps near the water on the Outer Banks and sounds, gathering oysters, one of their chief food sources, clams, mussels, and crabs. They fished continually in the shallow sounds from substantial canoes, hollowed from the tulip tree and white cedar by fire and scrapers, and used hand nets and spears to get fish. They also built elaborate weirs out into the sounds that trapped many fish. But they had in addition permanent village sites. These were based on small fields laboriously fashioned by the slash and burn method, and changed to new ones nearby as soil fertility (not high as the soil was thin) gave out. Corn, from which they claimed to be able to get three crops (though we suspect the third might not always ripen), was their main food product. Beans grew up the cornstalks. Plots of cucurbits were tended and were highly productive. Sunflowers were also grown for their oily seeds. Tobacco, which had a ceremonial significance, was grown in carefully tended plots near their ceremonial buildings.

Their houses were large, the longhouse derived from the north; long posts were inserted in the ground at intervals and were bent over to form a frame for a curved roof. Cross pieces were tied between them to make them firm, and a roof of woven mats added. The chief interior furnishing was a bench mainly for sleeping. Most of their life was carried on in the open air. A communal fire did for cooking in the clay pots that the women fashioned. They served their stewed meat and corn on platters. Of their wooden utensils we have little knowledge. A ceremonial building, as a base for their priests and a temple for the dessicated remains of their leading men, stood somewhat apart and nearby a circle of posts around which communal dances and other ceremonies were held. Their village settlements of some six to twenty longhouses might lie open, as did Secotan, well to the south of Pamlico Sound, or might be palisaded, with a narrow defensible entrance, as Pomeioc on the mainland somewhat to the south of Roanoke Island. Roanoke Island, a substantial piece of ground (though swampy and without as much solid land as in the twentieth century), was the nucleus of this Indian group. Its village at the northern end of the island (now long eroded away) was palisaded and had several cornfields close by. It was there Wingina had his home and from there he dominated such other groups as, from time to time, he could. His village of Dasemunkepeuc, on the mainland across Croatan Sound, was larger.

These people wore little in summer. A breechclout of skin or one or two apron skirts were all that was needed for man or woman; male children might be naked, or, if female, wore a rudimentary breechclout. But they believed in decoration: they tattooed their faces and rubbed dye into them; they painted designs on breast, arms, and legs; they wore chains of pearls or shells and armlets, and leg ornaments of the same; they hung pendants from their pierced ears, and, if they could get it, earrings and gorgets of copper hanging from their necks or placed on their heads. They could sew onto a netlike warp strips of rabbit fur to make a short light cloak. The chief might wear a puma tail when fully painted for war. The shaman, endowed with curative powers and a capacity for divination, might attach a bird's body to his head. He, especially, wore a "medicine" pouch attached to his waistband, but others probably had pouches for tobacco. The Indians are not known to have worn foot coverings. For colder weather they had mantles of deerskin, finely tanned, often decorated with colored designs.

Their weapons were mainly bows and arrows with which they could take deer and many small mammals. In war, besides the bow, they used wooden clubs. They certainly had a few stone axes, but stone was a scarce commodity, though they could find small pieces of quartz from which they could strike flakes for arrowheads or small tools. They knew of iron and had a few spikes salvaged from a Spanish vessel wrecked many years before. They had seen Europeans then. The Spaniards who annexed the Outer Banks in 1566 landed a considerable way farther north and themselves saw no Indians but may have been seen by them. There had been several wrecks on Wococon and in one case survivors got to sea in a patched-up craft but were driven back on land and drowned. But the close-up view of the two English ships, small by European standards, but enormous in relation to their canoes, was astounding. So were the English who were so richly clothed and endowed with many novelties in the way of equipment and weapons. Gunfire seemed like man-induced thunder and it was hard for them to understand how bullets could kill from a distance. They were to find that the visitors were continually inquiring, by signs or by attempting to find names for objects, far more than they could effectively tell about their country and its people. But they were to prove, in this area at least, well-disposed toward each other, and the spontaneous attraction that drew each to each demonstrated that whatever previous views the English had about the savagery of savages, these people were human and humane, even if very different in their level of cultural and material equipment from themselves.

The Indians kept out of the way until they saw whether the visitors meant to stay. To show themselves prematurely could invite hostile reactions. As it appeared the newcomers were intending to remain for some time—they may even have pitched some tents on shore— contact was desirable, if only to see whether commercial exchanges with them were possible. Certainly, trade with peoples of the interior was not unfamiliar to them. Stone, copper, and such things came from far inland peoples, though precisely what was given in exchange (dried fish? shell beads?) we cannot tell. But whether they previously had made any exchanges with Europeans is still unclear. Casual trading by French ships on the southeastern coasts had been going on for a long time.

Finally, three Indians approached in their boat. One came on shore and began calling unintelligibly to the English who were at that time all on shipboard. A party landed, made friendly gestures toward him, and induced him to come back with them to one of the ships. This indicated that he did not anticipate any hostility. He was welcomed, given a hat, shirt, and other useless objects, and was introduced to wine. Then he was returned to shore, and with his associates soon brought back a boatful of fish that he wished to have divided between the two English vessels. This favorable initial contact and exchange of gifts was enough to open the door to much more important visitors. A fleet of canoes appeared with forty or fifty men and from one of them emerged an imposing figure, whom they learned afterward to be Wingina's brother, who was acting as head of the group while his brother recovered from a wound. Granganimeo settled himself in some state, seated on a long mat, with his men around him and four other men at the seaward end of the mat. He beckoned the Englishmen to come to him, which they did, and he received them with elaborate gestures of goodwill. They gave him presents (he had come armed with a basket for the exchange) and he received them with dignity; finally they parted.

This traditional ceremonial exchange meant, from the Indian side, that relations had now been formally established and the parties could treat each other as equals. And this they proceeded to do. A few days later canoes appeared laden with goods for trade, dressed deerskins (chamois leather it seemed), tough leather (buff, probably not bison, though this was so called later), and undressed deerskins. The cape merchant of the expedition opened his package of merchandise and began to offer objects in it for skins. Granganimeo, who was there informally this time, seized on a tin dish which he clapped on his breast, after making a hole in it, as a gorget. For this the English obtained twenty skins and for a copper kettle, fifty. This was not sharp trading, the metal being more than the Indians would have acquired in some years of trading in the interior. They also wanted iron objects, hatchets, axes, knives, and especially swords but, for the time being at least, the Englishmen would not part with any even though they were offered many skins. The Indians took no offense at this, but behaved in a manner suggesting earlier trading contacts with Europeans, though, as stated above, it is impossible to be certain.

Granganimeo paid a social visit a little later and drank wine and ate meat and bread on board. A little later still he brought his bashful wife and small children with him—an unusual demonstration of trust. His wife, who was not tall, wore a skin cloak with the fur next to the skin and an apron skirt. A band of shell beads encircled her forehead (her husband also had a number of them) and loops of pearls hung from her ears to her waist. (Ralegh was to receive a little bracelet of them when the expedition returned to England.) Other women encountered had ornaments of copper hanging from their ears as did some children. Granganimeo himself had on his head a broad plate of copper, which he would not allow the Englishmen to remove. The Indian men and women dressed alike except that the men scraped the hair from one side of their head. Their color appeared yellowish and this was probably correct—sunburn, walnut oil, and the remains of pigment often made it hard to distinguish precise skin color. The hair of all adults was black, though that of some children was reddish.

Once trading was begun individual Indians came down to the shore with "leather, coral and divers kinds of dyes, very excellent"— the leather probably included dressed skins of other animals besides deer, possibly even bear; the "coral" was wampum, beads made of shell, conch especially, but cockle, mussel, clam, and oyster as well; and among the "divers kinds of dyes" probably would have been red dye from puccoon roots (which would have to be traded from the interior) and dogwood, a purplish color from pokeweed, and black from sumac. These were exchanged freely except when Granganimeo was present; then only he and the other elders (*weroances*), distinguished by copper gorgets, could trade. Granganimeo's wife came frequently, followed by a large group of women, she herself coming aboard with her children and a few others. Tribal discipline was carefully maintained; Granganimeo signaled by numbers of fires lit on the shore how many canoes were coming out to the ships so that the English would not mistake their intentions as hostile and take alarm.

Granganimeo sent the Englishmen daily presents of meat, fish, fruit, vegetables (squash, walnuts, gourds, and beans), and corn (the first crop, still white in the grain, was just ripening). They learned that the Indians inserted their seeds in the ground after working it over with wooden digging sticks, and themselves tried sowing seeds, peas and beans, which grew rapidly. There was some misunderstanding about the products, as Barlowe credited them with having both wheat and oats and misidentified some kinds of squash as melons.

After relations had been established on the Outer Banks, Barlowe took seven of his men in the pinnace's boat and worked his way up what is now Roanoke Sound to the northern end of Roanoke Island. There the men came to Granganimeo's palisaded village of nine longhouses. Because he was not at home, his wife ran out to greet them. She directed men from the village to draw the boat on land, carry the Englishmen ashore (they were getting wet as the water was rough and it was raining) and even bring their oars after them. The longhouse in which she lived was said to have five compartments, but longhouses seen in drawings made the following year show no such room-like divisions. She and her women took off the mens' clothes, washed and dried them (over what sort of fire?), and washed their feet in warm water, while she prepared food for them. When all were dried and dressed, she brought them into an inner room where was set out on the sleeping bench at the side boiled corn, boiled and roasted venison, and stewed, boiled, and roasted fish, along with raw and cooked squash and other roots and fruits. Barlowe believed they drank wine while the grape lasted, but he was wrong; on the other hand, he is probably correct when he said they flavored their drink with spicy herbs (ginger and black cinnamon were his own misleading descriptions) and sassafras. Clearly the men enjoyed the meal after hard shipboard fare. As Barlowe tells it:

> We were entertained with all love and kindness, and with as much bounty, after their manner, as they could possibly devise. We found the people most gentle, loving and faithful, void of all guile and treason, and such as lived after the manner of the

Golden Age. The earth bringeth forth all things in abundance, as in the first Creation, without toil or labor. The people only care to defend themselves from the cold in their short winter and to feed themselves with such meat [food] as the country affordeth. Their meat is very well sodden [boiled or stewed], and they make broth very sweet and savory: their vessels are earthen pots, very large, white [brown?] and sweet: their dishes are wooden platters of sweet timber. Within the place where they feed was their lodging and within that their Idol, which they worship [and] of which they speak incredible things.

Not all the things he mentions could be accommodated inside any of the houses of which we have other record. "Sweet" he uses to mean pleasant and agreeable, and applies it widely, but his description is so vivid and effective, as well as idealistic, that it formed a very fine piece of publicity once the expedition had returned to England.

Granganimeo's wife understood they were cautious about their safety and had some hunters disarmed as they came through the village entrance. Distressed that the visitors insisted on sleeping on their boat some distance from the land, she sent mats to shelter them from the rain, brought them food ready to cook, and had a number of men and women sit by the bank all night to keep them company. Although Barlowe was prepared to regard them as kind and loving beyond compare he did not, even so, dare trust them so far as to risk endangering the expedition through lack of precautions.

Barlowe gives additional details of their reactions to the English— the whiteness of their skin, the largeness of their ships continued to amaze them; they also continued to show great alarm whenever a firearm was discharged. Among his other impressions, their arrows had a sharp shell or fish tooth for points (many, in fact, were of stone); they had fire-hardened wooden swords and wooden breastplates, and clubs to which they fastened the horn of a stag or other beast. They carried their Idol with them to war "of whom they ask counsel as the Romans were wont of the Oracle of Apollo." They marched to war singing. They engaged in cruel and bloody wars, especially in recent years, so that the people were reduced in numbers and parts of the country were left desolate. But this latter information he could not have learned from contacts made before the linguistic barrier was broken.

We also have from Barlowe a good general account of the Outer Banks and of the sounds and islands in them. Of Roanoke, he says:

one [island] is sixteen miles long, at which we were, finding it to be a most pleasant and fertile ground, replenished with goodly cedars and divers other sweet woods, full of currants [small grapes], of flax and many other notable commodities, which we at that time had no leisure to view . . . [Other islands were] most beautiful and pleasant to behold, replenished with deer, conies [rabbits], hares and divers beasts, and about them the goodliest and best fish in the world and in greatest abundance.

Exactly what the rest of the expedition was doing while Barlowe examined Roanoke and other islands in Roanoke Sound and the opening of Albemarle Sound, we do not know. They were making, we may think, a more extended reconnaissance of the region, perhaps up Albemarle Sound, perhaps as far south as Secotan. But no record survives of the reactions of others than Barlowe and his boat's crew to the setting, prospects and, above all, people of the region. What we do know, however, is that they took on board, by what means we cannot say, two Indians—Manteo and Wanchese—to bring back to England. We can easily imagine Thomas Harriot, who was good at picking up an elementary vocabulary, meeting Manteo during some of the expedition's extended excursions and persuading him to go to England with them—if indeed Harriot was present. Manteo was a Croatoan, not a Roanoke, Indian living down near present Cape Hatteras, where his mother ruled a separate group. Evidently he was easily persuaded that everything English was attractive just as Barlowe persuaded himself that almost everything about the Indians was perfect. Wanchese was a different problem, as he was one of Wingina's subjects. Did Granganimeo persuade him to go with the Englishmen in the hope that when they returned, as they said they would, he or his brother would learn much more about these strangers? Or was Wanchese snatched up and taken prisoner when he was found alone away from his people? We cannot be sure which explanation is correct.

In any event, after a stay of a month or less, the pinnace was prepared to leave, taking samples of Indian products and the two Indians with them. Harriot would have left with Barlowe and White, so that the utmost could be gleaned from Manteo and Wanchese. The pinnace made a rapid voyage home and arrived safely in the west of England about the middle of September; her English passengers had been away only four and a half months. Whether Ralegh went down to meet them or whether they joined him in London we do not know, but their news of a favorable site and friendly people immediately set him moving to publicize what had been found and to exploit it in order to arouse interest at Court in a more extensive and expensive venture. An early priority was to learn what the two Indians could tell. If we have assumed that Harriot was probably with Barlowe it is largely because the Indians rapidly learned some English and Harriot, equally, some Algonquian, though whether he was already working on the phonetic alphabet that he eventually constructed to record the sounds of their speech is unknown.

Ralegh had not been idle while the ships were away. The Reverend Richard Hakluyt had returned from the Paris embassy to write for him, and for Hakluyt's master, Sir Francis Walsingham, an elaborate treatise that could be presented to Queen Elizabeth on the importance of colonizing North America as an essential part of the policy of English expansion with which he and those for whom he worked were identified. Hakluyt's "Discourse," which we know best as his "Discourse of Western Planting"—though he had a longer name for it—started by insisting that the English Protestant church should assert its claim to universalism as opposed to that of the Church of Rome, by engaging in missionary work, and where better than in North America? He set out to prove that the Queen had a valid title, mainly through the Cabot discoveries during Henry VII's reign, to North America. Spain was the usurper here and her flaunting of papal grants was irrelevant to English claims. Mainly, Hakluyt relied on economic arguments. England depended on continental sources of supply for basic commodities and luxuries alike. This demand could be satisfied from North America if colonists were sent there to work (and perhaps the inhabitants too). A great volume of trade could be built up with the inhabitants; in turn, they would supply many valuable products. England had surplus labor, which could best be employed in America. Under the Crown, a new English society could be established in this vast area that lay open to exploitation and settlement. He elaborated these points in great detail. But he felt that the Queen herself should take a hand in the venture as it would be difficult for private men alone to make rapid progress in building up an empire which, he implied, might soon rival that of Spain, especially, of course, if valuable minerals were found. It would be possible to collaborate with the inhabitants because they would respond favorably to kind treatment, compared with the cruelty the Spaniards were said to inflict on their Indian subjects. Why they should be willing to give up their land to large groups of colonists was not touched on.

This learned, persuasive, and valuable state paper was intended for the Queen, Ralegh, Walsingham, and only a few of the inner circle of officials who were sympathetic to American, and anti-Spanish, ventures. Its persuasiveness was limited by the fact that Hakluyt's specific information on eastern North America was very narrowly based and he had had to generalize widely about the Americas as a whole. Thus much of what he said was partly or wholly inapplicable to the area to which Ralegh's ships had gone. Moreover, for Queen Elizabeth to take on extensive royal investment in colonization at this time was quite unrealistic. She had too many problems on her hands with the Netherlands, with Spain, and with Ireland, and too little money to spare to attempt anything of the sort. But at least she might aid Ralegh substantially to bring about a breakthrough in this novel area of colonization and conquest some thousands of miles from England. Although the "Discourse" was finished before Barlowe arrived, about mid-September, it was presented to the Queen only early in October, when Ralegh knew that the results obtained by Barlowe appeared very favorable to the development of his project. From then on he could put his plans for colonial propaganda fully into effect.

So far we have concentrated on Barlowe and the pinnace. What of the larger ship that Amadas commanded? We have no journal of its proceedings after the first picture of the two vessels lying at anchor just inside the Outer Banks at Hatarask, or Port Ferdinando as the entry was now usually called. We suspect that it was soon found that the larger vessel could not move freely around the shallow Pamlico Sound and that at low tide she was not even comfortable at her first anchorage. She may well have sent out a boat to explore the sounds

and banks, but it is probable that she soon left the port and proceeded northward by sea to explore what further entries could be
discovered and what the people living there were like. We have a
garbled report from a man captured by the Spanish in 1585[2] indicating that *before* reaching Hatarask the English went ashore and were
met by hostile Indians who killed and ate thirty-eight of them! It is
clear that no such thing could have happened before they reached
the entry in the Outer Banks, as Barlowe described it. On the other
hand, it is not impossible that Amadas's ship went northward and
did meet Indians who were at least potentially hostile.

Another deposition, taken in Spain about 1596 from Richard Butler,[3] the Irishman who had been in Ralegh's service and who had
sailed with Amadas as corporal, is more specific, but he mixes up his
chronology and facts. Nonetheless we can get something of a story
from him. He rightly mentions the landing at Hatarask and goes on:

> From there they moved twelve leagues to the north and found
> a port, with a depth of nine feet, which the savages called "Ca-
> cho Peos," and these savages were enemies of those of Puerto
> Fernando [Hatarask].

From this we can make two alternative but tentative reconstructions,
the first being that the inlet was that known in 1585 as Trinity Harbor,
providing an outlet from Albemarle Sound, and that the hostile Indians were Weapemeoc, living on the north bank of Albemarle Sound.
There is no evidence that at this time they were Wingina's enemies;
moreover, twelve leagues is too far north for Trinity Harbor, which
we know in 1585 had on the bar only eight feet of water at high tide.
Butler makes no suggestion that the hostility of the Indians was
turned against the English, though it may have been if it was clear
they were allied with Wingina's people.

The more likely alternative is that they sailed farther north and
entered Chesapeake Bay, which was more than twelve leagues away
and had a depth of very much more than nine feet on the bar.
Fernandes should have known about the earlier Spanish attempts to
explore the bay and to establish a mission there, and of the final
expedition of revenge against the Powhatan Indians (as we later call
them) in 1572 after they had destroyed the mission. There is no
doubt that a likely reaction of these Indians to an English ship would

have been a hostile one, though it is doubtful that they would have been in contact, hostile or otherwise, with the Indians of Roanoke Island. The second reconstruction appears rather more attractive in view of later developments in that region.

From there Amadas is said by Butler to have sailed toward Bermuda in search of a Spanish prize but failed to find one. He was caught in a storm, and then sailed across to the Azores, where he again hoped to take a prize. But he was unsuccessful in the six weeks he spent in these waters and returned to England only because provisions were giving out. This is highly plausible as Fernandes considered no voyage worthwhile unless prizes, preferably Spanish ones, were taken, even though such captures were still open piracy. This would put the return of Amadas's ship well into November if Butler is correct, so that it could contribute little to the first phase of Ralegh's preparations for a colonizing venture.

In the meantime, considerable progress was being made in getting information from the two Indians whom Barlowe had brought to England. In mid-October we find them in Ralegh's household, dressed up in brown taffeta in the English fashion. They spoke but could not be understood and clearly were finding it difficult to adapt to the strange circumstances in which they found themselves. But by December they were cited as authorities on their homeland, for we hear of "some of the people born in those parts brought home into this realm of England by whose means and direction, and by such of her Majesty's subjects as were sent thither by the said Walter Ralegh, singular great commodities of that land are revealed and made known to us." That this was not an empty boast is shown by the material in Barlowe's narrative as it has come down to us (and which Amadas signed as well as himself). To his simple and direct account of the contacts made in North America was now added information that clearly derives from Manteo and Wanchese. They are referred to specifically as a source—"as these men which we have brought with us into England have made us to understand." A two-way exchange of information was now taking place and we are strongly inclined to give Thomas Harriot credit for this. The Indians were thus able to indicate something about the political geography and relations of the area.

To the north there was a great settlement called Skicóac and access to it could be had from Occam (Albemarle Sound)—but this was, in fact, beyond the Great Dismal Swamp and known, we think, only by hearsay to the Roanoke Indians. Toward the southern limits of Pamlico Sound Indian groups were at war with each other, the "Pomouik" and the Secotan, on the Neuse and Pamlico rivers, respectively; they also were alleged to be hostile to Wingina. Wingina may have attempted to assert some degree of hegemony over the Secotan, though this is conjecture, but they had recently repelled him. His influence seems to have extended at least as far south as Pomeioc on Wyesocking Bay and perhaps also comprised the Hatarask Indians from which Manteo came. It is very difficult for us to clearly distinguish tribal divisions and superiorities at this time, and noncommittal words like "group" are often used here instead. However, a clear picture of the sounds and the barrier islands enclosing them emerged from these descriptions even if they were not always accurate. This enabled Ralegh to demonstrate that his knowledge now encompassed a substantial region on the North American coast. But it did not bring out that swamps, swamp forest, and bare sandy deserts as well as fertile oases marked the area and that the waters of the sounds were too shallow for ships to sail in, nor do we think that Ralegh later understood this to be so. Throughout, his failure to see the land for himself, and the tendency of his subordinates to emphasize the advantages rather than the disadvantages of planting a colony there, weakened his planning. Such ignorance, however, did not prevent him from pushing ahead with large-scale arrangements for a settlement in 1585.

Planning the First Virginia Voyage

Ralegh had seen and understood only too well how Sir Humphrey
Gilbert had faltered in preparing for his last voyage. Many of the
persons and institutions that backed him were of little solid worth
and would sign promises but not come up with hard cash, while he,
himself, frittered away what he did assemble by incompetence and
delays—and with some considerable bad luck. Ralegh was determined to get royal support, or the authority of parliament, if he
could, for his venture; if he could not, then he would make sure, or
as sure as possible, that his backers had the intention and the cash to
support his voyage.

By now Ralegh was a member of parliament for Plymouth, along
with John Hawkins, the former raider-trader in the Caribbean, now
the clerk of the Queen's ships and very respectable. Ralegh had the
idea that an act of parliament confirming the Queen's letters patent
to him would be of great value in lending force to his efforts to raise
money, and, incidentally, would involve the Queen more closely in
his undertaking. His fellow members of the House of Commons
seemed to agree. They passed the bill in its preliminary stages,[1] but
with qualifications about Ralegh's power to take with him certain
classes of people. The House of Lords, however, did not pass the bill
and it dropped, the probable reason being that its members saw no
reason to repeat or qualify the Queen's patent, which was in itself
sufficient. Ralegh, however, obtained much of what he wanted by
bringing in the bill. The committee to which it was sent for scrutiny contained most of the members whom he wished to convince
to become his associates in his ventures—Sir Christopher Hatton
and Sir Francis Walsingham, who were influential with the Queen;
Sir Philip Sidney, who had supported Gilbert; Sir Francis Drake,

who was always ready to support new anti-Spanish ventures; Sir Richard Grenville, a distant relative of Ralegh's and possibly already his choice to lead the expedition if he could not go himself; and probably Anthony Rowse and Thomas Cavendish as well as others. A diarist noted that of those on the committee "many were to go in that journey." So Ralegh was at least assured of powerful and influential support, most of the members being rich and representing west country constituencies.

The bill also provided Ralegh with a valuable official-sounding piece of propaganda, the preamble citing the Queen's desire:

> that the knowledge of God and true religion might by her Highness' labors be propagated amongst foreign nations, the people of this her Highness' realm maintained and increased, and traffic [trade] to the most benefit and commodity of her loving subjects as otherwise should spend their time in idleness to the great prejudice of the Commonwealth be trained in virtuous and commodious labor....

It went on to claim that Ralegh's discovery of "an unknown land never heretofore possessed by any Christian prince or Christian people, the nearness whereof and infinite commodities of the same might yield unto this her realm of England the benefits before remembered and many others." We can be sure that every member of the House of Commons and House of Lords saw this, and that the rewritten narrative of Arthur Barlowe, signed by Philip Amadas as well as Barlowe, was circulated in manuscript (if not in print) among many of them. In addition, Richard Hakluyt was induced to add a number of practical recommendations to the copies of his "Discourse" that were made for especially influential people.

Ralegh consulted a military expert on what preparations he should make to establish the colony. He received an interesting if elaborate scheme for a strong, well-armed military expedition of eight hundred soldiers, a proportion of whom would make exploring excursions into the country,[2] while the remainder worked to construct a formidable fort, its fortifications enclosing a town on a peninsula or island. An experienced engineer would be needed to organize and carry through the building of the fort and settlement. There would need to be a physician "to discover the simples [curative qualities] of herbs, plants, trees, roots and stones, a good geographer to make descriptions of the lands discovered and with him an excellent painter, apothecaries and surgeons." Also desirable would be an alchemist (metallurgist) to assay metals, a lapidary to identify jewels, masons, carpenters, Cornish tin miners, and "some excellent husbandmen with all things pertaining to husbandry and all manner of seed corn." A hierarchy of officials was suggested, including a general in absolute command, a judge with full legal authority, and those with military ranking from colonels downward who should "all know their offices and what by duty they are to do." There would be a "high treasurer" with authority to receive all receipts and make payments. The admiral, too, would be accountable to the treasurer for the fifth part of all treasure found, which should go to the Queen. The soldiers were to be under strict discipline and were not to injure or exploit the Indians ("that no Indian be forced to labor unwillingly").

The details of the fortifications suggested need not concern us here, but for the town inside the expert said "I would have every street straight to every bulwark and to every gate and to the midst of every curtain so as standing in the market place [elsewhere described as "large for assemblies and to sit in if need be"] you may see all the bulwarks, curtains and gates." This was unlike anything that could be built in the area where Amadas and Barlowe had been in 1584. It was much too elaborate and in any case there was no building stone within very many miles. At the same time, its general design may have stimulated plans, and even experiments, in laying out designs for a settlement.

The handwriting of the military expert is very similar to that of Sir Roger Williams, a veteran of continental wars, who is known to have been in England at the time. He was evidently a member of a group of men who passed jocular remarks about each other. We have an example of this in "An ironical letter" written to Sir Roger Williams by Jack Roberts,[3] who had been with Sir Humphrey Gilbert in 1578. Extracts from it, if not fully intelligible because the persons cannot all be identified, show that the Virginia voyage was discussed and jested about in London at the time. It runs, in part:

Don Rogero. I have received a letter from you by John Winter [with Drake, 1577–79], and opening of it, I thought it to be

some old debt and reckoning of Jack Hannam [whose son was
later to be involved in an American voyage] for a breast of veal,
mutton and onions at the Green Lettice, or the woeful complaint of William Martin's soldiers for leaving them behind him;
or the lost will and testament of Father Lyster. Master Groome
hath obtained of the State of Venice the last of this month the
maintenance of two ordinary tables, and the relief of Mun Fel-
ton and five whores. Captain Shoute, Captain [Thomas] Churchyard [the poet], and Captain Story have sworn solemnly either
to raise the seige at Antwerp or to leave good wine and a tavern
so long as they live. Indeed Captain Churchyard should have
been withdrawn out of this action to be secretary to Amias
Preston in Master Rawley's voyage. A captain who though he
speak ill, yet he writes but badly. Old Morgan, Master Herbert and Father Lyster are resolute—whether Sir Francis Drake
and Sir Richard Greenfield go forward in their voyage or
no, they will drink burnt sack. And old Morgan told Herbert
plainly that a man is a man. And Master Herbert is of opinion
that old sack is better than new, and Father Lyster maintaineth
it. Captain Rich hath gotten during life, by help of the Recorder
[of London], that no man, whatsoever he be, shall have to do
with Midsummer Watch or Mylandgreene service but himself,
George Whetstone [with Gilbert, 1578] Master Skidmore and
Guy of Cardife stood to be his lieutenants: Whetstone was
favored because he was a poet, Master Skidmore served in
Fleetestreete and Smythfield these thirteen or fourteen years
upon his own charges. But for all that Guy of Cardife carried it
away because he did wear a red scarf upon his left arm. In truth
Master Skidmore took it so unkindly that he fell into a tavern
and presently one goblet was gone. . . . [These are jests about
the London trainbands.] Master Thomas Somerset hath given
away all that he hath to the poor people and is a priest in little
Amadas's ship in the voyage. . . . John Winter commends him
unto you hartily, and I love nobody but my best friends, George
and you; when you will rebell I am ready. And thus farewell
from Cepons at the Worlds End, where Water Pan was either
taken for a good musician or physician. I know not what day,
but a market day, A Friday, a fish day.

Perhaps this gallimaufry suggests that Sir Roger Williams was not taken too seriously by his pothouse friends, but the glancing references to the preparations for the voyage, however unhelpful about personnel, show that he was closely involved with what was going on. Ralph Lane and Philip Amadas, who designed the fortifications actually built on Roanoke Island, apparently did not derive a great deal from Williams's plan (if it was his), though they, Thomas Cavendish, and Ralegh may have found incidental suggestions that it contained useful in determining the type of person who should be taken on the voyage, and the plan may have suggested a few of the expedients for protecting the settlement that were eventually adopted.

Of much more significance was the fact that Ralegh decided that Thomas Harriot and John White should go on the expedition with special responsibilities. They were to note down and draw everything that would be of interest and importance—the Indian villages, cornfields and gardens, techniques for catching fish, religious edifices and ceremonies, types of individuals and their ranks, together with specimens and drawings of plants, animals, fish, minerals, and any other materials that could be of value in building up a picture of the country—as well as to survey the ground in detail and make a general map of the area. A detailed plan for just such a survey had been prepared for one of the voyages planned by Gilbert in 1582, but of course, had never been implemented.[4] But it is not unlikely that it was revived and modified for use in 1585. Such a survey had never yet been attempted for any part of North America and it did not follow precisely any precedents set by the Spanish. Harriot was already learning as much Algonquian as he could from Manteo and Wanchese. By the time the expedition reached its destination, he would be in sufficient command of the language to make extensive inquiries among the local people so as to enable him to compile a full discourse on their society and artifacts on his return. He would, too, act as advisor on navigational methods to be used on the voyage to America.

The elder Richard Hakluyt, the lawyer of the Middle Temple whom Ralegh is likely to have known for nearly a decade, contributed two memoranda that summarized the objectives of the forthcoming voyage and gave a number of practical suggestions for developing the settlement and exploiting it economically. Unfortunately this advice was not based on intimate knowledge of what could and could not be grown or obtained there. In one document he characterized the Indians, probably from having seen Manteo and Wanchese:

> The people be well proportioned in their limbs, well favoured, gentle, of a mild and tractable disposition, apt to submit themselves to good government and ready to embrace the Christian faith.[5]

This was, we suspect, intended as propaganda to be circulated among those who might be induced to go. But in another document, perhaps intended for Ralegh himself, he was much more frank. If the Indians opposed the colonists ("that seek but just and lawful traffic"), then severe measures should be taken against them. Alliances could be made by one group against another so as to divide and conquer. If this did not suffice,

> we will proceed with extremity, conquer, fortify and plant in soils most sweet, most pleasant, most strong and most fertile, and in the end bring them all in subjection and to civility.[6]

Here there is no suggestion that the colonists would be doing the Indians a service by living alongside them, so as mutually to learn from each other. The English would act just as the Spanish had done in creating their empire—proceed in amity with the inhabitants so long as they were docile, but kill, conquer, and settle, as suited the colonists, if they resisted intervention. In this statement much of the pious consideration allegedly to be given the native peoples was shown to be hypocritical and the naked imperial objectives revealed, though of course we cannot say that Ralegh agreed precisely with this particular formulation of the objectives of the expedition. It may warn us, however, against thinking that the interests of the inhabitants ranked before those of the settlers or that the latter were intended to be confined to small areas marginal to native settlements only.

The recommendations that the younger Richard Hakluyt added to his "Discourse" covered very comprehensively the stores the expedition would need, and the seeds and roots they must bring in order to provide food for themselves as soon as possible, along with livestock, hogs, rabbits, doves, domestic fowl, ducks, and—we may laugh at this—"turkeys male and female."[7] In addition, all sorts of specialist horticulturists would be needed if vines and sugar, for example, were to be grown. There would need to be expert fishermen and men to make them nets, butchers, bakers, and the rest. There would have to be soldiers, too, and men who could make and tend weapons. Specialists in fortifications would be required, as well as men who could prepare and package goods to be transported back to England as merchandise such as "joiners to cut out the boards into chests to be embarked for England." Then there would need to be men skilled in building and making the materials, bricks, tiles, and suchlike, for houses. And finally a string of craftsmen like barbers, laundrymen, and tailors, would be required to look after the settlers. In this spectrum of a whole society that he thought could be moved, Hakluyt almost forgot members of his own profession. As an afterthought, he added one or two preachers to keep the crews and settlers Christian, a physician, a surgeon, and an apothecary.

Ralegh was, if anything, soon overburdened with advice as if he intended to move a substantial part of the English people swiftly to America. Nevertheless, he received some valuable and practical suggestions for which he made provision. Nor did he have to rely solely on volunteers. In January he received authority to impress in Cornwall and Devon and at Bristol ships, shipmasters, seamen, soldiers, and equipment for his ships. How far he had to use these powers of coercion we do not know, but ships and men impressed in this way would not necessarily be very reliable elements in an expedition.

He was, moreover, making significant headway with the Queen. She knighted him at the Twelfth Night ceremony on 6 January and graciously allowed him to call the new land (all 1,800 miles long of it) VIRGINIA in her honor. He was able therefore to get a seal made with his arms as, the inscription indicated, the official seal of Sir Walter Ralegh, Lord and Governor of Virginia ("Domini & Gubernatoris Virginiae").[8] The choice of this name was to be an important landmark in American history given its prominence ever since, though we must continually remember that it was not confined to the area of the planned colony but applied to all the coastlines (and the interior behind) covered by Ralegh's patent once his colony had landed and established itself. So far, we have not found that the

3. Sir Walter Ralegh's Seal as Lord and Governor of Virginia, 1585.
British Museum, Department of Coins and Medals: redrawn for
D. B. Quinn, *The Roanoke Voyages* (Cambridge: Hakluyt Society, 1955).

Queen proved willing to contribute any money to the venture, Hakluyt's "Discourse" notwithstanding. What she did do was to allow 2,400 pounds of gunpowder to be delivered to Ralegh, and she let him have her galleass, the *Tiger*, variously rated at 140, 160, and 200 tons, for his service (though whether she charged him or let him have it freely we do not know).[9] But that was all. Essentially the venture was to be a private one, with the Queen's authority and blessing but little material help.

We have no authoritative evidence on how many men were designated to remain in America. The probable number is about five hundred. They would go in two installments, some three hundred perhaps, with Sir Richard Grenville in April, who could be expected to be established in June, and perhaps another two hundred under Amias Preston and Bernard Drake in June and be settled in August. What proportion were to be soldiers and what proportion civilians we also do not know. It was to be an entirely masculine venture, the men, soldiers, and civilians alike being paid wages for a term of service at sea or on land. What is reasonably clear is that it was not intended to be the final version of a series of colonial settlements but was to be largely empirical. Some men would be employed to see what could be grown; others, to determine what could be obtained for commercial use from the natural environment; and still others, to develop trade with the inhabitants. There was to be a strong emphasis on exploration, which would be carried out by parties of men, well armed in case of attack, but not necessarily taking offensive action against the people unless attacked by them. There would also be what we might call the survey unit, Harriot and White, with some civilian attendants, to carry out the surveying, mapping, and observation of all aspects of the area; this group would be given a guard of soldiers only when thought necessary. Soldiers would be necessary to safeguard the base settlement and its fortifications against possible attack.

The fact that Amadas's ship on her return to England in 1584 sailed down toward Bermuda and then to the Azores looking for prizes emphasizes an aspect of the venture that was, perhaps, the most pressing one of all, namely the use of the settlement as a base for raids on Spanish shipping.[10] Even if England and Spain were not yet at war, they were on the brink, and stragglers from the great Spanish *flota*, which sailed majestically through the Florida Channel in summer but often left a few ships, unable to keep up with the rest, to fall behind the convoy, provided an obvious target for attack. Indeed, it may have been contemplated, too, that ships should revictual at the colony on their way to or coming from attacking Spanish shipping in the Caribbean.

There were problems that could have been foreseen already. How carefully Amadas and Barlowe were probed about the anchorages available outside and inside the Outer Banks of North Carolina is unknown, but it cannot have been too carefully. The shallow entry to Roanoke Island was known, and it was clear only pinnaces and boats could come to it. It may be that there was little concept of the stormy character of the ocean waters off the Outer Banks and how they were to earn their later sinister title of "the Graveyard of the Atlantic" for the numbers cast ashore there, but open water, with no shelter visible, did not offer good prospects for a squadron riding at anchor at sea. If Amadas had entered Chesapeake Bay in 1584, he would certainly have found a very different situation—deep water harbors and shelter—but it seems uncertain that he did. The gilded picture Barlowe painted of the Outer Banks could easily have been clouded if serious consideration had been given to these matters. Even the suggested size of the projected settlement was unrealistic. Would three hundred to five hundred men be able to establish themselves on an island reckoned to be a mere sixteen miles long? Could any inhabitants expect to remain there? Was such a contingent not bound to invade the interior and settle on Indian lands, and do so by driving off the inhabitants or enslaving them? The more we examine the plans for the colony the less realistic they appear, though in fact we will find that circumstances scaled them down to more realistic proportions.

The 1585 Voyage

In contrast to the delays and inefficiency that had marked Gilbert's preparations, Sir Walter Ralegh's colonizing expedition was rapidly and efficiently assembled. Sir Richard Grenville, who was chosen to lead it, was a distant relative of Ralegh; he owned property in northern Cornwall but had more recently been in financial difficulties. He was evidently closely attached to Ralegh and named him first among the trustees to whom he confided his estates during his absence. Grenville had a strong personality and did not please everyone under him on the voyage, but he was efficient and it was not his fault that the ships did not keep together.

The flagship of the squadron (the "Admiral") was the *Tiger*, commanded by Grenville with Simon Fernandes as chief pilot and master. She had recently been rebuilt as a galleass, having had some of her older and clumsy upperworks removed, and sailed well enough, except that she proved to be of too deep draft to enter the Carolina Sounds. The *Roebuck*, a flyboat, was a broad-beamed, Dutch-type vessel of 140 tons burden; she was commanded by a Captain John Clarke who had sailed her for Ralegh for some time previously. She probably ranked as vice-admiral of the squadron. The 100-ton *Red Lion* of Chichester was under George Raymond of Weymouth, who was to prove unreliable. Thomas Cavendish, a rich young man from Trimley St. Martin, Suffolk, commanded his own small vessel, the *Elizabeth*, of 50 tons. He was to be high marshal, or judicial officer, of the expedition. The *Dorothy*, of 50 tons, belonged to Ralegh. We are not told who was her captain but it may well have been Arthur Barlowe. Philip Amadas, who was to act as admiral in the colony, was on the *Tiger*, as was Colonel Ralph Lane, who was in command of the soldiers of the expedition under Grenville. Lane had been specially released from an Irish command by the Queen to go on the voyage. Francis Brooke, treasurer of the expedition, was also there. The two pinnaces are not named, nor do we know their tonnage, but it would be in the region of 25 tons each. They would each be attached to one of the larger ships and be expected to keep company with her. They would be invaluable for exploration. It is roughly estimated that the total complement was about six hundred men of whom at least half were expected to constitute the first colony.

The vessels were well armed as they expected to pass through hostile Spanish waters in the Caribbean, but we have no details of their armament. Perhaps half the men who were to remain in America were soldiers. We know, roughly, how they would have been equipped. They would have a doublet and hose with a large cloak or coat, several shirts with neck bands, several pairs of leather shoes, and woolen stockings; and they would be armed with pistols and a caliver or a pike or halberd, with bows and arrows in reserve. They would have thick leather (buff) jerkins, leather or metal head-pieces, and probably a round wooden and leather target (or shield). Body and leg armor would be available for some of them. The officers would wear much more elaborate versions of the same type of clothing, embroidered and often with capes lined with silk. They would, on land at least, wear broad brimmed hats. They would also have full suits of armor for emergencies on land. The sailors would be dressed in a loose blouse and canvas slops (or breeches), with a cape of some sort and a woolen bonnet or cap.[1] Intending civilian colonists would have chosen the dress they habitually wore, unless Ralegh issued them some uniform suits of clothing before departure.

A considerable quantity of stores would be carried for the colony —artillery, small arms, gunpowder. There would be a good deal of iron and other metals, in bulk as well as in the form of tools and implements. The latter would include agricultural implements but apparently not fishing gear for the colonists. Stores to last the ships six months would be supplemented by dry goods to last the colonists for almost a year, a whole ship chandler's store indeed. There would also be a good supply of drugs, medicines, and spices. Substantial quantities of wheat and other grains would be taken, along with meat and fish, salted and some dried. How much in the way of building materials would have been carried is conjectural, probably not more than metal spikes and nails, a pitsaw or two, and a forge. The colonists would be expected to rely mainly on timber until they could make brick or tile for themselves, though some tile may have been brought for roofing. We know that the bulk of the food stores was carried on the *Tiger* and the remainder would be largely in the high-capacity *Roebuck* along with most of the settlers on these two ships, but possibly only some settlers and no stores with Raymond. Some of the seamen who sailed the vessels had been impressed, including some Dutchmen, and several of the commanders were tainted with piracy, Clarke certainly, Raymond probably, nor should we forget the record of Simon Fernandes. They would be an effective expedition only so long as they kept together and Grenville was able to assert his authority over the captains.

The fleet set out from Plymouth on 9 April. It got out of the English Channel without difficulty and sailed comfortably through the Bay of Biscay, but off Portugal it encountered a major storm. The pinnace with the *Tiger* sank and the expedition was scattered in all directions. This was to prove a major impediment to Grenville hereafter and eventually helped to alter the size and character of the colony. The *Tiger* was now alone as she made her way to the Canaries and rapidly across the ocean on the southeast trades to Dominica, which was sighted on 7 May—a passage from England to the Caribbean in less than a month, which was exceptional.

A rendezvous evidently had been arranged, on the advice of Fernandes, on the uninhabited southwest coast of Puerto Rico. There, in Guayanilla Bay, the *Tiger* dropped anchor on 11 May.[2] Grenville knew he would have to wait for the other ships if they kept to their arrangements and, of course, had survived the crossing. He decided to establish a temporary base camp on shore that would provide restful quarters for his men, who could put up tents and build light shelters. He threw up a hasty entrenchment around the camp and mounted a few guns in case the Spanish attempted to surprise him.[3] This was also good practice for Lane's men assigned to prepare the fortifications on Roanoke Island. A replacement for the pinnace was urgently needed. A forge was set up to make nails and trees were cut, carried to the site on small wooden trucks, sawed in a saw-pit, and rapidly shaped into a substantial pinnace that may not have been decked. She was then equipped with gear from the *Tiger's* stores.

4. John White's Plan of the Enclosure and Camp at Guayanilla Bay,
Puerto Rico, May 1585.
British Museum, Department of Prints and Drawings, 1906-5-9-1 (4).

The new pinnace seems to have been almost completed when the *Elizabeth* appeared on 19 May, she at least having kept the rendezvous. But none of the others ever made it. Another ship somehow got to the western end of Jamaica and there had an engagement with a French privateer, though the outcome is not clear. The same ship, or just possibly another, was in distress off the north coast of the same island at some point after using up all her stores. This area was uninhabited and as supplies were not available the captain turned twenty of his men loose on shore and sailed off; later some of them were picked up by the Spanish. This episode shows that at least one of the ships was more interested in taking prizes than in founding a colony.[4] The vessel here is most likely to have been George Raymond's *Red Lion*, but eventually she and the other two missing ships —we do not hear what happened to the second pinnace—seem to have proceeded directly to the Outer Banks and to have arrived there in mid-June.

Meanwhile Grenville had decided to exploit the Spanish islands in order to improve his resources. He attempted to acquire food supplies from the Spanish authorities on Puerto Rico who made contact with him, but though promises were made, the stores did not arrive and he concluded that an attempt would shortly be made to attack the encampment. So he abandoned it and sailed into the Mona Channel between Puerto Rico and Hispaniola. There he captured two small Spanish ships—welcome additions to his three vessels. One had little to offer in the way of stores but the other, which was making for San Juan to distribute goods brought from Europe, yielded valuable spoil. She was stripped of the cloth and other goods she had on board and her people ransomed at an inhabited place for livestock, hogs, calves, and horses to bring to the colony, as well as some foodstuffs.[5] In the meantime Lane took the other little vessel to Salinas Bay, near Cape Rojo, where he found two mounds of salt ready for removal. With the aid of the vessel's Spanish crew and some of his own men, he obtained a lading of salt. Lane's preoccupation with fortifications was shown by his construction of elaborate sand entrenchments around the area where the salt was,[6] though their value, in case of an attack, could only have been nominal.

Setting out with five vessels on 29 May, Grenville anchored on 1 June at the Spanish town of Isabela on the north coast of Hispan-

5. John White's Plan of the Enclosure at Salinas Bay, Cape Rojo, Puerto Rico,
May 1585.
British Museum, Department of Prints and Drawings, 1906-5-9-1 (5).

iola. There the inhabitants were evidently used to trading with intruding ships and were not prepared to regard the English as enemies. The governor of the place with others came on board the *Tiger*
to be entertained handsomely by Grenville. Having played the
pirate off Puerto Rico, he was now putting on the mantle of the
honest explorer and trader. After this a large party of Englishmen
went ashore and built two banqueting houses "covered with green
boughs" where they entertained the Spanish as lavishly as they could.
Not only compliments but also presents were exchanged before the
parties got down to plain trading. We suspect the English used Spanish money and goods taken from the richer prize to acquire more
horses, cows, hogs, sheep, together with hides, sugar, ginger, pearls,
and tobacco, among other things. The show of friendship did not
mean very much, but if there was a chance of making a profit from
strongly-armed visitors who were actually prepared to pay, the Spanish were ready to ignore long-standing orders to treat all intruders as
enemies.

During the visits to the island some of the other men concerned
with stocking the colony were uprooting plants of sugar cane, plantains, pineapple, mammee apples, and other fruits and vegetables.
These were placed in containers (dry vats) with soil and put on the
decks of the ships, the expectation being that at least some would
grow in the colony—though in fact none would, and in any case
most would die from salt spray on the sea voyage. John White, too,
was actively experimenting as he began his visual record of the voyage. He made a picture plan in detail of the first encampment on
Puerto Rico and another of the salt-taking episode, while he drew
detailed pictures of a land crab, hermit crabs, scorpions, fireflies, an
iguana, an alligator, a pineapple, mammee apples, plantains, and,
possibly later, a flamingo, all of which have survived as a brilliant
visual record of the Caribbean phase of the voyage.[7] Much effort was
wasted in collecting plants, however, because the English had no
conception of the actual year-round climate of the Outer Banks.
They equated it with that of similar latitudes in the Old World and so
had quite incorrect ideas about what would grow in eastern North
America.

The Spanish were able to gain from the prisoners who were ransomed at Puerto Rico some information about Grenville's activities,
most of it reasonably accurate. Grenville had made no secret of his

intention to establish a colony, but he had given no indication of where it might be located. Having left Hispaniola on 7 June, he threaded his way with some difficulty through the Caicos and Bahama islands before coming out into the Florida Channel. As he made his way up the Florida coast, his ships were reported to the Spaniards by the local Indians. When the evidence of his activities in the Caribbean and off the Florida coast was put together in Spain, the Spanish were able to conclude to their satisfaction that he had indeed gone to settle well to the north of the Spanish posts at Saint Augustine and at Santa Elena on Parris Island.[8]

On 23 June shoals forced the ships away from the coast, probably in the vicinity of Cape Fear. The Englishmen caught fish in a harbor that might have been that of Beaufort, North Carolina, and on 26 June entered an inlet at Wococon. The present island of Ocracoke may very well not represent the Wococon of 1585, because part of present-day Portsmouth Island and part of Ocracoke may have been joined at that time. Although it clearly looked like a good harbor to Grenville and his men, their sounding was inadequate and they brought the *Tiger* into such a shallow channel that she grounded in heavy seas. The writer of the main journal of the voyage attributed this mishap to "the unskillfulness of the Master, whose name was Fernando." Apparently other vessels also ran onto the sandbars but were got off rapidly, though the *Tiger* was in great danger of destruction. Ralph Lane tells us:

> The *Tiger* lying beating upon the shoal for the space of two hours by the dial [clock], we were all in extreme hazard of being cast away, but in the end, by the mere work of God, floating off, we ran her aground hard to the shore, and so with great spoil of our provisions saved ourselves and the noble ship also, with her back whole, which all the mariners aboard thought could not possibly but have been broken in sunder, having abiden by just tally above 89 strokes aground.[9]

It is hard to calculate precisely how much damage the supplies suffered. Certainly the wheat, rice, and salt on board got wet and were ruined. Other perishable commodities were also lost, but how far this prejudiced the welfare and comfort of the colony is not clear. But it was a bad beginning.

The next few weeks saw a fairly leisurely attempt to assemble information about the area and to discover what had happened to the other vessels. A few days were spent sorting out the damage to the *Tiger* and making essential repairs, which must have been adequate as we hear of no further trouble from her. On 3 July word of their arrival was conveyed to Wingina at Roanoke Island. Richard Butler told his Spanish captors that he had been one of those sent in a canoe,[10] though he probably meant a ship's boat, northward outside the Outer Banks to try to locate other vessels. They eventually reached Port Ferdinando where they found two of the missing ships, the *Roebuck* and the *Dorothy*. On 6 July John Arundell, who had probably been there in 1584, went with Manteo to Roanoke Island to follow up the early news and to have preliminary discussions about locating the colony there. Some soldiers were sent to search the island of Croatoan to the north where they found two men wandering on the sixth; they brought them back on the eighth with news that some thirty other men were loose on land, where they were dumped by Raymond about 17 June. He had at once set sail for Newfoundland to plunder fishing vessels. The thirty men he left behind were probably gradually rounded up over the next week or so. By 11 July Captain Clarke had come down from Port Ferdinando and joined Grenville; between them they would be able to decide what parts of the original plan could be retained. Grenville was evidently satisfied that the prospects were good but he waited for definite news from Wingina before making a move northward.

The crucial part of the voyage was now accomplished and an assessment could be made of what had been saved and what lost. Although we do not know how many men had died on the voyage, or precisely how many Raymond had accounted for, or who had been lost in the first pinnace, we can guess that, out of the estimated 600 men who began the voyage, close to 500 would have still been available. But with information from Clarke, who had probably been in touch with Wingina before he came south, Grenville would reckon that the 200 to 250 men he could still plant as colonists would be too many for the available land on the island and would be inadequately supplied with necessities from the stores remaining. We might guess, too, that some of the livestock as well as many of the plants collected in the Caribbean would have died by this time, further depleting available resources. By 11 July it is probable that it had been decided to leave only a hundred men or so under Lane on Roanoke Island. This would be enough to fulfill the objectives already indicated, provided, of course, that the colony was rapidly and effectively reinforced, and that relations with the inhabitants did not deteriorate quickly and fatally.

Although the journal recording Grenville's passage through the Caribbean and up the coast of southern North America is laconic enough except for a few graphic passages, John White was endeavoring to maintain a record of what could be found at sea.[11] He drew, for example, two great ocean birds, a tropic bird and a frigate bird, that had been shot and laid on deck in the positions in which they had originally been seen in flight. The seamen, too, were busy catching fish from the deck when the *Tiger* was not making rapid headway. These White drew as soon as they were caught so as to preserve something of their appearance in their natural habitat. His moonfish, grouper, grunt, soldier-fish, dolphin (Dorado), sharksucker remora (suggesting they took sharks as well), and triggerfish all bear witness to his skill in drawing biological specimens. His best pictures are those of the flying fish, which at many a time must have landed on deck, and of the Portuguese man-o'-war, the complex jellyfish, which he must have observed from the side of the ship as it floated in the water, because it would have been unrecognizable if it had simply been brought on board in a net. White had thus shown that he was not a mere craftsman but had a strong feeling for the appearance and function of a wide range of living creatures. It is possible to fault him on minute details, but in general no English drawings of the novel fauna of these waters were to touch his in quality for a very long time. Very soon he would have an opportunity to show what he could do with human beings in their natural environment.

All had not gone easily on the voyage. Just as Raymond had betrayed the trust placed in him, so there was dissension on board the *Tiger* that Grenville was unable to quell. There were those who thought Simon Fernandes was not as reliable a pilot as he made himself out to be, and there is more than a suggestion that Grenville did not favor him while Ralph Lane strongly supported him. On the other hand, Grenville had a serious falling out with some leading members of his company, most particularly with Lane. The division between them continued after the landing on the Outer Banks and

apparently led to threats against Lane by Grenville, who as general
had wide powers over his subordinates. But Thomas Cavendish, in
command of the *Elizabeth*, Captain John Clarke, captain of the *Roebuck*,
Francis Brooke, the treasurer, Edward Gorges, and gentlemen members of the household of Sir Francis Walsingham, Master Russell and
apparently Master Atkinson were all criticized or chastised by Grenville. What these quarrels were about we cannot tell, except that
Lane accused Grenville of "intolerable pride and insatiable ambition."[12] The dossier of complaints he sent back to Ralegh, however,
has not survived. These differences did not augur well for the sound
establishment of the colony. At the same time, whatever the dis-
putes, which persisted right up to the time of Grenville's departure
for home, the participants contrived to cooperate—at least on the
surface—and to get on with the business of settling Englishmen on
American soil.

Founding the Colony:
The First Steps

We might expect that just as soon as the realities of the establishment of a smaller and less impressive colony were spelled out, immediate steps would be taken to put them into effect. But this was not so. First of all, Sir Richard Grenville wished to see a reasonable part of the area and not simply be tied to the island chosen by Amadas and Barlowe as the most desirable starting point for settlement. His feelings were natural, but he also is likely to have been influenced by the plans that had been made before he left England for a second expedition, under Amias Preston and Bernard Drake, to bring out a further contingent of colonists later in the summer.[1] We do not know how many colonists were being considered but it may have been as many as several hundred more. Grenville could not know that this expedition would never arrive because in June, just before it was ready to leave, it was diverted to Newfoundland under circumstances that will be discussed later. In early July he may well have felt that he had a duty to find another place for this second batch of colonists to settle, as it can scarcely have been envisaged that they also should be placed on Roanoke Island.

These reasons—exploration and prospecting for a further site—explain the expedition that Grenville led across and around Pamlico Sound, beginning on 11 July. Grenville was in his tiltboat, a large London wherry that had been specially shipped on the *Tiger*. He was accompanied by, among others, John Arundell, now back from Roanoke Island with favorable news from Wingina, and John Stukely, one of the Devonshire gentlemen on the voyage. In the large, capacious pinnace constructed on Puerto Rico was Ralph Lane, with

Ships of the 1585 expedition at sea

Ships of the 1585 expedition approaching or at the Outer Banks

The Pinnace in the Sounds (Pamlico Sound and the
head of Albemarle Sound) 1585–86

6. Ships of the 1585 Expedition and of the 1585–1586 Colony, from the Maps
of John White and Thomas Harriot.
British Museum, Department of Prints and Drawings, 1906-5-9-1 (2–3).

Thomas Cavendish, captain of the *Elizabeth*, Thomas Harriot, in his role of scientific adviser, and twenty others. She was under sail, but Lane was to complain that she drew too much water and that she would not move to an oar. Philip Amadas, John Clarke, and ten other men were in one ship's boat; Francis Brooke, the treasurer, John White, and others, in another. The party comprised at least sixty men in all, and the flotilla must have made a colorful sight as it crossed the sound.

This was the first time that Pamlico Sound had been explored by Europeans. It is likely that the route was worked out for them by one of the Indians, probably Manteo, as Wanchese would have been recognized as a member of Wingina's group, to whom some of the villages were hostile. They first made their way to the northwest where they reached Pomeioc, a major village where Wingina may have had some influence. There they were well received and passed the night nearby in Wyesocking Bay; on the twelfth they explored Pomeioc freely. Some members of the party seem to have been taken to see the great lake Paquippe, now the much shrunken but still substantial Lake Mattamuskeet, inland from the village. That day John White was busy making detailed sketches of the village and drawing pictures of a number of its inhabitants. It was his first great opportunity, on this expedition at least, to make comprehensive drawings of an indigenous people at home. His patience and skill have enabled us to bring it to life.

Pomeioc, as shown in White's drawing,[2] was a closely palisaded village with an easily guarded entrance. The eighteen longhouses, of varying sizes, that it contained made it a large settlement for this area, conceivably the largest on the sounds. In the drawing, the roof mats of some of the houses are thrown back to reveal the sleeping benches inside. One unusual building with a stepped roof and pyramidal top may be the mortuary temple. A central fire is burning in an open space between the houses, around which a number of people are gathered. Men, women, and children appear, some in family groups, and, a unique feature, a domesticated native dog is shown. It is possible that some details were elaborated from comparable scenes White saw later; even so, he made a valiant and successful attempt to convey the character of village life in this drawing. He also made a detailed portrait of a woman and child, one of the more famous of his figure drawings.[3] The woman was the wife of a *wero-ance*; there is tattooing on her face, and her hair is cut short across her forehead and loosely knotted at the back. She wears a long chain of beads, with a single apron skirt in front. In her hand she is holding a gourd for carrying water. The child, her daughter, is not clothed, except for a skin girdle and a rudimentary breechclout. She is holding an English doll given to her as a present by the visitors. The fact that women allowed themselves to be sketched shows that trustworthy relations had been established. The drawing of an old man, wrapped in a deerskin mantle, gives a good impression of the ordinary inhabitant.[4] The mantle retains the hair, which was worn on the inside. His own hair is shaved on one side of his head, with a high roach or coxcomb in the middle. His features are compressed and worn. Cornfields are shown around the village.[5]

On 13 July the flotilla passed on in a southwestward direction and entered the mouth of the Pamlico River and then the Pungo River, its tributary. Some way upstream was a village—Aquascogoc—to which the explorers were directed. It does not seem that they were made especially welcome here or that White was able to make any drawings. Apparently some of the Indian men swam out and entered at least one of the boats, pilfering. After the party had set out from the village it was discovered that a silver cup, probably belonging to Grenville himself, had been stolen.

They reentered the Pamlico River and turned westward. Upstream they came to the important village of Secotan, the search for the site of which has so far met with no success. There the chief, perhaps the same one who had inflicted the earlier defeat on Wingina, received them favorably and made them welcome. As a result, White was able to make a fine group of sketches of the village and its inhabitants on which he later relied. His final drawing shows an open village nestled among silvery trees, with twelve buildings in sight, though more may have been concealed among the trees to the left of the drawing.[6] Again there are sleeping benches inside the longhouses, while a small communal fire marks the central walkway; on it are laid mats, on which platters are set out for a meal. In what is apparently an area set apart for religious observances, a perpetual fire was kept burning in the center of a group of stones or blocks of wood with some ceremonial purpose. A building later shown to be a mortuary temple is in the foreground. On the right foreground, a dance ceremony is being held around a circle of posts with carved tops; men and women are crouched down, ready to take the place of some of the dancers.

The most valuable feature of the drawing is the information it gives on Indian agriculture. Three patches of corn are shown on one side of the village—ripe corn, green corn, and newly-sprung corn. An amusing little structure in the plot of ripe corn is a bird-scarer's hut, raised above the corn. To one side of the corn there is a rich patch of squashes of various sorts, pumpkins and gourds among them. Then to the left of the walkway there are irregular patches of sunflowers and of tobacco well advanced in growth. As a summary of the more settled aspects of village life this could scarcely have been bettered (though, again, some details may well have been added from other villages seen later). Once more White was able to draw the portrait of a weroance's wife.[7] This time she is wearing a double apron skirt and has a headband of indeterminate material around her forehead; otherwise, she is decorated as the previous woman had been. Some of White's other surviving drawings, which are not specifically noted to have been made here, may also derive from this visit.

Between the drawings made at Pomeioc and Secotan, a very good picture of Indian life can be obtained, though the impression they give is somewhat deceptive. These people spent much of their time in the summer and autumn in camps on the Outer Banks and the shores of the sounds, collecting oysters and crabs and fishing, partly for food to be eaten, partly for stores to be dried for later use or even traded inland. Then, too, in winter, the men, and possibly the women, would leave the village to hunt in the forests well into the interior. It was on excursions such as these that they made contact with other Indian groups and where, most probably, old antagonisms and fighting developed between them, which could be sanguinary enough. There was also, as has been mentioned, intermittent rivalry between leaders of various groups for hegemony over others, which could lead to protracted strife. At times they may have fought simply to maintain the valor of their young men and the reputation of their group.

Grenville turned back on 16 July. It is probable that he at least examined the mouth of the Neuse River and what is now Core

Sound, if it was there then, before he reached Wococon once more. Amadas, in his ship's boat with eleven men, was detached by Grenville to go back to Aquascogoc and demand the return of the stolen silver cup. This was not forthcoming though the chief evidently promised to let them have it. In a revenge out of proportion to the offense, Amadas, Clarke, and their men set fire to the corn and houses and so wrecked a community whose hostility, as a result, might well react against the colony at a later stage. It was an unwise as well as intolerant act.

At last it was time to make a move to establish the colony. But though Grenville returned to his fleet "anchoring at Wokokon," as we are told, which suggests that the *Roebuck* and the *Dorothy* had come down from Port Ferdinando, it was not until 21 July that they set sail northward, probably occupied in the meantime with putting finishing touches to the repairs needed on the *Tiger*. And it was not until the twenty-seventh that all the ships were safely anchored off Port Ferdinando. On the twenty-ninth Granganimeo, once more as Wingina's envoy, came on board the *Tiger* along with Manteo, who is likely to have been at Roanoke Island helping to make final arrangements about where the colonists should settle. There is no suggestion that there was any objection raised to the Englishmen installing themselves on the island. We can envisage, though we have no direct evidence of it, that much gear was landed on the beach and placed on ground high enough to be safe from the tide. It is also likely that very soon the pinnace and the ships' boats were making their way into Roanoke Sound and into the cove on Roanoke Island, now eroded but then the northeastern tip of the island. From there their gear would eventually be carried a short distance to the site of the new settlement, using, for the heavier equipment, the trucks or gun carriages shown on the Puerto Rico drawing. Just how soon the site of the settlement began to be cleared of trees, a considerable task as they had not only to be cut but uprooted, is not clear, but the clearing was probably begun as soon as possible and involved stationing a band of men in tents on the site. Part of this may have been lightly timbered as it was probably the location of former Indian fields. Here the English would be for the first time in close proximity to Wingina's village on the northern shore and would begin to make contact with its inhabitants, probably under strict orders to maintain good relations and avoid intimacies or conflict at all costs.

On 3 August Philip Amadas, probably accompanied by Manteo or Wanchese, was sent out on the first exploring expedition to make contact with the numerous villages of Weapemeoc on the north bank of Albemarle Sound. There were at least ten in number of which White was to record the names of eight, which were under the hegemony of Okisko. White and Harriot may have been on the excursion, to which the pinnace would have been assigned. Here there was evidently much cleared land where a good impression of the nature of Indian agriculture and of Indian life could be obtained.

There was much other exploration done in these early days at the end of July and the early part of August. Richard Butler, who is not to be relied on but cannot wholly be ignored, gives a picture of what he said he experienced, remarking that it was difficult inside the sounds to make progress against the current from Port Ferdinando:

> The deponent disembarked and having encountered the natives of the territory, he went inland to investigate, leaving the 120 men who had left the ship with him, at the edge of the sea. He was in the company of the natives for about eight days and they treated him well. As he had had some communication with the two natives who had left with the English on the occasion of their first visit, he was able to understand a few words of what they were saying. He went inland for about twenty leagues [beyond the head of Albemarle Sound?] and then returned to his companions, who, he discovered, had also explored the interior. . . . On his return they embarked and wished to pass, but were unable to do so because of the current. Seeing that they could not proceed owing to the strength of the current, they crossed the current to the northern side. They landed and met some of the natives of those parts; they are the enemies of those of Puerto Fernando. They killed about twenty of them and captured some of the women whom they gave to the other savages. They then returned to where their ships were.[8]

It is impossible to analyze this in detail but it seems plausible that some hostility was encountered on this particular journey. If, in fact, Indians were killed and their women brought to Wingina as trophies, they would be acceptable as such because they could be assimilated into the community. At the same time this document suggests that the involvement of the English in the conflicts of the Indian groups began earlier and was more sanguinary than had been anticipated or is mentioned elsewhere, though this is far from being established. It also suggests, obscurely, that the flow of water in the sounds and especially down Albemarle Sound was a considerable impediment to movement.

In the English reports, however, all was sweetness and light so far as the country was concerned.[9] Apothecaries and merchants were discovering commodities that had valuable uses for the English—trees that produced rich and pleasant gums, fine grapes, drugs (not specified), several kinds of flax (one like silk), fine corn (high yielding—400 grains to the ear), whose cane was thought to make sugar, and clay like the Mediterranean *Terra sigillata*, which had medicinal qualities. Ralph Lane became lyrical and totally unrealistic when he said in a letter to the elder Richard Hakluyt, "we find that what commodities soever Spain, France, Italy or the East parts do yield unto us in wines of all sorts, in oils, in flax, in resins, pitch, frankincense, currants, sugars and such like, these parts do abound with the growth of them all." To Sir Francis Walsingham he reported a little later the discovery of a kind of corn that "yieldeth both corn and sugar, whereof our physician here hath sent an assay to our Lord Sir Walter Rawlleye." Such reports were bound to produce disillusionment and in the longer run did much harm to the prospects of successful colonization.

Lane, however, was not so unrealistic about the problems that the shoreline presented. Port Ferdinando had an entry with twelve feet at high water, "and the bar very short, being within 3, 4 and 5 fathoms water." This narrow entry would enable it to be easily defended and he proposed the building there of a sconce, or small fort, though this was never done because it would signal their location to any Spanish ships that might sail by. Another entry, Trinity Harbor, well to the north—White was to show it as an outlet from Albemarle Sound—had only eight feet on the bar at high water. Lane did not mention the small entry a little to the north of Port Ferdinando, to which White gave the name of Port Lane, but it may have been too shallow to be of any use. Concerning the shallowness of the sounds, Lane says only that the pinnace drew rather too much water to sail easily in them.

It was now time to send word home that the expedition had arrived. John Arundell was given command of one of the small and faster vessels, possibly the *Dorothy* or the larger of the two Spanish prizes, and set sail on 5 August to bring the first messages to England. We cannot tell how soon he arrived but he was received at Court, where Queen Elizabeth made him the first of her Virginia knights by knighting him at Richmond, as Sir John Arundell of Tolverne, on 14 October. Because Ralph Lane dated three of his letters 12 August, it seems probable that some of the other vessels sailed shortly after that date; the *Tiger* departed on 25 August, and the *Roebuck* in turn set sail on or just after 8 September.

Not only the intending settlers but also the craftsmen from the ships and, no doubt, some of the seamen, had already been well practiced in erecting fortifications at Puerto Rico. Thus it would not be difficult for them to undertake comparable work on Roanoke Island, rapidly and effectively, though on a more substantial basis than during the earlier experiments. Ralph Lane was an expert in fortification. It appears from a later reference that Philip Amadas also took some part in supervising the construction. Surviving documents, together with the archaeology so far done on the site (though the latter is an ongoing project), leave much to the imagination in attempting to visualize what was done. A considerable amount of imaginative projection is essential (which may prove incorrect as later archaeological work proceeds) to obtain anything like a full picture of the first English settlement constructed on North American soil.

In the first place, we must presume that a plan for an enclosure was worked out and surveyed on the ground. This would need to be large enough to contain all the necessary buildings for the colony, to give the colonists enough space to move about inside the enclosure, and to comprehend the whole inside such defenses as would seem necessary for the protection of the colony. The one or two indications that we have of the general enclosure, together with the examples we have from Puerto Rico, would suggest that a trench was excavated as the main barrier to intervention by the Indians—caution would suggest that some protection from them might conceivably be necessary, however cooperative they might appear. But the possibility that Spanish reconnaissance vessels might discover the settlement, even though it would be hidden from casual observation from the sea, had also to be kept in mind. These considerations would have governed the precise form of the enclosure.

The "old trench made by Captain Amadas," of which John White speaks later, would then have been the usual form the defensive barrier would take. This would, in its excavation, produce a bank of earth, rather sandy earth in most cases, that would provide a low embankment. Whether any firing step was provided inside this bank and whether there were regular projections in it to enable a patrolling sentry to make effective observation along a stretch of the enclosure, we cannot tell. What we do know is that provision was made for the construction of one or more strong points at a corner, or corners, of the enclosure. This, or these, would take the form of a major embrasure in the conventional star fort style, which was demonstrated at the top of the drawing of the salt taking near Cape Rojo. The excavation of Fort Raleigh has fully illustrated this and will be examined in detail later.[10] Provision had to be made for the mounting of cannon and also for the security and comfort of the guard that would be maintained there. The enclosure may, or may not, have been regular in form—the first enclosure in the Caribbean simply followed the natural lines of defense the site afforded. But a quadrangular or triangular outline would have been more usual according to European practice. In that case Fort Raleigh could be one of the two, three, or more strong points of a similar character. It would be natural to expect that the side of the enclosure facing east, toward the direction from which Spanish reconnaissance parties might come, was at least laid out regularly in a straight line. This might or might not be necessary for the other sides of the enclosure where protection against Indian intervention only might be provided. Because Fort Raleigh alone survives as an authentic reconstruction, nothing more can usefully be said about the enclosure, except that lines of stakes may have been planted, either as a palisade of pointed laths or poles outside the ditch, or even, as has been revealed in later excavations in Virginia, a boarded fence constructed around part of the defenses. But so far this is entirely a speculative addition. That a trench existed around at least the greater part of the enclosure may, in all probability, be taken for granted.

Inside the reconstructed strong point (which it seems best to call

Fort Raleigh for the time being) heavy wooden platforms would be necessary if guns as heavy as sakers were to be mounted (saker shot being later found by White on the site). Lighter guns could be supported on their carriages by carefully packed earth and could well have been swivel–mounted fowlers, which could cover a wide field, whereas the saker would be fixed to fire in one direction only. We wonder whether a "cavalier," considered by the 1585 document cited above as necessary "to command the field," was not added at the opening of the enclosure inside the strong point. This would be a small bank of soil, built higher than the defenses of the strong point itself and having its sides strongly reinforced by planks, on which could be mounted a further swivel gun that could act in the way that the 1585 plan proposed. Whether the remains of such a cavalier can be found among the reconstructed remnants of Fort Raleigh is a matter of opinion, which cannot be confirmed or wholly denied. What the reconstruction of Fort Raleigh did establish was that a guardhouse about 35 feet long by about 10 feet wide was placed inside the strong point. This would provide both for a constant watch at the strong point itself and for patrolling sentries inside the rest of the enclosure, if these were thought necessary as a regular precaution or as an emergency measure only.

These military precautions, we might consider, were primarily the work of the soldiers to be left behind by Grenville and by other men with military experience on board the ships. The houses inside the enclosure would perhaps be constructed primarily by the civilian settlers, a number of whom should have been craftsmen, with the aid of the skilled ships' carpenters and other craftsmen who were able to build the new pinnace so rapidly at Puerto Rico. Although we know that there were a considerable number of "cottages," roofed with rushes, constructed for the leading members of the colony (Thomas Harriot's, for example, is referred to, and Lane may have had a larger dwelling for himself), and although White could refer to them in retrospect as "decent dwelling houses," we have no further details of their construction or how they were laid out. It might seem likely that, in accordance with other early plans for settlements or forts, they were placed around an open space, a square, or even a circle, possibly some in pairs, some singly, and with openings between them. An open space in the center of the enclosure would be a sensible provision to avoid the men huddling together in closely placed buildings without an outlook or a place for recreation close at hand. It could also limit the advance of an accidental fire. Beyond the cottages there were other buildings. These were most likely to have been between the cottages and the eastern line of the defended enclosure. One of these was presumably the building that Grenville's fifteen men used as their headquarters ("the house wherein all their victuals and weapons were," as White was to be told in 1587).

From existing evidence we can suggest what some of them may have been. There was certainly a marshalsea or jail, as there was both a provost marshal and a deputy provost (the equivalent of military police) who would enforce discipline among the soldiers and probably execute the legal decisions of the marshal, the deputy left by Thomas Cavendish (the high marshal or judge, who did not remain in the colony), which involved imprisonment. This jail was equipped with hand-locks, a type of handcuff, and had inside it "bilboes," long iron bars fastened to the floor along which ran sliding leg-irons. There may well also have been a gibbet erected to act as a warning to possible capital offenders (we have an incidental reference later to men being found hanged).

There was also a store, with its keeper, which housed the supplies that Ralph Lane would issue as they were required, even though he lost "the most part of his corn, salt, meal, biscuit and other provision" when the *Tiger* went aground. Whether the store included arms and armor we do not know. A separate armory, with an armorer capable of repairing arms and armor, would be a sensible addition, though an entirely conjectural one. Thomas Harvey, as cape merchant, would also have had a warehouse for the storage of articles acquired by barter from the Indians or collected or even grown by the settlers. Because there was an undertreasurer left in the colony, we may conjecture that although the colonists, soldiers, and civilians alike would receive their basic rations from the store, they would be paid something in money (as they were all paid servants of Sir Walter Ralegh) in order to buy small luxuries from the warehouse so long as they were available and also to purchase small objects (or steal others) for individual trade with the Indians, even if this might have been officially discouraged. Thus, if we included a small treasury for the undertreasurer (securely lockable we would assume), we would account for between three and five such buildings, most of which would be appreciably larger than the cottages and at least as large as the guardrooms at the strong points. In addition, barracklike structures would be needed both for soldiers off duty and for servants. All the larger buildings would require more complex methods of timber construction on which we can offer no indications.

Entirely conjecturally, we may also suggest there was a work area inside the enclosure. The forge would be a necessity when iron objects—nails, spikes, tools, weapons, hinges, locks, and suchlike—needed making or renewal; the metallurgist had a furnace that could reach some 2,000 degrees Fahrenheit; the pitsaws must have been constantly working to provide usable timber (though they could have been located outside the enclosure). Such a work area would need to be insulated in some way from the flimsy timber dwellings and their fire-prone roofs but, apart from placing them at some distance and perhaps having a barrier of some sort between working and living areas, it cannot be suggested how this would be done. Finally, there was a question of whether any space was left inside the enclosure for the garden plots necessary to test the roots and seeds brought from the Caribbean and (in the case of seeds) from England. Clearly, a small number of men experienced in horticulture would have been included among the settlers. Similarly, though not inevitably, there could have been enclosures for raising domestic fowl and rabbits, a steady resource in English homesteads. These amenities might indeed have been provided outside the enclosure, where there would also need to have been enclosures for the surviving "horses, mares, kine, bulls, goats, swine, [and] sheep" acquired in Hispaniola, which could not be allowed to run wild.

The northeast shore of the island, as well as the northwest, has been eroded by wind and water so that it is no longer possible to indicate precisely the location of the "point of the creek" that formed the cove where equipment and men were landed. There was to be found at this place in 1588 a slipway or pier (or both) which marked the place where pinnace and boats could put in and from which the heavier gear could be transported on rude, wooden wheeled trucks such as are shown in the Guayanilla Bay drawing. Barrel-lined wells were also found there in 1588, but it would be reasonable to suppose that water was found inside the enclosure (though not yet located). It is just possible that the settlers had to carry their water from impermeable layers in the sandhills then existing between the enclosure and the north or northeast shore. If so, water barrels must have been busily carried day by day from wells to the enclosure, again on simple trucks. We can easily visualize too the well-worn track that must soon have appeared from creek to fort.

We have almost no indication of how the cottages were constructed. Simple pole and frame cottages, provided they did not exceed an area of much more than 12 by 16 feet, could have been rapidly erected and thatched, giving one room below and an attic above. Perhaps two of these joined made up the more generously sized cottages. They would need to be fitted with built-in settles, benches, and bedsteads at the very least. Hinges, latches, and locks we would expect to have been brought out from England for the doors. Whether chimneys of mud and timber were constructed for some or all of the cottages we cannot say, but they would provide necessary amenities for the winter months unless small charcoal-burning braziers (and we know charcoal was made near the enclosures) were used for heating. Cooking is likely to have been done communally, though Lane could have had his own cookhouse and so conceivably could a few of "the better sort" housed in the cottages. For the soldiers and servants some communal cooking arrangements would have to be made, for it is assumed that "the better sort" would have their personal attendants to look after their wants, including their sanitary needs. The rest of the settlers would also require latrines, which would be placed well away, one assumes, from the cottages. And then there would need to be trash pits. In early settlements refuse tended to be scattered around the house itself when it consisted of small broken objects and even animal bones, but in a closely confined settlement communal arrangements for the disposal of waste materials would be essential. If ever such middens were found, much more could be learned of the life-style of the colonists over the next ten months.

If the enclosure and most of the buildings were finished between 12 August and 8 September, or thereabouts, as would seem to be the time available for basic construction, it is evident that work must have gone forward in a well-planned and disciplined fashion. How far trees had to be uprooted inside the enclosure would depend on how much of the land had previously been used for Indian fields and when. In parts of the enclosure tree stumps could be left, but for the most part they would have to be cleared away. The amount of timber needed to be cut and shaped for poles and boards would be substantial; boards were usually split with an ax and wedges, but handsaws and pitsaws would be necessary to shape much of the timber. Perhaps, as shown on Guayanilla Bay, the larger tree trunks were brought in by the trucks already presumed necessary to carry heavy gear from the landing place. They were, in fact, almost identical with the gun carriages on which shipboard cannon rested. Nor when the ships sailed would work be finished. Each cottage would have to be furnished with utensils of pottery, pewter, and iron necessary for daily life, trimmed with such hangings as the occupants had brought with them, and supplied with bedclothes. That these were in most cases too simple and primitive for the taste of the gentlemen of the colony is evident from Harriot's description of their dissatisfaction with their life on Roanoke Island. We might expect Lane to have somewhat more luxurious quarters than the rest, though as a soldier he would be used to rough living. His field bed, however, could have been an elaborate one, with other accoutrements to match. Soldiers and servants in their barracklike buildings would have to content themselves with the minimum amenities—beds, places to hang clothes and arms, benches, tables from which to eat, and pottery and metal utensils for food. Even while exploration was continuing a certain amount of construction and repair would be needed inside the camp. Sidings for the houses might be Indian mats to begin with, but lath and plaster walling would probably be needed (or perhaps timber walling) as nights and days became colder. The daily occupations involved in keeping a hundred men going would require the attention of an appreciable number of persons doing nothing else.

It is our great misfortune that we have had to fit together so much of this very limited picture from imagination or analogy. Much more insight, but of a purely fictional sort, would be needed to bring this static picture (true perhaps only in bare outline) to life. It may well be that this attempt has taken us already too far along the road of conjecture. However, if this attempted reconstruction is to have any validity references to the "fort" must, in general, mean the enclosed area as a whole, and not simply our Fort Raleigh. The word could apply to the minor defenses around the settlement, to Fort Raleigh, or to comparable strong points, but each time it must be considered carefully in its context. This amounts to a major revision in the traditional manner of looking at the settlement whereby Fort Raleigh has been taken to be the fort and the cottages and other buildings to be in some way loosely appended to it.

Ralph Lane could write "From the new fort in Virginia" possibly as early as 3 September and certainly by 8 September.[11] In the meantime Lane and Grenville, whatever their differences, which continued to be reflected in the bitter letters Lane sent home by the ships, had long ago reached agreement about the number of settlers it would be possible to maintain in the colony, and had proceeded in the construction of the settlement on that assumption. This number was much smaller than had originally been planned—107 men besides Lane, with the addition of one other, John White, who is not on the list we have (perhaps he compiled it and forgot to include himself). We are told that Grenville, as he prepared to reembark on the *Tiger*, left "with them as much of all provisions as his plenty would give him leave," which was probably far from enough, even for the reduced number. He set sail on 25 August, arriving at Plymouth only toward the end of October, having taken a valuable Spanish prize on the way but claiming to have "possessed and peopled the same [her "Virginia"] to her Majesty's use, and planted it with such cattle and beasts as are fit and necessary for manuring the country and in time to give relief with victual, as also with such fruits and plants as my travail by the way thitherwards I might procure."[12] He thus indicated that at least some of the beasts obtained in the Caribbean had survived and were at the settlers' disposal, while he also, optimistically, suggested that plants brought from there would also flourish on Roanoke Island. As we know, they could not and did not.

But one ship still remained, Captain Clarke's *Roebuck*, until at least 8 September. On that day Lane wrote a last letter to Sir Francis Walsingham full of optimism, especially concerning the lands just explored to the west, possibly beyond the head of Albemarle Sound.[13] There, he noted, the population was thick, seven hundred persons having been seen at one place celebrating, presumably, their green corn festival which marked the completion of the main corn crop. This area, where he hoped to go during the winter, was some 140 miles inland. We cannot usefully guess where it was. He also sent with Francis Brooke, the expedition's treasurer, a full account of the voyage for Sir Walter Ralegh's use; most unfortunately, it has not survived. With the departure of the *Roebuck* the colonists were left to their own devices, but with the promise of a supply of provisions by the following Easter.

With one of Lane's September letters was enclosed a rough sketch map, which is our earliest cartographic record of the Roanoke Island region.[14] It might possibly have been drawn by Harriot, but its scale is very defective and unprofessional. On the other hand, it contains a considerable amount of topographical information. It extends as far south as Secotan and thus includes the area Grenville's party explored around Pamlico Sound, but it adds to the north and west Albemarle Sound, with the Roanoke and Chowan river mouths at its western end. It is confusing about the Outer Banks. "The port of St. Mary's where we arrived first" is given south of Wococon (and the name is derived from a Spanish map), whereas Wococon is shown much too far to the north. Products found in various places are specified—roots that dye red on Croatoan; "Galls," possibly merely oak galls but more probably the medicinal plant *Sabatia* (later drawn by White) near Shallowbag Bay; the grass that bears silk (yucca) in the marshy islets in what is now Croatan Sound; large red grapes in Weapemeoc; and a great store of fish in the fresh water in Albemarle Sound. Roanoke Island is named "The King's Isle" in honor of Wingina. The inlets through the Outer Banks are not rendered with any degree of accuracy. Entrances to Currituck Sound in the north and to the Neuse River in the south are indicated. The whole, however, served to give a fair impression of the layout of the water and land so far explored. We can compare it with the later engraving of a lost White drawing, "The arrival of the Englishmen," which shows a more polished picture plan of the same area, and which may have been cut from a more sophisticated version of this original sketch.[15]

By November all the ships were home and Ralegh had heard all the good and bad news that Grenville, Lane, in his reports, and others could tell or show him. He could gain some impression of the value of the work that had been done and could satisfy himself

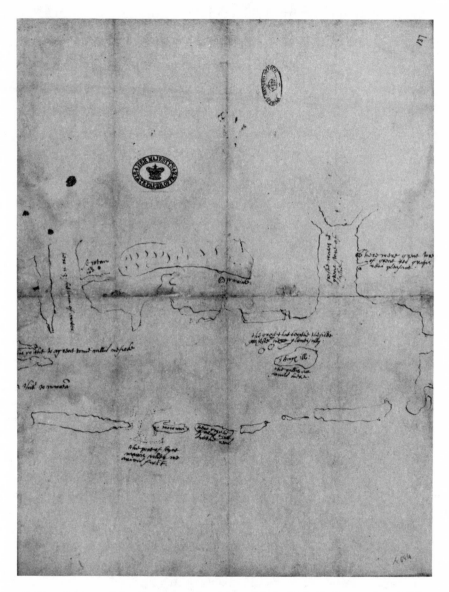

7. Sketch Map of the Roanoke Island Area Made Early in September 1585,
Possibly by Thomas Harriot.
London: Public Record Office, Maps MPF 584.

that, however many mishaps there had been, more than a hundred men were firmly located on American soil and taking an active part, he hoped, in preparing for the next developing stage in the colonization project.

A crucial change had taken place between the time the expedition sailed from England and when Grenville returned. The Spanish king had at long last retaliated against the English for their many pinpricks against his empire. Sir Francis Drake had robbed his Pacific possessions; many pirates had invaded the Caribbean and were stealing Spanish ships and their contents, as Grenville had done on his outward voyage. At the same time, many English merchants were peacefully trading with Spain for whale oil, leather, olive oil, wines, fruits, and products of the western empire brought to Seville in exchange for English cloth and tin, Newfoundland fish, and many other products. Many more English than Spanish ships were involved. Consequently, when, early in May, Philip struck at the English by placing an embargo on all their ships in Spanish ports and later seizing them, war had in fact begun. The Queen authorized the issue of letters of marque, turning piracy into privateering, and English ships were dispatched to seize as many Spanish vessels and their cargoes as they could.

In June, Amias Preston and Bernard Drake were ready to bring reinforcements and stores to the Roanoke colony, and, no doubt, to raid the Spanish Indies going and coming. On 20 June they were countermanded. They were ordered to go to Newfoundland instead, warn English ships there not to go directly to Spain with their catch, and to seize Spanish and Portuguese fishing vessels and return with them to England.[16] Thus, the small colony remained both unsupplied and unreinforced. The former can only have been a hardship, but the latter was more likely a blessing, as larger numbers would have added little to the effectiveness or otherwise of the English settlement at that time. On his way home Grenville had gone south toward Bermuda, where he had been fortunate enough to capture the rich straggler from the Spanish fleet, the *Santa Maria de San Vicente*, on which he placed a prize crew.[17] He took command of her himself, sailing into Plymouth on 18 October, and pleasing Ralegh, himself, and all the other investors in the voyage by recouping all they had spent, and perhaps more, from the value of the vessel and her cargo. Whatever else it might or might not produce, the Roanoke colony could enable ships returning from it to prey on the Spanish fleets. But for this reason the specter of possible Spanish destruction of the colony must also have arisen in the minds of the promoters.

The Settlers, 1585–1586

The colony established on Roanoke Island in September 1585 was in many respects a self-contained community, and the people who made it up demand as careful consideration as we can give them. We have a list of their names, but in most cases do not know either what they did in England or precisely what their position was in the settlement. Moreover, though we have some detailed evidence from Ralph Lane and from the work of Thomas Harriot and John White, we do not have any diary of the occurrences in the colony into which we can fit their activities as a systematic chronicle. We do know, however, that all of them either were hired by Ralegh for wages or had come as adventurers at their own expense and, consequently, as investors in the enterprise. All the indications are, however, that the great majority were in a real sense "servants" of Sir Walter Ralegh, under his lieutenant Colonel Ralph Lane, who as governor of the colony had very wide powers, including those of life or death over the men. Although we do not hear it referred to, it is probable that Lane was assisted by a council consisting of the gentlemen and the chief officials, but whether it would have had anything more than advisory functions is doubtful.

Lane was hot-tempered and did not deal easily with opposition; he was also, as we know from his letters, vain and boastful. As a professional soldier he tended to fall back on the use of force rather readily, instead of wasting time on diplomacy, and this may have helped to sour relations with his Indian neighbors. At the same time, it is clear that he was an effective leader in that he kept his men in good health if not always in good spirits. He is probably correct when he says that on the long voyage on the *Tiger* only 4 men out of 160 died,[1] a remarkable record for the time, and Thomas Harriot tells us only 4 out of 108, 3 of them delicate men, died during the nine and a half months they spent on Roanoke Island. Lane attributed the lack of mortality to strict discipline and careful organization. He was probably right. So we have to think of the colony as being under a type of military discipline and control, with little opportunity for individual enterprise and certainly no opportunity for mutiny, even if Lane could not stop a good deal of grumbling. Harriot, on the other hand, attributed the low mortality rate to the healthiness of the climate of the island and the country generally.

What it meant to be an "adventurer" can be glimpsed from what we know of the cape merchant Thomas Harvey.[2] A member of the Grocers' Company of London and a citizen of London, he claimed to have invested his own money and other sums that he borrowed in articles with which to trade with the Indians. We may hope that he had a larger and more varied stock than the *Falcon* had carried in 1578 for a similar purpose—a few unfinished, embroidered doublets, two pieces of calico, "and certain manilios of brass [and] certain Morris bells, which manilios and bells came into two firkins," a very trivial cargo indeed.[3] It is clear Harvey hoped to exchange the goods he had brought for the furs, skins, drugs, spices, dyes, fine timber, metals, and other goods that, he had gathered from Manteo and Wanchese, would be available when the colony was established. But according to him, he was to be disappointed and to lose all his investment. Whether this is strictly true we cannot tell as Harvey in later life did not prove to be an altogether admirable citizen.

But a number of the gentlemen with Lane were also adventurers. They would expect that precious metals or at least metals of some value like copper and lead would be discovered and that they would get a share of these in return for their investment. We cannot say whether, at this stage, they were promised land in the longer run if they remained in the colony, but it is possible that they were. They too were to be disappointed in the end, but from the beginning they were a source of some discontentment. Thomas Harriot had hard words for many of them. Some, he said, never moved from the island "after gold and silver was not soon found, as it was by them looked for," and they "had little care for any other thing but to pamper their bellies." Then, in a famous passage, he declared:

Some also were of a nice bringing up, only in cities or towns, or such as never (as I may say) had seen the world before. Because there were not to be found any English cities, nor such fair houses, nor at their own wish any of their old accustomed dainty food, nor any soft beds of down or feathers, the country was to them miserable.

The picture of Lane as a stern disciplinarian, keeping his colony under strict control, scarcely fits Harriot's picture of some of the colonists making no effort to take part in its work and complaining of the lack of amenities to be found in a pioneer settlement. Yet perhaps we can reconcile the two aspects if we separate the colonists into two groups, one composed of men who had come as soldiers and as minor officials with jobs to do and who were receiving pay for doing so, the other, the adventurers, who had paid in advance for what they expected to be a glamorous and profitable experience and who were not, to the same extent, amenable to discipline when their expectations were not satisfied.

It is probably justifiable to think of the soldiers as comprising rather more than half of the total number and, perhaps, forming two small companies of twenty-five to thirty men each, having Edward Stafford and John Vaughan as captains. They would probably take turns in providing the guards for the defenses and also be available for expeditions into the interior. At least some of those named as "Master," and so entitled to be regarded as gentlemen, would be enrolled in these companies with some subordinate rank, whereas others would be the semiindependent gentlemen who have been referred to already. But it is not possible to say which was which among the group comprising Acton, Marvyn, Gardyner, Snelling, Anthony Russe (Rowse), Michael Polyson, Kendall, and Prideox (Prideaux). We do not have the given names of some of them and they are hard to identify. And not all the gentlemen were designated "master" in the list: Marmaduke Constable, for example, was almost certainly a Yorkshire gentleman of that name,[4] and probably others were also passed over. But Sir Francis Drake had always maintained that it was necessary to have a few gentlemen in a military force to stiffen the rank and file, and, through the respect they engendered, make the rank and file more effective in warfare.

We cannot pick out many of the soldiers as such except for a group of five who had evidently come with Lane from Ireland and were Irish—his personal attendant, Edward Nugent, Darby Glande (or Glavin), afterward a soldier in the Spanish army,[5] Edward Kelly, and John Gostigo (Costigan?). Others could possibly be found in army lists of the previous years, but these are seldom available. That the soldiers were unruly and were punished is indicated by Harriot, when he says that "some for their misdemeanour and ill dealing in the country have been there worthily punished." Indeed, it is probable that one was hanged, and his corpse left hanging to intimidate others, for some misdeed or other late in the colony's history.[6] There is little doubt that the jail was used for offenders. But for adventurers who were not soldiers and merely proved uncooperative, punishment was scarcely possible or advisable except for very grave offenses.

There were, inevitably, a number of craftsmen whose presence we must assume but whose names we do not know. Among the more important would be the smith or smiths and the carpenter or carpenters (wrought-iron spikes were found at the fort site as well as an auger). There was a gunsmith and (or) an armorer, because weapons had to be kept in good order. There was a cook (or more than one), a baker, and a brewer (as we hear of them making beer from corn). John Brocke has been tentatively identified as a shoemaker and John Fever (of French origin) as a basketmaker.[7] There was also a thatcher, because the cottages were thatched and the job was a skilled one.

With Thomas Harvey were men engaged in administration. We hear of a keeper of the store and a master of the victuals, who would look after and dispose of the reserve of food and supplies accumulated for the use of the colonists. According to Harriot, except for the short time after the *Tiger* grounded when they were without food, the colonists were adequately fed, even if not at such a level as to satisfy some of the grumblers who have been mentioned. There was, too, some stringency toward the end of the colony's stay. There was an assistant treasurer, and Christopher Marshall has been tentatively identified as a former minor customs official who could have been he.[8] It may be that Harvey was also master of the store and that he had the duty of supplying the men's needs, at least in part. The position of master of the victuals, the basic food supply, indicates that they were under Lane's control and were issued as a ration under his ultimate supervision.

An important part of the function of all these officials was to acquire corn from the Indians in the autumn of 1585 to make up for food lost or damaged on the *Tiger.* It seems probable that enough was obtained to tide them over the winter adequately, if not with plenty, though whether a diet of corn and venison, the most likely constituents along with fish and oysters, would have agreed with all of their digestions remains an open question. Certainly they went short in late spring and early summer. So did the Indians at this time of year and they would not have much to spare for the colonists. It would seem, however, that they supplied Lane with some seed corn in the spring. To plant the corn his men would have spades and mattocks used for constructing the defenses and cottages (indeed, we can see mattocks being used in John White's drawing of the salt-taking episode on Puerto Rico), as well as a wrought-iron sickle, which was recovered from the fort ditch. Indian assistance was needed, and was forthcoming, for the technique of corn cultivation to be learned. Harriot describes it in detail.

It seems likely that each of the three fields laid out was of one or more English acres (forty perches by four) in size. Harriot reckoned that a field of corn would yield two hundred London bushels to the acre, five times as much as a field of wheat in England at that time. This was thought sufficient to maintain them over the winter of 1586–87 if they were not relieved. Probably the corn was planted in sequence in each field, several weeks apart, in Indian style, to provide a regular return of new corn from July onward. The first corn was forming from these plantings just as the colonists left the island in June 1586. How many of the men were skilled gardeners or agricultural laborers is unclear, but if specialized crops like sugar were contemplated, then a few experienced cultivators were clearly present. It seems most unfortunate that the first colony did not see the completion of a full year's cycle as then we could better estimate its viability, at least in foodstuffs. However, recent research has shown that the amount of productive land on the island was limited,[9] and that the area used for agriculture by the Indians was small, leaving most of it heavily forested, with heavy undergrowth, except where they had cleared it by burning the understory.

As "Admiral," Philip Amadas would have had a small crew of experienced sailors under his command to man the pinnace; these would be reinforced from time to time when crews for the boats left with the colony—at least two—were needed by exploring or trading parties. One of these boats would be permanently attached to the survey party so it probably had a small regular crew. It is likely that some of his men also learned how to use the local dugout canoes, which Harriot was to describe and White to draw, and may have acquired some, though we do not hear of any being taken back to England.

One group of specialists was of considerable importance, namely the "mineral men"—metallurgists and miners. The leading metallurgist in the list was Dougham Gannes, otherwise Joachim Ganz, a Jewish expert from Prague, who had been involved in the locating and working of copper mines in England.[10] He would be considered to be "Dutch" or German in the nomenclature of the time. He would be employed in testing any metal objects found in Indian hands— and they had a number of copper ornaments when first encountered in 1584—to find out whether the copper was of good quality and also whether these objects contained any gold or silver. Specimens for testing could probably be acquired from the Indians in exchange for European glass beads or brass decorations. He would also, of course, test any specimens found by explorers that might have a mineral content of value. Initially the miners would have been employed on the fortifications, but we do not hear of their being used elsewhere, except that Harriot reported the finding of "a veine of earth along the sea coast for the space of fourtie or fiftie miles, whereof by the judgement of some that have made trial here in England is made good alum," important in preparing cloth. It is likely that miners were employed to dig it out and have it tested on Roanoke Island, before bringing specimens to England. What were said to be "White copperas," niter, and "Alumen plumeum" (a fine type of alum) were also identified by the mineral men but mean little to us. It is possible that the men named in the list—Daniel (Daniel was the metallurgist on Sir Humphrey Gilbert's voyage in 1583 but was lost at sea),[11] Erasmus Clefs, Edward Ketchemen, Haunce Walters, Thomas Skevelabs, and Smolkin—included some German miners. But Ganz was clearly the man who counted in this group.

Harriot tells us incidentally, something about the work that was done in searching for and testing metalliferous substances. With regard to iron, he says that a number of places "we found neer the water side the ground to be rocky, which by the trial of a mineral man [Ganz or one of his assistants] was found to hold iron richly." The places he specified were in one case about 80 miles from the fort and the other, 120 miles. This would probably mean they were located in the basins of the Chowan and Roanoke rivers, and would bring the areas within the modern geological area known as the Talbot Terrace, to the west of the Suffolk scarp.[12] Inside this zone the rivers have high banks of clay and sand that contain bedded and iron-cemented clays whose color would reveal their iron content. This, effectively, is not workable so that the "mineral man" was being optimistic. Harriot says also "It is found in many places of the country else." Here he probably refers to bog-iron, which can be seen in the swampy areas and from which iron-founding attempts were made on the James River less than a quarter of a century later. It is workable but with much labor, even if Harriot thought it "a good merchantable commodity" considering the low cost of feeding men there and the abundance of timber and its increasing scarcity in England. Thus the idea of producing iron from American ore and timber and reexporting the bar iron to England was already emerging during this period.

Harriot believed he had identifed silver pieces among the ear ornaments of a weroance who lived some eighty miles away and who claimed to have obtained them from the interior. White grains of metal in the rivers were also thought to be silver. But there is no suggestion that specimens were acquired for testing. Harriot was quite mistaken about the presence of silver as there is none within range, though a few Spanish silver coins from wrecks may already have begun to circulate and to be used. It is just barely possible that a few tiny nodules were carried down by streams and made into beads.

Copper was a more important possible find. Copper was found in some quantity in the possession of the members of the Chowan tribe, and was the object of a late, though unsuccessful, search by Lane because the Mangoaks (Tuscarora) were said to have had access to sources of it. Of the two pieces of copper found at the fort, one in

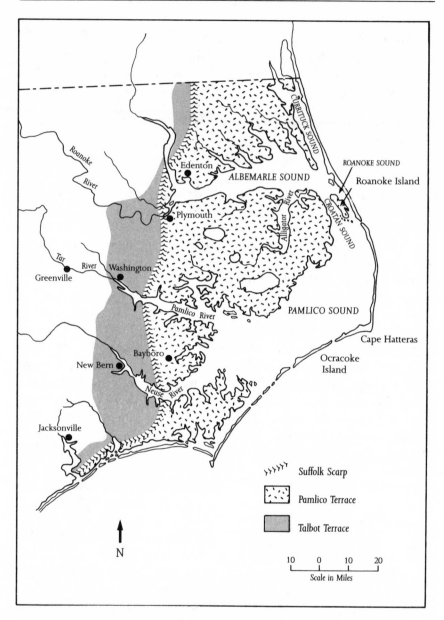

8. Location Map of the North Carolina Coastal Zones.
After V. Bellis, M. P. O'Connor, and S. R. Riggs, *Estuarine Shoreline Erosion in the Albemarle Sound Region of North Carolina,* Raleigh: State University of North Carolina Sea Grant Program 75-29, 1975.

the topsoil and one at the bottom of the ditch, both had been melted. A small piece of a crucible that was part of Ganz's equipment was found at the fort site. The melting of copper would also imply the existence of a fairly powerful furnace, capable of reaching the melting point of copper, some 2,000 degrees Fahrenheit. But it is clear from the narrative records that the colonists never reached a source of natural copper, though they may have picked up occasional small nuggets in the Chowan and Roanoke rivers. A discovery of copper in quantity could have helped to put the colony on an economic footing, but sources of natural copper in eastern North America were limited in number and yield. The deposits in the Virgilina district, penetrated by the Roanoke River, outside their range, may have been used by the Indians, but the colonists never had access to them.

Gold and silver in quantity would have made the colony a genuine success and would have attracted major support for further colonization in North America; their availability could even have attracted royal support. Many of the colonists had come out expecting to find gold or silver; when repeated efforts failed to locate any, they felt that their adventure was worthless and consequently reviled the whole project when they returned home. But these men would not have made successful colonists anywhere in eastern North America. Ironically, North Carolina produced an appreciable quantity of gold in the nineteenth century.

The leading merchant and craft companies of London were very much interested in the discovery of economically viable products. Incited by the elder Richard Hakluyt, they could have expected the colony to produce many things they could sell. Similarly, leading apothecaries—John Gerard was to do it later—liked to send younger men trained by them to identify medicinal plants and substances. Thomas Harvey, as a member of the Grocers' Company (which included apothecaries), would have been well aware of the kinds of spices and medicinal plants that the company hoped would be found. Thomas Bookener (Buckner) was later found to be a member of the Mercers' Company, which, although primarily concerned with textiles, was also very interested in dyes and minerals like alum used in the manufacture of cloth. He was to become a lifelong friend of Thomas Harriot.[13] A John Tuyt, who has been identified as a London apothecary, was probably the man of that name in the colony.[14] He would be of help in providing herbal medicines for the treatment of minor diseases in the colony, and he would be busy examining plants and trees for their medicinal properties and instigating their collection. These men, more particularly, perhaps, the apothecary, would be especially valuable to Harriot and White as they made their survey. We cannot be certain that any of the physicians and apothecaries (as they were mentioned in the plural), who were on the ships in August, stayed behind. The only guess about a surgeon is that he just might have been the "Haunce Walters" of 1585, because there was a "Hance the Surgeon" with White on his 1590 voyage.

Finally, it is worth noting that, if the Thomas Luddington who was a Fellow of Lincoln College, Oxford, was the man of that name in the 1585 colony, then it is possible that he was already in Holy Orders.[15] There is little doubt that throughout his stay Lane would hold regular services in the colony on Sundays, but, without a clergyman, these would consist only of the reading of extracts from the prayer book and the Bible, together with the singing of psalms. Bibles, the Book of Common Prayer, and the Psalms, which at that time were in a metrical version, generally appended to the prayer book, were undoubtedly among the colony's equipment. But if there was a clergyman, he would hold regular church services, with sermons and a communion service; in that case, the earliest Anglican observances on North American soil could be dated from the beginning of the settlement. Perhaps, if something more could be found about Thomas Luddington, this could be confirmed or denied.

Apart from Thomas Harriot and John White (in view of their responsibility for conducting a survey), the colony may be described as containing a good cross section of the Englishmen of the day. It probably had very few agricultural laborers, an essential component in any enduring settlement. It certainly lacked experienced fishermen and even huntsmen, as Harriot comments on "the want of English means for the taking of beasts, fish and fowl," which men experienced in these arts could surely improvise.

Its bias on the military side emphasized the colony's position as an outpost against Spain, as a possible base for ships operating against Spain, and a possible target for Spanish attack. It also indicates that the colony had to guard against the hostility of the native inhabitants.

If the Indians were universally as kind and loving as Arthur Barlowe had depicted them, there might seem to have been some overemphasis in this respect. If in 1584 Amadas had experienced some hostility in an area other than the Outer Banks, it would be more natural to take precautions. Indeed, Manteo and Wanchese may well have emphasized the wars between one Indian group and another and suggested at least that the English should help Wingina against his enemies. This, rather than concerns about the Spanish alone, could have influenced the colony's military aspect.

It must always be remembered that the intended colony was much larger than the actual one. The presence of three or four hundred men would have totally altered the balance of personnel and the circumstances under which they could establish themselves. Ralegh had an empirical temperament and it is not certain that in 1585 he saw beyond a single year or two of attempted settlement. If he already had in mind long-term plans for colonization, a very different setup would be required, even apart from the need for women and children to lay foundations for a viable community. It seems best to regard the 1585–86 colony as primarily an experiment in colonization rather than the first step in a carefully-thought-out program for establishing a lasting society of English people across the Atlantic.

It is interesting to compare the limited information we have at our disposal and the legitimate conjectures that can be made about the men who remained on Roanoke Island with the elaborate lists that the younger Richard Hakluyt added to his "Discourse" after Barlowe's return in September 1584. They assumed, from the beginning, the existence of large areas of cleared land and would have involved bringing at least the four hundred or so men we think Ralegh contemplated settling in the colony in 1585. It would be pointless here to give Hakluyt's whole list,[16] but a selection may be revealing. He said they would need specialists to grow sugarcane, vines, and olives; as well as gardeners, grafters (for fruit-tree grafting), fowlers, sea and freshwater fishermen, net makers, butchers, salt makers, cooks, bakers, brewers, men to grub up trees for export and sawmill experts to produce boards for them, carpenters for buildings, blacksmiths, pitch and tar makers, coopers to make barrels, dyers to search for cochineal and other dyes, brick and tile makers, thatchers, well sinkers, lath makers, barbers, laundrymen, shoemakers, bottle makers, and tanners. A certain number of these craftsmen we have found to be present or assumed were essential to the conduct of the settlement, and a number of others may also have been there. But this selection is worth giving to indicate the range of specialists it was thought might be essential or at least desirable. In such a small settlement, however, the more active and efficient men would take on a variety of roles, as in any pioneer venture. At the same time, Hakluyt's list shows that much care was given to preparing the colony and thinking ahead about what type of person would be most useful to take part in it.

Explorations

We have no journal of the colony between the departure of the ships in September 1585 and the beginnings of a narrative in the surviving version of Ralph Lane's report from March 1586 onward, which originally was almost certainly much longer. Consequently it is difficult, at times impossible, to follow by direct means the activities of the settlers during the period from September to March. We must attempt to do so indirectly, but the record is bound to be imperfect. Thomas Harriot wrote a full chronicle of the enterprise but it has completely disappeared. We can get some help from the general account of the country with which Lane prefaced his narrative of the last few months of the settlement's history, because he tells us a little about the characteristics of the various regions that his men had entered. We have to rely very largely on an interpretation of the map John White drew from the many detailed sketches and charts Harriot and he prepared in the settlement, though the map we have is likely to have been drawn after his return to England from a larger and possibly more detailed original.

The actual method of making such a map, as was constructed during the period between July 1585 and June 1586, had been laid down in the instructions for an earlier voyage that have already been mentioned. It must also be realized that at the time the map was being made, Harriot was making notes and White drawings of almost everything they saw in their travels. In the absence of photography, such procedures were the only way to obtain a comprehensive record of the features of a particular area and its inhabitants.

To begin with, it seems best to start with the map.[1] From the time of the first landing onward the pilots of the vessels anchored at Wococon and later at Port Ferdinando were evidently assisting in making a survey of the coast and the shoals and shores of Pamlico Sound. The outline of the outer shore between Cape Lookout and the Outer Banks opposite the outlet of Albemarle Sound was clearly the work of the maritime experts, passed on to Harriot and White. The same was true of the shoals inside Pamlico Sound and the greater part, at least of the outlines of the inner shores, of the sound traversed in the July expedition, already described. But these were clearly supplemented in detail by Harriot's sketches of the shores and rivermouths and, as has been seen, by White's many sketches of the villages and their inhabitants.

The location of the group of southern villages on the map, with a view of Lake Paquippe (largely conjectural), as seen from Pomeioc and the Secotan and Neuse rivers, all derive from this July enterprise. Its lack of precision—for example, in locating the site of Secotan—has given rise to difficulties of interpretation.[2] But Lane tells us that the reexploration of this area was left incomplete. His remarks on the passage from Roanoke as being "through a broad sound within the main, the same being without kenning [beyond view of land] and yet full of flats and shoals," is a good description of it even at the present time. He explains that, apart from the pinnace, he had only one large boat, the double wherry, which would carry fifteen men and which, he says, "drew too deep water for that shallow sound." He was evidently unwilling to trust to the goodwill of the Indians of this area—remembering the clash at Aquascogoc—unless he could return there in force. At the same time, the map shows the pinnace under sail farther north in the sound, apparently making for the entrance through the Outer Banks called Chacandepeco, just north of modern Cape Hatteras where Manteo's people lived and where his mother headed a small tribal group, so that the pinnace could apparently sail this far south across the sounds. It is probable that Harriot and White were able to sail in her to this point of the Outer Banks, as it would be a long row in a small boat, which we think they used for much of their survey work.

The most surprising thing to the modern viewer of the White map is the great eastward-pointing headland that projects from the Outer Banks in the vicinity of modern Rodanthe well to the north of Cape Hatteras. This was evidently charted by the seamen from offshore. It was called Cape Kenrick by the colonists, probably from the name of

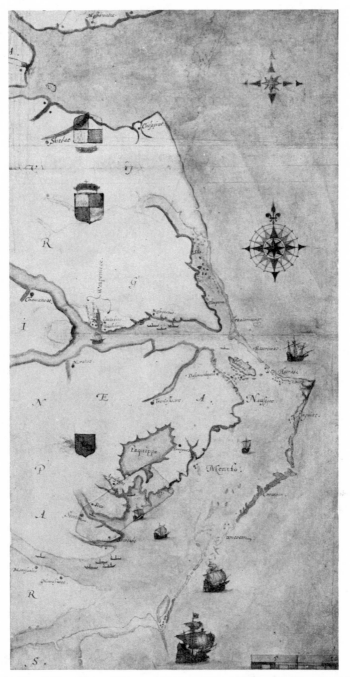

9. The John White–Thomas Harriot Map of Ralegh's Virginia, 1586.
British Museum, Department of Prints and Drawings, 1906-5-9-1 (3).

the lookout man on one of the ships who first sighted it. The high dunes to the north of it were named Kenricks Mounts. It disappeared in a storm before the 1730s and is now represented only by Wimble Shoals well out to sea. Working northward, outside the Outer Banks, we see clearly two of the inlets described by Lane earlier, Port Ferdinando, the main entry to Roanoke Island, and, only a little way to the north, Port Lane, which was too shallow for use except by small boats. Clearly, the pinnace could enter from Port Ferdinando and sail up Roanoke Sound to an anchorage on the eastern side of Roanoke Island. What is now Croatan Sound was blocked by a large number of small islets, probably mere clumps of grass-covered, salt-marsh peat. Whether the Indians could find a passage through them in their canoes we do not know, but it is unlikely that an English boat could do so.

Continuing northward on the outer shore we do not find Trinity Harbor where we would expect to do so. The widening of the banks at modern Nags Head is distinctly shown, both on White's map and on the engraving of "The arrival of the Englishmen" already mentioned. On the latter, Trinity Harbor is clearly shown at about the site of modern Duck, along with two other inlets somewhat farther north along Currituck Bank. But no inlet is clearly indicated on the White map until we reach the vicinity of modern Deals. Trinity Harbor remains something of a mystery. Had it existed as Lane described it, it could have acted as an outlet for some of the water from Albemarle Sound, but it could conceivably have closed up over the period between September 1585 and June 1586 during the constant series of changes involved in the retreat and alteration of the barrier islands.

It seems probable that seamen, too, had some share in delimiting the waters around Roanoke Island and the mouth of Albemarle Sound—with its shoal—as shown in the engraving "The arrival of the Englishmen." But to Harriot and White there remained the task of going over again many of these shorelines, plotting them in accurate relation to one another by surveying techniques and carrying forward the mapping up the Chowan and Roanoke rivers all the way north to Chesapeake Bay, some seventy-five miles to the north of Roanoke Island.

The earlier document, already referred to, tells us something of

how it was probably done. The surveyor would have with him someone to attend him "with pen, ink, paper and pencil, with black lead,
and Ephimerides [calendrical tables] or with some other calculated
tables to observe the latitude. Another to attend him always with an
universal dial [a precursor to the theodolite], a cross staff [used for
taking latitude sights], and a sailing compass [possibly rectified for dip
and variation]." So Harriot and White, each with his "writing table" or
notebook, Harriot with his plane table, and White with his drawing
board and array of colors, would need two or more attendants. It is
almost certain that they had a small boat at their disposal and that
the attendants may also have used the oars. They would move slowly
from place to place, with the primary object of getting the orienta-
tion of the map sketches correct, and then going on with their
numerous other tasks.

The proposed instructions for topographical mapping were very
precise. A table of map symbols was to be drawn to show differing
land forms and vegetation, and to mark shoals and obstructions in
water. The surveyor was told to "divide your plats of the country
into sundry particular cards of four sheets of Paper Royal [twenty-
four inches by nineteen inches] along by the sea coast according to
the bigness of the table of your instrument [the plane table] or as
you shall see cause for your best division of the bounds either by
rivers, headlands, etc." The completed sheets, keeping the same scale
throughout, were to be systematically lettered from south to north,
"multiplying your letters as occasion shall require till your whole
discovery be perfectly finished and set down in plat," that is, when
the sketches were reduced to fit together into a general map of the
region. Such a process, or something very like it, was used by Harriot
and White. In carrying out the survey they traveled very considerable
distances in order to get dimensions and directions correct, so that
from July 1585 to June 1586 they were almost continuously on the
move.

They had evidently almost completed the survey when they had to
leave, but not quite, because on the final map parts of the Chowan
and Roanoke rivers are on a somewhat larger scale than the rest of
the area (and may well have been drawn from impression rather
than survey). In general, however, this is the first surveyed map
to be made of any part of North America. Of course, the survey

sheets have not survived and we are very fortunate to have White's version of the completed map from his own hand, even though the technical side of the survey, and presumably the reduction also, would have been largely done by Harriot. At the same time, both men were doing a great deal of work in collecting material on natural resources, making notes of and drawing fauna and flora, and making a thorough examination of Indian society. We can at least be certain that they were not among the idlers about whom complaints were afterward to be made. Perhaps it was just because Harriot and his party proved it was possible to do so much and to remain active throughout the year that he was so severe on those who had fewer specific tasks to keep them employed.

Although Lane in his report stressed the discoveries that were made by the colony over the whole period of its existence, it is not clear whether most of his men moved very far from Roanoke Island between September 1585 and March 1586. Parties almost certainly visited a few of the villages lying on Pamlico Sound, to the west and southwest of Roanoke Island, and it is likely that they had some contact during the winter with the Weapemeoc villages along the northern shore of Albemarle Sound. In these cases the object would be to obtain corn, deerflesh, and fish from the villages in order to supplement their slender stocks, though these included barley, oats, and peas—their wheat had been ruined when the *Tiger* grounded. We have almost no evidence of what objects were offered in exchange but they probably would include metal knives and tools as well as trinkets of brass and other metal (casting counters among them), colored cloth, and pieces of copper. How easily the Indians took to the trading for European goods apart from copper is not known, but clearly the colonists obtained sufficient corn to keep them tolerably fed over the winter. The position was to be different in the spring, when both Indians and colonists went short. What the Indians *could* supply, but this was early in summer, is shown by Arthur Barlowe, describing presents sent by Granganimeo, "fat bucks, conies, hares, fish, melons, walnuts, cucumbers, gourds, peas, and divers roots and fruit ... and of their country corn." Even if Barlowe's identification of melons and cucumbers is wrong, and the peas were beans, the list is impressive. But supplies of all but venison and fish, and to some extent corn, would diminish rapidly from late October onward.

The colonists would also attempt to acquire other goods from the Indians through trade—in particular, furs and skins. This was primarily the task of Thomas Harvey, the chief merchant; but, according to him, he was unsuccessful in it.[3] Again we can refer to Barlowe for what was offered, comprising "leather [dressed skins], coral [wampum], divers kinds of dyes very excellent." Decorated skin mantles were especially attractive to the English. Harriot tells us that "deerskins, dressed after the manner of chamois [leather] or undressed, are to be had of the natural inhabitants thousands yearly by way of traffic for trifles." How many were bought is wholly unknown. It is likely that a few bearskins were also acquired as there are several references to bears being plentiful. But evidently there was no development of a fur trade as such, for Harriot says that they only obtained two marten (mink) and not a single lynx skin. He ignores the considerable muskrat population though he refers to the numerous river otters seen if not killed. Nor did he get skins from raccoon. But he collected all the information about furbearing animals he could and acquired specimens of some of them. Clearly, the colonists failed altogether to induce the local population to engage in trapping and killing of furbearing animals for commerce. The Indians used various dyes, some of the sources of which Harriot is able to specify, but they were not thought worth trading for as Harriot doubted whether they would prove "merchantable," even if they would be useful to colonists in residence.

Pearls were the one product that was especially sought from the Indians. They consumed such large quantities of oysters that pearls, though not frequently found in *Ostrea virginica* today, were accumulated in some quantity. More important were the pearls from the freshwater mussel. These appear to have been plentiful and were acquired easily from the local people though some were spoiled because they were not removed from the shell until after the oysters and mussels had been cooked. However, Harriot tells us that "one of our company, a man of skill in such matters [a lapidary?], had gathered together from among the savage people about 5000," from which he had picked the finest and made a chain. This was intended to be a gift for the Queen but, as discussed later, was lost in the colonists' hurried departure from the settlement.

In all this Harvey should have been prominent, but evidently he did little to justify his position as chief merchant. He and the keeper of the store must have been responsible for purchasing most of the major supplies of corn, venison, and fish for the colony. It might seem that individual settlers could buy trinkets in the store or dispose of personal articles (or those they could steal) and that some trading was done by individuals but perhaps, apart from acquiring a certain number of pearls by barter, not very much. Clearly, however, trade with the Indians was not the great source of goods or profit that had been forecast. Their surpluses were small and they were not induced to develop any substantial market economy by the settlement, even if Harriot considered that a very large quantity of dressed deerskins could eventually be obtained from them.

Lane's one major initiative before the end of 1585, possibly in late October or early November, was to send a party of men to explore the area to the north of the sounds, namely, what is now part of the state of Virginia. This group evidently contained a military element and its leader, whom we cannot identify, could have been one of Lane's captains. Lane only describes him as "Colonel of the Chesepians." Harriot and White were especially important members of the party. The special attraction of the area to the north was the "city" of Skicóac, which Barlowe says, based on the account of Manteo and Wanchese, was the largest Indian settlement in the whole region. If, indeed, Philip Amadas had found the entry to Chesapeake Bay in 1584, there would be an even greater incentive to explore the area as ships found the approaches to Roanoke Island so limited and dangerous.

It would seem that this expedition made its way northward through Currituck Sound because so many islets, and in one place a shoal, are marked on White's map. It is clear that they had the pinnace and one or two boats or canoes. Because "sho." (for shoal) is shown on the map, they may well have hoped to continue up the sound but instead sailed through the opening shown where the Outer Banks terminate. On the map the upper part of Back Bay is shown somewhat out of scale, and the territory from the opening in the Outer Banks to the coastal area bordering Chesapeake Bay is featureless. This would be explicable if the party was taken through the inlet and followed the coast northward to Cape Henry. This stretch of coast is well delineated on the map, and Cape Henry (not yet named, of course) is clearly indicated. This is the first record of an English entry into Chesapeake Bay.

There then followed some exploration of Lynnhaven Bay. On the map its two arms are rather formally indicated, with the village of Chesepiuc, evidently a village of the Chesapeake tribe, clearly shown between them. Recent excavation of a residual village site in this general area suggests that it was Chesepiuc, though so far no European artifacts have been discovered there.[4] It would then appear from the map that the party proceeded along the shore until it came to the Elizabeth River, which it ascended and up which, about fifteen miles from shore, was located Skicóac, the chief village of the Chesapeake tribe. Harriot indicates that traveling was not always easy, and he is evidently speaking particularly of this expedition when he says, "in all our travels which were most special [important or significant] and often in the time of winter, our lodging was in the open air upon the ground." It might appear that they went ashore and slept where they landed and that in the interior they often, if not always, had to make do with what shelter they could find in the open. They evidently made close friends with the Chesapeake tribe and had a base near them for a time. They were able to explore, probably from the water, the Nansemond River, though the indication on the map of what were apparently two Nansemond villages without names might suggest they did not make any close contacts with this tribe.

They appear to have made a cursory excursion across Hampton Roads to define the James-York peninsula, with an island in the bay off Hampton Roads—it may have been Old Point Comfort displaced. So far as the Eastern Shore was concerned their information can only have been oral. The map shows an east-west shoreline, with three villages marked and two named, and indicates the continuation of Chesapeake Bay only as a broad stream entering the northwest corner of the map. For this area it is highly probable that White made sketches and drawings of people, villages, and fauna and flora, though nothing of this portion of his work has survived. But this section of his map is an important record of the travels of this party, which indeed represented a "special" exploration. The return journey must have ended the same way it began—by entering Currituck Sound as soon as an opening could be found.

Lane's report of the colony's discoveries stresses the value of the accounts he had of the area to the north. He says that the journey was about 130 miles, which might approach accuracy if we were to trace the coastal journey from Roanoke Island to the Nansemond

River. But his report is confusing. He says "the passage to it was very shallow and most dangerous by reason of the breadth of the sound and the little succour that upon any flaw [a sudden storm] was there to be had." This would certainly apply to Currituck Sound but not to the offshore coasting that has been indicated. As for the discoveries he says:

But the territory and soil of the Chesepians, being distant fifteen miles from the shore [i.e., the location of Skicóac], was for pleasantness of seat, for temperature of climate, for fertility of soil, and for the commodity of the sea, besides multitudes of bears, being an excellent good victual, with great woods of sassafras and walnut trees, is not to be excelled by any other whatsoever.

The presence of the English party evidently created great interest in the region and, according to Lane, the leading men of the adjoining areas, "countries of great fertility . . . all came to visit the colony of the English which I had for a time appointed to be resident there." They included the Iroquoian Mangoaks (probably here Meherrin), "Tripa-nicks and Oppossians," whom we cannot identify with certainty, (though one or other may have been Nottoway), and so greatly enlarged the scope of English-Indian contacts. Harriot gives us no further clues as to the characteristics of the region but Lane's summary comments are probably based largely on his expert information. From that time onward the occupation of the Chesapeake country was to become a long-term objective in the English colonizing plans.

When this exploring party returned, probably toward the end of February or early in March 1586, the settlement on Roanoke Island awoke with early spring from its apparent winter lethargy. If its men grumbled it was probably not entirely without reason, as food, if adequate, was probably monotonous, and we hear the settlers were short of clothes (though they could have adapted substitutes from deerskins easily enough). We still cannot wholly explain Lane's inaction over the winter because if the weather was favorable in the Chesapeake it must have been a mild winter on Roanoke Island. The explanation may rest, at least partly, on his relations with his Indian neighbors, which we can leave for the time being, and his feeling that, with a party away, he could not take too many risks if he, himself, went exploring. But because the pinnace was evidently with the Chesapeake party his own freedom of movement was somewhat limited.

By this time Lane had learned much by hearsay from the Indians about the Chowan tribe and its great leader Menatonon, and also many rumors about a people known as Mangoaks, who lived far into the interior. Relations on Roanoke Island between Lane's settlers and Wingina's tribe deteriorated as time went on, but in March 1586 the two leaders were still on speaking terms. Lane admitted to Wingina that he intended to search for these strange, and rich, Mangoaks, as well as to visit the Chowan people, and the chief encouraged him to do so. Lane also asked him for a guide to their territory. Lane tells us that Wingina was playing a double game: on the one hand, he encouraged Lane to go inland and allowed three of his men to accompany him; on the other hand, he sent word to the Chowan tribe and to the Mangoaks that Lane intended to enter their country. The first is probable enough but the second is very dubious. Moreover, Lane says Wingina told him that Menatonon was arranging a hostile expedition against the colonists, "certifying me of a general assembly even at that time made by Menatonon at 'Choanoke' [Chawanoac] of all his *weroances* and allies to the number of 3000 bows, preparing to come upon us at Roanoke, and that the Mangoaks also were joined in the same confederacy, who were able to bring as many more to the enterprise." Menatonon later told Lane that at the same time Wingina was reporting to him that Lane intended to destroy his people. We cannot trust Lane's account fully, and certainly Wingina's figures were wildly exaggerated, if they had a basis in fact. Whatever the precise truth was, Lane decided to act, because at last he was ready to explore inland. He took the pinnace and his wherry and "light horseman" (which he also calls a wherry) with a substantial number of his men up the Chowan River to Chawanoac. (White's map shows the pinnace only at the head of Albemarle Sound but probably she could have sailed all the way.)

Apparently the Chawanoac people did not anticipate Lane's approach. He seems to have burst into the village with his men and, meeting with no resistance, seized Menatonon, who was paralyzed in the legs, and placed him in "a hand lock," or handcuffs. The sight of perhaps forty Englishmen, a number of them in armor and with guns and swords in their hands, must have been frightening as well as unexpected. Because Lane makes no mention of chiefs of other tribes being there, and certainly no Mangoaks would have been present, the assembly may have been merely a tribal council. Menatonon appears to have taken the whole affair very calmly as there does not seem to have been any bloodshed and Lane assured him he meant him no harm. Despite this inauspicious beginning, where Lane displayed his belief that potential differences could best be settled by a show of force, the two men reached some basis for mutual understanding. Almost certainly this was achieved through the efforts of the interpreter, who was probably Manteo, as he was best placed to soothe the chief's fears. Lane does not give a straight-forward account of this highly dramatic episode, and in failing to do so he reveals his inadequacies as a writer. He does make it clear that for several days the two men had long and interesting conversations. Menatonon told Lane much about the country to the interior and to the north, some of which appears to have misled Lane almost as much as, or more than, it informed him. But this assessment may be unfair because in his narrative Lane is recollecting oral discussions of which he may not have had adequate notes.

Briefly, this is Lane's story. In effect, Menatonon told him that a three-day canoe journey northward up the Chowan River followed by a four-day passage overland would take him to the territory of a powerful ruler whose lands bordered the sea but who had his seat on an island. This ruler had great quantities of pearls—Lane describes in some detail how they adorned him and his men in an elaborate fashion. Menatonon said this ruler had visited him two years before and exchanged with him pearls for copper. The Chowan leader presented Lane with a rope of such pearls, blackened by fire, which he afterward lost at his departure. Menatonon gave Lane the impression that this ruler had commerce with white men, and he promised guides to conduct Lane and a party to his area. Lane decided that he would attempt to go there as soon as he had received supplies from England. He evidently suspected that this ruler lived on the great bay found by his party of "Chesepians," as he said he would send a bark and two pinnaces from the supply fleet to enter the bay from the north. He himself, with two hundred men, indicating the size of the reinforcements he expected, would travel overland from the Chowan, setting up an elaborate chain of small forts (sconces) at intervals on the way. He must have concluded that Chesapeake Bay was much farther away by land than it actually was, but there seems little doubt that he was being directed to the territory of Powhatan, or his immediate predecessor, in the Virginia Tidewater. This added a further objective to the already enunciated desire to follow the lead of the wintering party and turn from Roanoke toward the Chesapeake area.

Menatonon directed Lane's attention not only to the north but also to the west. He told him that up the Moratuc River (the Roanoke River), beyond the territory of the Moratuc tribe, he would find a great nation—that of the Mangoaks (which we know to be a derisive Algonquian name for the Iroquois tribes of the interior, but here used most frequently for the Tuscarora). The Mangoaks had much copper, so much so that "they beautify their houses with great plenty of the same." He would have to pass up the river, against a violent current from the west and southwest, and with many twists and turnings. For thirty miles it was "as broad as the Thames betwixt Greenwich and the Isle of Dogs," when you would come to the town of Morotico, the chief town of the Moratuc tribe (near modern Plymouth), and beyond that again to the territory of the Mangoaks. Lane was told that thirty or forty days' canoe travel beyond Morotico he would come to the head of the river "which springeth out of a main rock in that abundance that forthwith it maketh a most violent stream." Moreover, beyond that "this huge rock standeth near unto a sea . . . so that the waves thereof are beaten into the said stream. so that the fresh water for a certain space groweth salt and brackish." Moreover, up the same river there is a province "to which the said Mangoaks have recourse and traffic . . . which hath a marvellous and most strange mineral." This they call "Wassador, which is copper. but they call by the name of Wassador every metal whatsoever." The place is called Chaunis Temoatan and the metal there "is very soft and pale," not like English copper which is "redder and harder." The people of Chaunis Temoatan, it was said:

Take the said metal out of a river that falleth very swift from the rocks and hills, and they take it in shallow water. The manner is this they take a great bowl by their description as great as one of our targets [a small shield] and warp a skin over the hollow part thereof, leaving one part open to receive in the mineral. That done, they watch the coming down of the current and the change of the colour of the water and then suddenly chop down the said bowl with the skin and receive into the same as much ore as will come in, which is ever as much as their bowl will hold, which presently they cast into a fire and forthwith it melteth, and doth yield in five parts, at the first melting, two parts of metal for three parts of ore.

Lane was thus presented with an alluring range of prospects. First of all, the Mangoaks had copper (and some natural copper could indeed be found in the Roanoke River basin in the Virgilina district, not an impossible distance away). Second, he was assured that the Mangoaks got copper in great quantities from the people of Chaunis Temoatan, far inland, in a mountain range. The copper, pale and soft, sounded much more like gold than copper in the tale. Moreover, the copper was obtained when the headwaters of the river were in flood when it could be tapped by panning the effluent so as to gather up metal and other matter by the simple technique of placing a skin bowl in the water and subsequently separating out the contents ("melting it" he said, which would not be necessary with alluvial copper and which no Indians in eastern North America could do), so that some two-thirds of the contents would be pure metal. The elaboration of this tale suggests that copper did indeed come from a great distance, perhaps from lodes in the Appalachians, possibly from the great trade network in Lake Superior copper the limits of which are scarcely known. And beyond that again was what sounded like the South Sea, the intruding Pacific of the Verrazzanian hypothesis.[5] At last, here were objectives that were worth making every effort to search for and that would stir the gentlemen and, indeed, every colonist into anticipation and action. The orbit of Lane's ambitions was thus extended to the widest possible extent, far beyond the expectation of his sponsors, Ralegh among them.

For Lane there were two possibilities: one a route to a great bay and harbor to the north, the other, a chance to reach a tribe that had much copper of its own, and had access to a people far inland who produced the copper (or gold) from swift-flowing water. Menatonon may have passed on all these tales in good faith, but whether they

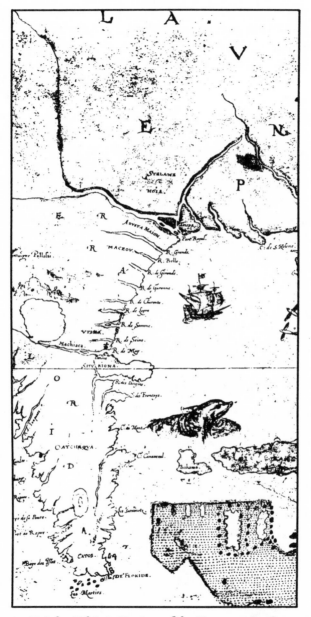

10. John White's Version of the Verrazzanian Sea.
Extract from John White's General Map of Southeastern North America,
British Museum, Department of Prints and Drawings, 1906-5-9-1 (2).

rested on anything more than myth and hearsay is difficult to assess. We can suggest, however, that Menatonon did have some knowledge that copper could be obtained in the basin of the Roanoke River itself. Lane incorrectly thought of the Chowan River as flowing from the northeast and the Roanoke River as flowing from the northwest. Instead, the two rivers follow, after some of the twists and turns of the Roanoke River of which Lane was aware, a parallel northwest-southeast course, at times little more than twenty miles apart; but, whereas the Chowan is only a short stream, the Roanoke continues. Some 150 miles up its course, in what is now Granville County, sources of natural copper and traces of silver were found in the matrix of copper that was worked out in the Virgilina district in the nineteenth century in the greenstone schist through which the Roanoke River had cut a channel.[6] This would be scarcely worth stressing if it was not to be alleged that in the early seventeenth century the Chawanoac tribe had access to sources of copper on a river, which, if the information was correct, can only have been in this area.

The Roanoke River expedition, Lane decided, must take precedence over everything else. He must, if at all possible, have a major discovery to report to the supply fleet that had been scheduled to arrive by Easter (3 April) and that might easily appear before the month was out. At the same time, although Lane left Menatonon after two days' talk, but exacting "a ransom agreed for" (no doubt in corn and perhaps a little copper), he did not, in spite of being greatly impressed by his wisdom and knowledge, wholly trust in his continuing friendship. Evidently Lane was impressed more by the number and strength of his warriors and feared that, if he was attacked by them, the settlement would have little hope of survival. Consequently, he took Menatonon's son Skiko as a hostage (conceivably leaving an Englishman in exchange, though this is not known) and sent him down to Roanoke Island in the pinnace. Henceforth, his own energies were wholly devoted to the expedition to the Mangoaks, and beyond them toward Chaunis Temoatan itself, even though Skiko was to tell him that it lay so far beyond the Mangoaks that it would be definitely out of his reach.

Closer to the colony Lane had his own problems. What we must assume had been amicable relations between the settlers and the occupants of the Roanoke Island village became less easy. The absence of a journal, and Lane's vagueness about the continuing relations between his men and the Indians, make it difficult to follow exactly what happened. Both Granganimeo and another leading *wero-ance* in the Roanoke group, Ensenore, are described as having been continuously friendly until their deaths in the spring of 1586. On the other hand, Wanchese, who had left the colonists and returned to his own people, became hostile to his former hosts (or captors, as he may have come to regard them) some time after August 1585. Manteo cooperated closely with the settlers throughout and accompanied them on some of their expeditions, but he is likely to have spent time with his own people on Croatoan Island about fifty miles to the south. Wingina is depicted by Lane as unreliable, his manner varying between friendship and hostility. He is frequently accused of treachery and of attempting to raise the peoples of the whole area against Lane, later reverting to a measure of cooperation, and finally deserting Roanoke Island and establishing himself as a hostile power at Dasemunkepeuc on the mainland on Croatan Sound. As the contacts of Europeans and Indians are examined, some clarity in their relationship may emerge, but they remain difficult to disentangle so long as we have only Lane's confused account of what was clearly a crucial issue for the continuance and prosperity of the colony.

Lane was elated by the prospect of a deep harbor to the northeast on Chesapeake Bay, but he was inspired to immediate action only by the hope of obtaining metals, possibly precious metals, in the interior. He knew of the Algonquian tribe, the Moratucs, who lived in the lower reaches of the Roanoke River, and expected them to guide him to the territory of the Mangoaks, very much farther upstream. And he wished to make the expedition at once. His men must decide:

> I did refer it to the greatest number of voices whether we
> should adventure the spending of our whole victual in some
> further view of that most goodly river in hope to meet with
> some better hap, or otherwise to retire ourselves back again.
> And for that they might be the better advised I willed them to
> deliberate all night upon the matter and in the morning, at our
> going aboard, to set our course according to the desires of the

greatest part. Their resolution fully and wholly was (and not three found to be of the contrary opinion) that whilest there was left one half pint of corn for a man that we should not leave the search for that river.

This is a valuable sidelight on Lane's methods. He might lead his men to the Chowan village on his own initiative, but when it came to a major issue of this sort, he was prepared to take a democratic sounding of his men's opinions. With their backing he felt he could set out on this hazardous expedition.

The pinnace was sent back to Roanoke Island, presumably with a bare minimum of rations for her crew. The wherry and the light horseman were loaded with as many men as they could safely carry, together with two mastiffs, great dogs which were valuable for hunting and of which the Indians were afraid. We can assume the men wore armor to protect their heads and the upper body and that all had calivers as well as swords and daggers. There were some thirty in all (Lane had wished to take forty). They found the entry to the wide Roanoke River beset with difficulties from the beginning. The two pairs of oarsmen in each boat had to row against a strong downstream current and must have been frequently alternated. It is difficult to estimate how many miles a day they could make, though Lane indicates something like thirty to thirty-five miles. Twelve hours' rowing at three miles an hour would appear to have been possible but far from easy where the current was swift, though it probably moderated somewhat as they progressed.

Lane expected to get corn and fish from the Moratuc people, but found that they had left their villages empty, taking their women and their corn, so that no food was to be found. Two days upstream (or was it three as the chronology is confused?) they heard Indians shout, they thought calling to Manteo, but he said that the sounds were in fact war cries and took up his caliver in defense. He was right, for as the leading boat, the light horseman, turned toward the shore a hail of arrows descended on them, but harmed no one, glancing off their buff coats or armor we may assume. The boat was brought to land and under cover of the men in the wherry the light horseman's company clambered up the steep banks to come to grips with their assailants. But they were unable to do so. The Indians faded into the woods. Lane established a strong camp on shore—

"making a strong *corps de garde* and putting out good sentinels." In the morning they had to decide whether to chance finding an occupied village before nightfall or to abandon the venture. The men chose the latter course because there was virtually no food left. Before they set out, they killed and prepared the two mastiffs for eating; on them they were to subsist for more than a day, aided by the fresh young leaves of the sassafras tree, the only edible substance they could find. The expedition was a failure and Lane would have been wiser not to have attempted it without adequate supplies, though clearly his men were prepared for adventure after their long period of inaction over the winter.

Once turned downstream—it seems very difficult to guess just how far they had gone, probably well beyond the town of Moratuc, near modern Plymouth—they rowed rapidly in one day "down the current as much as in four days we had done against the same" so that by nightfall they were at the mouth of the river, near where it enters Albemarle Sound. They camped in safety on San Souci Island, around which the Roanoke River divides, and rested, chewing on sassafras leaves because the dogmeat was gone. They awoke on Easter Eve, 2 April, to find that the water of Albemarle Sound was so rough and broken that they could not proceed without great danger of losing their boats. They thus spent a hungry day and second night on the island. By the next day—Easter Sunday, as it happened—the storm had subsided and the sound offered a clear passage.

The weakened crews traveled thirty-five to forty miles farther down and across the sound to Chepanum, one of the Weapemeoc villages well known to them. But there, again, they found no Indians in the villages, To save their lives, they ate some fish discovered in the weirs. By that time some of the men in the light horseman were, as Lane said, "far spent." Thus refreshed, they were able to continue on to Roanoke Island and regain the settlement. The utmost effort, Lane is at pains to stress, had been made to reach the Mangoaks and their copper, because Joachim Ganz ("Master Yougham") insisted that "copper, seeing the savages are able to melt it [but were they?] ... is one of the richest minerals in the world." What Ganz meant was that such copper, being soft, must be very pure, and his own experience in Central Europe and in England had made him aware that copper was in great demand and of appreciably high value.

Lane returned to the colony convinced that Wingina had set both

11. Engraving of the John White–Thomas Harriot Map of
Ralegh's Virginia, 1590.
Theodor de Bry, *America*. Part 1. Frankfurt am Main, 1590, plate 1.

Americæ
pars, Nunc Virginia
dicta, primum ab Anglis
inuenta sumtibus Dn. Walteri
Raleigh, Equestris ordinis Viri
Anno Dni M·D LXXXV regni Vero
Serenis: nostræ Reginæ Elisabethæ
XXVII
Hujus vero Historia peculiari
Libro discripta est, additis
etiam Indigenarum
Icomibus
A W A
O
I
K
A
Skicoak
E A P E
E O C
Chesepiooc sinus
Comokee
Apasus
OCCIDENS
SEPTENTRIO
ORIENS

the Moratuc and Weapemeoc peoples against him, that he had induced them to leave their villages and thus deny him food so that he and his men would starve. And in his eyes, too, Wingina had very nearly succeeded. We cannot totally accept Lane's word for this, even though he could have obtained such information from Manteo and later from Skiko. It may be that part of the reason for the Indians' departure was that it was the hunting season when the men and probably the women, after a severe winter and before the sowing season, took off to hunt in the interior. If Wingina had had something to do with the abandoning of the villages, it may have been because he had made them fear for their women and older people at Lane's hand if they left them behind. But we have no clear evidence of this. In any case, it would be unwise to accept everything that Lane says about Wingina as being absolutely true.

The exploration record of the colony is thus very mixed. Little effort was made to map in detail the sounds to the south. The Chowan River was not explored to its source. The expedition up the Roanoke River was undertaken too hastily and without adequate preparation even though it was seriously hampered by the Indian boycott. The colony's most successful achievement was to redefine the coast to the north of the Outer Banks along the southern shore of Chesapeake Bay and up the Elizabeth River. Lane's visit to Chawanoac was, however, a notable one. Overall, the White maps show that a substantial segment had been added to our knowledge of the coast and interior of eastern North America. It was unfortunate that the limited exploration of the interior from the head of Albemarle Sound did not reveal the region beyond the swamp forests and bring to light the fine piedmont country of modern North Carolina. Despite its limitations, however, the achievement of the colony is all the more remarkable when compared with the failure of any Europeans to follow it up effectively for much more than half a century.

The Final Phase

The last few months of the colony's history are a series of ups and downs, breathing spaces and crises. There was exasperation at the failure of the relief expedition to arrive by Easter and a critical shortage of supplies for the colonists, punctuated by an armed clash with the Roanoke Indians. These circumstances illustrate very well the varying problems with which even an experimental colony such as this had to contend. Ralph Lane's resourcefulness in keeping his men healthy—even if he could not prevent their growing discontent with their lot—shows his competence as administrator. Few early settlements of this size were able to survive in such good health for so long. On the other hand, whatever view we take of Wingina and his advisers, there is little doubt that Lane's actions inflicted long-term damage to the relations between the colonists and the inhabitants. This would make it difficult, and perhaps impossible, to establish further colonies on Roanoke Island or in the surrounding area unless, indeed, the Indians were subjected to severe coercion or even wiped out. These considerations may appear too drastic a judgment to make before the history has been taken any further, but it is not unwise to have them in mind, as they may help us to view later events in a better perspective.

Lane's story is that in March, before he made the expeditions already described, Wingina had planned to desert Roanoke Island, leaving his fields untilled, and to remove himself from all contact with the colonists. At the same time he was, as has been noted, alleged to have been conspiring with the tribes who were supposed to be concerting a great attack on the colony when Lane burst in on Menatonon at Chawanoac. Wingina also was held reponsible for inducing the Moratucs to desert their villages during Lane's venture

121

up the Roanoke River. While he was away, it was alleged that he circulated very widely the rumor that Lane and his men had either starved on the journey or been killed by the Moratucs and Mangoaks. He was also said to have contemned the Christian God, which previously his people had appeared to reverence based on what the colonists had told them, because He could not protect them from starvation or from death at the hands of their Indian enemies. But Lane's return, hungry but unharmed, with all his men, including three Roanoke Indians besides Manteo, showed all this propaganda to be false.

It was mainly this that made Wingina alter his attitude. This change was assisted by the death of the remaining *weroance* of Wingina's tribe, Ensenore—Granganimeo had evidently died earlier and Ensenore was to follow him on 20 April only two weeks after Lane's return— who still favored the colonists, suggesting that Wingina had to take some notice of the elders, the *weroances* who were his advisers. In any event, Wingina now became cooperative out of respect for Lane's achievement, or so Lane says. Whereas it seemed to Lane that, if the Roanoke village had been deserted in March, the colonists would have had no fish weirs, "neither could our men skill of the making of them" and they had not "one grain of corn for seed to put in the ground," now everything changed. Ensenore's opinion in his last days is said to have been vital. He and at least some others believed the Europeans to be dead men who had come back to live for a time on earth, and because of their power the Indians could not destroy them. The Indians therefore must help and not hinder the colony.

Moreover, at this time the status of the colonists was greatly enhanced by the actions of Menatonon, who sent a message to the head of the Weapemeoc group, Okisko, commanding him, as Lane claimed "to yield himself servant and homager to the great *Weroanza* of England, and after her Sir Walter Ralegh." This implies that Menatonon had been told a great deal by Lane (or perhaps, by Manteo) about Queen Elizabeth and Ralegh and had been so impressed with what he heard that he was willing to have his associates submit themselves, in some vague respect, to English authority. It is difficult to know how much this meant, but at least it indicates that Menatonon had some degree of influence, perhaps even authority, over the group of villages of Weapemeoc, the territory along the fertile north bank of Albemarle Sound. Moreover, Okisko acted on his command. He sent twenty-four of his leading men to Roanoke Island to inform Wingina and Lane that "they were ready to perform the same . . . and . . . were to acknowledge Her Majesty their only Sovereign."

The practical result was that Wingina agreed to set up weirs at Roanoke Island for the use of the colonists, which his men rapidly did, and "in the end of April he had sowed a good quantity of ground [with corn], so much as had been sufficient to have fed our whole company (God blessing the growth) and that by the belly-[full] for a whole year." Besides that, "he gave us a certain plot of ground for ourselves to sow." According to Lane this "put us in marvellous comfort," for by the beginning of July they could be self-sufficient. Moreover, Wingina planted his own corn on Roanoke Island and also at his other principal village, Dasemunkepeuc, across Croatan Sound on the mainland, so that he could not easily desert either place in order to isolate the English.

This episode raises some interesting questions. It would appear that, hitherto, Lane had not obtained possession from Wingina of any land on Roanoke Island other than that containing the settlement and the space immediately around it—there had been no major transfer of land to the Europeans. It also shows that land was either available in a semicleared state (being formerly used by the Indians) or else was hastily cleared by the slash and burn method to provide a very considerable area of new agricultural land by the end of April. If it was newly cleared it is most probable, because it was done in such a short time, that the tree roots were left in the ground, although the availability of European mattocks, axes, and spades would have greatly assisted the Indians' progress. Wingina, too, must have been able to acquire seed, or had concealed it, if he could sow this ground for the colonists. If they themselves had no seed corn it is interesting to speculate what they could have sown in the ground allotted for them to cultivate. A limited amount of dried peas and beans are the most likely seeds to have been still available, but we cannot guess how far they were able to make use of this land for potential food production. Moreover, the problem of supply for May and June, if relief did not come, was one that still threatened disaster. Good relations with the Indians seemed essential. Through trade, the colonists hoped to get some of the meal made by the

Indians from the root of the arrow arum, which the English called "Cassada," presumably identifying it with the "Cassava" or manioc of Central and South America, though it was not the same. They also found their new weirs were not reliable as they often failed to trap any fish. The colony could still be driven into severe straits if not actual starvation.

In the meantime, even immediately after the Indians helped so considerably to put the colonists on a continuing basis, Wingina was giving them cause for anxiety. At some time during the spring he had changed his name from Wingina to Pemisapan, perhaps to stake his claim to be a war leader. Moreover, after Ensenore's death on 20 April, he behaved in a less friendly manner especially after the fields had been sown. Wanchese, with one of the *weroances*, Osocan, and another member of his group, Tanaquiny, apparently soon showed their hostility to the colonists as well. Finally, Wingina decided to desert his village on Roanoke Island and take all his people to Dasemunkepeuc. Although Lane admits that one reason for his doing so was to arrange to make a second sowing of corn there, he gives away what we can take to be the primary reason: the steady pressure on him by the colonists for food in a season between early spring and summer when the Indians themselves went short. Lane says that he wished "to withdraw himself from my daily sending to him for supply of victual for my company, for he was afraid to deny me anything, neither durst he in my presence but by color [pretense] and with excuses, which I was content to accept for the time, meaning in the end, as I had reason, to give him the jump once for all. But in the meanwhile, as I had ever done before, I and mine bore all wrongs and accepted of all excuses."

It does not require much reading between the lines to realize that, by this time, the pressures of the colonists on Wingina were becoming intolerable and that, despite all his attempts to placate them, their constant demands were wearing him down. He was, rightly, beginning to fear that Lane might eventually take violent action against him. For all his explanations, Lane was no diplomat. He believed in pressure and, if pressure failed, in force. He had clearly made this obvious by the time Wingina departed from the island.

The account of the final confrontation comes entirely from Lane, so that its details should be viewed with some caution, though it may well, in essentials, be correct. Lane's story, then, is that Wingina (as we will continue to call Pemisapan) retired to Dasemunkepeuc partly to intrigue further against Lane. Lane had foiled an attempt by Skiko to escape and had imprisoned him for a time, even threatening him with execution, determined to keep him, just as he had earlier refused a ransom of pearls from Menatonon for his return. He claims that his action made Skiko a confidant of Wingina, who believed Skiko would help him, at least with information, against Lane, whereas Lane had, he claims, won him over to give information on what Wingina was planning and doing. The story he heard was that Wingina was now so rich in copper obtained from the colonists for supplies and assistance over the past ten months that he could bribe the Weapemeoc people and the Mangoaks to come down to his village, under cover of a commemorative religious assembly, and from there make a mass attack on the colony. This would yield them more copper and many other things as spoil. It was said that he sent a similar invitation to the Chesepians, but this is unlikely. There is no reason to disbelieve what Lane says about the Weapemeoc people. The reply Wingina received from them was that Okisko would not join with Wingina but for the time being would take those loyal to him away from their villages. Other Weapemeoc villages, however, would agree to join Wingina of their own accord.

This shows that Okisko's hegemony was not unlimited; indeed, it was largely nominal and thus should act as a warning against considering the Indian groupings as tightly consolidated confederacies. As for the Mangoaks, some skepticism must be maintained. Would these Iroquoian people, already said to be rich in copper, be willing to come to the coastal area at all or would they be acceptable as allies to the Algonquian peoples there if they did? This remains dubious and perhaps Lane is exaggerating or was merely misinformed on this point. However, it was reported that the Mangoaks had accepted the promise of a bribe. They were to assemble with the dissident Weapemeoc villagers and come to Roanoke on 10 June and, after diplomatic maneuvers by Wingina to bring his men to the island to settle issues between them and the settlers, cross over Croatan Sound and attack and overwhelm the colony.

As often with Lane's narrative, there is some discrepancy in his chronology. But, according to him, Wingina had promised to come over with his own men to discuss issues between them on 31 May, well before his allies were to have joined him. But probably the date 10 June was incorrect—it first appeared in print as 10 July and was later altered. The overall strategy, according to Lane's information, was that when Wingina and his men came to the island they would attempt to attack and kill the leading men in the colony. When they had begun their attack, fire signals would alert those of his allies who remained at Dasemunkepeuc to cross the sound in their canoes and complete the destruction of the settlement, dividing the spoil obtained there.

Lane is very specific about Wingina's own part in the plan. Tanaquiny and Andacon, two of his lieutenants, with twenty men, would attack Lane's house at night, set its reed thatch on fire, and kill Lane as he ran from the burning building. Other parties would do the same for Thomas Harriot's house, and for the remaining individual houses in the "town" (the only case where we hear the word used). At the same time larger parties, presumably, would attack and overwhelm the guards at the defensive works of the settlement.

On learning this, Lane tells us he decided to take the initiative himself. He informed Wingina he intended to visit him briefly for a specific purpose. He had heard ships had been sighted to the south (though he had not) and would go himself with a party toward Croatoan to meet them and hunt on the way. He wished to borrow some men from Wingina to hunt and fish for him and to buy four days' provisions for the expedition, even though Wingina had been refusing to sell anything to Lane and may already have sent men to wreck the fish weirs on the island. Apparently this move disarmed Wingina, who knew that Lane had in fact dispersed some of his men to forage for seafood. Prideaux and the provost marshal, with ten men, had been sent with the pinnace to live at Port Ferdinando, while Captain Edward Stafford, with twenty men, had gone in the wherry to Croatoan (here named "my Lord Admiral's Island," in honor of Lord Howard of Effingham, the lord high admiral of England) to try to feed his men and also to keep watch for any shipping that might appear. Others were sent to the mainland to live on the prepared arum roots ("Cassada") and on oysters. This left Lane with only some fifty to sixty men under his direct command; at least twenty soldiers among them would be needed to maintain the guard on the defenses. He thus appeared to be playing into Wingina's hands, almost, we might say, inciting him to carry out his planned course of attack.

Lane's actual strategy was a night attack on 31 May, a "camisado" as he called it, because the soldiers left the tails of their white shirts hanging behind to alert those who followed them and prevent them from confusing them with the enemy. The first part of the plan went wrong. At nightfall the light horseman under its master (Captain Vaughan?) was to seize all the canoes that were on their way to Dasemunkepeuc, presumably returning from fishing, for Lane's own use. But one resisted. The men in the English boat attacked and captured the canoe but, in the fracas, decapitated two of its crew. The alarm was thus given to the village. Lane's men, approaching by water, exchanged shots with the villagers; they claimed to have killed three or four of them, but the rest made off into the woods. The English had now taken the military initiative, but without a major success in the first phase.

The next morning, 1 June, Lane gave Wingina no time to recover. With twenty-seven men in the light horseman and a canoe (this party included his "Colonel of the Chesepians" and the sergeant major, his field officer), he landed at Dasemunkepeuc and announced he had come to complain of some of the previous night's events (alleging an attempt by Osocan to release Skiko on the island). Lane entered the village and, when in the middle of a group of Wingina's leading men, gave his watchword "Christ our Victory" and he and his guard immediately fired on the surrounding Indians with their pistols. The Colonel of the Chesepians struck Wingina with a pistol ball and others were killed. While Lane was preoccupied with trying to safeguard the individuals known to be Manteo's friends (including, we can assume, those who had been on the Roanoke River venture), Wingina, wounded, managed to spring to his feet and run into the woods. Lane handed his long pistol to his Irish "boy" (who has not been identified), who managed to shoot Wingina again in the buttocks, but still he ran forward. Another Irishman, Edward Nugent, and the deputy provost took off in pursuit. Nothing was known for a time, and Lane even thought he had lost both Wingina and his own men. But then Nugent reappeared carrying Wingina's head in his hand.

This daring and sanguinary action solved Lane's military problems as the news of Wingina's fate spread soon enough to deter his allies from approaching his village. We are not told, either, of how the remaining Roanoke Indians reacted to the death of their chief. It is probably safe to speculate that, because the killing had been limited to Wingina and a small number of his leading men, the remainder submitted to Lane, especially as some had been dubious supporters of Wingina. If Wingina is to be set up as a martyr to European brutality, then much of Lane's account of his plots must be discounted, and perhaps at least some should be taken as not fully established. Yet the hostility shown to the settlers can be said to have justified Lane's action as aggressive self-defense, more particularly as it was not accompanied by any mass killing of the Indians and quite probably was followed by some attempts at reconciliation, which certainly Manteo, Harriot, and others would have desired. But the surprise attack was, in its own way, a parallel kind of treachery to that with which Lane credited Wingina. Opinion on the justifiability of his actions, however, is bound to remain divided. Nevertheless, on 1 June 1586 the colony was given a new lease on life, by whatever violent means. Over the next week at least the question of survival must have seemed to be decided.

If there is any way to describe the situation of the colony in early June 1586 it is one of waiting. Because "the first supply" (as it would have been called in Jamestown in 1607) did not come at the beginning of April as had been planned, or at the end of April as Lane had hoped, he and others must have wondered whether it would come at all. The sowing of cornfields and the obtaining of fish weirs before the end of April indicated that the settlers had been skeptical enough to plan realistically for an uncertain future. At least they had laid the basis for survival. And, for the time being, the threat of being overwhelmed by a vast array of the native inhabitants, which had loomed ominously over the colony from March onward, had been lifted.

But questions remained. Would Lane's domination over the Roanoke Indians prove temporary, and would it be succeeded by a long period of guerrilla warfare that would be difficult or even impossible to end? Would the influence that Lane claimed to have established over the Weapemeoc and Chowan Indians be maintained? It is evident that he had some doubts about this, as demonstrated by his continued retention of Skiko. Would Menatonon reverse his policy toward the English when Skiko was eventually returned, as he surely would have to be? Then there were practical concerns. Would the colonists remain in good health, and would the disruptive factions among them be contained if they were left in isolation? How, too, would a group of colonists, even though it contained a number of specialist technicians, be able to supply itself from native sources, with clothing and weapons—especially gunpowder? To do so, would they have to make drastic changes in their way of life? Above all the question was, if they were cut off from England, could they learn to live with the Indians? That is, could they sufficiently comprehend their way of life to learn from them and to establish with them a relationship halfway between hostility—which could not be ruled out entirely as the Indians respected and engaged in warfare themselves—and the converse strategy of turning Indians into part-Europeans?

Not all these questions may have been in the forefront of the minds of either Lane or Harriot, but they probably were aware of them in some degree. So to "waiting," as we have characterized the outstanding feature of the situation in June, must be added "forethought," involving concepts both fearful and demanding, but perhaps affording to a small group of the settlers, Harriot and White among them, some attractive and exciting prospects.

Rescue and Frustration, 1586

The year 1586 was a difficult one not only in the colony but also outside it. There was much overlapping of plans and events, and considerable confusion resulted from both accident and the lack of well-thought-out action. The first colony came to an end almost by accident. A second colony was, in one sense, frustrated and its make-weight substitute destroyed. Ralegh's Virginia, sown with such a flourish early in 1585, became a wilting plant in 1586—even a dying one, it may seem to us—before the end. Yet the impact of the first colony was not to be lost. In succeeding years its significance grew as more came to be known about its achievements. In a real sense it opened up the New World to Englishmen and provided a starting point from which English American colonies were to grow, even if continuity was lost.

In many ways the year 1585 had been decisive for Elizabethan England as it saw her launched, though not yet formally at war, into a struggle with the immensely stronger Spanish empire. The seizure in May of the English merchantmen in Spain had provoked a series of English reprisals. One, as we have already noted, deflected the reinforcement that had been intended to strengthen the Roanoke enterprise. Amias Preston and Bernard Drake had indeed reached Newfoundland in time to warn English fishermen not to return with their catches to Spain. But they had done much more. They met with George Raymond's *Red Lion*, the errant ship of Sir Richard Grenville's fleet of 1585, and together they had plundered harmless Portuguese fishing vessels, brought a string of them to England, and imprisoned their crews, in revenge for what Spain was doing, or was supposed to be doing, to English seamen in Spain. Moreover, they had swept far enough southward in the Atlantic to capture several valuable Portuguese sugarmen coming from Brazil. The Portuguese were forced to pay heavily for having been invaded by Spain in 1580. The prisoners were charged with some unspecified crime and lay rotting in jail until, in the spring assizes at Exeter where they were being charged, they spread the jailfever—typhus— among those present in court. If any prisoners survived, they had the grim satisfaction of communicating the fever so that not only the judges but also Bernard Drake, one of their captors and recently knighted for his feat, died in a tragedy that left its mark on English annals.[1] But the achievements of Preston, Drake, and Raymond had netted them great profits that overshadowed the long-term puny profits to be obtained by sending Englishmen to colonize the eastern shores of North America.

On the other side of the ocean, the Spanish in the Caribbean— especially those in Florida—had learned of the apparent destination of Grenville's fleet of 1585 and the planting of a colony some place beyond Florida on the North American coast. Some of the ships had been observed as they emerged from the Florida Channel and Pedro Menéndez Marqués, the efficient and ruthless governor of Spanish Florida, who a few years before had rounded up more than a hundred Frenchmen in what is now South Carolina and executed almost every one of them, was most anxious to track down the English colonists and assure them the same fate. But his resources were limited. He did obtain a ship late in 1585, though she got no farther north than Cape Fear and found no English. The Spaniards had expected to find them somewhere in the vicinity of Saint Helena Sound, where the French had been before.[2] The governor now decided that the English must have installed themselves on what had been a Spanish missionary objective in 1570, namely Chesapeake Bay, and he was prepared to go to look for them as soon as he could assemble the ships and men to do so. Had he had more resources it is possible that Ralph Lane might have been found and attacked before June 1586 and his colony wiped out.

The principal English riposte to the Spanish challenge in 1585 was the preparation of a major fleet under Sir Francis Drake. In the end it comprised more than thirty vessels, including some twenty-five ships, apart from pinnaces, and involved much royal money and several royal ships, as well as vessels financed by courtiers, gentle-

men, and merchants.[3] Setting out in September, this fleet terrorized
in turn Vigo, Santiago in the Cape Verde Islands, Santo Domingo, the
oldest European city in the New World, and the important port of
Cartagena. Drake had released many European and Turkish galley
slaves at these last two ports and at one point was said to have been
carrying with him some three hundred South American Indians who
had helped him at Cartagena as well as a number of black, predial
slaves. His objective was to cross the Isthmus and sack Panama as he
had planned in 1573. No doubt for this he needed as many men as
he could round up, but fever and other diseases soon killed many of
his own men and the released captives were probably used in part to
replace them. So in the end he neither made this attempt nor attacked the strongest port in the Caribbean, Havana, whose destruction would have harmed the Spaniards far more than anything he
had done previously.

Drake may or may not have been asked by Sir Walter Ralegh to
destroy St. Augustine and the fort at Santa Elena (San Marcos) because of their possible threats to the Roanoke colonists—as has been
suggested, they were very real threats indeed. But it may have been
what he heard from Spanish prisoners that made him concern himself with North America at all. We now know that after his return to
England Drake told a foreign visitor he met at the Court that:

> when he established that Captain Marchio [Pedro Menéndez
> Marqués] in fact had organized an expedition to Virginia in
> order to root out utterly the British colony which had not yet
> consolidated its settlement there, Drake followed suit by put-
> ting to sea himself and set course towards Virginia, with the
> object, commendable of course, of rescuing Ralph Lane (the
> undoubtedly distinguished leader of that colony) and his peo-
> ple from death.[4]

This may well have a good deal of truth in it. A decision had been
made that in January 1586 a frigate would leave Spain to bring supplies for Florida and then to make a reconnaissance of the coast to
locate the English colony. Later this was augmented by the decision
in December 1585 that two vessels, one a strongly-armed frigate,
should come with arms, supplies, money, and men, so that from
Florida a major attack could be mounted against the English estab-

lishment, which was thought to be much more powerful than it was. But certainly in the spring of 1586 reports of an impending attack on the English in North America would be current in the Caribbean and could easily have reached Drake. But that his objective was to "rescue" Lane is less certain; more likely, it was to reinforce the Roanoke settlement. He would have expected both a large number of men to have been left and further reinforcements to have arrived. He would have known before he left England in September 1585 that Ralegh intended to send out reinforcements to the colony in 1586. It is also likely that he had on board a member of the 1584 voyage under Amadas and Barlowe who would have been able to indicate to him where the colony was to be located.

Drake certainly decided that, instead of attacking Havana, he would destroy the Spanish hold on Florida. On 28 May he appeared with his great force, swelled by a number of small captured vessels, off St. Augustine and proceeded to attack the fort and make preparations to take it. But Menéndez Marqués was a shrewd tactician. After a vigorous token resistance, he and his garrison, with almost all the inhabitants of the little town, faded into the woods, and Drake's major plan was frustrated. But having missed the garrison he destroyed every vestige of the town, picking up a few Frenchmen who had been prisoners and a handful of black slaves. Later, the Spaniards were amazed to learn that, before destroying them, he had stripped the houses of doors and windows, locks, and similar articles—everything that might be of use to the Roanoke colonists when he found them. He then decided to proceed to Santa Elena on Port Royal Sound where there was another Spanish garrison, apparently not knowing there was also a small one on the St. Johns River. They put in at various points along the coast—the Spaniards said three places, the English two. They did not enter what they thought was Port Royal because the pilots said the bar was too shallow, though that was a mistake (perhaps they were at the Savannah River), but they did put into Saint Helena Sound, to which the Frenchmen could have directed them. There they obtained from the Cusabo Indians, who had many earlier contacts with the French, masts, fresh water, and firewood. Finally on 8 June Captain Edward Stafford on Croatoan (as Lane said, but almost certainly on John White's Pacquiac Island [the southern part of Hatarask] south of Port Ferdinando) believed he had sighted ships.[5] He lit a great fire which Drake's men saw. Drake sent a skiff ashore to investigate and found Stafford and his men. Contact had been established.

Hearing that reinforcements and supplies for the colony had not yet arrived, Drake at once penned a letter to Lane offering:

> the supply of our necessities to the performance of the action we were entered into, and that not only of victuals, munitions and clothing, but also of barks, pinnaces and boats, they also by him to be victualled, manned and furnished to my contentation.

Lane said Stafford conveyed this in a day by marching overland some twenty miles. This does not make sense if Stafford was stationed on Croatoan well over fifty miles south of Roanoke Island, but much more probably on Kenricks Mounts (a high dune) or at Cape Kenrick on Pacquiac Island, as already suggested.

Lane's reaction was very mixed—one of the Drake journals says that the settlers thought "we had been a new supply." The letter from Drake and the events that followed when contact was made after the great fleet arrived and had found some holding ground "in the road of our bad harbor" made all clear. When the two men met on 11 June, they found they had much to discuss. Drake could not have known that so few men would have been left in 1585, as John Arundell had not arrived with the news before he left England. His actions at St. Augustine had clearly shown that, even though he anticipated a Spanish attack on the colony, his objective was to help strengthen the two or three hundred men he expected to find, augmented perhaps by as many again in the spring of 1586, so that the Spanish could be repulsed when they appeared. It was for this he had surely brought the furniture of the town of St. Augustine and proposed to leave freed black slaves and probably other men (had he still some South American Indians on board?). With more men, more arms (as he had captured so many Spanish cannon), and a number of small vessels to give the English mobility in the vicinity of their base, resistance could be effective and the Spanish force defeated. Instead of a reinforced colony Drake found just over a hundred discouraged men, short of food even if they expected crops to be available within a few weeks. Many of them were discontented, having failed to find sources of precious metal or even copper and no richly endowed Indian groups from whom they could accumulate wealth. On Roanoke Island they were condemned, as most apparently thought, to an agricultural existence and under threat from Indian attack.

It was clear that Lane wished to leave Roanoke Island but he did not want to return to England without some more tangible achievement to present to Ralegh, as otherwise he would be deemed to have deserted his post. Even to contemplate leaving now was to deny the chances of reinforcement arriving a little later. But Drake's news of the breach with Spain, his own aggressive actions, and the riposte that Spain was likely to make against England may have convinced Lane that Ralegh was simply unable to get permission for ships to leave England to make the voyage. The two commanders worked out a plan between them that would meet to some extent their several objectives. Drake would take to England "a number of weak and unfit men," men, we may suspect, who had not necessarily become debilitated so much as finally disillusioned with the prospects of the colony—among them was Thomas Harvey, the cape merchant.

In addition, Drake would leave Lane skilled oarsmen, craftsmen, and others, and also "so much shipping and victual, as about August then next following, would carry men and all my company into England when we had discovered somewhat that for lack of needfull provision in time left with us as yet remained undone." This somewhat obscure statement meant that, when properly equipped, Lane would explore Chesapeake Bay, reverting to his earlier plans for doing so. Small boats, skilled masters, and, we might add, a sufficiently large vessel to make the Atlantic crossing safely, with a supply "of calivers, hand weapons [pistols and possibly swords and daggers], match [for their matchlock calivers] and lead, tools, apparell and such like" would enable him to do so successfully. Drake had no great shortage of such things though he was not well supplied with food. The arrangement was that Lane's officers, including his vice-treasurer and the keeper of the store, should board Drake's ship, the *Elizabeth Bonaventure*, with their notebooks and list what they needed; these wants would then be supplied, "together with the bark *Francis*, of seventy tons, equipped with supplies for 100 men for

four months," the estimated time for the search of Chesapeake Bay
and the return to England. With the *Francis*, owned by Drake himself,
under Captain Thomas Moore would be two fine pinnaces and four
small boats, with two experienced ship masters, one of them the
celebrated pilot Abraham Kendall and the other Griffith Herne, who
has not been otherwise identified. Drake had consulted his own
captains about this, and they had agreed with the plan. What was to
happen to the equipment and men intended to reinforce the colony
was never indicated. His blacks and his released prisoners would
presumably have to go to England.

The large fleet anchored off Port Ferdinando must have made a
fine array, such as was not to be seen in eastern American waters for
very many years. The great *Elizabeth Bonaventure*, of 600 tons, was the
Queen's ship and Drake's flagship, and the *Primrose*, of 400 tons, was
part-owned by John Hawkins and commanded by the leader of the
Northwest Passage voyages of 1576–78, Martin Frobisher, and the
Galleon Leicester, of 400 tons, commanded by Captain Francis Knollys,
brother of the man who had disrupted Sir Humphrey Gilbert's expedition in 1578, must, in particular, have made a noble sight. The *Aid*,
of some 350 tons, was also a fine ship, belonging to the Queen. The
Tiger of perhaps 200 tons, a merchant ship of the same name as
Grenville's 1585 flagship, was under the command of Captain Christopher Carleill, who had planned an American voyage in 1583–84,
but had brought his ships no farther than Ireland. His interest in
America remained active from the time his pamphlet was published
in 1583 until his death in 1593, shortly before which he had collaborated in another propaganda tract (left in manuscript) on the possible occupation of what is now New England.[6] This was to be his
only experience in North America. There were twenty other ships,
with a great flotilla of small pinnaces and other small craft, Drake's
own and others taken on the latter stages of the voyage. The large
vessels were all anchored well out to sea, the small ones inshore,
some of them probably inside the slight shelter offered by the inlet
Port Ferdinando. This fleet must have greatly impressed any Indians
who saw them with the power of England and her Queen.

On 13 June the *Francis* was being laden and a number of the
colonists had gone on board to arrange for the transfer and stowage
of the supplies that were to be left. For the time being it was not
intended to disturb the colony itself, because the *Francis* would be

anchored nearby until the colonists were ready to leave in her for their expedition to Chesapeake Bay and then home, while the pinnaces and boats would give them ample room to transport their goods from their island base to the ship before she set sail. But this was not to be. On the thirteenth, when Drake and many of his captains were still on shore conferring with Lane, a tremendous storm broke. As one of the journals described it, this was accompanied by "thunder and rain, with hailstones as big as hens' eggs. There were great [water] spouts at the seas as though heaven and earth would have met."[7] The colonists had never seen a storm like it. It may have been an early hurricane as it lasted three days, which is exceptional for a storm at that time of year. Because their anchors would not hold, the four great ships were forced to put to sea at once. The *Primrose*, for example, broke an anchor of 150 hundredweight and many cables snapped. All the vessels were put in danger "in avoiding the coast." Many of the pinnaces and boats were smashed against the Outer Banks or sank. When the storm abated after three days most of the ships came back to the roadstead if they still retained sufficient anchors and cables, including the *Elizabeth Bonaventure* herself, which had to pick up her commander and others left on shore.

Drake then discovered, to his and Lane's dismay, that the *Francis* evidently had been in such danger that she had put far out to sea and did not return. This completely altered their plans. On board the *Francis*, engaged in the lading and in learning how the ship operated, were a number of Lane's leading men—we do not know how many, but there were probably twenty or more. This meant that Lane had to revise completely his own plans, though it was still possible for him to envisage adapting them to meet the new circumstances. He declared his willingness to go on with the venture and Drake again offered to cooperate. After discussions with his captains he offered Lane another ship, the *Bark Bonner* of 120 to 170 tons, apparently owned by William Hawkins. But she was much larger than the *Francis* and could not enter Port Ferdinando. Lane, probably after consulting some of the men who had coasted into Chesapeake Bay in 1585, decided she was too large to make the attempt. Thus he made up his mind to abandon the settlement, as Drake offered, alternatively, to take the remaining colonists home.

It is likely that this decision was reached early in the day on 17

June. Suddenly Lane had to uproot the colonists who were still established in their settlement on Roanoke Island, with all the gear and gatherings of nearly a year's occupation. Drake mobilized a number of boats to take them off. Because the waters of the sounds were still very rough and the seamen were impatient to begin the return voyage, the fort and "town" were evacuated in great haste. The colonists speedily gathered together their possessions. Lane, Thomas Harriot, and John White, among others, would be especially heavily burdened. But the sailors had been sent for men, not impedimenta. Some of them threw packages overboard rather than give them space in preference to men. They had no respect for Lane. Some of his goods went into the water, including the chain of pearls he had been given. Also thrown out and thus destroyed were some of the notebooks and drawings that Harriot and White had laboriously assembled. This loss must have been heartbreaking for Harriot and White and certainly humiliating for Lane.

The boats ferried the remaining colonists out to the ships. Lane and White went on board with Drake, while Harriot may have found himself on the *Primrose* though the evidence that he did so is purely circumstantial. The pickings left for the Indians must have been very considerable in quantity. Incidentally, Manteo chose to go with Lane; apparently so did another Indian from his group, Towaye. Although we have no evidence of why they did so, Manteo may well have meant to assist with the interpretation of what Harriot and White had managed to save—a fairly substantial amount—of their collections. Perhaps he had other considerations as well, such as the promise of rewards from Lane and Drake. It may be merely that he had enjoyed living in England.

Finally, on 18 June, the fleet set sail. Not all the ships went directly to England so they did not keep their formation on the return voyage. At least a few went to Newfoundland to refresh themselves with fish. But the *Elizabeth Bonaventure* made directly for England. On board her John White found a fellow artist and cartographer, Baptista Boazio, who had been Christopher Carleill's page, but who now appears to have transferred to Drake's ship. Boazio made remarkable drawings of the ports that Drake had entered, one of which, that of Santiago, survives in its original form.[8] White gave Boazio copies of a number of his drawings, among them a turtle, a fish, and an alligator, which he used to decorate the engraved versions of his plans and his general map of the voyage when he returned to England.[9] After a reasonably fast passage, the *Elizabeth Bonaventure* "arrived at Portsmouth the eight and twentieth of July 1586," the narrator of Drake's expedition adding, "to the great glory of God and to no small honor to our Prince, our country and ourselves." The colony had returned safely to England and Lane was not prepared to admit he was discouraged, as a report states:

> I have seen and studied some letters which Ralph Lane recently sent to a friend from the royal ship who also helped him (for she was standing by off Portsmouth at the time) in which he remarks on the fact that plenty of precious metals and stones are to found in Virginia, a region which he intends to make for again soon.[10]

In the meantime Sir Walter Ralegh had been expanding his interests and offices, and still more, his responsibilities with them. In 1585 he was appointed Lord Warden of the Stannaries and High Steward of the duchy of Cornwall, which gave him the oversight of the tin mines in Cornwall and extensive jurisdiction over the population concerned with mining. As lord lieutenant of Cornwall he was ultimately responsible for the militia forces there and for their mobilization in time of war. As vice-admiral of Devon he was concerned with jurisdiction in maritime cases and with the spoils that privateers were bringing in from Spanish ships, while at the same time discouraging piracy on vessels of other nations. Although he was able to delegate much of this authority, henceforth the supervision of the southwestern counties was to take up an appreciable amount of his time. Moreover, in 1585 he was increasingly involved in the plan to split up a large part of Munster, devastated by rebellion and war, among English settlers. Indeed, almost at the precise time of the colonists' return, he was named to head a syndicate of "undertakers," as adventurers in Munster were called, to mobilize those gentlemen in Somerset, Devon, and Cornwall who were interested in acquiring lands there, while within a year he was, himself, to receive a vast commitment to develop a new colony in Ireland. He was also engaged in acquiring, and apparently in having built, ships to take part in the lucrative privateering war against Spain, and several of his privateers were active in Atlantic waters by the time the colonists reappeared.

In November 1585 Ralegh had undertaken to equip and send a supply ship to the Roanoke colonists to reach them by 3 April 1586. As we have seen, it had not arrived by 18 June. We have no clear evidence to suggest whether, and to what extent, he was at fault. His other preoccupations may have led him to delay somewhat in dispatching the vessel; the English Channel was difficult to sail from during the winter months,[11] and, if the ship had not set out by mid-March, she might be held back further by the frequent storms of that period. The ship's company, too, is not likely to have resisted attempts to take some Spanish prizes as she passed through the Caribbean. These are mere speculations, but any one of them, or several in combination, could account for the failure of the ship to arrive in time. This was enough, as we have seen, to wreck all the effort that had been put into the establishment of the first English settlement in North America.

We have only one clue as to the time of the ship's expected departure, namely a note of a letter (though the letter itself is lost) from the Queen to Ralph Lane, dated 20 March 1586, which she would have carried.[12] But Richard Hakluyt says that the ship did not leave until after Easter (3 April), which would seem to place at least some of the responsibility for the delay on Ralegh's shoulders. All that is known about her is that she was of 100 tons burden: we do not even know her name. If we estimate that she left on, say, 5 April, and took approximately the same length of time as Amadas and Barlowe (seventy-eight days), she would have arrived about 22 June or about four days after the colony had gone. However, Philip Amadas had had to make a closer examination of the coast north from Florida than she, with a pilot who would have been on one of the earlier voyages, should have needed. In 1585 Sir Richard Grenville, for all his delays in the Caribbean, had taken only seventy-nine days to reach Wococon, while some of his vessels had already arrived at Port Ferdinando. If the supply vessel did leave before the end of the first week of April, she ought to have arrived before 18 June. All Hakluyt says is:

Immediately [within a week?] after the departing of our English colony out of this Paradise of the world, the ship ... sent and set forth at the charges of Sir Walter Ralegh and his direction, arrived at Hatorask, who, after some time spent in seeking our colony up in the country, and not finding them, returned with all the aforesaid provision into England.

So now we have a third set of Englishmen exploring Roanoke Island and the Carolina Sounds, but this time we know nothing of where they went or how the Indians reacted to them. Did they, for example, find anyone who could speak some English? The answer would seem to be that they did not because they continued their search, when any Roanoke or Croatoan Indian, who spoke even very little English, could have told them that Lane had departed. Further, not all the colonists left with Drake. One of the Drake journals provides us with a little sidelight that is not reported by Lane; its author says that all were taken off the island "except three who had gone further into the country and the wind grew so that we could not stay for them." We might imagine that at the point when Lane had decided to remove his colony a little later to search Chesapeake Bay, and before the storm, the three men had been assigned to convey Skiko back to his father Menatonon. It may well be that Menatonon wanted them to work for him and so they were not released. Had they gone back to Roanoke Island and found the settlement deserted, they would be faced with a critical situation; unless they were waylaid by the remnants of Wingina's band, we would expect that they would try to make their way back to Chawanoac and, if they did so, remain there. The men from Ralegh's ship evidently found no trace of them. They may well have thought from the disorder in which we believe the settlement was left that Lane had been driven off by some cataclysm and had taken to his boats, especially as traces of the storm may still have been evident. The "some time" spent by the ship in its search could not have exceeded a week or ten days, and her return to England probably took place about the end of August, a month or so after the colony's return.

The supply ship was not the only or even the major contribution to the continuity of the colony that was planned for 1586. A major expedition, which was intended to raise the number of the colonists to three hundred or more, which had been the original plan in 1586, was being prepared. Whatever news Grenville had brought of the unsuitability of the harbor in the Outer Banks and the difficulties that the roadstead off the banks might present, it is possible that even then a deeper harbor to the north, the Chesapeake Bay that Amadas may have found in 1584, was the ultimate objective. Once more Grenville was to lead the expedition, and it is likely that he was willing, as he had been in 1585, to invest some of his own possessions in it. He had done very well from the prizes taken on his return voyage and hoped to do still better on the next occasion. The desirability of a North American base for carrying on the privateering war against Spain, now that it was official and was being encouraged by the Queen, was very much greater than it had been in 1585. He could rely on major assistance in money, supplies, and, probably, ships from Ralegh, now established in his new position of authority in the southwest. Consequently, Grenville appears to have moved from his country house at Stowe to his town house in the North Devon town of Bideford, a port on the River Torridge from which there was a good channel into the commodious Barnstaple Bay, though with a treacherous bar where the conjoined rivers Torridge and Taw enter the bay.

Fortunately, because we have no English narrative of his preparations or his voyage, we have a brief account by an expert Spanish pilot, captured on the *Santa Maria de San Vicente* in 1585 and taken with him in 1586.[13] Pedro Diaz tells us that Grenville fitted out "six ships, one of 150 tons, and the rest from 100 down to 60 tons . . . with 400 soldiers and sailors and provisions for a year." A local diary gives us some indication of the timing of the expedition, saying that "on 16 April . . . Sir Richard Grenville sailed over the bar with his flyboat and frigate, but for want of sufficient water on the bar, being near upon neap, he left his ship."[14] What this means, apparently, is that one of his vessels, the flyboat most likely, went aground and Grenville had to leave her for a time until she could be floated off. The expedition's departure was thus delayed until perhaps the beginning of May. We have little information on his ships: the flyboat is likely to have been the *Roebuck*, Ralegh's flyboat, and the frigate the larger of the two Spanish prizes taken in the Caribbean on the way out in 1585, but this is not certain. Arthur Facy was captain of one ship, with John Facy as master, while Grenville would command the flyboat as his flagship. Unfortunately we know nothing of the men he brought with him. Of the four hundred Diaz mentions, perhaps two hundred were intended as colonists and, judging by the preference he showed in selecting Lane's men in 1585, many of them would be soldiers. We have no idea how many were intended to be genuine colonists, craftsmen, miners, horticulturists, farmers and so on, or where, as he had some knowledge of the Outer Banks, the sounds, and the area beyond them, he intended to locate them. It can scarcely have been on Roanoke Island, which could only support about a hundred men, if that. We are led to suppose that he may have intended to seize some of the more fertile land occupied by Indian groups, possibly the village land of the Weapemeoc area. If so, conflict and forced removal of part of the Indian population was being contemplated. Otherwise, it might be assumed that his objective was the Chesapeake.

It is necessary to remember that, if all the plans of 1585 had been implemented, up to six hundred men might have been installed, and this could not possibly have been done without clearing the Indians from large areas of their settled lands. It appears desirable to stress this aspect of the English attempts at colonization during the years 1585–86; otherwise, it is easily forgotten and a misleading impression is conveyed that the whole purpose of the settlement was to intrude peaceably on land not occupied by the inhabitants without significantly disturbing their traditional society. The small number of men Lane actually had with him in 1585–86, and the scientific projects that were undertaken by a number of them, have tended to obscure this aspect of potential appropriation of land from the Indians and their removal from some part of their territories.

To begin with, Grenville showed no sense of urgency in his voyage.[15] He proceeded almost as if his commission to capture Spanish ships entitled him to act the pirate. He robbed an English ship, coming from Spain, of wines owned by Breton merchants, then took two French vessels bound for the Spanish Netherlands, one of which, the *Julian*, he sent back under a prize crew to Bideford. He later took a Dutch flyboat, which he incorporated in his fleet. In all cases his excuse was that the ships were trading with the enemy,

Spain, though the English courts later did not endorse his actions. Our chief authority for the voyage remains Pedro Diaz, the pilot taken in 1585, on whom he appears to have relied because he knew the Atlantic routes well.

In the Madeiras Grenville attempted to obtain water at Porto Santo; when the islanders resisted, his ships, now seven in number, fired cannon at them before sailing off without water. It was probably at this point that he began to realize he must hurry to get to Lane's assistance, whether or not the supply ship had arrived. His own intending settlers may well have been getting restless with the delays. It is likely that he took Diaz's advice and decided to try a direct run to the North American coast, taking the risk of being becalmed in light or no winds north of the belt of trade winds that normally carried vessels from the Canaries to the West Indies. The crossing appears to have been successful but we cannot tell precisely how long it took or where he made his landfall. Infuriatingly, our English source (Richard Hakluyt) says only that it was "about fourteen or fifteen days after the departure of the aforesaid ship" of Ralegh's. All we can say is that it should, therefore, have been about the middle of July, though it could have been a little later.

Grenville was astonished to find neither Ralegh's ship nor Lane's colony at Roanoke Island. We are told that he traveled into various parts of the country looking for them but did not find any traces. He also undertook some expeditions of discovery on his own account. According to Hakluyt, "After some time spent therein, not hearing any news of them, and finding the place which they inhabited desolate," he set sail after fourteen days. Again, the absence of a precise date is most exasperating. Pedro Diaz tells us a little more, though it does not always coincide with this brief English account. He reported that they found two hanged bodies, one of an Englishman and one of an Indian. Was this a sign of dissension on Ralegh's ship and a record of some conflict with the Indians? Or was it a grim record of an episode from Lane's last days on Roanoke Island of which we know nothing? Diaz said that they eventually captured three Indians, all they were able to see in their travels. This might suggest that the Roanoke Indians remained in hiding and that Grenville did not go very far away on his own excursions, because the area, as we know, was well-inhabited. Of the three Indians taken, two managed to give Grenville the slip, but one was retained. Moreover, he knew a little English and therefore had been in contact with Lane's men. From him they obtained the news that the colony had been taken away by Sir Francis Drake—though we feel that the naming of the English admiral was done by Diaz rather than by the Indian. This is likely to have been the Indian who was named Raleigh (or Rawley) and remained in Grenville's service until 1589. He became a Christian and his christening in Bideford parish church is recorded on 27 March 1588. He lived for just over a year after that and was buried in the churchyard on 7 April 1589.[16]

The impression that Diaz gained of Roanoke Island was unfavorable. Lane's men had been in poor condition and very short of food, "for the land produces little to eat, having nothing but maize, and of that little and the land wretchedly poor . . . There is plenty of timber and the soil is sandy, liable to be inundated and marshy." He had to obtain his information at second hand, and so did not know the quality of the soil there, "beyond that it appears fertile and well-wooded." He said that on Roanoke Island "they have a wooden fort of little strength and it is on the inside by the water." The fortifications indeed were not very strong, though the statement that the location was "by the water" is confusing. But Diaz did not see the fort or the island at first hand as Grenville kept him away from it. We are thus left with very many questions about this visit to Roanoke Island. Grenville would have found that the Indians and the men of Ralegh's ship had cleared anything of value from the site that had been left behind on Lane's hasty departure. We can be sure the Indians had reaped Lane's cornfields as soon as they were ripe. When he returned to Spain, Diaz said: "The reason why the English have settled here is . . . because on the mainland there is much gold, and so that they may pass from the North to the South Sea, which they say and understand is nearby, thus making themselves strong through the discovery of great wealth." He thus expressed the wishful thinking of the Englishmen among whom he resided for several years, and indicated the myths that were current about Ralegh's Virginia.

After leaving Port Ferdinando, Grenville may have sailed southward, as a number of ships were sighted off Santa Elena, still occupied by the Spanish, some time in August, but it is not certain that these were Grenville's. He did attempt to repeat his success in 1585 in picking up a straggler from the Spanish fleet between Bermuda and the Azores but without any result. By this time there was sickness on board, and at least some of his ships put back all the way to Newfoundland to obtain fresh fish, which they did on Conception Bay, on the east coast. This action suggests that the disease was scurvy and that fresh food was the best remedy. But Grenville was not to be robbed of prizes. He sailed back to the Azores, robbed a small interisland boat, apparently taking some people from it (who Diaz says died), and picked up a jettisoned cargo of West Indian hides at Villafranca. Finally, with the aid of another privateer, he captured a rich Spanish frigate from Puerto Rico off Terceira. At last he was satisfied, and in December (perhaps on 26 December, the date Diaz gives) he returned to Bideford with his Spanish prize "laden with sugar, ginger and hides."[17]

In 1586 Grenville had indeed shown more concern with privateering than with colonization, even though he, like Ralegh, had also been negotiating for land in Munster, which he was to take in hand to colonize over the next few years. He had brought some forty Spanish prisoners to England and, in February 1588, the two pilots that he held, Pedro Diaz (under the name of Pedro de Santa Cruz) and Francisco de Valverde, sent a complaint to Spain that of the twenty-two persons he had at that time "he treats [them] as slaves are treated in Algiers, making them carry on their backs all day stones and other materials for a certain building [probably improvements to his manor house at Stowe], and at night he chains them up."[18] Twenty others were said to have escaped or died. If this is true, Grenville would scarcely have had much respect for the inhabitants of America had he remained there as head of a colony.

We have no direct evidence of Ralegh's reactions to the return of his first North American colony with Sir Francis Drake at the end of July 1586. He must have been greatly disappointed and also angry, angry at Lane for leaving with the colony, even though there were many extenuating circumstances that Drake, as well as Lane, could explain to him. He would be angry, too, that his own ship had failed to reach the colony in time, though we do not know whether he or others were primarily to blame for this. Above all, he must have been furious that Grenville had gone off on what might well be a fool's errand, an expensive expedition in which he had a substantial stake. He could not anticipate what action Grenville might take, more particularly whether he would leave another colony there or not. As the year went on and Grenville did not return, he also must have become anxious about the safety of that expedition.

Later in the year, Ralegh's attention was being drawn more and more away from North America to Ireland. By the summer he probably had set his heart on acquiring lands that were adjacent to an established port, and he hit upon Youghal, a small town at the mouth of the fine River Blackwater which had a good harbor and adequate housing. He also thought the river would give him access to some excellent lands in the interior where there was an old castle, Lismore, which might be rehabilitated. He knew this part of Ireland from his earlier days there and he had influence with officials in Dublin, so that by October 1586, he was able to get a very high priority in the surveying of part of the land he coveted, while the burgesses of Youghal, to whom he would have already offered his protection, appear to have assisted in his project.[19]

At the same time there is no doubt he would have taken very seriously the reports that Lane, Harriot, White, and no doubt others brought him from Roanoke Island. Lane was told to write a long report of what he had done by way of both a chronicle and an apologia. What we have, as Richard Hakluyt printed it in 1589, is clearly only a series of major extracts from it. But so far as it goes, for all its incompleteness, it is invaluable as a record. Ralegh, however, must have been struck by Lane's conclusion:

> The discovery of a good mine, by the goodness of God, or a passage to the South Sea, or some way to it, and nothing else can bring this country in request to be inhabited by our nation. And with the discovery of any of the two above showed, it will be the most sweet and healthfulest climate, and therewithal the most fertile soil, being manured, in the world. And then will sassafras and many other good roots and gums there found make good merchandise and lading for shipping, which otherwise of themselves will not be worth the fetching.

This was a brave, salutary, and, to Ralegh, somewhat bitter conclusion. Virginia would not be a profitable plantation colony where men, as his servants, would work for him thousands of miles away. Some other solutions must be found. It is probable that he was interested in the reports of plentiful metal in the interior, even if it was only copper, though even there the evidence brought back was far from conclusive. There were no sources of natural metallic copper in England or Wales, and ore, to be smelted, had to be present in quantity, which was in no way indicated in the accounts he had heard. Copper, gold, and even pearls must be discounted as short-term sources of wealth.

Now that England was actively at war with Spain in western waters, the report of the existence of the deepwater entry to Chesapeake Bay and the assurance of a major deepwater harbor there was more attractive because it could provide, as evidently the Outer Banks and Roanoke Island had wholly failed to do, the location for a major base that could operate against Spain in the west. Just at this time, too, the same consideration was in the minds of the Spanish: they also knew the bay and greatly feared that, if the English occupied it, they might be dangerous to their fleets and hard to dislodge. From this time on, for some four years, there was to be a race—a snail's race, perhaps, we might regard it in retrospect—for Chesapeake Bay between England and Spain, with neither in the end prepared to spare the resources from major sea-fighting elsewhere to occupy and man it.

If Ralegh's commercial and strategic interests were given a dose of cold water by Lane's report, which we have little doubt was corroborated by men such as Amadas, on whom Ralegh could depend perhaps more firmly than on Lane, his intellectual interests were aroused and excited by the results of the great labors of Harriot and White. They had brought him a map on which he could rely for accurate topographical information on the area, insofar as he would concern himself with it in the future. White had brought a large number of drawings, perfected from his sketches when adverse weather interfered with the survey. Harriot had a mass of notes about the inhabitants of the country and about almost every aspect of its resources. It is true that both of them were very disappointed, to put it mildly, at the loss of some of their precious materials in the last rush away from Roanoke Island, and furious with the sailors for their part in it. It is apparent, however, that Harriot had saved his journal. They also took back many specimens, though not all were carefully labeled, or the labels had washed off in the hurried departure. Charles de L'Écluse, the eminent natural historian, was able to acquire a few when he visited England a little later, but found difficulty in assigning them to the correct source.[20] It is not stretching the imagination too far to think of Ralegh, with Harriot and White, laying out these objects and pictures in his apartments in Durham House in the Strand where he now lived. White is almost certain to have given Ralegh finished versions of many of his drawings and Harriot to have furnished him with copies of a selection of his more interesting notes, together with a version of his journal. These also would have been exhibited to Sir Francis Walsingham, who had had so much to do with getting backing for the voyages in 1584 and 1585, though perhaps they discouraged him from taking any further part in the venture. White was almost certainly commissioned to make a set of his drawings for Walsingham and, apparently, at least one other person at Court, though it does not appear that anything was presented to the Queen herself. Of her reaction we have no evidence whatever, but at least she could consider she was wise not to have involved herself deeply in the undertaking, which was as yet far from being an asset to her power, and she did not participate in the voyages that were to follow.

White, we may consider, set to work with Harriot to make a coherent set of reference material on the maps and survey, while Harriot was also required to turn his journal into a systematic history of the 1584 and 1585–86 ventures. The work they put in Ralegh's hands has disappeared without trace, and there is nothing now in Harriot's surviving collections of all that he collected. But that he continued to work in Ralegh's household at these and other tasks there is no doubt.

At the end of the year, too, or in the very first days of 1587, Sir Richard Grenville went to London to explain how he had fared and how he had complicated further dealings with Virginia by his actions there.

A Colony Which Died

So far nothing has been said of Sir Richard Grenville's positive actions on Roanoke Island in July or August 1586 in attempting to maintain an English presence in the area. We have no direct information on the reactions to the deserted condition of the island of the substantial number of men he had intended to leave there. It would not be difficult to imagine that the majority of them would be totally unwilling to remain, especially as it would have become plain to them, once they had understood that Sir Francis Drake had had to take Ralph Lane off because help had not arrived, that they might not be effectively supplied. They would also have seen that Grenville himself was primarily interested in privateering. Richard Hakluyt, whose vague and unsatisfactory note on the 1586 expedition is our only English source, states that Grenville was "unwilling to lose possession of the country which Englishmen had so long held [an overstatement, surely]," and that "after a good deliberation he determined to leave some men behind to retain possession of the country." Hakluyt says (apparently correctly) there were fifteen of them, but according to Pedro Diaz: "in the said fort [on Roanoke Island] he left eighteen men and . . . left in the said fort four pieces of artillery of cast-iron and supplies for the eighteen men for a year."[1] Hakluyt tells us they were "furnished plentifully with all manner of provision for two years," but he gives no names. Diaz says that "in charge of them he left a Master Cofar [Coffin?], an Englishman, and another called Chapeman," neither of whom has been identified.

The men Grenville left behind are likely to have been volunteers, ready to leave the rough life on shipboard to take their chances in what seemed a virtually uninhabited wilderness, especially if they were promised monetary rewards if they remained until they were relieved. Among their stores may well have been luxuries that they did not ordinarily see. It was bad strategy on Grenville's part. If he could not spare a number of men comparable to that under Lane, it would seem to have been futile to leave such a small number in such a vulnerable position. However, he would not have known of the Spanish threat, nor of the potential hostility of the Indian population. By keeping out of his sight to the extent that they did, they totally misled him, and his captive (the Indian he named Raleigh) evidently did not succeed in warning him of the danger in which he had placed these men. In establishing this post Grenville compounded his mistakes in starting so late and taking so long on his journey. The 1586 voyage would therefore lead to tragedy.

The only further information we have about this "second colony," as we should probably call it, comes from John White upon his return to Roanoke Island in July 1587. He found "the fort razed down." Precisely what this means cannot be satisfactorily resolved.[2] The houses in the "town" had not been demolished, but they were in very poor condition. Squashes had grown up in the clay floors and were providing food for deer; otherwise, the structures, including the upper rooms, were intact. Clearly the settlers had been gone some months, but that is all we can tell from this direct evidence. It may be that the rectangular enclosure, excavated in 1965, represents an attempt to create a more modest defensive work, which was not completed or put to use.

White learned more as he probed the friendly Croatoan Indians, through Manteo and probably through an appreciable knowledge of the language which he may well have developed by this time, judging by the inscriptions on a number of his drawings.

What happened, though we cannot tell when it happened, was that the Indians of Aquascogoc and Dasemunkepeuc—the latter village was inhabited by Wingina's men but we cannot be certain that he had also dominated Aquascogoc as well—joined forces with the much stronger Secotan Indians of the Pamlico River and planned to eliminate the weak English settlement. Whether this came about because of any aggressive action by the colonists, or whether it arose from the enmity engendered during the last weeks of the residence of the first colony, we have no means of telling. However, thirty picked men landed on the island and hid themselves behind trees "near the houses where our men carelessly lived," thus seeming to have abandoned the fortifications. The raiding party counted eleven of the fifteen colonists at home. Therefore, two Indians, apparently unarmed, came into the open and asked to speak with the two leading Englishmen, whom we might think would be Diaz's "Cofar" and Chapeman, making friendly signs to them. The two men came out to meet the Indians, but while one of the Indians held one of the Englishmen in an embrace, the other, with a wooden sword that he had hidden under his deerskin mantle, struck him on the head and killed him. This was probably the leader of the little band.

The second Englishman, who was still free, ran back to his companions. The remaining twenty-eight Indians immediately joined the other two and chased the Englishman to where the rest of the colonists had now appeared and were taking up their arms. While a rain of arrows fell from the Indians' bows, they managed to establish themselves in the house where their weapons and stores were kept. This was perhaps a larger building in the "town." But they were unable to make a stand, as the attackers soon set the reed-thatched roof on fire. The Englishmen were then forced to take up any weapons they could lay hands on and run from the house. They seem to have given a good account of themselves among the trees surrounding the settlement. One of them was struck in the mouth by an Indian arrow and died. One Indian was hit by an incendiary arrow, possibly fired from a musket or caliver, and he, too, died after a time. The fight continued for an hour. Although the tree cover favored the attackers, the Englishmen slowly retreated to where their boat was secured, all the time being shot at by arrows, some of which struck home but not fatally. It is possible a few of the men had managed to put on their morions or even breastplates, but this is somewhat unlikely. The Indians had expected to kill all of the colonists at their headquarters and had not bothered to immobilize their boat, which lay in a cove not far from the fort. The Englishmen were able to reach the boat and hold off the Indians while the nine survivors boarded it. They then set out for Port Ferdinando, the main entrance to the sounds from the Outer Banks.

By the time they had rowed a quarter of a mile, they sighted the four men who had not been in the "town" coming from a creek where they had been getting oysters, perhaps to the south near

Shallowbag Bay. They probably had a small skiff of their own because they were soon taken on board the larger boat. All thirteen of them put off for the Outer Banks. They landed on the small island shown on White's map as lying between Port Ferdinando and Port Lane, "on the right hand of our entrance," where they remained for a time (we cannot say how long). It was their last known resting place.

We are not told in any source what kind of boat Grenville left with the settlers. In view of their number, we presume that it was not a pinnace, but, because nine could row out in it and take four more on board, that it was somewhat like Lane's wherry, capable of holding fairly comfortably all fifteen men while their numbers were intact. The chances are that they took with them the skiff or canoe we have assumed the additional four men to have had. They would have no stores whatever, apart from any crabs and oysters they might have been able to gather on the sound side of the island before they left. It is also tempting to assume that they were able to rig some sort of sail on their boat. A mast and a sail might already have been stowed on board. Otherwise some jury rig, made from oars or fish spears and their shirts, is the best they could have attempted. They eventually departed from their temporary refuge, to which the Indians, busy looting their possessions, did not follow them. But no one would willingly set out into the ocean off the Outer Banks without some sail to supplement their oars.

This was the last that was seen of them. They were thus the first "Lost Colonists" if we exclude the three men Lane left behind in June 1586, who evidently had not joined them. It is probable that they were lost at sea. They may have found refuge with an Indian group either north or south of Port Ferdinando. They did not join Manteo's Indians on Croatoan Island to the south. Just conceivably, they might have reached Cape Henry and made contact with the Chesapeake Indians. Had the Powhatans found them they would have been summarily killed. All we can say is that the "Second Colony" came to an abrupt and, probably tragic, end. The vivid narrative of the fight and their escape is a tribute to the eloquence and powers of observations of the Indians from whom it came. How did they obtain such details? Were they observing the Dasemunkepeuc Indians so very closely that they could follow these events in such detail? Or is it possible that one or two were even among the attackers and successfully covered up this fact? Most probably, the story of the attack and its result was told among the tribes with whom the Croatoan Indians were still in friendly contact and came to them orally in a tale that would likely become part of the lore of the members of the groups who took part. At least we can say that the events described fully illustrate Grenville's lack of wisdom in leaving such a weak party behind, men who were able to fight bravely and effectively once they had recovered from the initial surprise, but whose ultimate fate we have no hope whatever of learning.

Surveys of Man and Beast

The World of Nature

No area of eastern North America was so thoroughly examined for many a long year as that of Roanoke Island and its hinterland by Thomas Harriot and John White during the period from July 1585 to June 1586, and no survey of its kind would be done again until long after the American Revolution. The character and nature of their cartography has already been illustrated, but the survey went far beyond the mere defining of the area's outlines, however important that task was and however well it was done. The survey filled in the outlines in a most remarkable way. At the same time, we are forced to recognize at the beginning that we do not have all the evidence they then collected. Their day-to-day note books, lavishly illustrated, and their early drafts of a comprehensive survey were partly destroyed in the flurry of leaving the island with Drake's men in 1586.

Both White and Harriot hoped someday to make up for this lost segment of their survey by returning at leisure, but for neither was it possible. Although White did spend a brief time on Roanoke Island both in 1587 and 1590, he had other and more immediate things to do. Further, the portfolio of finished replicas of his original drawings, which has been miraculously preserved (a fire in 1865 charred the edges of some of the drawings and they were drenched with water but survived), formed only part of his output. His family had a further and fuller set of drawings; a son (apparently there was a younger John White who could have had a hand in them) and other members of his family made copies of many of the originals that are now lost.[1] Finally, a set of replicas was given to Theodor de Bry to engrave for his fine edition of Harriot's small book, A briefe and true report of the new found land of Virginia, which appeared in 1590. The book itself is our fullest account of the survey and supplements the White drawings. But it was not all he had on hand, only a quick and brief summary for promotion purposes, written in 1587 and first published in 1588. We have also lost the detailed treatise on the Indians and the chronicle of events that he tells us he prepared. He did add some further notes on Indian life to the engravings in de Bry's edition, but that is all.[2] It is a great deal, however.

Ecology as a concept and a term may belong only to the last century or so, but in their way the surveying pair were ecologists. White showed in his depiction of Indians fishing a complex relationship between the plants of the seashore, the life of the littoral (crustacea, etc.), the fish of the sounds, and the birds of the air—all comprehended inside a scene of communal human activity. Harriot, though he broke up his little book into subject sections, conveyed throughout it a sense of the whole environment, man and nature, even if the concept had not yet found a term to describe it.

Because his immediate aim was promotion, Harriot spoke first of the things that settlers might gather, grow, and sell, then of the use that the inhabitants already had made of nature by their horticulture and by their use of plant life to sustain themselves. Then, detaching himself from man, he wrote about the native trees, birds and fishes, with such mammals as he knew of, while in parallel White recorded them in line and water color. Next he turned to the practicalities of economic exploitation—metals, stone (or, rather, the absence of), brick, lime (from oysters), and the all-surrounding timber. Finally, he observed the Indians with the eye of an intellectual. He saw something, if not all, of their relationship to the soil and their reactions to English encroachment, and expressed the optimism of the European Renaissance man that these people who could look after themselves so well, as White illustrated with his pictures of Indian activities, could also take in the Christian faith and European techniques where these were relevant and acceptable. The truth about both the physical environment and the society of the inhabitants was more complex and the prospects for settlement less favorable than he imagined. But his critical sense did not allow him to rhapsodize; rather, it enabled him to show what he had seen and to evaluate it with reasonable optimism, while omitting the less favorable circumstances, except for his account of the disease-carrying capacity of the Englishmen, which neither he nor his contemporaries could under-

❧ A briefe and true re-

port of the new found land of Virginia: of
the commodities there found and to be rayfed, as well mar-
chantable, as others for victuall, building and other neceffa-
rie vfes for thofe that are and fhalbe the planters there; and of the na-
ture and manners of the naturall inhabitants : Difcouered by the
Englifh Colony there feated by Sir Richard Greinuile *Knight in the*
yeere 1585. which remained vnder the gouernment of Rafe Lane Efqui-
er, one of her Maiefties Equieres, during the fpace of twelue monethes : at
the fpeciall charge and direction of the Honourable SIR
WALTER RALEIGH Knight, Lord Warden of
the ftanneries ; who therein hath beene fauou-
red and authorifed by her Maieftie and
her letters patents:

Directed to the Aduenturers, Fauourers,

and Welwillers of the action, for the inhabi-
ting and planting there:

By *Thomas Hariot*; feruant to the abouenamed
Sir Walter, a member of the Colony, and
there imployed in difcouering.

Imprinted at London 1588.

12. Title page of Thomas Harriot, A briefe and true report of the
new found land of Virginia (London, 1588).

stand, any more than twentieth-century man understood quickly the deadliness of radiation.

Harriot and White were primarily interested in objects—the artifacts of human life, the products of nature, and their possible utilization by and for European settlers once they came into living contact with the soil of North America. This is what gives White's pictures their immediacy, their impression of being the thing he saw, as far as he was competent to record it. They ignore the implications of settlement and, except in one section of Harriot's tract, the whole question of relations between Europeans and Native Americans on which so much was written then, and still more later. Consequently, it is permissible to consider both the human and nonhuman elements in the survey together, to demonstrate not only their fullness and comprehensiveness but also their considerable limitations.

It is not surprising that Harriot should start with "the fertility of the soil." Here the primary illustration was the ease with which the Indians could grow crops, the quality and yield of which was, by English standards, very ample and boded well for the future of agriculture in the hands of colonists. The really impressive crop was maize. Indian corn was planted "without muck, dung or other thing, neither [do they] plow nor dig it as we [do] in England." The preparation of the ground by men using long peckers (not mentioned by other early observers), of course, followed the long process of burning down the trees, leaving their roots to decay and finally clearing the ground after a number of crops had been grown in the interstices. Harriot is speaking of matured garden plots, the result of a long period of labor of which he does not seem to have been aware. The women followed with short wooden peckers and went over the ground in detail, clearing it of weeds and obstacles. They burned the rubble on the fields (thus providing a little in the way of potash for fertilization, but not doing so consciously, as they did not disperse the heaps of ash over the ground). They worked systematically over the plot, placing four grains about an inch apart, and laying down the seed carefully in rows, each group of seeds a yard apart, each row another yard apart. In the intervening ground they planted seeds of beans, squashes, and "melden" (a salt-bush [Atriplex] or lamb's-quarter [Chenopodium album]). It is certain that beans were grown up the cornstalks and perhaps added to the little groups of corn seed. His mel-

13. (a) Bird Eating an Ear of Maize; (b) Skink. After John White.
British Museum, Department of Prints and Drawings, 199.a.3 (104b, 126).

den would appear to be a local weed that was tolerated in the cultivated area because of its value as a salty flavoring.

Harriot claims that one crop of corn could yield two hundred bushels to the acre as opposed to a maximum of forty bushels an acre of wheat grown in England. But these figures, by modern reckoning, are much too high. He also thought double-cropping was sometimes achieved. For English settlers, however, corn was the thing—"you which shall inhabit and plant there may know how specially that country corn is there to be preferred before ours." He goes even further: "Besides the manifold ways in applying it to victual, the increase is so much that small labor and pains is needful in respect of that which must be used for ours." He even claims that one man could prepare and plant in one day enough corn to keep him for a year.

Harriot is assuming that a small field of one acre was sufficient to feed a village. (White shows no outer limit to the plot appearing in a drawing of Secotan, and in one version of a drawing of Pomeioc shows three cornfields, apparently larger, surrounding the village.) Besides being ignorant of the time and difficulty involved in preparing a smooth field (the slash and burn period took much longer), Harriot was unaware that the villagers did not have the capacity to use the land indefinitely without manuring it; thus they had to shift their fields every few years and so again undergo the long process of clearing, which he took for granted. Indeed, Ralph Lane also took for granted that the land prepared and sown for him by the local people in the spring of 1586 was available without earlier work, when clearly it must have been a former Indian field that had become fertile again. A long-occupied site like Chawanoac shows, under excavation, that Indian occupancy did not involve moving the village when fields became barren. New fields, or fields restored to fertility over time, could be worked on an extended site as they were needed.

If Harriot tells us how corn was grown, White shows it growing. In his drawing of Secotan we see the corn plant emerging from the soil in the latest sowing; no other plants are visible. But White shows, too, that corn was planted in three different sowings: in July one is ripening, one is half-grown, and a third is emerging from the ground. A hut among the ripening corn where a boy bird-scarer sits adds a human touch to the picture. But White is also able to demonstrate what the corn was like in a drawing (surviving in a copy) of a bird pecking an ear of corn. This, the experts tell us, was corn of the "Eastern Complex," eight- or ten-rowed flint and flour corn, in which multicolored grains were common, as in this example. It had been grown for centuries in eastern North America.

It is clear, too, that Englishmen copied Indian methods of cooking the corn. It was boiled alone or used as a constituent in an animal-vegetable stew, and made into meal (they would have used hand-mills rather than the slow pestle and mortar methods of the Indians) and bread. It also proved to make acceptable beer. There is no mention of the digestive upsets that were to afflict some later settlers as the result of an almost wholly corn diet. But clearly to Harriot and White, corn was the staple that made colonization basically possible. They both seemed confident that Englishmen could grow it them-selves once they had learned local methods of planting and usage, not to mention the storage of seed, which is taken for granted.

Harriot tells us that both beans and peas were grown, and that they grew up the cornstalks. Of course, no peas were cultivated, but smaller and larger bean varieties seem probably to have been in use. At the time the distinction was not always clearly observed in En-gland. The special character of the American "runner" beans and their difference from European broad beans does not appear to have excited comment.

Sunflowers, which were grown for their seed and oil, impressed Harriot with their size. The cucurbits were also impressive. There were sufficient varieties among them to lead him—mistakenly—to add melons and cucumbers to the squash, pumpkins, and gourds that were already present. White shows us that at Secotan the squashes were carefully segregated and grown in close profusion. Sunflowers, on the other hand, were planted in small separate patches, detached from the cornfields.

After corn, it was not a food but a drug that attracted the most attention from Harriot, namely the native tobacco, Nicotiana rustica. His description was the first to appear in England, though tobacco had been in use there before his time. He remarked that it was sown by itself, as indeed it is shown, like sunflowers, by White. This Uppo-woc, which the Spaniards, he said, called "tobacco," is "an herb . . . the leaves thereof being dried and brought into powder, they use to take the fume or smoke thereof by sucking it through pipes made of clay into their stomach and head." According to Harriot, it had positive qualities: "it purgeth superfluous phlegm and other gross humors[3] [illness, in fact], openeth all the pores and passages of the body, by which means the use thereof not only preserveth the body from obstructions, but also, if any be, so that they have not been of too long continuance, in short time breaketh them, whereby their bodies are notably preserved in health and know not many grievous diseases wherewithall we in England are oftentimes afflicted." He recognized its sacred character among the Indian population, but said "we ourselves during the time we were there used to suck it after their manner and also since our return, and have found many rare and wonderful experiments [experiences] of the virtues thereof." Certainly Harriot and his associates brought Indian pipes to England and had them modified as acceptable smoking implements. He became an inveterate smoker and his papers are full of notes to purchase tobacco. He also led Sir Walter Ralegh to bring it to Court as a fashionable habit, and indeed long after continued to supply Ralegh and the earl of Northumberland, his later patron, with the choicest varieties he could find. The Court reaction against tobacco under James I, who believed it was a pernicious poison, left him and his circle unmoved. The myth that he and Ralegh introduced tobacco into England is a different matter—seamen and seafaring areas had known of it long before. But Harriot included tobacco with corn, squashes, beans, and sunflowers as "among the commodities for sustenance of life."

It is difficult to say whether Harriot overemphasized or underestimated the importance of agriculture in Indian society. According to some modern scholars it was vitally important, but among such littoral peoples as these fishing likewise held a special position in their economy. This was also true of traditional hunting, for deer and bear, and gathering of wild plants. The inhabitants of many towns and villages moved most of their people to sources of crustacea and fish in the summer; they spread out to gather wild plants and roots; they dispersed again in winter to their hunting grounds. Some may have lived the year-round in primitive camps near oyster and mussel beds. Some towns and villages (tidy and compact in White's drawings) were stable and long-lasting—Chawanoac, as already indicated, is known to archaeologists as an example of the latter. Others were shortlived and could be packed up and carried to a new site. The village on Roanoke Island was quickly deserted in the spring of 1586 and the people simply enlarged their chief town of Dasemunkepeuc to accommodate a larger population.

Nor was there very much land there that could be used for long-term agriculture. The humus cover was thin on Roanoke Island; any lengthy disturbance, together with the winds sweeping over the island in fairly frequent storms, soon left areas of naked sand, as was also true of the Outer Banks. Once the ecological balance of the natural vegetation was seriously disturbed, the land became largely useless. It might seem that the colonists of 1587 realized this and regarded the thick humus of the area north of the borders of the Great Dismal Swamp as a preferential location for a permanent colony. Besides, the extent of the unusable swamp forest—not taken note of by Harriot—and of the great swampy fringes, the wetlands, of the islands and shores inhibited extensive settlement. Harriot and White could not see or apprehend the whole picture either of Indian life or of the possibilities for settlement, honest and thorough as they were.

Harriot's interest in language and his mastery in some considerable degree (though he was modest about it) of the Algonquian language made it possible for him to find out what natural products the Indians used. The section in his book on roots is interesting because it shows how much the Indians subsisted on vegetable products. The groundnut (*Openauk*)—the source of the myth that the colony brought the potato to England—the tuckahoe (*Okeepenauk*), the duck-potato (*Kaishúcpenauk*), with the arrow-arum and golden club (*Coscúshaw*), from which the poison had to be removed before they were edible (he gives some detail of how this was done), and angelica (*Habascon*), all filled a place in the diet he proposed for the colonists as did wild onions, which grew in abundance. The most amusing was his *Tsinaw*. A medicinal root of great value in the herbal pharmacopoeia of the period was China root, an oriental smilax. To the English, the greenbrier, which they found in profusion in the Roanoke area, appeared similar if not identical to it. They were continually asking the Indians about China root, and whether the local smilaxes were the same. The Indians may not have had a name for it

but hearing "China" so often they learned to say it themselves—as
Tsinaw—and for once Harriot was naive enough not to recognize its
origin and believed it to be the Indian name. The hemexia, a smilax,
was later known as S. pseudochina, while the thorny greenbrier was
also considered to be closely related, as it was. But this root had a
market in Europe (the Spanish brought other dried varieties to Europe, as salsaparilla, where it was much prized), but for medical rather
than dietary use. White added to the brief repertoire of medicinal
plants drawings of the Sabatia, a gentian, and of a milkweed.

Fruits, too, he stressed—his chestnut was the coastal chinquapin,
his walnuts were both the hickory (in several species) and the black
walnut. The latter did not grow freely near the coast, but because it
was sought for in the interior for food and body oil, trees from its
nuts tended to grow around some Indian villages, though the Indians depended much more on the locally-plentiful hickories. Both,
however, formed a food supplement much valued by the inhabitants. To Harriot the persimmon was equated with the English med-
lar and like it "not good until they be rotten." The prickly pear (his
Metaquesúnnauk) then so flourished along the Outer Banks that its
fruits were large enough to be edible (it was already being cultivated
in Spain). Grapes—both the small summer grape and the muscadine
(with perhaps other kinds)—he thought were not only pleasant to
eat but could form the basis for a wine industry, though he was
mistaken in this as later colonists did not find them of more than
domestic value. The wild strawberry he found in profusion, but
probably on his travels, especially in the Chesapeake Bay area, as it is
not common near the coast farther south. He recognized mulberries
from the red mulberry (if not the correct species for silk production), crabapples, and huckleberries and cranberries (as "Hurts"), and
what was probably the peppervine (Sacquenúmmener) he saw the Indians boil for a long time before eating it to remove the poison. He
thought some of the seeds of reeds and grasses were edible—he may
have identified the wild rice, but this is far from certain. The wild
peas he found on his travels can only have been the rather negligible
beach pea, because its peas are so small. The Indians made much of
acorns from several species of oak (Segatémener, Osámaner, Pummuckóner,
Sapúmmener, and Mangúmmenauk), which they treated in various ways
before cooking, even making bread from them.

14. John White's Drawing of the Sabatia, a Member of the Gentian Family. Now known as the Large Marsh Pink (*Sabatia dodecandra* [L]), it is still found on the Outer Banks.

In all this Harriot demonstrated his thoroughness in disclosing how the Indians exploited natural products, but he also revealed how completely they used them and so modified some of his emphasis on their cultivated plants. He also showed a certain naiveté in expecting potential colonists to subsist on arum roots, acorns, and the like, which would be scorned by Europeans and were, in fact, not used by the early settlers, unless perhaps in time of famine. Of course, walnuts, hickories, strawberries, and a few other fruits would be agreeable as food supplements, just as they would in England. But whether a colonist would be attracted by some of the things he described is very doubtful. Thus, there is a certain lack of subtlety in his promotional efforts and we can see the intellectual and the linguist dominating the publicist.

When he came to wild animals Harriot could naturally stress the deer—indeed, they formed a basic food supply for Indians throughout eastern North America; the small white-tailed Virginia deer was prolific and not too hard to run down with dogs or shoot with arrows or calivers. There were also plenty of rabbits (coneys, as the English called them): technically, the marsh rabbit and the cottontail might be hares but for practical purposes they were just rabbits. (Unlike some propagandists for colonies, he did not advocate the construction of rabbit warrens to grow rabbits for food.) He was able to do little more than name other edible and inedible animals. He had eaten two smaller sorts (raccoon and opossum?) for which he had names (Saquénuckot and Maquówoc) but only when they were caught by the Indians. The gray squirrels the colonists caught themselves and ate. They realized that in the winter hunts, which he does not specify further, the Indians tracked down and killed bears. The black bear, Lane had noted, was especially plentiful in the area explored by the Chesapeake party and for centuries it remained the major source of food and fur on the fringes of the Great Dismal Swamp.

Altogether, Harriot had named no less than twenty-eight kinds of wild animals, but could go no further in describing actual specimens. In fact, this entire section reveals how the settlers had wholly failed to develop the fur trade with the Indians. Arthur Barlowe had stressed that they were offered furs and skins in 1584, but in this regard Harriot speaks only of deerskins. It is difficult to find an explanation except that the Indians may have regarded the greed of

15. Black Bear from the Great Dismal Swamp, 1983.
Bear Photographed at Parker's Ferry, fall 1983.
Photo by Mike Voss, *Ahoskie News-Herald*.
Courtesy of David S. Phelps.

the Europeans for furs as reprehensible; normally, they killed only as many beasts as they needed, recognizing their kinship with the animal world. It perhaps is significant that not a single wild animal appears in White's varied gallery of pictures, although there is one domesticated dog in the drawing of Pomeioc village. There is a touch of humor in Harriot's mention of dogs as food: "their wolves or wolfish dogs. . . . I have not set down for good meat, least that some would understand my judgment therein to be more simple than needeth." He admitted that he could recognize the difference in taste between the Indian dogs and the colonists' own mastiffs, which, as we have seen, they were forced to eat on the Roanoke River expedition, and perhaps others after their return. Although he had heard the natives ate "lion" (puma), he never saw one, but White shows a chief decked out for war, with a clearly identifiable puma tail as decoration.

Harriot was happier with birds. Turkeys he had known in England in their domesticated state. White did not leave us a picture of any, nor of the mourning dove or "partridges" (bobwhites), but Harriot's cranes appear, as White drew a sandhill crane and a pelican head, together with one shown flying aloft in the fishing scene, though not his geese (Canada, brant, and snow geese) but the swan is represented in White's trumpeter swan. For the rest Harriot said that he had identified forty-eight birds and had caught, eaten, and drawn eight kinds of waterfowl and seventeen land birds. White's pictures support him here. We have from White several loons, a surf scoter, a red-breasted merganser, a bufflehead duck, the bald eagle, and a somewhat indeterminate gull (making seven at least); and of the land birds, the red-headed woodpecker, downy woodpecker, grackle, bluebird (?), towhee (twice), thrasher (probably twice), Baltimore oriole (?), eastern redwing, barn swallow, eastern cardinal, yellow-shafted flicker, blue jay, and possible cuckoo and junco (making, with the brown pelican, seventeen including possible duplications). Incidentally, Harriot's statement that "we have the pictures as they were there drawn with the names of the inhabitants [those the Indians gave them]" is only one of two references to his collaboration with White in the combined verbal and visual survey. His "parrots" (Carolina paroquet), "falcons" (duck hawk), and merlin (pigeon hawk) are not among White's surviving illustrations.

To those familiar with the abundant bird life of the coastal area and the winter accession of swans, geese, and ducks, Harriot's list and White's representations comprise an elementary bird book of no insignificant proportions. We might wonder that, though Harriot records the large numbers of wintering swans and geese, he makes no mention of whether the settlers succeeded in killing a substantial number of them for food. But this may be implicit in his remarks on their quantity.

He was happy, too, with fish and his cooperation with White is evident in the combined record from their survey. Harriot states that the sturgeon was plentiful from February to May and White made a drawing of one, though again no reference is made to the accumulation of sturgeon and its preservation during the period of short rations in the early summer of 1586. It was later to save the Jamestown settlers at a critical period. The run of "herrings" is also noted: Harriot remarks on their size, as well he might because both alewife and shad are much larger than the Atlantic herring. The sturgeon and "herring," he says, "we found to be most delicate and pleasant meat." Lane had complained that the settlers had lacked the means of catching fish and had induced Wingina to have weirs built for them, but surely no great skills were required to take these herring—at least during their spawning season. Should we say that soldiers, administrators, and intellectuals did not make good fishermen at that time, or was Lane exaggerating the inability of his men to succeed, without Indian aid, in procuring food supplies of fish from waters that were, from White's fishing picture, swarming with them? His "old wives" were sheepsheads, as White demonstrated, his mullet was the striped mullet, and his "plaice" one of the many flounders, all three shown by White. Rays (sting ray and skate) also appear in his fishing scene. White even put an improbably large hammerhead shark in his view of fishing in the sound—small ones have been seen in the sounds, the larger only off the Outer Banks. Harriot says that he ate many other excellent fish but had only the Indian names for them. For twelve more they have the pictures "as they were drawn in the country with their names," of which White supplies the bowfin (or mudfish), white perch, striped bass, drum, needlefish, gar, catfish, burrfish, croaker, and puffer, making at least ten; in addition, a few in the fishing scene are identifiable, though others are not.

Harriot goes on to describe the Indian fish weir—"a kind of weir made of reeds which in that country are very strong [cane stakes]" and which White shows in detail, with the traps inserted in the long line of staked obstructions. Harriot speaks too of "the other way, which is more strange, ... with poles made sharp at the end, by shooting them into the fish after the manner as Irishmen cast darts, either as they are rowing in their boats or else as they are wading in the shallows for the purpose." White again lets us see this practice—the incredibly skillful striking of fish by men wading with long "darts" or spears. With an artist's license he also allows us to see the fish on the point of being struck. The Indians in the canoe he shows have a stone on board on which they can cook fish (shad?) straight out of the water (was the fire also used as a lure at night?) and a hand net, which we may suppose they used to land wounded fish struck by the "dart" throwers, or even to catch crustacea, such as the spider crab and other crabs shown on the shore near the canoe. Once more, between them, Harriot and White provide us with a very creditable survey of marine resources.

When Harriot comes to the life of the seashore he is mainly brief and dismissive. He fails to stress the large part that oysters played in the Indian diet, even if he later recognized the presence of their shells as a source of lime. Mussels are passed over without reference to the distinction between the freshwater mussel, which produced the best pearls and was found in the rivers where fresh water predominated, and the common sea mussel, which was mainly of value for its edibility. But mussels, like his periwinkles and crawfish ("crevices"), were common property to England and the New World. What did attract him was the creature that John Smith was to call the king crab (though the zoologists have stolen the name for another representative of the family). Harriot used its Indian name, Seékanauk, "a kind of crusty shell-fish which is good meat, about a foot in breadth, having a crusty tail, many legs like a crab and her eyes in her back. They are to be found in shallows in salt waters and sometimes on the shore." He may have found the impressive horseshoe crab edible but others have not. Certainly it was unique, and still is. The three eyes on its carapace were a residual feature of its long history on earth and, if not inactive, were probably of little value in finding its way. The Indians used its spiky tail to tip their fish spears, and White in his fishing scene shows one scurrying along the verge of the water.

Harriot concludes his section "Of Fishes" with "tortoises," remarking that there were both land and sea varieties: "their backs and bellies are shelled very thick, their head, feet and tail, which in appearance, seem ugly, as though they were members [limbs] of a serpent or venomous, but notwithstanding they are very good meat as also their eggs. Some have been found of a yard in breadth and better." Had we only this description we should not be very well informed, but White takes us into the world of the box tortoise, the terrapin, and the sea turtle in three of his finest drawings and also places the sea turtle in the water in his fishing scene. What distinguishes the three White studies is the care that has been taken to display them in significant detail and to present them in a highly decorative style. What he does not do is to give any indication of their scale. His terrapin is spread out so that its 4 to 5.5 inches occupies a whole page in his album. His box tortoise (now usually referred to as a turtle) is smaller and is seen from the side, but though it occupies only half a sheet it is nevertheless about, or larger than, life size (4.5 to 6.5 inches). The finest of all is his sea turtle, which ranged to even larger sizes than Harriot noted, being recorded at anything from 31 to 47 inches in length. The rich coloring and the lively appearance of this drawing makes it stand out even among some many fine representations (though the legs of his terrapin have been somewhat distorted for decorative purposes). This turtle in the sixteenth and seventeenth centuries laid its eggs all the way along the Outer Banks (though now it does not do so north of Ocracoke) and must have provided excellent flesh as well as eggs for Indians and settlers alike. We can see a few crabs scuttling through the White pictures of fishing but "tortoises" bring to an end all that Harriot had to say on the natural history of the area.

By way of comparison, neither John Smith's account of the Chesapeake for the early years of the seventeenth century nor William Strachey's version of his survey of water and land fauna (except in touches) have the freshness and critical authority of Harriot's work.[4] We may suspect that he had lost many of his notes because for parts of his treatise he spoke of depending on his memory, but his natural history material, together with whatever set of the White drawings he had at hand when he was writing, left him adequate scope to give a fair and full conspectus of natural resources. White, too, went beyond economic value in his depictions, especially of birds. He also extended the range of his observation to include at least one snake (of somewhat indefinite character, probably a milk snake) and a three-lined skink, nor did he ignore the humble lamprey.

Honest man that he was, Harriot did his best to set out for intending colonists of the future the commodities they might find that could be exported to provide for their sustenance. But his presentation must have seemed very limited and unlikely to provide much gain, even if the settlers could, if they had to, live on Indian cultivated products and on the abundant wild life of the region. Few would go, and rightly so, unless they had something of value to export. The first item in Harriot's list was "silke of grass or grass silke," not perhaps the most likely ingredient in economic success. This "groweth two foot and a half high or better, the blades are about two foot in length and half inch broad. The like groweth in Persia." It should be cultivated even though much of it grew wild—"which also by proof here in England, in making a piece of silk grosgrain ("Grogran") we found to be excellent good." In the first place, it is clear he knew nothing of silk cultivation in Persia and, secondly, though a silk-like (or linen-like?) fabric could indeed be made from the leaves of the yucca (*Yucca filamentosa*), it was not silk and, regardless of experiments made with it later, it never did nor could provide the basis for an industry. His silk was almost a complete mirage. White's milkweed (*wisakon*), with its fluffy, silky seed pods and its stringy stalk, was another candidate, though Indian uses were primarily medicinal.

He then goes on to "worm silk"—saying that "in many of our journeys we found silk worms fair and great, as big as our ordinary walnuts." If these were cultivated and mulberry trees planted (he evidently did not distinguish the red mulberry from the "Chinese" [and European] species), another silk industry could emerge. Here, of course, he is completely at sea and seems to be referring to the tent caterpillar or fall webworm, with their characteristic webbed constructions. This then was another mirage. And so indeed was his suggestion, about which he did not appear very positive, that both hemp and flax grew and could provide crops in the land he had traversed, even if he admitted there was not much of either in any one place. There were certainly specimens of wild flax (but with yellow, not blue, flowers) and Indian hemp (*Apocynum*) if he could have recognized it, but his idea that these native varieties could be developed to provide sailcloth and cordage for shipping was a mere guess.

From misty riches to be gained from dubious plants Harriot turned to equally nonexistent minerals—a fifty-mile vein along the coast identified in England as "roche alum," valued in the cloth industry. But nobody has found a deposit containing this aluminum-potassium compound anywhere in the coastal areas. (Rock alum was obtained from alum stone in Italy but compacted clay can give illusory impressions.) Other minerals he cited were "white copperas" (a zinc compound), "nitre," a not too carefully-defined mineral at that time, and "plume alum." All of these are equally ambiguous and unidentifiable, though the iron sulphide (his "copperas") could well have been isolated from the clay deposits on the Upper Chowan and Roanoke rivers, as already suggested.[5] Either Joachim Ganz was a charlatan or Harriot used his own judgment in identifying substances of which he knew nothing, as mineralogy was, except for the ores of a few specific metals (copper and iron among them), a very little-understood science at this time.

As for his next product, *wapeih*, a clay like the Mediterranean *terra sigillata*, and prized for its supposed medicinal properties, there was clay indeed but no more valuable than other clays anywhere. Its use for poultices, diarrhea, and the like is not recorded nor would it have been of much, if any, help in these areas.

Harriot was much more in line with reality when he stressed the potential of the coastal area to produce pitch, tar, resin, and turpentine. There were considerable stands of long-leaf pine, loblolly, and other conifers among the hardwoods of the swamp forests, and these were to finance much later activity—almost the only paying product of the area—for a long time. It was not for nothing that North Carolina came to be called the "Tar Heel State." But the exploitation of timber for such products required time, capital, and the slow development of techniques of economical production.

From the French discovery of the medicinal virtues of sassafras in the early 1560s and its exploitation by the Spanish colony in Florida after 1565, there had developed a whole pharmacopoeia in which sassafras was the specific cure for many diseases from syphilis to sore throats. In 1577 this was set out in Nicolas Monardes's book, translated by John Frampton with the alluring title *Joyfull news out of the newe founde world*, of which Harriot had a copy with him. Sassafras, which the Indians called *winauk*, was plentiful—"a kinde of wood of most pleasant and sweet smell," as most would agree today, but scarcely "of rare virtues in physic for the cure of many diseases," as Monardes claimed and to whom Harriot refers his readers. This was indeed a salable product and for a generation commanded high prices in England and elsewhere. It was later to be exploited in the Virginia colony. But those who dug up the roots and peeled the bark soon found, as tobacco planters were eventually to find to their cost, that overproduction could bring down the price—from several shillings a pound to a few pence—if too much was produced and imported. In view of the high esteem in which sassafras was held at that time, Harriot's recommendation made good economic sense.

The same was true, within even narrower limits, of his commendation of cedar wood (eastern white cedar [Thuja], red cedar, and southern red cedar [Juniperus]), "whereof if nests of chests be there made, or timber thereof fitted [made fit] for sweet and fine bedsteads, tables, desks, lutes, virginals and many things else (of which there had been proof made already) to make up freight with other principal commodities will yield profit." There was no doubt that cedar in bulk, or finely sawed into boards, or even made up by expert craftsmen on the spot, could find a market in England—after all, cedar chests are still very much prized. But he was shrewd in assessing cedar in the trunk as a subsidiary commodity in the makeup of a cargo, for in the small ships of the time a lading of timber alone could rarely yield a high profit if it had to be carried thousands of miles. But cedar was, indeed, to be exploited later, just as the experiments made after the return of the colonists in using it for fine joinery—"sweet and fine bedsteads, tables, desks, lutes, virginals and many things else"—had evidently proved it was worthwhile, and thus gave him some grounds for commending the exploitation of this rich natural product.

Harriot also saw a future for the deerskins which the Indians "dressed after the manner of chamois" and were willing to exchange for English products. Clearly he was overoptimistic when he says that thousands of dressed (and also undressed) deerskins "are to be had of the natural inhabitants yearly by way of traffic for trifles," and this without depleting the supply of deer available for exploitation. No doubt the Indians did and could dispose of deerskins of either sort, but the idea that they would concentrate a large part of their effort on killing deer for their skins or that their women would devote much of their time to dressing and painting them in exchange for European bells, needles, toys, and other trimmings, with which they would soon be satiated, was wholly mistaken. Harriot's view presumed that commercial activity could be stimulated rapidly to become a major facet of Indian life. In the very long run, perhaps, it could and would in some areas of North America, but the facile assumption that it could be done with the scattered population of the coastlands was unrealistic, even though it did offer small scale exchanges of a realistic nature. At that time, Indian belief in the affinity between themselves and the natural world could well have inhibited large-scale slaughter of animals except for food.

Civet cats, and the civet that they secreted—products of Asia—were much appreciated in Europe as a base for scents that were greatly needed in an insanitary society. Harriot had found a dead skunk and smelled where another had been, but his olfactory senses were not too refined if he identified their effluvia with civet. Or perhaps he was referring to the muskrat, with its less powerful secretion. Nonetheless he noted the existence of such animals, and their possible exploitation, in his list of recommendations.

It has been shown that iron was present in the banks of the Chowan and Roanoke rivers. Nodules of iron oxide (red ocher) were used for body paint. Harriot says that a rocky deposit was found about 120 miles from the fort (on the Roanoke River?) which a "mineral man," Ganz or another, determined to be rich in iron. Iron was also said to be found in many other parts of the country (as bog iron?). Harriot thought it could be exploited, because, apart from feeding the men engaged to remove it and provide timber to smelt it, it could be produced cheaply, without the high costs of timber in England. This too the Virginia Company 1607 thought and put much money and effort into trying.

Lane (as we have seen) had been obsessed with the potential of copper deposits, which he had never seen, and with the possibilities of gold being found with the copper. Harriot, too, though less uncritically, placed copper high in the potentialities of the area. He says that 150 miles into the mainland they had found Indians with small plates of copper (clearly the Chowan tribe) who spoke of others farther inland "where as they say are mountains and rivers that yield also white grains of metal which is to be deemed silver." He did see two small pieces of silver hanging from the ears of a chief living about 80 miles away (was this among the Chesapeakes?). And this chief told how copper and silver were found in water in this way. This was much less than Lane had said about the Mangoaks and their mysterious suppliers at Chaunis Temoatan. There seems no reason why—when the Roanoke River cut through the greenstone schist in the Virgilina ridge (about 200 miles northwest from Albemarle Sound), which held quantities of copper ore and also some cuprite or copper oxide (which would attract the Indians as a dyestuff)—traces of native copper should not have remained in the river bed and even, with the cuprite, in the banks, but this whole area is now under water (in Kerr Lake) and it may never be established that this was so. Even Lane, we noted, heard that at least most of the copper came from the mountains twenty days beyond where he himself had been. Either natural copper deposits in the mountain areas were being worked on a small scale or Lake Superior copper, traded over such vast areas down the Mississippi-Missouri basins, might have overflowed as far east as the piedmont. A variety of copper sources, most producing small quantities, seems most probable.

Pearls seemed to be another source of wealth. Harriot found the mussel pearls of little quality, though perhaps he did not search far enough. But one man collected about 5,000 from the Indians, presumably both from mussels and oysters (which the Indians ate in such quantities that the few pearls to be found in them must have accumulated relatively quickly). The pearls collected during their stay were, as we have seen, lost at their departure in 1586. Pearls were, however, not to be an economically important product for early settlers in any part of the Americas north of the Caribbean.

There were gums (from the sweet gum and other trees) and apothecary drugs which seemed potentially profitable. But if there was indeed an apothecary with them, as has been suggested, he did not make much of those, apart from sassafras, that were found. Dyes were more attractive, because the Indians used a good variety for body decoration. Sumac, yielding black, was familiar in England but more plentiful in the Roanoke area; there were reds in the seeds of *Wasewówr*, possibly pokeweed, in roots called *Chápacor*, not unlikely to be dogwood, and in the bark of a tree called *Tangomóckonomindge*, which may be the same but has not otherwise been identified. He does not mention the puccoon or bloodroot, which tended to be traded from the interior to the coast as a preferred red dye or, indeed, the red ocher, to which reference has been made. Harriot would have liked to think that some of these red dyes, which all the sources named produced, would be valuable in the finishing of English woolen cloth, but he was not sure. He might perhaps have made some more experiments in this field, even though he draws attention to the extensive uses of vegetable dyes, and, probably, minerals, by the Indians, which White was to illustrate graphically in so many of his drawings. And while he was thinking of cloth, he suggested that woad (*Isatis tinctoria*), still the major source of blue dye and recently begun to be imported into England from the Azores, should and could be grown by settlers, as should madder (*Rubia tinctoria*), which produced a reddish dye. Here he was on not too unfirm ground, but these plants needed heavy soil, and the sandy topsoil of Roanoke Island and adjacent lands would probably have not sustained them for very long.

In total, what Harriot suggests as products of commercial importance for the future amounts to very little indeed. He is saying, whether he intends to or not, that settlers will find little to exploit that is already there. If they are to make export crops by agricultural work it must be from nonindigenous plants—though sugar and citrus fruits might yet flourish. (In November 1585 Sir Richard Grenville still had this idea.)[6] The colonists could get food from native crops but little of value to sell, even if Harriot's more optimistic notions were confirmed.

Harriot correctly believed that settlers would need all the guidance they could get on the materials that were available for establishing themselves in dwellings and for erecting any subsidiary buildings or defenses they might find necessary. Accordingly, he reserved what he had to say on trees for this section of his book. First and foremost were the oaks, which, he said, were "as good white timber as any can be," even if he did not stress their great size and the enormous labor required to obtain planking from them, though of course younger and slighter trees could be used for posts and poles. The colonists probably had brought at least one pitsaw in 1585 but water mills would be more effective. He also stressed the utility of fir trees—loblolly, long-leaf pine, and several others—which he said, rightly, could make fine masts. The "sweet wood," *Rakíok*, from which the Indians burned and scraped out their dugout canoes, he admired because it was both soft and durable, enabling vessels large enough to carry twenty men to be made from it. This was almost certainly the tulip tree (*Liriodendron tulipifera*), unknown in Europe. Cedar, he had already specified, but he repeated something of what he had said earlier, and of cypress (juniper), he said, "is also a wood of price and no small estimation." Indeed, both cedar and cypress from America were taken to England and naturalized well before the end of the seventeenth century—trees at Syon House and Sherborne Castle, occupied, respectively, by the earl of Northumberland, Ralegh's friend, and by Ralegh himself, may well be descended from trees taken from Roanoke Island or, more likely, from the Jamestown colony.

Maple receives only cursory attention: witch hazel and maple are said to have been used by the Indians for bow staves. Certainly witch hazel was. The abundant ilexes appear only as holly suitable for making birdlime. Willows were appropriate for making weirs and traps for fish "after the English manner," which apparently none of the colonists could do. The Indians made theirs of cane, which worked very well. Beech and ash would make casks, cask hoops, and the wooden parts of ploughs if they were needed. Elm was self-explanatory, and so, after Harriot's earlier explanation, were sassafras trees (their function in building was not specified). The sweet bay, which seems to have been his *Ascopo*, had a hot, spicy bark, though he did not make clear what it could be used for. He had Indian names for many more trees but had no means of identifying them, nor would it be necessary after what he had said of others.

When he came to other building materials he was less surely at home, as he may not have considered this aspect in detail while he was in Virginia. He did stress that there was no stone anywhere near the seashore, except for a few pebbles brought down into Albemarle Sound. In their travels some had seen hard, "raggy" (rough-surfaced?) stones, great pebbles, and a kind of gray stone like marble, of which the Indians made hatchets to cleave wood. Indians said there was plenty of stone inland. What was found were clearly erratics brought down from the piedmont by the rivers, though Lane's expedition may have seen rock outcrops farther up the Roanoke River. Stones were rarities among the Indians of the coastlands—one crude stone ax and a few rough stones to support cooking pots have been found on Roanoke Island—and were traded from the interior. As an after-thought, Harriot reported that one man found a bed of hard "rag" stone some 120 miles away, but he did not know where nor do we. Quartz pebbles (jasper) from streambeds, flaked for arrowheads by the Indians, were not valuable to him.

Brick was another matter. There was clay on the island and in various other parts which would make good brick. Certainly brick was made on Roanoke Island, though the specimens so far found were not of the highest quality; many had broken, and others had been used for sharpening tools or weapons. Clay from the banks of the Chowan and Roanoke rivers would make brick of better quality. Lime too was no problem, as oyster shells were so plentiful—middens having largely been cleared for liming fields at later times—

while he also remarked that there were places along the shore, presumably inside the sounds, where oyster shells lined the water in unlimited quantity.

The making of the settlement in 1585 had given Harriot's associates experience in timber construction, but he does not appear to have shown any interest in techniques of construction or in what sorts of dwellings it was possible to build quickly. We are almost certain White drew the 1585 fortifications and settlement in detail, but that these drawings were among those lost in June 1586. He was evidently not at Harriot's side to remind him of what exactly had been done and how effective or otherwise the construction had been over the ten months it had been occupied. Settlers could gain a good deal from Harriot but he is of more interest to us now as the scientist trying to scale down his survey to the level of the ordinary colonist. But his ambition to publish went far beyond this small volume—significant as it is as the first English book based on first-hand observation in any part of North America. He said that he and White had not been able to draw all the birds seen and even eaten "for want of leisure" but that "after we are better furnished and stored upon further discovery, with their strange beasts, fish, trees, plants, and herbs they shall be published."

The survey was not completed in the time they had had and much had been lost at their departure (though he did not stress this). But he and White hoped to come back to continue their collaboration so that in the end a great illustrated handbook on the natural resources of North America could be completed and published. This was a noble aspiration but one that was never to be achieved, even though a fragmentary selection of one aspect of the survey, notes to engravings of some of White's Indian drawings, did, in the end, see the light and helped to bring him a measure of international fame.

The nature and nurture of the new land may not have come to light fully in what Harriot and White have left us, but they had, between them, made an imperishable beginning.

The World of Men

The world of men as John White and Thomas Harriot saw it before it was influenced by European intervention is in many respects the fullest and most complete panorama in the history of North America after 1500. Both partners kept a clear eye on the people who inhabited the area into which the English intruded and were able to transmit in line, color, and words more than we can ever know again about these people, who were never to be seen subsequently in their natural environment. It is, of course, the visual evidence that is irreplaceable. Nowadays, the archaeologist can tell a great deal about the material life of the people with whom he is concerned. But when a world was dependent on perishable, wooden articles of everyday life, the main structures of indigenous society cannot be revived, nor indeed can the appearance of the people be envisaged. All studies of the Late Woodland peoples at the last stage of their independent existence must go back to White's drawings and be aided by Harriot's words, even if we have more literary materials on the Virginia Indians of the early seventeenth century, though none that regarded them so closely and so dispassionately.

White had been trained in London in a school of practical painters. The guild of Painter Stainers where a John White appears in 1580 was composed of men who decorated houses and furnishings with paint. This is not to say they were house painters. The interiors of Elizabethan structures were elaborately decorated and this required artistic skills beyond those of the routine craftsman. Further, pageants, masques, and plays increasingly played a part in Elizabethan life and needed men of artistic skills to create the scenes and extravaganzas with which they were filled. White branched out from this area into wider fields. He was able to see the work of foreigners like

Cornelius Ketel and Lucas de Heere who were in London in the 1570s, and above all to link up with Jacques Le Moyne de Morgues. Le Moyne was a French painter who had been trained at the French court in developing the art of the miniaturist into the realistic representation of flowers and birds, as well as portraits. Moreover, he had been in North America in 1564–65 until chased away by the Spanish, making drawings of Indians and no doubt of fauna and flora. He had settled in London as a refugee Huguenot after the massacre of St. Bartholomew in 1572.

How and when White met Le Moyne we do not know, but he was influenced by Le Moyne as a painter and absorbed in the subject matter of his paintings. He learned from him but did not copy his style: like a true artist, he developed his own. This showed some outside influences from continental examples of paintings apart from those of Le Moyne. Yet much of the method White learned was original. His use of watercolor in a wide range of colors and with careful techniques employing both line and wash had not hitherto been developed in England. He may have learned something from what appears to have been another of his skills, the making of estate and house plans. These, if drawn on the ground by survey techniques, were often afterward highly colored in watercolor to demonstrate to owners of property the special characteristics of the buildings, fields, and vegetation of their lands; because they were attractive as well as useful, they were also often employed as wall hangings. Maps, too—and topographical mapping was developing fast in England in the 1570s—were normally colored in wash to bring out special features and enhance their appearance, whereas figures and scenes were added even to subjects and plans whose primary purpose was utilitarian. Somehow White picked up these skills and combined them into a distinctive technique and style, with touches of Mannerist exaggeration and formalizing, though we do not know where and from whom he learned them.[1]

After an Eskimo had been brought to London in 1576 by Martin Frobisher and was painted by Ketel and de Heere, his oriental features inspired someone to employ John White to accompany Frobisher on an Arctic voyage in 1577 to make a full record of these Asiatic-looking people who might guide the English through the supposed Northwest Passage to Asia. White's drawing of an encounter between English and Eskimo—a band of the Thule Inuit—in Baffin Island we have in a copy or an original. His picture of a captured man was done slowly and carefully on the spot after his capture: the same was true of his picture of a woman and child picked up later in a brutal and insensitive manner. He showed how these people lived, though most of his paintings of them were lost. Yet he illustrated his unique talent for bringing out the features and clothing in minute detail, which was to stand him in good stead in the Roanoke colony.[2] A small book of engravings of these Eskimos was published in London in 1578. Because no copies of it now survive, we cannot reconstruct precisely what it contained, or whether White's name was ever mentioned as the maker of the drawings on which the engravings were based. But sufficient copies and derivatives of engravings from it have now been traced, and linked to the surviving White Eskimo drawings, to make it clear that the book circulated in the Netherlands and Germany, at least, though no traces of its use in England have so far been found. White, even if not publicly recognized, had made a mark in the portrayal of exotic, if unwilling, visitors to England well before his employment by Ralegh to go to North America. He, at least, would have known of White's earlier achievements.

His sketches on the 1584 expedition are not extant, but there is little doubt that he made many notes and drawings of what he saw and that these gave him some idea of what to record when he returned fully equipped in 1585. We have already followed his voyage through the Caribbean and caught a glimpse of the valuable record he made, which could supplement or even replace the written narrative. But it was when he came to the Outer Banks that he really set about making, not merely the arduous map surveys we have noted, but also the intimate and revealing—and above all sympathetic—drawings of Indians and Indian life. These are among the most valuable records of all the Roanoke voyages.

White's quick sketches were probably first made with black lead in small sketch books that he could carry about easily, with notes of colors and details to be worked up later on. But once installed on Roanoke Island he was able to draw from life as well as to work up his field sketches into finished drawings, using all the skills he had learned during his formative period as a practical craftsman in England and on his Arctic voyage. Excellent examples of drawings that must first have been done rapidly as sketches and notes are those of the villages of Secotan and Pomeioc, made during the first brief visit of Sir Richard Grenville in July but clearly developed afterward on Roanoke Island when the colony had been established. Into them he put a comprehensive picture of native life in its untouched (we might say uncontaminated) form. So too some of the portraits of persons from these villages must have had a similar history.

In the case of both village drawings, he is able to give us a picture taken, as it were, from above the site, looking obliquely across it, so that all the details can be picked up in partial perspective. The setting of feathery trees into which Secotan is placed gives the picture its context.[3] It allows the houses to intermingle with the forest and illustrates how the clearings were cut out of the surrounding wood-land—the insignia of a Woodland culture that had existed in eastern North America for more than 1,500 years before this time. A wide central path runs through the village but only a few of the houses are arranged systematically along it, ending with two houses lying ob-liquely across it. Four houses are indeed set end-on to the path and one on its side whereas four others are scattered through the wood-land, and there is the suggestion that this open settlement may have been larger than he shows. It has a casual, unplanned appearance, combined with sharp differentiation of functions in its layout. A freshwater pond, dug for the purpose, is shown at the top of the picture, and the cornfields, already commented on in connection with Thomas Harriot's description of corn cultivation, are shown on the right-hand side of the picture. The longhouses are shown from various angles owing to their irregular distribution and display clearly their pole and frame construction, with their mat coverings in place. The ends of all but one of them are open and the sleeping benches down each side are visible. Window openings are also shown in the sides. For their dimensions we must rely on Harriot, who is cited below. These are the first and only directly-observed longhouses of the coastal Algonquian Indians and as such reveal much about their character, if not a great deal about their interior contents. The large house with the closed gable end and a door opening in the middle of this, as it is adjacent to the cornfields, may have been where the dried corn and other produce were stored for winter use.

The following text labels appear within the drawing:

Their rype corne

Their greene corne

Corne newly sprong

Their sitting at meate

The place of Solemne prayer

The house wherin the Tombe of their Herounds standeth.

SECOTON

A Ceremony in their prayers w strange iestures and songs dansing abowt posts carued on the topps lyke mens faces.

16. John White's Drawing of the Open Village of Secotan.
British Museum, Department of Prints and Drawings, 1906-5-9-1 (7).

In the version of this picture that was engraved, evidently from a different model, a closely packed patch of squashes and gourds is growing in what, in the original version, is a bare area, surrounded by a loose fence of upright stakes. Clearly any fires would be too dangerous to be laid inside the fragile structure of the houses, and the fire shown on the central path, between one group of houses, was used communally for cooking purposes. The main cooked food was corn, usually combined with other vegetables and meat and fish constituents into a stew. No cooking pot is shown here. The bird watcher's hut in the ripening cornfield is a platform on stout legs, on which is erected a pole and mat shelter, tall enough to allow the watcher to sit and look out over the bird-threatened grain. On the main path, somewhat below the houses and some distance from the first of them, mats are laid on the ground and people are eating from large platters of clay or wood laid on them. They are sitting in various postures on the ground, and the inscription, "Their sittinge at meate," indicates that this was a normal practice. This is not documented elsewhere.[4]

At the bottom limit of the corn patches there is a path and beyond it a row of posts set far apart in the ground, evidently to mark a boundary. This boundary might appear to be that between the ordinary living area and that devoted to communal and, especially, religious activities—the one, of course, was not distinct from the other. On the left-hand side of the main pathway there is another fire, evidently maintained for ceremonial purposes and labeled by White "The place of solemn prayer." Around it are various ill-defined shapes, which may be of stone or wood, having some ritual function. The small house to the left of this is probably associated with the activities of their priest or shaman. In the foreground is a high but short-sided longhouse, which is described as "The house wherein the tombs of their 'Herounds' [weroances] standeth." In the center, on the pathway, five figures are crouched down, heads bent forward looking toward the right where there is a circle of wooden posts with carved tops, and around which a dance is being performed. A single crouched figure on the right suggests that he or she, like those on the path, is waiting to take part in the dance in due course. This is captioned "A ceremony in their prayers with strange jestures and songs dancing about posts carved on the tops like men's faces."

White was to elaborate some of these features in later pictures. The engraved version adds to the spaces between trees and houses on the left, irregular patches—two in each case—of tobacco and sunflowers.

The whole assemblage is the nearest thing we have to a view of Indian life in progress without any trace of European intervention. The figures are engaged in the normal tasks of watching a fire, possibly mending a tear in a mat on one of the houses, squatting to eat, standing guard with bow and arrow, or participating in the complex ceremony of crouching and dancing described above. The lightness and airiness of the drawing conveys very well the nature of the people who were scattered throughout the woodlands of eastern North America at this time, having little of permanence in many of their habitation sites and yet creating in them a communal presence that revealed a closely-integrated society, even if one that could move itself rapidly and effectively from one site to another in a short time. In this single picture White shows us more about the character of Woodland Indian life than could many thousands of words.

The other village of which White gave us so much detail, Pomeioc (or Pomeiooc), is very much more an enclosed social group (except that in a copy of his drawing cornfields—not shown in the surviving original—were added outside the village).[5] Here the longhouses are jammed closely against one another, nine of them as large as the largest in Secotan, but seven of them of smaller sizes (and these have the gable ends closed with door-like openings). Some of the houses are covered with bark instead of mats. One very large structure has a quite different type of roof, tiers of mats rising to a pyramid-like top and the rest totally enclosed by mats or bark. This building is thought to have had some ceremonial and religious function but it is not clear precisely what—to call it a temple might be to assume too much even though in a later note Harriot does so, and indicates one of the adjacent houses as the chief's dwelling. Some of the small houses are probably storehouses, but the whole represents a much larger and more closely-knit social group, emphasized by the palisade of stout posts that surrounds it. The entry is a narrowing track which beyond the palisade is marked by an interlaced, cane border. Here the central space around which the houses cluster is much larger, proportionately, than that for Secotan; at its center a major fire is burning and many of the inhabitants are seated around it. Family groups, usually a man, woman, and child, stand near some of the houses. Several men are standing armed as if they are acting as sentinels, though there is no such figure at the entrance. Others are lounging around in casual postures, one of them with a medium-sized, sharp-nosed dog, the only representation of this domesticated animal we have for eastern North America. The pond was, as Harriot says, dug out to provide fresh water, if there was none nearby.

The villages of Secotan and Pomeioc clearly represented a way of life that was characteristic of most of the coastal bands, though not all of them appear to have had year-round residences. Some small bands lived in primitive shelters near the shore, subsisting almost wholly from gathering and using whatever shelter the woods could provide in winter weather. The population of the villages too was depleted, probably drastically, twice a year: in spring and early summer many moved to the shores where crustacea and fish were most easily taken in quantity and camped out there; in winter most of the men and probably some women went on long-distance hunts into the forest. We cannot tell how far they followed the practice of the Virginia Indians of clearing the understory in the woods by controlled burning so as to leave rides open for the chase. This would have been possible only in open woodland such as that found on Roanoke Island, and not in the swamp forests covering much of this area.

Harriot's own note on the longhouses might very well suggest that merely estimating size from appearance in the White village pictures is an inadequate measure. He says:

> Their houses are made of small poles made fast at the tops in round form after the manner as is used in many arbours in England, in most towns covered with barks, and some with artificial [i.e., manufactured] mats made of long rushes from the tops of the houses down to the ground. The length of them is commonly double to the breadth. In some places they are but 12 and 16 yards long and in other some we have seen of 24.

According to this, houses would range from 36 by 8 feet to 72 by 36 feet. This would seem to accord with observations of other travelers farther north. We should probably assume that an extended family of relatives occupied each house—remembering that the society was matrilineal and therefore relationships were not those of a European patrilineal social order.

Harriot's summary on the villages indicates that generally they were not large, especially near the seashore. They contained from ten to twenty houses, with the largest seen (Skicóac) having only thirty. In some of the enclosed villages—White did not draw one— bark covered the stakes forming the palisade; others had the open pole palisade of Pomeioc, and still others were undefended settlements like Secotan. Whether these were characteristic of one group rather than another is not known: they may have been merely choices made pragmatically when a village was established and developed.

White reinforced the village pictures with individual studies based both on rapid sketches made during the early explorations and, thereafter, on more thorough examination at his leisure on Roanoke Island and nearby. Notable among these was the fishing scene, clearly composed from many sketches and not intended to be wholly realistic as it shows the fish through the water.[6] Low sandy shores in the distance and a beach in the foreground delimit a narrow channel. A fish weir runs out into the water, the lines of canes focusing on a rectangular trap inside which fish are shown. Two similar weirs are seen in the distance. A large dugout canoe shows men cooking fish on board (on a stone?) while others are propelling the boat with long paddles; several of them are using nets, a long pole net and a small hand net. In the mid-distance are men using long spears or darts, tipped, we are told, with the tail of a spider crab, in order to spear fish—the water being only knee deep. Overhead a brown pelican and two swans are flying. On the near shore plants are growing down to the water, with a horseshoe crab and hermit crabs moving along the edge. The whole joins the human and the natural world closely together, marking their interdependence and the exploitation of nature by man.

One facet of native custom that clearly fascinated White and Harriot related to their method of preserving and displaying the dead, or at least dead chiefs, and possibly the elders, of the groups. This was the mortuary temple.[7] In the drawing one of the longhouses is

The manner of their fishing.

17. John White's Composite Drawing of a Fishing Scene.
British Museum, Department of Prints and Drawings, 1906-5-9-1 (6).

shown with the mats drawn back from the gable; inside is a platform, raised more than halfway up the sides of the building, on
which are lying pale, skeleton-like forms, the heads toward the front.
Behind them is a row of large covered baskets of rectangular shape,
carefully covered. At one side near the front is an idol, a squatting
figure not unlike a European, wearing a large hat and brightly colored paint or covering. He is not too-well defined in the drawing so
perhaps White had merely a glimpse of what was there and the
actual figure was quite different. Below the platform two deerskin
mats are laid on the ground. White gives this description of the
picture, the fullest he adds to any of his drawings:

> The tomb of their *weroances* [whom he calls "Cherounes"] or
> chief personages, their flesh clean taken off from the bones save
> the skin and hair of their heads, which flesh is dried and en-
> folded in mats laid at their feet, their bones, also being made
> dry, are covered with deer skins, not altering their form or
> proportion. With their "Kywash," which is an image of wood
> keeping the dead.

The engraving takes a different view, this time from inside the building. We see the structure of poles and bent boughs making the
curved roof with their ties and the supports of the platform, two
stout posts, which maintain the structure on which the bodies are
laid. They are more sharply defined but in general follow the form of
the original drawing. Where the engraving differs is in placing a
priestly figure on the ground, tending a small fire beside the mats on
which, presumably, he lay. The notes attached by Harriot say of the
idol "Kiwasa":

> For they are persuaded that the same doth keep the dead
> bodies of their chief lords that nothing may hurt them. More-
> over under the foresaid scaffold some one of their priests hath
> his lodging which mumbleth his prayers night and day, and
> hath charge of the corpses. For his bed he hath two deer skins
> spread on the ground: if the weather be cold he maketh a fire
> to warm by withal. These poor souls are thus instructed by
> nature to reverence their princes even after their death.

Here, White shows a desire to penetrate further than he usually did into the inner concepts and beliefs of the people, and his drawing certainly brings into graphic relief one of their formal ceremonial practices. There is a note of condescension, which is also unusual for him.

His other communal activity is much less graphic and original but more human. It shows a young man and woman sitting on the ground at the side of a mat, eating with their hands from a dish of boiled corn.[8] The cheerful appearance of the woman brings her to life. The accompanying note to the engraving says that, having laid their food on the ground, "the men upon one side and women on the other" they eat "Maize sodden [boiled or stewed], deer's flesh or some other beast and fish." Harriot adds: "They are very sober in their eating and drinking and consequently very long-lived because they do not oppress nature." Thus Harriot shows his own preference for a simple diet and his belief that adherence to it lengthens life. This fits in with what we know of his personal austerity in later life, mitigated only by his reliance on tobacco.

Other communal arrangements were not forgotten. A setting similar to the fire scene in the Pomeioc picture is given for "Their manner of praying with rattles about the fire."[9] The picture is one of White's most impressive group portraits. A man is seated orating at a fire (the smoke almost obscuring his features), around which a group of men and women, also seated, are listening attentively and waving gourd rattles in time with what must have been a rhythmic speech. The whole group is absorbed in the ritual and there is a real sense of group participation. According to the note attached to the engraving of White's drawing, this ceremony took place "when they have escaped any great danger by sea or land or have returned from the war" as a joyful token of their deliverance or victory. In fact, it was probably a tradition by which a recital of past history, true and mythical, was woven into a celebration for which there is no precise parallel in eastern North America. The leader was possibly the shaman of the group who was in some sense the guardian of its history and the recorder of its feats in battle.

White's largest and most ambitious drawing was that of the green corn ceremony celebrated around a circle of posts very much as seen in the Secotan drawing.[10] Fourteen men and women decorated with paint, some holding twigs and some rattles, are dancing around the circle of posts—on the tops of which are carved faces of men or superhuman beings. In the center are three women around whom the ceremony revolves. Such a ceremony was widely practiced among Woodland Indians, though the Secotan drawing is the only early representation of it. According to the notes on the engraving, the participants included not only the local groups but also visitors, who were distinguished by marks on their shoulders indicating the village or tribe from which they came (and, indeed, a later engraving substantiates this). It might appear that at the corn ripening there was a sequence of ceremonial exchanges between the villages to make up a series of such dancing ceremonies. The precise function of the young women in the middle of the circle is not known, though perhaps they are symbols of fertility.

The boat-building technique (represented by an engraving only and not by a drawing) demonstrates another communal activity, the hollowing of a canoe from a tree.[11] Harriot's notes tell of the slow, patient process of burning through the trunk so as not to damage the main body of the tree. When the tree had fallen, every branch (and, of course, the top) was carefully removed by fire. The tree trunk was then lifted and placed on a stand, made from branches laid between two sets of crossed and tied posts like a saw-horse. The bark was scraped off and the hollowing process begun. In the engraving, sharp shells, conch and scallop we suspect, are shown being used as scrapers, first to remove the bark and then, after fires have been lit in the trunk, to hollow out the interior by scratching at the charred wood, until the whole interior of the tree has been excavated. The wood of the white cedar and the tulip tree was especially suited for this purpose as the inner layers are not necessarily as hard as the outer. The art and craft of making these canoes—some of them, we are told, large enough to hold twenty men—was a task for the winter, when leaves were off and the sap was down. Judging by the number of canoes seen and, indeed, needed by these people, the making of the dugout canoes was the major industrial activity of many of the coastal groups. How seaworthy they were is not evident, but they could be used freely on the sounds for much of the year. No sails were seen; long and short paddles and poles were used to propel them.

Besides these more elaborate scenes are several showing day-to-day activities. "The broiling of their fish over the flame" details the making of a primitive broiler.[12] "They stick up in the ground 4 stakes in a square room and lay 4 posts upon them and others over thwart the same unto a hurdle of sufficient height." They laid the fish on this structure and lit a fire underneath, "and other fish they hang on sticks set upright in the ground" and placed them against the barbecue frame. Evidently the fish was cooked slowly over a small fire so that it would not burn. Harriot compared this with what he knew of Florida, where the process was one of drying fish for storage. Here, he claims, there was no storage, rather, all the fish was eaten when cooked. Not all subsequent writers are sure this was so, as dried sea fish could have been a valuable product for trade with the interior.

In another domestic scene a pot is boiling over a fire.[13] "The women," Harriot tells us, "know how to make earthern vessels with special cunning and that so large and fine that our potters with their wheels can make no better." The making of large cooking pots was certainly an old and valued art in the area and the method of doing so had not changed for centuries. The shell tempered clay was coiled from the bottom upward and was shaped as it was built up by fabric (string wound around dowels) tools, which left impressions on the pot. At the bottom tip a cap or point of clay was placed to complete its conical shape. The art was in maintaining an evenly balanced structure and then baking the pot upside down on a slow fire. Such a pot was found and reconstructed when the foundations of the 1585 fort were being excavated on Roanoke Island. For cooking purposes the pot was placed on a heap of earth, point (or knob) downward, to keep it from falling over, and then sticks of wood were placed carefully around it so that the heat reached the pot evenly. "They or their women [suggesting men took some part in cooking] fill the vessel with water and then put there in fruit, flesh and fish and let all boil together like a gallimaufrey, which the Spaniards call *olla podrida.*" They then put the food into dishes and set it before the company and "then they make good cheer together."

Corn is a prominent ingredient of the stew shown in the drawing. Harriot uses the occasion to preach one of his favorite doctrines—abstinence: "Yet are they moderate in their eating whereby they avoid sickness. I would to God we would follow their example.

For we would be free from many kinds of diseases, which we fall into by sumptuous and unseasonable banquets, continually devising new sauces and provocation of gluttony to satisfy our insatiable appetites." Harriot might indeed be a modern dietitian. He may obliquely be casting aspersions not only on English overeating in general, which in the moneyed classes was notorious throughout Europe, but also on his fellow colonists who gobbled up their stores so fast that they had to suffer hunger in the end. Against such practices he set the Native American example.

The remainder of White's pictures is a gallery of individuals, some sketched in brief visits, such as those to Secotan, Pomeioc, and Dasemunkepeuc (though he may well have visited the latter village on a number of later occasions). Although his pictures of communal life on Roanoke Island—depicting both the inhabitants and the settlers—have disappeared, we can probably conclude that most of the drawings of the individuals that survive were carefully drawn, with the full knowledge of their subjects, on Roanoke Island or nearby. The other group of missing drawings is that made during the winter visit to the Chesapeake country, which we might assume he gave to the colony that he brought out to settle there in 1587.

The respect he showed for individual personality in these drawings was outstanding and makes it clear that he was being wholly objective. They were not "mere savages" but men and women he had come to know and to esteem.

The aged man of Pomeioc is typical of his drawings of individuals.[14] He shows an elderly man "covered," as the note to the engraving says, "with a large skin which is tied upon their shoulders on one side and hangeth down beneath their knees, wearing their other arm naked out of the skin so that they may be at more liberty. Those skins are dressed with the hair on and lined with other furred skins." The man is lean, wrinkled but clearly healthy and vigorous. There is just a suspicion of hair on his face and the note says that, whereas young men vigorously scraped away any facial hairs, the old let them grow, though "to say truth they come up very thin." The fact that the man wears a deerskin mantle lined with other furs indicates that the people were able to provide warm skin clothing when the climate demanded, as it did for only a few months of the year, and that they were far from being "naked savages."

One of White's most attractive drawings is of the wife of one of the *weroances* of Pomeioc and her daughter, the latter holding an English doll in her hand.[15] The woman's appearance was characteristic of the region "for they wear their hair trussed up in a knot and have their skins pounced" or, as we would say, tattooed; "they wear a chain of great pearls or beads of copper or smooth bones, 5 or 6 fold about their necks, bearing one arm in the same [while] in the other they carry a gourd full of some kind of pleasant liquor." Harriot finds some difficulty in describing their single apron skirt, which is drawn up almost to their breasts and reaches below their knees, with nothing to compare with it behind. In the picture, this is elaborately fringed at the edges and inset with beads or pearls behind the fringe. With the woman is a little girl of seven or eight. Harriot writes about young girls in general "wearing about them a girdle of skin, which hangeth down behind, and is drawn underneath between their 'twist' and bound above their navel with moss of trees between that and their skins to cover their privities." The basic breechclout was thus worn by female children of prepubertal age. (The children after about the age of ten, we are told, wore deerskins as their elders did.) The girl's doll is dressed in Elizabethan costume, evidence that some real effort had been made to find acceptable gifts for different groups in the population.

Another woman, this time from Dasemunkepeuc, is dressed like the woman of Pomeioc, though she does not wear the headbands adopted by women of other villages and is not tattooed on the legs.[16] The women of this village were distinguished by their "strange manner of bearing their children quite contrary to ours. They taking their son by the right hand bear him on their backs, holding the left thigh on their left arm." The child shown with the woman in this picture is holding onto her back with one hand, while she is firmly holding his right arm over her shoulder. Clearly the child would have to exert himself to avoid placing his full weight on a single arm, and this may have helped him to develop his strength at an early age, although his mother has tucked his left leg under her other arm. This left her freer to move about than the English fashion of holding the child to the breast, and forced him to become more independent. The male child here is naked.

The Secotan women were designated as "of reasonable good proportion," suggesting that White and Harriot preferred their appearance to the women of some other villages.[17] In the drawing the woman wears the decorated apron skirt but this time it is the double variety, the second skin covering the rear. Harriot remarked on how well the deerskins were dressed, so perhaps this group excelled in this art. The hair is cut across the forehead in a fringe; the rest, which is thin and soft and not overlong, falls down around the shoulders, and the woman wears a decorated headband. She is elaborately tattooed, and her neck chain is either tattooed or painted on. The ear decorations are "chains of long pearls and some smooth bones" thus pulling down the lobes somewhat, but the nails are kept short. Harriot takes the opportunity of commenting on the facial appearance of the women in general: "they have small eyes, plain and flat noses, narrow foreheads and broad mouths." And, indeed, these features are characteristic of White's women, though their features are individualized and vary in some degree from person to person.

Harriot clearly liked to watch the Indian women: "they are delighted with walking in the fields and beside the rivers to see the deer and hunting of fish." He seems to regard them as mainly decorative and not, as in reality, occupied much of the time in the fields, in dressing skins and decorating them, in making pottery, besides maintaining their households and families. This might suggest that Harriot did not penetrate far into the domestic economy of the household or considered it of less importance than the appearance and leisure activities of the women. But in giving them so much attention White showed his desire to carry back with him a collective picture of persons, female as well as male, who could interest his sponsors in the individual villagers, and not simply their communal life. The degree of trust he inspired, in having such close contact with the village women, is also impressive.

White's men are even more sharply individualized, as has been suggested in the case of the old man of Pomeioc.[18] The priest is one of them. Those of Secotan (and there were clearly a number) "are well striken in years and as it seemeth of more experience [that is more cultivated in knowledge] than the common sort." They have a distinctive haircut and some ear hangings. But their most exceptional external feature is their dress: "they wear a short cloak made of fine hares' skins quilted with the hair outward"—these were made from rabbit skins cut around and around by the makers and then sewn into a net base, so as to give the impression of woven fur or cloth. The cloak was the priest's sole garment, we are told, but he would also wear a breechclout. They are described as being "notable enchanters" or wizards, who "for their pleasure frequent the rivers to kill with their bows and catch wild ducks swans and other fowls." The stress on leisure activities is also typical of White and Harriot's refusal to be limited to a purely economic or professional view of the people they pictured and described.

In contrast with the serious and dignified priest, there was the posturing "flier" or "conjuror" or "juggler" as he is variously described.[19] He was what later explorers would call the "medicine man," the shaman who could cure bodily and mental illnesses and forecast events by reading signs in the earth or heavens. Harriot says they "use strange gestures and often contrary to nature in their enchantments," though what he means by "contrary to nature" is not explained, except that "they be very familiar with devils of whom they inquire what their enemies do or other such things." Certainly, foreseeing the future was one of their functions, but how they communicated with their "devils" is not indicated. Like other men, they shaved the sides of their heads, leaving only a crest or roach, and fastened above one of their ears "a small black bird as a badge of their office." In the drawing it looks very much like a common grackle. They wore a girdle and tucked in a skin to cover their sexual parts. The drawing shows a grinning animal mask in the center of the skin, though the animal is not identifiable. Attached to the girdle was their medicine bag, though it is unlikely that either Harriot or White penetrated into its contents: they had to leave that to the imagination, though, among other things, it would certainly include tobacco for use in curative and ceremonial functions.

Two male leaders complete the gallery. One is a *weroance* of Roanoke, conceivably one of their particular friends, Granganimeo or Ensenore, who died at an inopportune time.[20] This is an elderly man, with deep wrinkles in his face. His hair is shaved, as the shaman's was, on the sides, leaving only a roach or cockscomb erect down the middle. The rest of the hair is worn long and trussed up in a knot at the back. They did not paint or tattoo themselves but hung pearls or copper beads or smooth bone from their ears. The au-

18. John White's Drawing of a Shaman ("The Flyer").
British Museum, Department of Prints and Drawings, 1906-5-9-1 (16).

thority of such men was marked both by a chain of great pearls, copper beads, or smooth bone hanging from their necks, and, more precisely, by a breast plate of copper, a gorget, hanging from a string. This would have been stone or natural copper but it was soon replaced by a larger plate of European copper, cut square, obtained from the colonists and shown as such in the drawing. From later reports it would appear that, before the Europeans left, a hierarchy, as we might term it, of gorgets had been established: the largest for the chiefly leaders, smaller for *weroances*, or counselors, and smaller still for lesser men. There was no distinction in basic costume between the *weroances* and the better-ranking women, as both used the double apron skirt. The note brings them to life: "moreover they fold their arms together as they walk or as they talk one with another in sign of wisdom." The counselors collectively had power to advise but evidently not to impose their will on the ruler, whose authority—at least in matters of war—was absolute.

The most striking figure of all is the chief,[21] here almost certainly Wingina, dressed for "their general huntings" (about which we could well learn more, though this is the only place they are mentioned) or for "their solemn feasts"—such as the dance ceremony already discussed. His dress may be taken as typical of chiefs in general. Their hairstyle was similar to that of the other men, but the roach was more striking and they stuck a long feather in the top, with two shorter feathers at the sides, reaching out over their ears. In the drawing clearly these appear to be turkey feathers. Their ear hangings were elaborate: heavy pearls, a claw of some great bird, or something else that struck their fancy. They either tattooed or painted their forehead, cheeks, chin, body, arms, and legs in patterns. Here extensive use of body paint strengthens the gaudy but impressive picture, with its predominance of red, which might in this case be red ochre. They wore a chain of copper beads or pearls around their necks and bracelets of the same materials on their arms. There were scarification spots under their breasts from which they let blood when they were ill (such odd interpolations adding to our knowledge of customs not detailed elsewhere). Around their middle they wrapped the skin of a beast so that the tail hung down behind. In the picture, the tail is clearly that of a puma or mountain lion, probably encountered on a winter hunting excursion at no great distance. The man in the drawing carries a cane quiver, with his bow ready bent in one hand and an arrow in the other. "In this manner," we are told, "they go to war or to their solemn feasts and banquets." Although their recreation was said to be hunting deer, when going to battle their war paint was elaborated so that they could look as "terrible" as possible.

This gallery, then, introduces us to men and women whom we can see in the group pictures, and in the engraving which shows the back markings indicating places of origin.[22] This system appears to be unique to this area. We get to know these people and to accept their differences from Europeans while at the same time seeing in them the common humanity which they share with them. There is no suggestion of inferiority: they were as fitted to their own surroundings as Europeans were to theirs.

Time after time we must regret that we do not have more of Harriot's detailed notes. What he says about the layout of native society makes more precise what is mentioned about it in the writings of both Arthur Barlowe and Ralph Lane. Harriot enables us to see for ourselves not great groupings of villages under a single lord, but rather a variety of hegemonies:

> In some places of the country one only town belongeth to the government of a "Wiróans" or chief lord [here he excludes the advisers from the title of weroance and confines the word to a chief], in other some 2 or 3, in some 6, 8 and more. The greatest "Wiróans" that yet we had dealing with had but 18 towns in his government, and [was] able to make not above 7 or 800 fighting men at the most.

This enables us to see Wingina as an aspiring ruler of a small number of villages who hoped by diplomacy or war to enlarge his lordship, and probably reckoned that the Europeans would help him to do so, though he was mistaken in this because they had no desire to upset existing relationships between the indigenous groups. The eighteen-village-chief was possibly the head of the Weapemeoc group, which contained most villages on the White-Harriot map.

With his special interest in language, Harriot noted "the language of every government is different from any other, and the further they are distant the greater the difference." This dialectal variation would apply, of course, only to the southern Algonquian groups, and not to the Iroquois. The Secotan group was the most southerly to have been encountered (though coastal Algonquians may have occupied a thin coastal strip appreciably farther to the south), and the Chesapeakes the most northerly. It is clear that at the time Harriot was more interested in the form of the words he wrote down (he may already have devised a form of his phonetic script) than their exact meaning, especially when they applied to living creatures. He can be credited, in turn, with giving the native peoples some English words to incorporate in their vocabulary, though we have seen one of them, "China," backfire on him in the form "Tsinaw." Nevertheless, his reference to dialects is an example of his scientific method.

His account of Indian warfare is also interesting:

> Their manner of wars among themselves is either by sudden surprising one another most commonly about the dawning of the day, or moonlight, or else by ambushes, or some subtle devices [though it is a pity he did not detail them]. Set battles are very rare, except it fall out where there are many trees, where either part may have some hope of defence, after the delivery of every arrow, in leaping behind some or other.

Le Moyne had shown, in his engraving of French Florida in the 1560s, that the Timucua and adjacent tribes in Florida engaged in set battles, in which the French also participated as allied combatants on one side or another, as Champlain was later to do in Canada. This was no part of the intentions of the English. Whatever antagonisms may have arisen between them and particular groups, notably with Wingina's, they do not appear to have taken sides in aboriginal conflicts. Had they done so the work of carrying out the survey would have been made much more difficult, if not impossible. As it was, Lane's wrangles with Menatonon and with Wingina may have hampered them to some extent, but not appreciably. They were fortunate, when with the Chesapeakes, to keep out of the range of the Powhatans, who could have proved dangerous enemies. But there is little indication that either White or Harriot were attacked or received with overt hostility during their research, even though this involved prying into Indian lifestyles, customs, and environments. The objects of the survey were peaceful; relations with the people they met were uniformly designed to develop a portrait which did not flatter or distort. This attitude was, almost without exception, an objective one. It would be interesting to know whether Manteo helped them, as he clearly could work with both Europeans and his fellow people in a cooperative manner. No doubt White's pen and brush and Harriot's questions in probably halting, if precise, Algonquian, created a great deal of curiosity, but evidently on the whole a friendly curiosity, and one that paid tribute to their patience and devotion to their task.

Englishmen and Native Americans

The whole question of the attitudes of the Native Americans toward Europeans and of Europeans toward them is a complex subject on which many different views have been expressed.[1] The Roanoke expeditions and attempted colonies represent the first sustained set of occasions when Englishmen and Native Americans came into contact for substantial periods of time. The question of the interrelationship between the peoples is one of great interest both for itself and for the future of continuing relations in the seventeenth century, even if it cannot be assumed that there was anything like complete continuity in this respect between what happened from 1584 to 1606 and what occurred later at Jamestown and elsewhere. Something of that relationship already has emerged in the narrative, but it may be worth elaborating to bring out, if possible, shades of differences in the approaches of individuals and groups on both sides toward each other. It may even be worthwhile to look back briefly at Christian, European, and, specifically, English attitudes toward non-European peoples in general.

For many centuries Christians of all shades and colors had been taught that non-Christians were barbarians, having taken over the Roman concept that the peoples outside the Empire were, by definition, inferior and could be classified as such. So those who were outside the Christian orbit (with the Muslim in a special category of intolerable deviants from Christianity) were outside the pale of what could be regarded as civilization and were, in fact, barbarians. Consequently, they must be treated as inferior because they had not chosen to become Christians, if the option of becoming so had been offered to them. If they were purely pagan, untouched by Christian contact, attitudes might remain somewhat ambiguous, and in the sixteenth century were still open to debate.

The concept of savagery versus civilization was something different: it was not an old sentiment but it was one that intensified in the early modern period as national groups became more self-conscious and as elites within them took on themselves the responsibility, or as they would have regarded it, the duty, of setting standards and drawing lines between savagery and civilization. In these circumstances, urbanized, educated Europeans, giving close allegiance to a monarch and to a sentiment of nationality, tended to regard as inferior any groups inside or on the borders of their own society who were markedly different in their customs and way of life. Thus, they could be treated harshly or brought less violently into the mainstream, or so it seemed, of national civilized society.

Such an attitude was held by some Elizabethan Englishmen toward many of the Welsh. It could be applied to the rude northern peasantry of England itself, with its penchant for living at least partly by cross-border robbery and plunder. Above all, it could be made to apply to the Irish.[2] Gaelic society and its mores might have a long history, but it seemed chaotic, irrational, and savage (even if Christian) to many Englishmen of the time, even if to a few of them it seemed to have its own rationale and to be acceptable on its own terms—at least within certain limits. An Irishman could be civilized, it was felt, if brought sufficiently under English influence, either by conveying him to England or by gradually bringing his people under closer English control in Ireland itself. The strength and resilience of the Irish resistance to this notion (and their own confidence in the superiority of their native society) often led Englishmen to continue to believe in their savagery or to blur their potentiality to become civilized. At least some of the Roanoke colonists had had experience in Ireland, notably Ralph Lane, who after 1586 was to resume his career there and indeed to die the knighted muster-master-general of that country just at the time when the last flickers of Irish resistance were dying.

The term "ignoble savagery" has been developed in recent years to indicate that the "savages" were outside the sphere of "civilized men." "Ignoble," if the term was used in this connection, meant that "savages" were common people, of strange habits, who were not "gentlemen," not that this implied any special stigma, but merely stated a social fact.

Christianity has always been ready, in theory and at times in practice, to recognize what might be described in a modern phrase as upward religious mobility, the transformation of barbarians into Christians by missionary activity. The pagan who moved into the Christian ranks, the ignorant superstitious rustic who could be induced to accept at least some of the ministrations of the church, ceased to be outside the pale of Christianity, though how far they might be allowed to move inside it depended on circumstances that might vary greatly. The mendicant orders had as their origin and purpose to bring Christianity both to barbarians and to persons inside or adjacent to their own society who might, even if nominally Christian, be regarded effectively as savages.

The new access to Oriental societies—Hindu, Buddhist, Confucian, and Shinto—as well as to animists of various sorts, brought problems to the Christian churches that hitherto had not been realized. How could these peoples be induced to give up their supposedly false gods when they were as firmly wedded to them as the Muslim to Mohammed? It was not until the 1540s that a new militant order, the Society of Jesus, was created to confront the rising tide of heresy inside Catholic Europe and also to find sophisticated means of penetrating the strange non-European societies, which aroused the missionary impulse to new and more wide-ranging endeavors than ever before since the early spread of Christianity. If in the East Indians were brown and Chinese yellow, color in itself could not prove an effective barrier to missionary activity, in spite of old physical and social inhibitions. The Asiatic societies must be treated on their own merits.

The Americas, however, offered very special problems. On the one hand the Spanish invaders were prepared to ride roughshod over all previous standards of civilized behavior in order to obtain wealth in bullion and jewels or even in power over agricultural workers in the more advanced areas. The *conquistadores* might well regard all American religions as those of devil worshipers with whom there could be no compromises. They must be wiped out with their (often) bloody rites. For churchmen, and indeed for the Spanish state (as the Catholic Kings made Roman Christianity the keynote of their society), some less drastic attitude and some more humane policies must be developed if the indigenes were not to be wiped out and if all

concepts of the Christian tradition of conversion of the barbarian
were not to be eliminated. There was, of course, the fact that Iberian,
and indeed much of Christian Mediterranean society, had turned a
blind eye to the position of black slaves. They were extensively used
and the Portuguese brought in many thousands of new ones from
Africa in the fifteenth century. Theoretically, such people, if they
accepted Christianity fully, ought to have been given at least nominal
freedom. In practice, blacks came to be regarded as subhuman, below the concern of Christians even as barbarians. Would the Native
Americans be placed within the same category?[3]

The long debates that were to take place in Spain toward the
middle of the sixteenth century as to whether some races of mankind were condemned to natural slavery, as Aristotle had argued,
proved inconclusive, but they showed the depth of the intellectual
dilemma with which the new imperial regimes were faced. In fact,
long before these debates were concluded practical steps had been
taken by both church and state (though it is difficult to separate them
in Habsburg Spain) to produce policies that opened up the possibilities of conversion to the Native Americans. The very fact that Pope
Alexander VI and Columbus had labeled the native peoples of the
Americas as oriental "Indians," and that the name stuck so firmly that
we still use it, had certain consequences. The peoples of the Americas had to have some rights to protection from extreme spoliation
and destruction. Thus, from 1500 down to the New Laws of the
Indies in 1542 (and the recopilatión of 1573), the state made attempts
to curb the excesses of exploitation of these peoples and eventually
to give them some recourse in law against severe oppression.

At the same time, it was felt that areas and peoples in the line of
advance (itself curbed from 1543 onward) should not be subjected
to massacre and enslavement merely because they were not already
Christians. The mass baptisms in conquered Mexico proved to be a
means of giving the Indians some slight measure of protection as
Christian Indians, while laying them open to punishments for not
being fully orthodox ones. Dominicans, Franciscans, and ultimately
Jesuits urged that pagan Indians be reached by missionaries before
they were subjected to secular conquest. Many attempts were made
to do this—for example, in western Florida, where Father Cancer
was killed by the Indians in 1549, and on Chesapeake Bay in 1570–

71, when a Jesuit mission was wiped out by those later known as the Powhatan Indians. This may have been because the local Indian priests wanted no rivals and could inspire deadly hostility against them or because the reputation of the Spanish as brutal and ruthless conquerors had spread so far that any representatives of Spain were treated as the forerunners of lay invaders.

In Spanish Florida after 1565 secular dominance over Indian tribes was normally first established before missionary activity was attempted. Indians who were bribed by gifts or, alternatively, brought within the tax-collecting net of Spanish officialdom, might be subjected to missionary activity aimed at integrating them into the hierarchical system established throughout the Spanish Indies. By this, a white elite dominated economically and administratively a subject but not wholly unprivileged Indian society that was at least nominally Christianized. The Indians of the Southeast proved difficult to convert. The Jesuits failed completely between 1565 and 1573 and withdrew. The Franciscans took their place. After 1573 conversion in the Sea Islands, where they concentrated, was slow, but gradually a simplified form of Christian doctrine was worked out and communicated to the Indians by the friars, along with restraints and alterations in their own customs (monogamy, for example), which would make the continuance of semiautonomous Indian societies tolerable to Spanish Christians. There were to be many rebellions before much progress in missionizing was achieved, but by the 1580s the friars were making progress as far north as St. Catherine's Island and working hard, though so far to little effect, with the Indians of Port Royal and St. Helena Sound. Indians who failed to eject the friars and yet refused to accept their perversion of traditional mores were forced to escape into the untouched interior.

On the other side of the coin, French would-be colonists between 1562 and 1565 (at Port Royal Sound and the St. Johns River), and in their intermittent contacts in the St. Helena Sound area in the 1570s, had made few attempts to turn Indians into Calvinists, even though some of them may well have wished to do so. For the most part they accepted Indian society as it was, studied it, traded with the Indians, fought with and alongside them, and were generally regarded by them as white invaders who might be tolerated for the goods they brought and the aid they gave without interfering with customary social habits. The very temporary character of French intervention may have created the impression that at no time would they seek to change Indian religious beliefs or social habits. This contrasted sharply with both Spanish tradition and practice.

How far Englishmen were affected and influenced by Spanish and French experiences in the Americas by the time the Roanoke voyages were begun is difficult to evaluate. From 1555 onward there had been available descriptions in English of the activities of the Spanish in the New World, at first favorable and later unfavorable. In 1563, and again in 1582, Jean Ribault's brief account of French Florida (mainly, in fact, modern South Carolina) had helped to induce a favorable attitude toward the inhabitants. A number of translations in the late 1570s and the early 1580s had given specific information on Spanish conquests and achievements; primarily in their own words, and therefore basically favorable by implication. From 1578, however, the man who had tried above all to create in Spanish ruling circles a sense of shame at the early cruelties of his countrymen in the Caribbean islands and on the mainland of Central America, Bartolomé de las Casas, had become known in northern Europe through translations of his *Brevissima relacion de la destruycion de las Indias* (1552) into Dutch (1578), French (1579), and, as *The Spanish colonie*, English (1583).[4] This had given the English much ammunition to fire against the godless treatment of the Indians by the supposedly godly Spanish.

Francis Drake had long taken the view that the Indians were unduly repressed by the Spanish and almost always succeeded in maintaining friendly relations with them both in the Caribbean and in the Pacific. Sir George Peckham, however, in his *True reporte of the late discoveries . . . by Humphrey Gilbert* (1583), had taken a sterner view.[5] The Indians "would easily be brought to civility." But, if they did not, Scripture gave Christians the right "to plant, possess and subdue." The savages must grant the English, when they planted colonies, "quiet possession." This should be done by "offering to live peaceably among them," though the settlers must resist any attempt to keep them out, after first giving them assurance (before missionary work was begun) of "benefit, commodity, peace, tranquillity and safety." To begin with, indeed, they must be regarded and treated as savages, but if they were complaisant and cooperative they might gradually become civilized and learn to live as equals (perhaps) alongside Europeans, or so the implication seemed to be.

Both Richard Hakluyt, lawyer, and Richard Hakluyt, preacher, had written treatises, still unpublished in 1584, on the need to cooperate with the Indians for economic ends,[6] but the younger Richard was concerned, especially in the "Discourse" discussed earlier,[7] that every effort be made to induce them to become good members of the Church of England. To him and to many of the clergy (who thought about the matter at all), it was vitally important that the English church should not be at a disadvantage before the Roman church in engaging in missionary activity, as Catholic propagandists had continually poked fun at them for their failure to carry their Protestantism outside England. Hakluyt regarded as legitimate only such policies and treatment of the Indians that would lead to conversion, and he was prepared to denounce the Spanish in unmeasured terms for their cruelties while saying very little about their missionary efforts or about the attempts by the state to give the Indians some limited measure of legal protection.

No prior consideration of Indian rights to their own territory is contained in the basic documents of the English colonizing projects—either in the grants to Sir Humphrey Gilbert and Sir Walter Ralegh, or even in Ralegh's subgrant to the City of Ralegh associates in 1587. Englishmen were to be thrust into land that was assumed to be virtually empty and where there was plenty of room for them, without necessarily disturbing the inhabitants unduly, but with no recognition whatever given to their indigenous rights of occupation. By implication, therefore, Peckham's view that, if English intrusion was resisted, the Indians must be forced to give way before the settlers was assumed to be the basic one. At the same time, during the continuing relations between the English and the Indians of the Outer Banks and coastal plain from 1584 onward, many attempts were made to limit friction between the peoples and to replace it by friendly cooperation. But this can only be understood, if at all, by taking each leader on his own terms and examining his individual interpretation of these preconditions. Thus Arthur Barlowe, Sir Richard Grenville, Ralph Lane, Thomas Harriot, and John White all had somewhat different concepts of what the relationship might be and on how it could be maintained. Ralegh did attempt to maintain some degree of detachment. He wanted to have land and colonists on North American soil but he was prepared to let his agents experiment with the precise ways in which this could be done. He cannot be credited with a single policy toward the indigenous peoples apart from the overriding consideration that some of their land should pass, as peacefully as possible, but pass, from the hands of its possessors into those of his English servants and agents.

The account of Arthur Barlowe, as edited by Ralegh or Harriot for propaganda purposes, provided almost too idyllic a picture of the little Indian world into which he had intruded in July 1584. Recall, for example, his phrases: "We were entertained with all love and kindness and with as much bounty, after their manner, as they could possibly devise. We found the people most gentle loving and faithfull, void of all guile and treason, and such as lived after the manner of the Golden Age." Moreover, the Indians were willing to trade with the skins and other things they had. They had appeared to offer, or Barlowe assumed they had offered, an invitation to the Englishmen to come and stay among them. Apparently this impression was not dispelled by Manteo or even Wanchese as they became understood toward the end of 1584, or, if so, it was carefully covered up. The 1585 expedition set out believing that friendly and cooperative relations with the Indians of Roanoke Island, the sounds, and the Outer Banks were already assured, and that their presence would not be resented or opposed. It is true that Grenville's crude revenge on the people of Aquascogoc in July 1585 may have caused both English and Indians to have doubts about the efficacy or even intention of proceeding peacefully, but it did not prevent the colony from being installed on old Indian fields on Roanoke Island. Indeed, we hear of no serious differences developing during the ensuing months, though it may be noted that we have very little direct information on the happenings of those months, and the picture, as it unfolds on Roanoke Island and its neighborhood in March 1586, is startlingly different. Mistrust and dislike had emerged on both sides and a threat of hostilities hung over the settlers and the colony, at least so far as Lane's narrative conveys it, though Harriot's account suggests a continuance and dependence of contact at an intimate level between the leading men of Indian society and at least the intellectuals among the colonists.

It seems desirable to examine in as much detail as possible Lane's changing attitudes, so far as we can discern them, from materials mainly supplied by himself. To some extent, his position appears to have been ambivalent. On the one hand, there is a degree of condescension toward his Indian neighbors. Menatonon is very perceptive "for a savage," but at the same time Lane is generous in his appreciation of what Menatonon told him about other tribes and about the great harbor to the north. He also respected his tactical advice on exploiting the copper sources in the interior as well as on reaching the harbor. When we consider that Lane burst into the village of Chawanoac when the chief was conferring with other tribal leaders and that he seized him and held him as his prisoner, and yet at the same time held confidential discussions with him, it is possible to see how mutual respect and understanding developed between them in this unlikely environment.

Yet Lane remains always the soldier, continually assessing the changing situation of the colony in military terms. He takes the precaution of bringing Menatonon's son Skiko to Roanoke Island as a hostage, despite his high opinion of the chief, and imprisons him when he attempts to escape. Eventually, however, he gains the boy's confidence and so acquires vital evidence about Wingina's conspiracy against him at the end of May 1586. Not long before that Skiko revealed that Menatonon had coerced the Weapemeoc high chief Okisko into submitting himself to Lane as a subject of Queen Elizabeth (whatever that implied). The triple relationship between Lane, Menatonon, and Skiko became in a sense an association of equals, each individual respecting the other and exchanging confidences, while still retaining a degree of caution on how far they could trust each other in extremity.

The course of Lane's dealings with Wingina is clouded because he does not reveal the nature of their earlier relationship and how it altered from friendship in September to hostility in March. During part of this time Wingina and Harriot had developed a close association which evidently differed very much from Lane's. Clearly, the settlement took root with the permission and, quite probably, the active assistance of the Roanoke Island Indians, who appear to have donated old fields and some woodland to the newcomers with every sign of goodwill, and may even have lent physical help in clearing some of the trees and undergrowth from the site. If there was such assistance, Lane would have paid for it in gifts of English trifles or metals, and the chief is likely to have been compensated much more handsomely. We would expect that mutual curiosity would have brought the two groups, living so close to each other, into reasonably intimate contact, yet we do not know whether Lane laid down any rules for the visits of Indian individuals to the site of the colony. Whether his men, on their part, were free to enter the Indian village we cannot tell. There may have been a little pilfering on both sides and some individual trading.

Life on the site undoubtedly became boring and monotonous for soldiers and gentlemen alike. They would be tempted by curiosity to pry into the details of Indian life and ceremony. In normal circumstances trouble could arise when the colonists made sexual overtures to the female occupants of the village. Harriot, however, tells us that the Indian women did not attract Lane's men. They seem to have attracted him, so the attitude of other men appeared surprising to him. (Some, indeed, could have been homosexual in their preferences.) But he may not have known everything that occurred as he was away from the colony much of the time. Certainly the possibilities for minor and mounting friction existed through mere propinquity, though opportunities for friendly associations and mutual understanding also increased.

What is thought to have brought about a major rift is corn supply. In September 1585, and for some time thereafter, the villagers would probably have had a surplus of corn from Wingina's two villages, at Roanoke and Dasemunkepeuc, but in spite of payment for it by copper, which appears to have been made, the amount available would decrease as Lane's requests increased. Consequently, the suspicion arises that requests actually turned into demands the Indians could not meet unless they surrendered some of their precious seed corn or themselves went short. When many of the villagers disappeared during the winter for the traditional annual hunt into the interior for deer and other animals, Lane may well have misconstrued this as a sign that they wished to reduce contact with him and his colonists. Certainly, at this time there would be less association and little or no trade. The Indians were probably back by early March, refreshed after gorging themselves with meat, carrying new skins, and feeling generally more self-reliant, just when the colonists were beginning to chafe at inaction. It was during this period that a breach between them developed and Wingina deserted the Roanoke Island village. Lane, wishing to give the Indians no further cause for complaint, apparently left it vacant.

Apart from the group exploring the Chesapeake area, the relative inactivity—so far as we are aware—of Lane's main party at the settlement during the winter is difficult to understand, as it might appear from all other indications that the weather was mild. Perhaps, inertia had set in; soldiers and gentlemen simply did not wish to move. Or it may well have been that growing suspicion between Indians and English led Lane to be cautious about leaving the fort and town with too few defenders.

What must be recognized is that, as far as we know, during the early months of the colony there were few obstacles to the widespread cartographic activities of the survey party under Harriot and White. Thus, as the Englishmen moved up and down the sounds and shores and penetrated into the villages to sketch and survey, they steadily developed their picture of the whole area. And as they did so, mutual curiosity between the survey party and the Indians about what the English were doing and how the Indians lived and thought continued. The Indians were amazed when Harriot showed them some of his instruments and what could be done with them. This, together with the obviously pacific attitude of the party, apparently encouraged almost universal cooperation from the inhabitants but not, most probably, from the Secotan and Aquascogoc people, who may not have readmitted them after the events of the previous July, when Grenville reacted so sharply against a minor theft. There are, however, hints of friction and opposition to their activities in some other unspecific places.

Lane was weak, having sent the strong party northward under his "Colonel of the Chesepians," and also being without the pinnace (and Philip Amadas in command of it?) and possibly one of the boats. The initial contacts that this group of men made with the Chesapeake Indians after they rounded Cape Henry cannot be particularized. They appear to have stopped at two villages, Chesepiuc and Apasus, on or near Lynnhaven Bay and from them could determine the precise location of Skicóac. The pinnace would have been able to enter the Elizabeth River, but may not have been able to proceed far upstream, and a boat may have been needed for the rest of the journey, some fifteen miles to Skicóac. There, contacts between the explorers—the leader of the party, Harriot with his now good knowledge of the language (even if the local dialect was different in some respects), and White with his sketching apparatus—and the village evidently developed rapidly. The implication of the little we know is that relations with the head of the group, a chief probably with hegemony over a number of villages in addition to those indicated on White's map we would think, were soon established on a friendly basis. Gifts would have been exchanged and the desire of the Englishmen to remain in the area for a time made known. They were evidently either invited to accept accommodation in the longhouses in the village or else given space outside it where an encampment could be erected. It is known that they were visited there, as Lane has already been quoted as saying, by a number of tribal leaders from the interior. It is interesting that they included, besides the Mangoaks (Meherrin probably in this case) representatives who may have been from more southerly Algonquian tribes but none from the Powhatan Algonquian group across the bay in the peninsular areas where the Powhatans were dominant.

Harriot and White were probably able to move about a good deal if the winter was mild (as it probably was because Lane made no complaint about it). It would appear, from indications that have already been noted, that the soil was fertile and easy to exploit. After they had spent some time with the people and probably made friends with the ruling elite and others, an invitation was apparently extended to the English to settle in the vicinity of Skicóac. At this stage it may even have been indicated that a mixed group of men, women, and children would be most acceptable. Previously it has appeared that the concept of the mixed community was the brainchild of White, in collaboration with Ralegh, after his return, but this is not clearly documented. It could very well have originated at Skicóac itself. Such a community would offer much less of a threat to the internal security of the tribe than a garrison of men alone, and would, if it developed, become a source of strength against the tribe's enemies, especially as the English had guns and could probably demonstrate their effectiveness by shooting some of the numerous bears that Lane said were found in the area.

Although there is an element of supposition in all this, it is kept within the limits imposed by the documentation and by the circumstances of the creation of the 1587 colony. It does, therefore, appear that it was possible for the members of the survey party to develop an association with the Chesapeakes, on a basis of equality and mutual friendship, which was paralleled only by the idyllic relations (brief and artificial as they were) that Barlowe had recorded for the Outer Banks and Roanoke Island in 1584. If the Chesapeake chief wished to have an English settlement to strengthen his own position as well as his friendship with the survey party, this did not mean that the invitation was any less sincere, or that White, Harriot, and the rest would have contemplated it unless relations with these Indians had been especially close. Long-term association with an Indian group was thought by the English party to be, in this case at least, desirable and unaccompanied by the strains between Lane and the Roanoke Indians, which, apparently, were already evident before the party left Roanoke Island.

Lane's account of the friction that had developed between him and Wingina by March 1586 is not prefaced by any clear indications of how it had come about, though it has been suggested that pressure for corn supplies was a major factor. His view of Wingina is an external one throughout, and the Wingina whom Harriot portrays is a very different personality. He was Harriot's friend, curious, receptive, if somewhat apprehensive, but capable of emotional contact with an Englishman. Did Lane not see and try to develop this aspect? At the same time, Lane was ready, once the Chesapeake party had returned, to set out exploring himself. He is not entirely convincing, as it has been suggested, in his declaration that Wingina had already begun hostile intrigues against him throughout the interior, which he proposed to visit. Was there a meeting of Indian chiefs at Chawanoac which was inspired by Wingina to thwart Lane or was it simply a gathering of Menatonon's dependents and associates concerned with purely local affairs? It appears wise to remain skeptical. Lane himself stresses his personal dealings with Menatonon, as has been shown, and does not reaffirm his allegations that Wingina was behind the meeting or that it was organized to plan his overthrow. Similarly, he may be inclined to exaggerate Wingina's influence on the Moratuc Indians in leading them to boycott and even attack Lane's men in their journey up the Roanoke River, or even to accept

Wingina's influence on the Weapemeoc Indians leading to their absence from their villages when Lane was returning exhausted from
his ordeal. The Indians who were away from the latter villages may
still have been hunting in the interior.

Another possible explanation is that because the English left behind a deadly and mysterious sickness at many places they visited,
perceptive Indians might have tended to avoid the English so as not
to be contaminated. Lane blamed Wingina's sinister influence for the
events of March yet, such was the shifting sequence of his relations
with local Indians, that by April he was again cooperating with Wingina and in that month the chief provided him, as has been shown, a
fish weir and men to assist in sowing cornfields sufficient to maintain
the colony into 1587 if relief did not come. This particular shift Lane
attempts to explain by pointing to a sharp division in Wingina's own
councils. His *weroances* were in part antagonistic to attempts he had
made to hamper Lane. Granganimeo, who had been so friendly with
Barlowe, had died but he had passed on to Ensenore, another aged
weroance, his theory of the nature of the Englishmen. They were men
who had died but had been allowed to return for a short period to
earth. They had supernatural instruments, such as guns and ships, at
their disposal, but most alarming and significant was their capacity to
spread disease from a distance. They would use these powers if
opposed violently. Continued friendship, or a show of it, was essential, but in due course the strange white men would soon disappear
and return to their status as dead persons and everything would be
as it had been.

Harriot does give us some indication that a theory of this sort was
in fact propagated. But it might not have been supported by the
tribesman who had stayed in England for some months. Wanchese
had left the colonists and rejoined his own people as soon as he
had come back with Grenville. He had returned with no feelings of
friendship towards the Englishmen, probably because he had not
been made as much of as the intelligent and adaptable Manteo while
he was in England. He could state that theirs was a country on earth
inhabited wholly by white men like these, and one that, for all its
marvels, stank and had many noxious aspects and occupants alongside its grandeur and mystery. To him, England was real and the
Englishmen he had seen in their natural milieu he had, apparently,

not come to like. His status under Wingina was not that of a weroance, but he could provide evidence, in the face of mere theorizing,
against the supposed supernatural nature of the colonists. He could
depict their society as a purely human one, with many aspects, apparently, that did not appeal to him.

Lane claims that all Wingina's inhibitions were removed after Ensenore's death on 20 April and that from then on the chief was preparing a major campaign against him and his men. His account is a
tribute to Wingina's ingenuity and organizing skill, whether or not
his range of connections was as wide as Lane indicates. It is very
doubtful indeed that he could have involved the Mangoaks in the
politics of the coastal Algonquians, for these Iroquoian people (Tuscarora) would be unlikely to involve themselves in such affairs in
association with Wingina's people, who were of different linguistic
stock and traditions and were, even though they traded, their traditional enemies. Lane's reactions to the developments in Dasemunkepeuc, already indicated, show that he regarded Wingina as a worthy
antagonist and did not underestimate him. Because he did so he
took the drastic course—killing the chief—as the minimal action to
bring the colony a considerable measure of safety.

As Drake's arrival relieved Lane of further responsibility for Indian
relations, it is impossible to calculate what he would or would not
have done to secure his position further, but the total record of his
dealings with the Indians is not, so far as the evidence (chiefly historical) goes, a wholly unfavorable one. It is that of a military man,
estimating his opponent's strengths and weaknesses and exploiting
them to his own advantage. His attitudes toward the Indian population were not aggressive: he admired the political capacity of chiefs
like Menatonon and even Wingina and, when at peace, appears to
have treated individual Indians well, taking a number with him on
his Roanoke River venture. Apparently he remained on excellent
terms with Manteo throughout; otherwise, he would not have opted
to return to England with Lane for a second time. All the same, he
appears to have had few general views on Native Americans. He took
them as he found them. As "savages" they were not unworthy opponents or allies, but he does not indicate that he had any specific
views about their future relationships with the English, as Harriot
had.

Apart from John White, Thomas Harriot provides us with the clearest and fullest account both of the Indians themselves and of English attitudes toward them and the character of the relations between White and Native Americans. Harriot's exceptional intelligence is undoubted. He saw more of the life of the peoples of the Roanoke Island area and the southern Chesapeake than anyone except White and so had a better opportunity to assess their temperament and character and to assess the future possibilities of relationships between the two peoples. In the first place, he was "in dealing with the natural inhabitants specially employed." In the second, he stated in his *Briefe and true report of the new found land of Virginia* (1588) that, besides his summary account there, he had written "a large discourse" concerning them. This has not survived but the notes that he supplied for the engravings of the White drawings in 1590 are probably brief excerpts from this lost treatise, which would have been of the greatest interest and value.

Harriot's task, to study and describe the Indians, is a mark of the intellectual curiosity of his master Sir Walter Ralegh and of their joint interest in learning everything possible about the indigenous peoples before the English had affected their society fundamentally. To know the peoples in whose territory you intend to intrude might be regarded as farsighted common sense, but it also represents an objective scientific curiosity that is evident throughout the surviving work of White and Harriot and that was later to be shown by Ralegh himself in his dealings with the inhabitants of the Orinoco basin. At the same time, though it is necessary to emphasize the scientific approach of both Harriot and Ralegh toward the problem of relations between white men and the natives, it should not be forgotten that Harriot, through his upbringing and training, was, however favorably inclined to the open-minded study of indigenous peoples, an educated Englishman. As such he had the ingrown preconception that English, Western, Christian, and state-organized society was superior to anything that might be found outside Europe. Consequently, it was almost inevitable that he should take the view that the best future for indigenous North American society lay in its gradual assimilation of European values and techniques, while necessarily retaining some appreciable part (but how much?) of the character of its own society and outlook. He is scarcely to be reproached for this.

All anthropologists admit that, when a Western culture makes contact with a technically primitive one, the observer from the West begins to alter that society, and that it is a virtual certainty that his successors will attempt to do so consciously for commercial, religious, or political ends. With these limitations, inevitable ones it might appear, Harriot's views of the Indians are of the greatest value, mainly because of his attempts to be as objective as possible.

The basic point of his *Briefe and true report* is "that they in respect of troubling our inhabiting and planting are not to be feared." Instead, "they shall have cause both to fear and to love us that shall inhabit with them." What he is saying, in effect, is that the English have enough to offer the Indians to bring about good and even loving relations between them, while at the same time the planters are evidently so strong and capable of overpowering the Indians if they wish to do so that an element of apprehension (for so "fear" implied at this time) will remain in the relationship on the Indians' part.

Harriot's descriptions of the Indians as people and of their villages is a concise epitome of what had been learned from his survey previously. His evidence that in most cases the hegemony exercised by any single chief was small throws an important light on their political structure. Hegemonies might range from a mere two villages (Wingina's when the English arrived) to a maximum of eighteen (Okisko of Weapemeoc). The most powerful, he thought, could call upon some 700 to 800 armed men. At a ratio of one to five, this meant a population, for that ruler, of about 3,500 to 4,000 persons. If this was Weapemeoc, the population in that area was dense given the character of native settlement patterns. Lane appears to have estimated that in June 1586 some 1,500 bowmen could be mobilized against him, but as he includes not only Mangoaks but Chesapeakes, neither of whom can be considered likely allies, this may be a considerable exaggeration. If it was true, it would represent populations dispersed over a wider area with a density as high as or approaching that of Weapemeoc. Internal warfare among the Indians was, he said, very rarely in set battles, but rather in ambushes and hit-and-run raids. The English were not worried: "our discipline, our strange weapons and devices ... especially of ordnance great and small" would defeat them. At the time he wrote he may not have known the fate of Grenville's men in 1586: they could not even attempt to bring their four cannon to bear on their enemies when they were surprised, and escaped merely by the good luck of reaching their boat ahead of their attackers, apparently without even using their handguns. Indian skill in evasive ambushes and stratagems was to be evident long after settlement had developed in Virginia and elsewhere.

Harriot's most significant assessment of Native American capacity is to credit them with intelligence, competence, and the ability to assimilate European techniques and concepts:

> In respect of us they are a people poor and, for want of skill and judgment in the knowledge and use of our things, do esteem our trifles before things of greater value. Notwithstanding, in their proper manner, considering the want of such means as we have, they seem very ingenious [perhaps "having high intellectual capacity"; certainly "talented"]. For although they have no such tools, nor any such crafts, sciences and arts as we, yet, in those things they do, they show excellency of wit.

Here he fully recognized the innate ability of the people, which he closely observed over an extended period. At the same time, he recognized in Indian society what may be described as a Neolithic level of social development, to which could be added, he thought, the refinements and developments of the advanced (Iron Age) society which he and his associates represented (if it is to be put into twentieth-century terms). He admired the Indians for their skills in exploiting more effectively than Englishmen could their relatively limited resources and artifacts. He expected them to develop rapidly English standards of commercial value, even though Lane suggests Wingina was already doing so by hiring mercenaries with the aid of the surplus copper he had accumulated from trading with the English.

There is an element of naiveté in Harriot's approach to the native assimilation of English practices and concepts:

> And by how much they, upon due consideration, shall find our manner of knowledge and crafts to exceed theirs in perfection, and speed for doing or execution, by so much the more is it probable that they should desire our friendship and love, and have the greater respect for pleasing and obeying us.

He was convinced that the Indians could be approached effectively only by allowing them to pick and choose which elements of European culture, material or otherwise, to absorb into their society—not by forcing European ideas and practices on them. Harriot's belief that the superiority of European ways of thinking and doing things would automatically lead them to accept the authority of the settlers and indicate that even the "conversion" of Native Americans into Europeans (by acculturation) would continue to leave them at a lower level in the mixed society, as they would strive not only to please, but also to "obey," the colonists. His view, however enlightened, contained an element of exploitativeness. Overall, he concluded, if such "means of good government be used that they may in short time be brought to civility and the embracing of true religion."

If Harriot was to have some doubts in later life about the theological subtleties of Christianity, the simple outline of the beliefs and practices of the Church of England were evidently sufficient for him at this time to lead him to consider introducing them to the Indians by example. His basic mistake was to consider the Indians as largely passive. This was far from being the case. Their willingness to choose to accept or adopt some limited aspects of white society was combined with a proud, even arrogant preference for their own values and customary way of life. As for the native religion, Harriot indeed appreciated its animistic character but failed to apprehend the unity of the people, the world of nature, and their gods into a single synthesis, one that was accepted as all-embracing. There was no question of its divisibility into segments that could be detached from one another and reintegrated with an infusion of white men's concepts and institutions.

"They believe," he said, "there are many Gods, which they call Montóac [manito, equivalent to either supernatural power or being] but of different sorts and degrees: one only chief and great God, which hath been from all eternity."[8] This supreme being, when he proposed to make the world, first made instruments for its creation and government, and, after that, "the sun, moon and stars as petty gods" and the principal evidences in his hierarchy. The waters were made first and from them all creatures derive, "visible and invisible." Mankind arose from a woman who fell from the sky and was engendered by the gods to produce the human race.

Such myths have been found elsewhere in North America but

there is some suspicion that by the late sixteenth century they may
already have received some slight contamination from Christian concepts by gradual infiltration from the Caribbean and Central America
over almost a century of Spanish penetration there. At the same time,
there is considerable support for the view that the supreme being
and the creation myth, in varying forms, was part of an indigenous
cosmology.

Harriot proceeds:

> They think that all the gods are of human shape and therefore
> they represent them by images in the forms of men which they
> call *Kewasówak*: one alone is called *Kewás*. Them they place in
> houses appropriate, or temples, which they call *Machicómuck*,
> where they worship, pray, sing, and make many times offerings
> unto them. In some *Machicómuck* we have seen but one *Kewás*, in
> some two, in other some three. The common sort think them
> to be also gods.

This is very informative. Clearly images did play a considerable part
in their ceremonial (though possibly White only caught a glimpse of
the image in the temple he drew and did not know how to depict it
accurately). What Harriot fails to explain is how these images of the
gods were associated with the dessicated bodies of their dead leaders
and what part these and, respectively, the priest and conjuror or
shaman played in religious observances. He was mistaken if he believed that gods were recognized only in human form. Animal life
and even inanimate life had qualities that to Europeans would have
seemed almost supernatural and their capacities for good or evil had
to be taken into account in carrying on their daily lives.

With regard to the Indian view of an afterlife, he informs us:

> They believe also [in] the immortality of the soul, that after this
> life as soon as the soul is departed from the body, according to
> the works it hath done, it is either carried to heaven, the "hab-
> itacle" of gods, there to enjoy perpetual bliss and happiness, or
> else to a great pit or hole, which they think to be in the furthest
> parts of their part of the world toward the sunset, there to burn
> continually. The place they call *Popogusso*.

Certainly their concept of a life beyond life was very general, but the doctrine of rewards and punishments after death does not appear to have been universal and might be taken as evidence of some degree of Christian contamination, conceivably, in this case, carried down from Jesuit teachings on the Chesapeake in 1570–71. However, it might be valid to recall Ensenore's view of the intruding Englishmen as men from another world permitted to return to earth for a short time, and equipped with various means—natural and supernatural—of imposing their authority. How does this fit in with any concept of heaven or hell (of a sort) for all eternity? It seems anomalous in Harriot's scheme, and, if Lane reported it correctly, it suggests that "the other world" was somewhat different from its articulation in Harriot's report of Indian cosmology. Perhaps it was not basically so as Harriot also heard tales of men returning from the dead—one man dead and buried, after a wicked life, returning to earth after being saved by one of the gods from "hell," and again a man rising from the dead and giving an account of a pleasant and homely "heaven" where he met his father, but was given leave to return to earth to extol the pleasures of the other world. Such tales were not uncommon in a society where clinical death could not be clearly established except in the case of their great men, chosen to be skinned, eviscerated, and preserved, who if they were not, in fact, dead were almost immediately killed by this treatment.

Harriot maintained that between the weroances and the priests, the ordinary people were made to obey by threats of the fear of "hell" and of the perfections of "heaven." At the same time this did not avoid (any more than in Christian society) physical punishment for wrongdoing, for thieves, whoremongers, and others were punished by death, forfeitures, beatings, and so on, as Jacques Le Moyne de Morgues illustrated in his sanguinary engraving of the execution of a Timucua Indian sentry who did not keep guard.

Harriot claimed he had conversed with Indian priests, who told him what he was to record about their religious beliefs. He professed to find them somewhat loosely attached to their own beliefs and cosmological theory and "that they were brought into great doubts of their own, and no small admiration of ours, with earnest desire in many to learn more then we had means for want of perfect utterance in their language to express." The last point is of interest as it is the

only place where Harriot admits that the subtleties of the Algonquian tongue, when applied to abstract topics, were somewhat beyond him. It is possible that this limitation makes his transmission of
religious ideas and cosmological concepts less reliable than usual.

As a man whose interests were basically scientific, Harriot naturally tried to satisfy the curiosity of the people with whom he spoke
about his technical equipment, such "as mathematical instruments,
sea compasses, the virtue of the lodestone in drawing iron, a perspective glass, whereby was showed many strange sights [its precise
nature is not known], burning glasses, wildfire works [fireworks],
guns, books, writing and reading, spring-clocks that seem to go of
themselves, and many other things that we had." He formed the
impression, rightly or wrongly, that these things "so far exceeded
their capacities to comprehend the reason and means how they
should be made and done that they thought they were rather the
works of gods than of men, or at the leastwise they had been given
and taught us of the gods." He carried this still further by saying that
this "made many of them to have such an opinion of us, as that if
they knew not the truth of God and religion already, it was rather to
be had from us, whom God so specially loved, than from a people
that were so simple as they found themselves to be in comparison of
us. Whereupon greater credit was given unto that we spoke of concerning such matters." What cannot be known is whether this reaction was shown by the common tribesmen or whether it was confined primarily to the *weroances* and priests or, indeed, how deep it
went. The impact of instruments and their appearance as magical
and therefore god-given would appear to have rather a limited range
of appeal. Curiosity indeed could be expected: a sophisticated de-
duction from seeing such things less so. But at the same time, everything Harriot says on this subject is of exceptional interest because it
is the first known report of the interaction between an educated
Englishman and relatively unsophisticated Native Americans and because it is more direct than anything of its kind to be recorded for
many years to come.

In the course of his travels Harriot was willing to act the missionary and he gives some impressions of this teaching of the basic
elements of Christianity and of the use of the Bible. Here he speaks
as a simple believer, as his own reservations did not emerge until
later life:

Many times and in every town where I came . . . I made declaration of the contents of the Bible; that therein was set forth the
true and only God and his mighty works, that therein was
contained the true doctrine of salvation through Christ, with
many particularities of miracles and chief points of religion, as I
was able then to utter, and thought fit for the time. And although I told them the book materially and of itself was not of
any such virtue, as I thought they did conceive, but only the
doctrine therein contained, yet would many be glad to touch it,
to embrace it, to kiss it, to hold it to their breasts and heads,
and stroke over all their body with it, to shew their hungry
desire of that knowledge which was spoken of.

This acceptance of the book as a god, or god-giver, rather than the
words contained in it indicates that he appealed to ordinary people
as well as to the elite, and suggests that he achieved some appreciable degree of eloquence in expounding scriptural material in the
native language. He does not take into account that the impact of his
teaching was probably very temporary.

His picture of Wingina is startlingly different from that of Lane, to
whom he was the clever but sinister intriguer. To Harriot he was a
close friend. Harriot called on him when he was in his own village
on the island; he accompanied him from time to time to other
villages. When he came to visit Harriot he remained "to pray and
sing psalms, hoping thereby to be partaker of the same effects which
we by that means also expected"—which implies a measure of devo-
tional activity in the settlement not otherwise suggested. Wingina
was twice very sick (with disease brought by the English?) and so
gave up hope of being helped by his own priests that he "sent for
some of us to pray and be a means to our God that it would please
him either that he might live or after death dwell with him in bliss."
He recovered, and presumably gave some credit to Harriot's God.
Other individuals when sick did the same. Through Harriot, and he
surely can be believed in this, the Indians were profoundly influenced by the concepts and magic exercised by the Englishmen's
God. The mention of others who might pray for Wingina suggests
that Harriot was not alone in being able to use the local language for
religious exercises.

Similarly, when corn began to wither during drought, the Indians

would come to ask the English to pray for its welfare, promising
rewards from the harvest if it flourished—though Harriot cannot tell
us if there were any results as the harvest in 1586 was not ready by
the time he left. Indeed any sickness, losses, "or any other cross unto
them" they would impute to English intervention, regarding it as a
penalty for displeasing them.

The most striking effect of Englishmen, principally the Harriot-
White surveying party it might be assumed, was the introduction of
sickness to the villages, when "within a few days after our departure
. . . the people began to die very fast, and many in short space: in
some towns about twenty, in some forty, in some sixty, and in one
six score [120], which in truth was very many in respect of their
numbers." Owing to the shortage of the incubation period, the disease in this case, if Harriot is correct, cannot have been measles
or smallpox (ten to sixteen days for the latter), and was therefore
probably some form of cold or influenza. The introduction of epidemic disease was the worst thing the English and other Europeans
could and did bring with them to North America, as it was to destroy whole populations over the next fifty years, and to go on doing
so after that.[9] This sickness was quite new to the Indians and they
did not know how to cure it; nor could the English deal with it
either, even if it had little, or no serious, effect on them.

Harriot's information about the incidence of this disease is very
strange. He says that it infected only those villages "where we had
any subtle device practised against us." If this was so, Harriot's progress, as that of Lane during the spring of 1586, may not have been
quite so painless and friendly as previously has been supposed, particularly if many places were affected. What is difficult to believe is
that villages that were wholly friendly escaped, while those that were
not suffered. This suggests a strong strain of belief in the irrational
in Harriot himself, which is not surprising as his generation was
brought up to accept witches and sorcery as part of the nature of
things, outside and beyond religious beliefs, and he recorded his
belief in miracles. If it was not miraculous, there seems to be no
obvious explanation of the phenomenon he reports, except that it
was only an illusion that such villages only were affected. He says that
Wingina, after seeing this disease infect three or four villages, alleged
that it was the work of God; it even appears that he and others

wished the English to have the same disease affect and cripple villages that were hostile to themselves. Through this misty glimpse there is conveyed an impression of rivalry and hostility between villages and between hegemonies for which little other evidence survives. Harriot insists he asserted that requests to call down evil or disease on other peoples were ungodly and could not be done, but he found it difficult to convince those who came to him with such requests that this was so. The Englishmen, they insisted, could indeed do such things, and shoot their disease with invisible bullets into the far distance.

The epidemics and their supposed incidence only in hostile villages helped to develop and reinforce the feeling that in some way the English must be godlike. According to Harriot, "some people could not tell whether to think us gods or men," especially because they did not see any of the colonists die or even any individuals that were particularly sick; "they noted also that we had no women amongst us, neither did we care for any of theirs." Lane confirms that only 4 out of 108 colonists died, 3 of whom were chronically sick, so that the healthiness which puzzled the Indians was evidently the result of good hygiene and discipline on Lane's part. The colonists' apparent indifference to the Indian women is singular. It may be that this lack of interest (if what Harriot says is to be accepted) kept alive the belief that the visitors "were not born of women, and therefore immortal," or else "that we were men of an old generation many years past risen again to immortality," which had, according to Lane, been Ensenore's opinion. But some took a more sinister view, namely that more of the same kind would come and kill them and take their places. This concept may have grown (perhaps with Wanchese's assistance) when Drake's fleet, the supply ship, Grenville's squadron, and Grenville's holding party arrived in rapid succession, and, if it had become dominant, could explain why the last of these was chased away. The white man must, perhaps, be made to leave them alone.

Harriot says that many of his own people began to believe in the supernatural nature of the outbreaks of disease, "especially some astrologers, knowing of the Eclipse of the Sun, which we saw the same year before on our voyage thitherward which unto them appeared terrible." Of the astronomer–astrologers on the voyage we know nothing, but astrology was so prevalent in England, and the belief that eclipses portended disasters so general, that it is not surprising that there were such harbingers of doom in the colony. But this is the only hint we have of their existence or their views. They paralleled the Indians' medicine men ("their physicians") who sucked coagulated strings of blood from sick bodies, alleging that these were the invisible bullets with which the English inflicted the disease. This indicates that the Indian shaman was willing to counterattack, and to build up resistance to those who placed too high a value on English attributes and skills.

Certainly these views of English and Indian interactions bring us below the surface of events. They show some contact at a moderately deep level and above all the development of magical concepts, first on the Indian and then on the English side. Ideologically, whatever the Bible message may have meant, a number of people on both sides of the fence shared similar preconceptions about natural and supernatural causes. The communicated disease, however its incidence was to be explained, was only too real and too much a portent for the continuance of European contact to be regarded as desirable.

Harriot concludes his report by saying "there is good hope they may be brought through discreet dealing and government to the embracing of the truth and, consequently to honor, obey, fear and love us." The combination is significant. The Native Americans could be confirmed in their belief in the superiority of the English to themselves, but they must not only love, but continue to obey and be apprehensive of them. They would remain, to that extent, allies and friends, but still in some appreciable degree subordinates. But he admitted that violent actions by some colonists before they left (and he does not seem to be thinking only of the killing of Wingina, though that would affect him as he had known him so well) might have antagonized some, because men had been killed "upon causes that on our part might easily enough have been borne," and the killers deserved punishment. He could only hope the rest of the inhabitants would not hold this against the English in general.

In many ways Harriot's is an extraordinary document, the first attempt to probe, by personal contact, into the minds and beliefs of a North American people. Harriot got some little distance with his probing, but not as far as modern scholars would have liked. Language remained a barrier to full comprehension. The revelation of Indian misconceptions about English powers, and of the equally uncritical acceptance of those powers by some of the colonists, refutes the assumption that Englishmen approached the question of relations with the Indians in a purely rational light. This applied even to Harriot, most rational of the Elizabethans. Whether such credulity helped or hindered mutual understanding must remain moot.

From Lane and Harriot we have their words—even if they are not always compatible—but from John White we have only pictures and actions. His drawings speak loudly of his goodwill toward the native peoples whom he pictured, and of his immense care to record them faithfully without either exaggeration or reduction. His actions are left to speak for themselves. As we will see, and we must here anticipate, the whole 1587 project, and its performance as far as he oversaw it, paid tribute to his belief that not only were Native Americans and white Europeans compatible, but also that in the future they could look forward to living side by side—men, women, and children from the British Islands alongside villages comprising men, women, and children of indigenous North American stock. His belief and hope are evidenced by the people he gathered around him for the voyage in 1587. His sincerity about not only the bountiful land but also the kindly and bountiful people must have been wholly convincing to induce husbands and wives—some with small children, some pregnant—and others to voyage into the almost unknown and plant themselves among, and indeed at the mercy of, many greater numbers of Indians in the Chesapeake region where he had lived for a few months but of which he and Harriot have left no verbal or graphic record whatsoever.

White believed he could live in his European community beside and with the Chesapeake Indians, but he was no pacifist. He took cannon and light ordnance; he took handguns; he took armor for himself and so, most probably, did others. He was prepared for defensive war, but he did not expect it from his hosts. His attitude of trust was evident up to the time he left his stranded company on the shores of Roanoke Island. He was apparently justified in his belief. The Lost Colonists, if our informants are not wholly misleading (and it is difficult to see that they are), had nearly twenty years of cooperative living alongside and mingling with their hosts. When they were destroyed it was by a jealous potentate who wiped out Indian and white alike on account of fears fostered by his priests that they represented a potential challenge to his power in some new manner.

There is much that is both naive and attractive about White's view. He showed none of Harriot's skeptical abstraction from Indian beliefs and concepts, no fear of the effects of communicable disease, no concept that the Chesapeakes might kill his men and absorb their women and children into their own tribe. The small amount of evidence that survives—and it is very limited indeed—suggests, as we have indicated, that his optimism was justified and that, at least in certain limited circumstances, white and Indian could live together and mutually assimilate some features from the society of each. Greater knowledge, however, might engender greater skepticism.

The question of the Indians who came to England between 1584 and 1586 is an interesting and important one, but it is not one on which the evidence is very clear. From the beginning, Manteo emerges as an exceptional individual. He would appear to have joined Amadas and Barlowe at some point on the Outer Banks before they reached Port Ferdinando or else happened to be there at that time and joined them out of interest and curiosity. As a member of a ruling family in a small tribe, he had the advantage with the English of some elevation of status. He could be treated as a gentleman, even though he was considered to be a "savage" one. There is no indication that he was ever anything but fully cooperative. It would appear that he adapted rapidly to the strangeness of English life and soon learned to speak enough English to make himself understood (it is thought with the close cooperation of Harriot, whether or not Harriot was with the 1584 expedition). He proved willing to give, in time for Barlowe's narrative to be compiled and circulated in December 1584, a substantial amount of information (much of which we have from no other sources) about the political and topographical disposition of the tribal groups of the sounds and the adjoining territories, so that from that time onward he was an invaluable guide to those preparing the 1585 expedition. It is probable that Ralegh took a personal interest in him, and there is no doubt, even if documents do not state it precisely, that he, Harriot, and White formed an effective working partnership, and that, indeed, in what Harriot and White did, individually and collectively, he was frequently an active third partner. It is highly probable, too, that it was his status and his connections with other Indian groups that enabled the survey to proceed so smoothly and with so relatively little friction (though, as has been noted, Harriot indicates that there was some of which we lack the details).

During considerable parts of the ten months the first colony lasted, Manteo probably was active in his own tribal group on Croatoan Island where his mother ruled, and took on himself the duty of informing his own people about what the presence of the colony implied and, as far as it was possible to convey it, about the strange atmosphere and the complex society that he had experienced in London and elsewhere in England. There is no suggestion anywhere that he considered the English to be anything but men, not supernatural beings, but he may well have been still puzzled by many of the institutions and customs of the novel European society. Thus he was prepared, perhaps even anxious, to go with Lane (on board Drake's ship) to England in June 1586, having been assured, no doubt, that the evacuation of the settlers was not the end of English activity in the area and that he would be able to return.

In England, between July 1586 and April 1587, most probably Manteo collaborated closely with Harriot in compiling his linguistic materials and in improving his English. In view of his later baptism, we are entitled to conclude that he concerned himself—to some extent at least—with understanding the tenets of English Protestant Christianity, and received some instruction in elementary theology. He gives every indication of having had intellectual leanings and his discussions with Harriot on cosmology, and with his spiritual mentor on theology (whoever he was), would have shed light on the differences between the Native American outlook on the natural and supernatural worlds and that of the Renaissance Englishman. At a more practical level, it seems probable, once White had decided what kind of colony he wished to establish, that Manteo was able to furnish invaluable advice on what the colonists should and should not carry with them and how they should comport themselves with their Indian hosts. Evidently he did not disapprove of the plan to settle alongside the Chesapeake Indians, and indeed may have provided information of value to White and his associates about them.

Significant as was his return to Roanoke Island with White in 1587,

Manteo receives no mention in White's journal. But once White was marooned with his colonists by Simon Fernandes, we know that Manteo went down to his people on Croatoan accompanied by White, who was now seen to depend very much on him. Later, when White was back on Roanoke, there occurred an unfortunate episode (detailed below), when some of Manteo's people were mistakenly attacked by the English. He evidently came to Roanoke Island in time to smooth things out and assuage bitter feelings on their part. By his handling of this episode Manteo shows himself to have been no mean diplomat and statesman. That this was recognized both by Ralegh in England and by White on Roanoke Island is shown by his formal admission in a baptismal ceremony on Roanoke Island into the Church of England, demonstrating that he was willing to accept (at least superficially) what he had learned about Christianity in England. He would act as a nominal convert for the clergy in England, to be paraded by implication in Hakluyt's published version of White's narrative in 1589 as a successful result of missionary activity (as indeed the baptism of one of Drake's liberated Turks in London had been not long before, showing that even Muhammad could give up his converts to the English Church).[10]

More significant was the entrusting to Manteo by Ralegh of the lordship and government, under the English crown, of the Island of Roanoke and its surroundings. Manteo's acceptance of this role will be treated as an indication that the area was about to be completely evacuated by the English, and that he was designated to become a major ruler of the area, not merely a member of a chiefly family of a small isolated tribal group. It may be that the party of Englishmen left behind to await White's return acted as some (temporary) limitation on his authority in the Roanoke area, because we have no evidence that he attempted at this time to assert his authority over the remnants of Wingina's people, perhaps in order not to involve the English party in local conflicts. Their presence may also have prevented him from making Roanoke Island his own base, so that he continued to operate from Croatoan. We may suggest also that his new hegemony may not have been acceptable to the Weapemeoc and Chawanoac tribes. White's complete failure in 1590 to discover any traces of Indian occupation of the island (apart from casual looting of materials left there by the colonists) indicates that it had not become a place where Manteo resided. His continued sheltering of the Englishmen, indicated by the messages they left for White to find in 1590, shows that he continued to feel a strong sense of responsibility toward them, and would suggest, when contact with White was finally lost, that he brought them into his tribal group on Croatoan. But if this slight indication suggests that he had not lost his affinity for the English, he does not appear to have built upon that a community such as White had envisaged emerging in the Chesapeake's territory. Unless a majority of the Croatoan Indians, with a leavening of English, moved away from the island, his descendants were living, when John Lawson saw them in 1701, just as any other Indians he encountered in the Carolinas, uninfluenced by the English, except perhaps for a slight mixture of European blood. In a sense, then, it can be said that Manteo's long sojourns in England may have gone for little or nothing. He was not, in any degree, permanently anglicized.

Manteo almost certainly went to England in 1584 of his own volition; Wanchese more probably was sent by Wingina (from his sickbed) or Granganimeo to spy out the strange land from which the visitors had come. Barlowe, however much he would have desired to take back Indians who could act as informants on language and conditions, would not have risked his friendship with the Roanoke Indians by seizing a hostage. Before the end of the year Wanchese and Manteo, both dressed in English clothing, were seen at the English court, but neither were heard to speak on this occasion. It seems very likely that Wanchese was treated as an inferior by Manteo and that he did not supply much information for the use of the 1585 expedition. Back on Roanoke Island, he left Grenville as soon as he could to rejoin Wingina and, it has been suggested, stood out against the attribution of supernatural powers to the English colonists. He was, however, only a warrior and not a *weroance*. Wingina must have been torn between the intellectual and emotional attraction that Harriot undoubtedly had for him, Lane's authoritarian dealings, and Wanchese's countersuggestions that the English were human and vulnerable. Certainly Wanchese appeared to Lane between April and June 1586 as a chief instigator of Wingina's hostility. Lane would, it seems, cheerfully have had him killed at the time of his intervention in Dasemunkepeuc. In 1587 he was to appear as the self-appointed

leader of his tribal group after Wingina's death, described as an enemy of the Grenville holding-party, and an active opponent of further colonization. He disappears thereafter, to emerge in late twentieth century Indian revival literature as the true Indian, determined to
uphold his people's traditions against the invader, whereas Manteo is
demoted to the position of collaborator with the intruder. These
categorizations are largely irrelevant to the conditions of the years
1584–87, but they are just worth noting. At least it can be said that
Wanchese returned from England unacculturated.

Towaye, the Indian who decided to sail with Manteo, left for England with Drake in June 1586 and returned with White in 1587. This
is all that is known about him. But it establishes that he spent a year
in the company of Englishmen at sea or on land and presumably
reacted to this experience in some way or another. He was either a
member of Wingina's group who disagreed with the majority and
favored the English in the last clash, or else he was brought from his
own group by Manteo to act as his associate and, perhaps, attendant.
Nothing more can be said. As for the last Indian known to have been
taken to England, he was one of three caught by Grenville in the late
summer of 1586 and the only one who did not escape. He appears
to have lived at Stowe or at Bideford in a Grenville household and to
have become to some extent acculturated. Evidently it was intended
that he be brought home by Grenville in 1588 and, when preparations for Grenville's new expedition were well advanced, he was, on
27 March 1588, baptized in Bideford Parish Church with the name of
"Raleigh," which certainly lacks originality.[11] He did not accompany
White in that year and lived on with the Grenvilles. But he did not
survive very long, as there is a record of the burial of "Rawley" on 7
April 1589. As a Roanoke Indian who became absorbed into an
English community and lived there from late in 1586 to the spring of
1589, he was the only Indian taken to England who lived there long
enough to strike some roots, but how deep they were we shall
probably never discover.

Of the four Indians discussed, it can be said that Manteo was
largely and Raleigh perhaps wholly acculturated. Wanchese resisted
acculturation, while nothing can be said of Towaye's reactions. At
least three of these Indians returned to their homeland and presumably left some traces of their life in England on their own people. We
would expect Manteo's contribution to have been a major one, but it

may indeed not have been so. His presence had ceased to brood over Roanoke Island by 1590.

No simple summary of English-Indian relations seems possible. According to the evidence that we have, the English did use pressure on the Indians, but it was not excessive and the violent action of which we have details was limited to the minimum force necessary to secure the safety of the colonists. This may not be the whole story as both Harriot, who is reliable, and Richard Butler, who is not necessarily so, speak of attacks that brought about more Indian bloodshed than is openly admitted by Ralph Lane. At the same time, there is no doubt that whites and Indians made a deep impression upon one another. The Indians were impressed by the techniques of the white man, to the extent that they regarded them as supernatural. The disease that flowed from them they viewed as something sinister and unnatural, whereas they were willing to accept a Christian god into their pantheon if he and the faith in him were expounded to them. Harriot is not convincing when he suggests that they would be willing to give up their old gods; he is so when he explains that they, or a few of them, could regard the God in the Book as a powerful spirit and one who could be admitted as such.

So far as status relations were concerned, all the English sources suggest that it helped to be a chief or a *weroance*. Such men were given much more credence or account than simple warriors. The respect for rank, endemic in English society, was also evident in relations in North America. In general, however, the Indians' primitiveness was accepted as a mark of some degree of inferiority, either that of the outsider, the "savage," or, at a friendly level, as something above that of a servant but below that of an equal. This is evident even in the accounts of Harriot who, nonetheless, had a high opinion of Indian intellectual and technical potential. The concept of equality appears clearly only in White and in him by implication rather than explicitly.

The overall effect of contact, however, remained governed by the fact that Englishmen, from Ralegh downward, regarded it as their right to intrude on American soil and to occupy such parts of it as they felt necessary, ultimately without regard to the desires of the inhabitants. It was therefore an expression of the imperialist, conquering mentality, in which indigenous rights were a marginal luxury.

A Colony Is Formed and Lost

A Colony Launched

Initially, Ralph Lane's return to England, even though with his company virtually intact and well, is likely to have infuriated Ralegh. Why did they not wait for his ship and Sir Richard Grenville's additional colonists, which could have brought the colony new strength and capacity to survive and expand? Whether the long interrogation Lane (and probably his other military associates) underwent mitigated his anger we cannot tell. Lane was required to put on paper the full story of events, the partial version of which has been related earlier.

Lane's premature departure from the colony revealed that establishing a band of Englishmen in what had been deemed a virtually empty and spacious area was not going to be nearly as easy as the optimism engendered by the Amadas-Barlowe voyage had suggested. For one thing the habitable space was simply an illusion. There was on Roanoke Island and in its vicinity little open or openable land, and what there was was already thickly inhabited. The indigenous people were numerous and warlike. Lane could consider himself fortunate that he was not attacked more systematically, even if we may also be sure he exaggerated the dangers in which he had been placed and his own ingenuity and skill in avoiding being crushed by taking the military initiative into his own hand. This made it clear that no idyllically peaceful future could be assured for any colonists left in Lane's place.

Lane's optimism focused mainly on one area: the region to the north where his "Chesepians" had wintered. There, there was deep water with space and friendly Indians. Moreover, he was hopeful about the prospects of metal—copper certainly, and gold possibly—in the interior, and felt there was even the chance that the Pacific was not far to the west after all. But these latter considerations were evidently far too much wishful thinking to make them worth further investment. The Chesapeake Bay question was the one to be pondered over. England's sea war was now open and expanding, and if there really was an effective port and anchorage, which did not suffer the defects of the Outer Banks and the lack of protection that ships riding in the roads must face, it could now be thought of as a possible base for anti-Spanish raiding, though with cautions and reservations. Had it not been for the capture of the *Santa Maria de San Vicente* on Grenville's return voyage in 1585, the whole venture would have been a crippling failure. As it was, Ralegh's ship's lading might not have been brought back nor was there a chance that her expenses would be covered, while a great question mark hung over what Grenville would do once the primary object of his voyage, the reinforcement of the colony, was frustrated by the absence of the settlement he had gone to reinforce. Would he defy the evidence of failure that confronted him and leave several hundred men, perhaps, to try again, or would he abandon the colonizing objective and come home with his force intact? He might indeed send home further prizes, in addition to those which had already, we must presume, reached Bideford, but doubts about the validity of the seizure of these prizes were to arise very soon.[1]

To questions about the future of a Roanoke colony were joined questions about the result of Grenville's voyages. Ralegh was rich but he was not anxious to throw money away and not only had many duties been thrust on him, but also the real problem of setting up his Irish colony had to be faced. Settlement in Ireland was not thought to be as speculative as an American colony it is true, but it was at least as onerous, and to be launched on a scale larger than anything that could be planned for North America. Ralegh was by now assured of his vast estate in Munster. The English privy council, mainly under pressure from Lord Burghley, had decided on the precise terms under which land was to be taken up. Grantees ("undertakers") had to plant freeholders and tenant farmers under rigid terms of clearing and fencing land and bringing specified numbers to their estates within a limited time. Ralegh's agents were busy in the West Country raising recruits for the scheme. Nothing like it would be attempted in North America for a generation. Of course, Ralegh could leave a great deal to his agents, who appear to have served him well, and inducing farmers to go to Ireland, only a day's sail from Plymouth, was much easier than expecting them to make their way into an unknown wilderness, as they thought, in America. Munster and its plantation was the greatest disincentive Ralegh could have had at that moment from entertaining further elaborate plans for American colonization. At the same time his genuine interest in the reports he received about the Roanoke voyages set him to devising ways and means of carrying on the project once he knew what had befallen Grenville and his expedition.

In any event, there was one major obstacle to a further colonizing plan. Lane had returned, if not exactly discouraged, at least skeptical about further prospects. Many others had come back with much less favorable views than his. Thomas Harvey was to spread about the complaint that his spell as cape merchant had ruined him financially because there was nothing to buy or sell.[2] But the majority of the colonists were saying that they had been badly governed and that the country itself was useless. Some were bragging about great exploits that they had never performed. Others maintained that no effort there was worthwhile. Most damning of all was that the gentlemen who had been brought out to stiffen the military element and to provide a measure of initiative in the exploration and exploitation of the country seem almost uniformly to have given the Roanoke colony a bad name: the living conditions were primitive; the food was poor; there were none of the amenities that civilized and cultivated men were used to; above all, there was no gold nor any sign of it, and without gold what was the point of suffering discomfort, even hardship, in a strange land with nothing better to offer than indigestible corn and wild, untamed people? Thomas Harriot was to scarify such ex-members of the colony in the pamphlet that he sat down to write toward the end of 1586.

Some had chafed at discipline:

> Of our company that returned some for their misdemeanour and ill dealing in the country have been there worthily punished, who by reason of their bad natures, have maliciously not only spoken ill of their governors, but for their sakes slandered the country itself. The like also have those done which were of their consort.

We could well do with further knowledge of what Lane had to contend with from such men. As we already have seen, Richard Butler claimed that even before Grenville's return a party he was with had attacked an Indian group, killed men, and brought women to be bartered off as gifts to other local Indians.[3] Such conduct may well have broken out from time to time, though we can sense that Lane made every effort to keep it under control until the very last stages. Even then perhaps he acted with more force than was necessary, as Harriot laments:

> Some of our company towards the end of the year shewed themselves too fierce in slaying some of the people in some towns upon causes that on our part might easily enough have been borne withall.

Whether he is speaking here of Lane—apparently not, as Lane had read and approved his book before it was finally published in 1588—the violence of the military and the upper-class treatment of supposed "inferiors" or even opponents (witness the willingness of Grenville to take violent punitive action against a minor infringement by the Indians of Aquascogoc in July 1585) were disruptive. Restlessness and arrogance certainly were rampant and when restrained brought complaints of too sharp disciplinary action.

Harriot might be technically a gentleman, as he had a university degree, but he had no respect for gentlemen colonists who were unwilling to suffer the minor discomforts and hardships that he evidently tolerated without complaint. His scorn for these men had no limits:

> Some also were of a nice [sheltered, we might say] bringing up only in cities and towns, or such as never (as I may say) had seen the world before. Because there were not to be found any English cities [some may have gone with visions of new Tenochtitlans to be discovered], nor such fair houses, nor at their own wish any of their old accustomed dainty food nor any soft beds of down or feathers, the country was to them miserable and their reports thereof according.

The bad press given the Roanoke colony by the returned colonists, or the majority of them, could scarcely have been worse, while at the same time the Munster lands were advertised as accessible, already cultivated if neglected, with old castles and houses merely needing rehabilitation. In 1586 it appeared that many of the things Virginia lacked, Munster offered—even if reality there proved harsher for many than was anticipated. Perhaps the greatest hardship Lane's colonists suffered was psychological: they were cut off from their homeland, without means of contacting their friends and relatives and above all without the great alternative to isolation, the expectation of coming home rich, which would have smoothed away many of their cares.

Once he had interrogated Lane and probably some of the gentlemen colonists and instructed Lane to write a detailed account of his experiences, Ralegh could turn to the more exciting and positive results of the colony's experience—the map, the pictures, the detailed notes, and the specimens that Thomas Harriot and John White had accumulated. Harriot had been brought into his household, most probably in 1583, to apply his theoretical knowledge of mathematics to the practice of sailing across the globe. Evidently he had been a great success both in correcting existing navigating formulas and in inducing experienced seamen to learn somewhat more sophisticated means of finding their position and of carrying out observations at sea. Gentlemen, too, had picked up something of this new fashionable art of navigation so that they would not be wholly at the mercy of masters and pilots when they should happen to gain command of a seagoing vessel. But when the opportunity of going to North America presented itself, Harriot's lively mind had turned to the task of hurriedly acquiring empirical knowledge that he might be expected to apply to a survey of the unexplored lands. Like the all-purpose intellectual that he was, Harriot studied surveying, mapmaking, botany (learned from herbals and the new-fangled Monardes), the elements of geology as they were known at the time (perhaps more to practical builders and architects than to academics), and the like. Sir Francis Drake had demonstrated through his wide-ranging investigations how much could be brought back from a world-encompassing voyage besides gold and jewels. Harriot too may have had some contact with the new topographers. Christopher Saxton had brought out his remarkable atlas of England in 1579, showing for the first time in extensive detail the layout and variety of his native land. This could well have inspired Harriot to attempt something of the same for the new America.

But one cannot place Harriot into the picture of inquiring intelligence and ignore White. If he began as a craftsman in paint, he had clearly learned many things besides. He had almost certainly taken part in some estate surveys and knew the field techniques in practice that Harriot was only learning in theory. He too had a lively and inquiring mind and it is clear that in conjunction with Harriot he had developed his interests along more practical lines. Harriot remained somewhat academic in his concerns: he was determined, for example, to master the linguistic intricacies of the Algonquian language, so different in its concepts and construction as well as in its vocabulary from anything he had encountered among Europeans at Oxford and in Ralegh's company in London. White was more interested in becoming competent to portray the incidents of daily life and to bring out the minutiae of the life-styles of the Native American peoples among whom he happily traveled.

Harriot and White were ideal partners for the survey, though we have no idea how they met. Ralegh almost certainly was made aware of White through the work he had done for Martin Frobisher in the 1577 Arctic expedition. He may even have been employed by Ralegh to survey some lands that were coming into his possession. Whether Ralegh knew Jacques Le Moyne de Morgues in 1583 or 1584, White's mentor then or later, we do not know. But by the time they returned to England in 1586 a perfect partnership had developed between White and Harriot, each supporting the other in his interests and achievements, and cooperating especially in the making of the map. The only flaw in their presentation of the New World to Ralegh was that, because some of the notebooks and drawings—so carefully collected and filed—had been dropped into the waters of Roanoke Sound in the hurried evacuation of the colony, gaps remained in what to both partners must have seemed an almost-completed enterprise, broken though not destroyed by sheer chance and misadventure.

It is not difficult for us to imagine what took place between Ralegh and his two faithful servants as soon as possible after their return and after they had assembled all they had brought back. It may have been difficult for Ralegh to spare as much time as he wished to examine the results of the survey but there is no doubt that his restless intellectual curiosity was stirred by them in a unique way. He was now living in Durham House in the Strand and allocated to Harriot a chamber that became for a time, we may assume, a laboratory for the study of the Roanoke enterprise. The map Harriot and White could show him probably was in sections and on quite a different and larger scale from the one that has survived. On it would be information on vegetation and on Indian occupation which the three could go over in detail from place to place, illustrated by the drawings White had made and the notes Harriot had written. Their long seminar may have taken many of the broken days and nights that Ralegh's duties and responsibilities allowed him. He had met Manteo and Wanchese before and now, Manteo, who had returned with the colonists, must at times have made a fourth partner to their deliberations. The contribution of the new visitor, Towaye, to these discussions, if any, is not known.

If it was exciting for Ralegh to see the New World vicariously in this way, it must also have been disappointing as the picture cumulatively developed. The existence of many occupied villages in what had appeared to be a reasonably empty land into which colonists could be intruded without too much displacement of native society must have seemed an unforeseen obstacle to extensive settlement of Englishmen. There is no reason to believe that Ralegh intended the removal of the inhabitants (though the same cannot be said of Grenville's projections). Moreover, the lack of open ground, with the great areas of swamp forest that were useless for short-term occupation, must have been an unsatisfactory revelation, as must the shallowness of the sounds and the narrow and shifting nature of the Outer Banks and their attendant shoals. Ralegh, too, was greedy as well as being intellectually involved in the whole range of contemporary human interests and knowledge. The gold some expected and Lane still half hoped for was simply not there and if copper was to be found in the end it would not amount to a great deal more than the iron that Harriot assured him was also present. The negative side, as revealed in detail, was a disturbing and depressing one, after so much optimism had emerged from the Amadas-Barlowe reconnaissance.

At the same time there were compensations. The healthy condi-

tion of the colonists throughout their stay indicated that this was
no Caribbean death trap, which privateers were finding drastically
trimmed the numbers of their fighting men with unknown but often
fatal diseases. It is especially interesting to us that there was no hint
of the malaria which became such an impediment to the development of the Cheapeake colonies later. It was clear that, with care and
discipline, Englishmen could live healthier lives in America than in
England. A further benefit was that, where soil was cleared, it was
very fertile, even if, as we suspect, the corn sown for Lane in April
1586 was planted in discarded Indian fields. The stress on the enormous yield of maize and its function as an all-purpose grain food was
important. A basic food crop to a grain-sustained people like the
English was of supreme importance, whatever minor defects a corn-
supported diet might prove to have in practice. The promise of
sassafras and other medicinal drugs was clearly attractive and would
keep Ralegh interested in trade with North American peoples for a
long time to come. But was there much else? Certainly not, if riches
were to be acquired rapidly—there was nothing more and probably
less than was to be gained in Ireland, except no doubt advantages of
climate and prospects of a wider range of cultivable crops. Just as
Ralegh was committed to stimulate and organize agriculture in Munster, so it must have seemed to him that agriculture was to be the
main resource if American land was to be settled and developed.
The attraction of sending farmers, rather than soldiers, or miners,
or craftsmen, must have presented itself to him as the pictures
and the expositions of White and Harriot informed him—in the kind
of detail that had never before been available to an English overseas entrepreneur—about the resources of the new land across the
ocean, even if many of its possible resources remained undeveloped,
even unproven.

To whatever Lane had said about Chesapeake Bay, Harriot and
White were able to add much more. As we have seen, they had
entered the great bay between Cape Henry and Cape Charles and
had followed a line of harbors from Lynnhaven Bay to the Elizabeth
River and to Hampton Roads (though whether they entered the
latter is open to speculation). Here was an expanse of water that
might accommodate any number of deep-draught vessels (insofar as
the term applied to ships of that time). Moreover, it was sparsely

populated. The Chesapeake tribe was credited with only three villages, though we would think that they must have had some more.
George Percy was to comment twenty years later on the open spaces
covered with strawberries that he saw;[4] John Smith was to remark on
the enormous size of the trees spaced along the Elizabeth River.[5] It
may well be that the understory was kept clear by the Indians for
hunting, but for whatever reason it was apparently not dense. Moreover, this area to the south, below the sandy fringes from Cape
Henry westward, had rich soil, as the Great Dismal Swamp had
already retreated some way, leaving behind deep peaty humus from
which rich crops could be raised. There can be little doubt that all
this had been tested thoroughly by Harriot and White, and that they
had detailed drawings and data to establish it, which were not published then or later—indeed, they were deliberately concealed. This
raised still further the prospects of establishing a farming colony in
this area, especially as the Indians had maintained friendly relations
with the "Colonel of the Chesepians" and the surveying party during
their winter residence there and had been able to keep them supplied with food without difficulty or friction. In saying this a good
deal of inference must be used but it is consistent with what we
know from other elements later in the story.

Ralegh was eventually left to deliberate on these matters. One
thing we know he did was to consult the younger Richard Hakluyt,
then back at his diplomatic task in Paris. Hakluyt was sent a summary
of the conclusions Ralegh had reached from his discussions with
Lane, Harriot, and White and was asked for his opinion. Hakluyt had
also been investigating renewed Spanish interest in western North
America and had sent Harriot a copy of his pamphlet reprint of the
account of the expedition of Antonio de Espejo into New Mexico in
1582.[6] Moreover, he had told Ralegh he had obtained a map of these
discoveries and promised to send it to him. André Homem was
working on it, apparently making a copy. This seems to have been a
map relating to the earlier expedition of Francisco Chamuscado in
1581, which must have been intercepted by a French privateer on its
way to Spain and acquired for Ralegh. It was later to be in Harriot's
possession though it has wholly disappeared. This was not irrelevant
to possible further enterprises in eastern North America. John White
was fitting together his and Harriot's detailed map into a general

picture of this extensive shoreline, and not doing so very well, judging by the surviving copy of that map; in it he accepted the long-
enduring concept of the Verrazzanian Sea. This, Verrazzano believed,
jutted into western America and made some part of eastern North
America accessible to the Pacific. The Carolina Sounds were now
known for what they were, but who knew whether the great Chesapeake Bay, when properly explored (as John Smith thought until he
reached the fall line on the Potomac), might not reveal the water-
shed between east and west and lead Englishmen to New Mexico or
even to Francis Drake's New Albion? In the light of knowledge that
was available to Spain if not fully to the rest of the world, these
concepts must have seemed fanciful to the utmost degree, but Ralegh had a strain of fancy in him, a desire to believe in the unlikely or
even impossible, as later exemplified in his search for El Dorado. We
can be quite sure that this question was propounded between Ralegh and Harriot in the months following the colony's return and
that the revival of the Verrazzanian concept on White's general map
was one result of these discussions.

But if Hakluyt was involved with Ralegh in such speculations he
was also being fully briefed on the reports of Lane, Harriot, and
White, and his opinion asked about the possibilities of directing
further colonies to America and, if so, where, while the advantages
of the Chesapeake were evidently raised with him. His answer came
clear and forthright in his letter to Ralegh of 30 December 1586:

> If you proceed, which I long much to know, in your enterprise
> of Virginia, your best planting will be about the bay of the
> Chesepians, to which latitude Peter Martyr and Francisco Lopez
> de Gómara the Spaniard confess that our Cabot [Sebastian,
> rather than John, and spelled "Gabot"] and the English did first
> discover, which the Spaniards hereafter cannot deny us when-
> ever we shall be at peace with them. And your voyage of Anto-
> nio de Espejo bringeth you to rich silver mines up in the coun-
> try in the latitude of 37 ½°.[7]

The last sentence ties up the two areas, Chesapeake Bay, which he
would have been told opened at 37 degrees north latitude, and the
western discoveries, not so long before, of rich silver mines (they
were in their turn to prove elusive) in New Mexico in the same or

nearly the same latitude, though Ralegh would have been amazed at the size of the landmass that lay between the two had he been able to distinguish reality from speculation.[8]

At that point, before Hakluyt's letter reached England, Ralegh would have received news of Grenville's return to Bideford in December. It is probable that the two men soon communicated with each other and met as early as it was convenient for them to do so, Grenville most probably coming to London. He did not come empty-handed as he had one rich prize from Puerto Rico to show for so much wasted effort, but his report must have given Ralegh considerable disquiet. (We do not know when his own, ineffective, supply ship had come home and what the information reported by her captain had been.) Grenville could state that the physical installations on Roanoke Island were indeed intact but that virtually no Indians were seen during his own explorations, which, as previously noted, were never specified. This was probably what led him to abandon his plan to leave a substantial colony behind him. As has been indicated, the half measures he had taken, leaving a handful of men behind under Coffin and Chapeman, were intended to mark the continued occupation of the area until further measures could be taken to abandon or develop the colonial enterprise. Because Grenville knew nothing of the circumstances of the first colony's departure, he had to be informed about them as well as about the discussion that had been underway, based on the reports received, for the previous five months. What he, and perhaps his captive Indian, had to contribute to the discussion we do not know, but it was clear that he was not willing or able to return in 1587 even to repatriate his handful of settlers, as his Irish properties—if not as extensive as those of Ralegh—were now ripe for development and would take all the time he could spare. It is possible, however, that he was willing to prepare a privateering squadron which might, under other leadership, make a call at Roanoke Island on its return voyage.

Ralegh had to make a decision: to renew the settlement on Chesapeake Bay on some basis to be worked out, or to abandon it and bring Grenville's men home, or to find some interim solution until major efforts might be undertaken to appropriate a substantial part of the region to his and the Queen's uses. He was helped to select one of these alternatives by the attitude of John White and a few others who had been with him on Roanoke Island. Whereas the majority of the colonists were sorry they had gone and were determined not to return, White had become so attached to the idea of living there that he was anxious to go back. Not only that, but he declared his willingness to lead a colony back to the promised land, for this is what North America had become for him. We may probably conclude that the consensus of the reports Ralegh had received since the return of the first colony was that a second colony (ignoring Grenville's men on Roanoke Island) should be one of self-supporting families, farming land there; rather than become dependent on Ralegh for maintenance, they should be capable of producing for themselves. White and Harriot had no objection to Roanoke Island except that it belonged to the Indians and their expulsion from it would continue to cause bad feeling between them and the English. The Chesapeake, on the other hand, seemed to offer land that could be appropriated for a colony with the consent of the Indians who nominally occupied it but who had land to spare within which a white community could be accommodated. We are not ignorant of the fact that hunting land, even if sparsely occupied, was as much a part of the heritage of a particular Indian group as cultivable land, but in this case the main source of game was to the south of the Indian settlement area, in a region that was otherwise uninhabitable, namely the Great Dismal Swamp, which Indians could penetrate in their canoes or through precarious passageways and where bears, rather than deer, were the chief objective for flesh and furs.[9] This, theoretically at least, made it easier for them to contemplate the intrusion of a white community into hunting land that was not a necessity for them and that was therefore less highly regarded. To some extent this is guesswork, but it seems to be borne out by what very little we know about Chesapeake society, and by the long background of prehistoric occupation of an area on the edge of the swamp where game was present in great numbers if only the specialized knowledge to kill it was available to the peoples who lived around its borders.

The Irish factor again stood in the way of the free recruiting of men for a further North American colony. From Cheshire and Lancashire down through the English midlands and along the southwest from Cornwall to Hampshire, busy agents of "undertakers" for the Munster plantation were engaged in recruiting settlers, mainly farmers if they could get them, for this venture. In these areas there was not much hope of a rival venture of the same sort for North America because the apparent attractions of the nearer settlement seemed obvious. The sphere of possible recruitment was thus confined to the southeast, or appeared to be so. London was thus the objective of White and his associates in attempting to find men who would bring their wives and children out into the wilds to try a hitherto unparalleled venture in North America. At this time London was a mélange of new and old occupants. Population was growing in England as a whole, but the basic wool and cloth industry was not expanding and though new small industries were springing up in many parts away from London the employment they offered was still limited. London had industry, new and old: London was the center of commerce and offered the opportunity of trading in goods, wholesale or retail, large- or small-scale, while its shipping was employing increasing numbers of men on shore as well as on the ships that sailed into and out of the Thames.

London, too, had an elaborate system of trade guilds. The twelve great companies were the preserve of the rich and those who were getting richer; only exceptional luck and backing could insert a man into one of them. The hundred or more lesser livery companies, as they were called, covered trades prosaic and exotic, skilled and menial, but all involved apprenticeship, then employment as a journeyman, and finally, with luck and drive, an independent mastership. But even this amounted to little in the menial trades. Unskilled labor coming in from the provinces and some skilled men displaced in their own towns provided illegal competition to the established craftsmen. They, in turn, might be glad to get out of London and try their hands at something quite different in another environment. Nor were they necessarily narrow specialists in their own crafts. London was a city of gardens, large and small, and many of the men of the humbler as well as the greater trades grew some of their own foodstuffs. If they were not agriculturists they or their wives were at least not wholly incapable of raising garden crops, and from such accounts as White could give them, the raising of crops was a great deal easier in North America than in England, with better weather, higher yields, and differing crops, all pointing to some easier degree of subsistence. In England, too, such men were wholly debarred from hunting—even if in London they would have little opportunity to do so—by laws restricting such activities to country landholders. They might keep a few "conies" or fowl for their family's food but that was all. And meat was dear in London. Fresh fish was not easy to obtain either, though there were usually herrings and dried salt cod to be had. The chances of a wider diet of game and fish were particularly attractive to townsmen. Apart from that, the city had many physical and moral disadvantages repugnant to many of its inhabitants.

It was from this class White himself had sprung. It was true that at his back was a Cornish family of some little substance in Truro, but that had led only to his apprenticeship, if we are correct, in one of the minor guilds, the Painter Stainers', though one with more opportunities than many for upward mobility. He himself had escaped to pastures new in 1577, in 1584, and in 1585–86. He had pictures to make after these episodes which were salable to greater men—and there is little doubt that he was busy copying his drawings for sale almost from the moment he landed—and could dispose of them in London among the merchant class as well as through his contacts with great men at Court. Such men as he, too, would in the course of time accumulate a modest capital, buy a house or two, a garden plot, a building site, which could, when sold, finance a place in a colonial venture in America or, indeed, in Ireland. But to Londoners Ireland was almost as far away as America, whereas to people of Bristol or Chester it was almost next door. It was, therefore, among such people that White went looking for possible recruits. It is especially difficult to trace families of this level of society. The lesser guilds did not necessarily keep such meticulous records as the greater ones; time and the Fire of London in 1666 had dealt more hardly with them. Many men in this class had common names and can be identified only by chance in parish registers and wills. But William S. Powell has at least indicated something of the context of White's London life.

White had a wife, though she may have been dead by 1586. He had a daughter Elenor, and it is probable he had a son John,[10] though perhaps he was born later of a subsequent marriage. Elenor was of an age to marry—over sixteen and under twenty, we might assume from contemporary examples—and her chosen husband was a member of the Tilers' Company, Ananias Dare, a brickmaker as well as a tiler, who had had an illegitimate son, not an infrequent thing to happen in a crowded city, but who was like White himself a man of some little substance. This much has been found, and it is probably a good lead into the stratum of society in which White found most takers for his plans to lead a farming, self-reliant settlement to America. For if White could assemble families who would sell their possessions and thus finance their own enterprise, he would have people who would be freer than those going to Ireland, who would be controlled by "undertakers" and limited by rigid terms of plantation. White's kind of people could make their own rules and live their own lives, provided Ralegh, as supreme lord and governor of Virginia, as he was to remain until 1603, would allow them to do so.

Clearly Ralegh was willing to respond. He could provide them with shipping and some means of defense, but he was not, at the time, anxious to commit himself to capital expenditure in maintaining a colony. The men who took his wages in 1585 offered no material return for it, so far as we can ascertain, when they returned in 1586. This was capital invested in manual labor and protective guards that produced not a single penny in profit. Material profits came from captures on the high seas and if they paid Ralegh's initial expenses in 1585 it is doubtful whether similar captures did quite so much for Grenville in 1586, though it is not impossible that they did so and repaid something of what Ralegh had contributed as well. The report that Harriot and White brought back was also a dividend of a sort. But to sponsor a colony that would be self-supporting once it reached America was a different matter. The colonists could fend for themselves and perhaps, in turn, send back products that would enable them to maintain something like English amenities by their sale and the return of commodities they could not make or acquire on the spot. Above all, they would keep Ralegh's authority alive and open up the prospects of further developments on the Chesapeake if and when opportunity offered.

Some other indications in Powell's provisional identifications suggest the area from which colonists were to be drawn. Members of

the "great" companies were not always rich and powerful: they might
be young journeymen out of their time, with no opportunity to set
up as a master; they might have committed some offense, such as
especially, getting into debt, which made it wise to leave the country;
or they may simply have been sufficiently adventurous to jump over
the counter and take their chance in a new land. If we suspect that
Thomas Harvey of the powerful Grocers' Company became cape
merchant in 1585–86 because he had something to hide in America,
we might say the same about the William Brown, goldsmith, who
could have been recruited in 1587 (or he could have been a brother
of the Maurice Browne who had also been from a London family
and followed Sir Humphrey Gilbert to his death in 1583).[11] Another
member of such a company, William Nicholes of the Clothworkers'
Company, could have come to America because a relative (brother?)
joined the managing group of the colony; the latter was to remain in
London and continue his support for the ventures at least into 1589.
Further research on the London City Companies and especially on
the manuscript parish registers and in the wills in the London Guild-
hall may well reveal other "possibles" and "probables."

London was not an ideal place for people to live. Although it
attracted those who lived elsewhere, who crowded into it, to the
old-established Londoners it might well seem to be a place to get out
of as it became more crowded and plague-ridden. And for good-
living people it also held many unsavory aspects. Thomas Lodge, a
voyager himself, and Robert Greene, the prose writer and satirist,
combined to write A looking glass for London, published in 1594, which
contained some exaggeration indeed, but more than a hint of why
some people might not wish to stay in that city if they could help it.
They wrote:

> O London! Maiden of the mistress isle,
> Wrapped in the folds and swathing clouts of shame:
> In thee more sins than Ninevah contains,
> Contempt of God, despite of reverent age;
> Neglect of law, desire to wrong the poor;
> Corruption, whoredom, drunkenness and pride.
> O proud, adulterous glory of the West!
> Thy neighbour burns, yet dost thou stop thine ears.
> Th 'larum rings, yet sleepest thou secure.

London awake! For fear the Lord do frown.
I set a looking glass before thine eyes.
O turn! O turn! With weeping to the Lord,
And think the prayer and virtues of thy Queen
Defers the plague which otherwise would fall.
Repent O London!

The work of William S. Powell indicates that at least thirty of the families' surnames (of course, many of them common ones) appear in the more accessible London records of the time and adds weight to the assumption that members of the new colony in preparation were recruited primarily from London.[12]

Essex too, the great agricultural neighbor of London, was another obvious source of colonists, especially those who were familiar with working the land. The county records of Essex (at Powell's hands) have turned up a few suggestive names. Mark Bennet, the husband-man, seems not unlikely and would fit into the agricultural pattern. The fact that James Hynde and William Clement were in Colchester prison together and the same two names appear in the list of colonists is very suggestive. The Thamesside parishes of Essex and indeed the county as a whole would seem to be a very likely recruiting ground.

One of the unexplained associations of this group of would-be colonists is with Portsmouth and the Isle of Wight. This may be simply because Sir George Carey, the self-styled "governor" of the island and a friend of Ralegh, wished to give the colony some assistance and perhaps to use the Chesapeake as a base for his privateers. But it may have quite a different implication. In 1586 many too hopeful settlers arrived in Munster expecting to find their lands laid out for them, but the survey was far from complete: many of the "undertakers" had not complied with the legal preliminaries and were wholly unable to cope with freeholders and tenants. Some of these people stuck it out and remained in Ireland until they could get installed. Others speedily became disillusioned, or did not have the resources to enable them to stay, and returned to England. One of the ports to which they could well have come was Portsmouth and we might think that perhaps from among them were recruited men and women who had turned from Munster to North America.

Such speculation will not take us far, but any ideas that the White colony had its bases in the West Country are certainly false. A few individuals may indeed have had roots there, like White himself, and may have drawn in relatives and friends but there is little or no evidence of it. The present indications are that it was a colony of Londoners with possibly some accretions from Essex and Hampshire, and conceivably, from some of the other southeastern counties as well. These counties are among the best-documented in the country, but they are also among the most thickly-populated, so that searching for men and women with common names is to jump into a morass. There are scores of John Whites alone to be found, though we are on moderately firm ground with the one we have. Powell makes a number of ingenious suggestions that could add to the number of identifications, but he would be the last to assert that we are certain even of so much as has been suggested here, beyond the few basic facts of the essentially London character of the colony.

The last month or two of 1586 were hectic ones for John White. The decision to form the new type of colony may have been made in principle as early as October or at latest November 1586, even though final plans for the actual voyage are unlikely to have been completed before Grenville's return. He must have had the support and aid of other returned members of the colony, even though they may not have all intended to come back to America. The role of Simon Fernandes in these formative months is unknown but it might seem that he took an active part, probably in helping to get shipping and to enlist sailors for the forthcoming voyage: if he was married in the city of London, as seems likely, he may indeed have contemplated bringing his wife, and possibly family, to America. But no student of his personality and actions can believe that he was wholly sincere. From the first he may have supported the new venture in hopes of exploiting it for himself as its admiral and without any real intention of helping to make the proposed settlement a permanent one or its interests paramount.

The fact that the men White gathered around him in December 1586 and became publicly associated with in January 1587 are virtually unknown, except for Fernandes and White's son-in-law, Ananias Dare, illustrates the point already made: that is, we may assume from the context of affairs, that these men were all, or almost all, Londoners. They came from the virtually unknown London lower middle class, men who had some little substance in the city but who for some reason were attracted by the chance of getting to a new land graphically and fully illustrated by White (whose drawings must have circulated widely in copies) and by the enthusiastic reports of Thomas Harriot, together with the powerful backing of Ralegh.

An entirely new type of organization was being put together and for its creation we probably have to thank Ralegh himself. What it offered the participants was incorporation under Ralegh as the Governor and Assistants of the City of Ralegh in Virginia. This would give them some status as a body of men capable of raising money and of distributing land and so would make it possible for them to raise subscribers among their friends who would stay at home (though the commitment to pay dividends to subscribers was one that was not easy to formulate). Ralegh assured those who would go on the voyages that they could distribute as much as five hundred acres each, a very large farm in England at the time, to any family or independent individual who went. If five hundred acres of wilderness, or of land already belonging in some manner or other to the native peoples, may not seem much to us, it was a fortune in prospect to the type of intending settlers that we have considered as most likely to take part.

What is not clear, and probably never will be, is whether all those recruited were to enjoy full status in the colony from the beginning, or whether some were to come as servants to others and win their freedom and land only after a period of working for them. A minimum investment in money and goods would seem to have been a necessary condition of acceptance as a full participant. In that case, those who were prepared to come but did not have that minimum could only proceed as dependents of a colonist who was better off. So we can assume, though we cannot prove, that the intending participants were grouped in two classes: those who could pay their way fully and those who must literally work their passage by sea and land like the indentured servants of the next century. This did not preclude the financing of individuals or families by relatives or investors who did not themselves wish to come. As we do not know anything about the business arrangements in detail, we can only speculate. It is impossible to find out what the minimum subscription was for a man, or for a family, but it cannot have been too small. These people intended to sell their property, or borrow on the strength of it, and they were not coming to America without adequate equipment or assurance of money behind them to finance future supplies when they arrived. Thus the venture can be thought of primarily as a bourgeois undertaking, that of a mainly middle-class group which was not satisfied for some reason with its prospects at home and, at the same time, was enticed by the prospects abroad, despite the bad reports put about by the majority of Lane's colonists when they returned to England.

There is no doubt that a primary incentive was land, land in quantities that small capitalists could never hope to acquire in England. There was also the attraction of novelties in both climate, foodstuffs, and animal products, which seemed to assure them of a better life for less effort than in London, Essex, or elsewhere in southern England. There is no hint in the surviving materials that intending colonists had an ideological reason for leaving England, but it is not at all impossible that some of them, possibly the majority of them, had such a reason. The Anglican Church had existed for nearly a generation and during that time had not, in the opinion of many people in England, especially in the southeast, become sufficiently Protestant. Throughout that period, the hierarchy had become more traditional and powerful. All efforts in Parliament to obtain concessions in the way of a more nontraditional prayer book and of some measure of participation in church affairs for laymen had been stifled. Preaching was frowned on and, if the Bible came off the presses regularly and in remarkable numbers, it was less and less, it seemed to many, the basis for a reformed church as they desired it to be. Already some puritans had broken away from the church and were carrying on an illegal Presbyterian system in secret, in which participation of the laity and the discarding of bishops had already begun and for which some had already suffered punishment.

There is no specific reason to believe that the would-be colonists were puritans of any extreme sort, though a few may have been, but removal to an atmosphere in which it was possible to work out a less restrictive church organization based on a more purely Protestant ethic could conceivably have acted as an additional incentive. After all, it was among just such middle-class commercial circles that Protestantism had come to England and was to remain most firmly entrenched. Thus speculation of this sort is not without some possible justification. It is something we must bear in mind even if the indications are not, so far, evident. These were clearly not Separatists, for if they had been, Ralegh could scarcely have encouraged them, but they could very well have been Protestant purists and the opportunity to create a Protestant type of worship was a very real prospect in any North American context even in the 1580s.

The founding documents for the creation of the new project were two. One was the contract (we cannot call it a charter as documents of this character were issued only by the Queen) creating the City of Ralegh in Virginia. This we do not have, and the lack of it hampers much of what can be said with confidence about the organization of the venture. From an indirect source (the grant of arms discussed below) we can reconstruct its essentials. By it, Ralegh relinquished his authority over an undefined portion of his claim to North American land to a syndicate to which he gave corporate status. Our greatest lack is in not knowing how specific it was with regard to location. We can only speculate that it comprised the lands and waters that lay to the north of Roanoke Island and between it and Chesapeake Bay, but whether it made any definition of the western extent of this territory there is no indication whatsoever. For Roanoke Island and territories adjacent to it, other plans were in prospect. We must assume that one limitation to the grant was made, and that was the reservation of land around one or more ports on Chesapeake Bay for ultimate development as a shipping base or bases for Ralegh, his associates, or even for the state, to be used primarily as a strategic reserve for maritime forces in the event of the continuance and widening of the struggle with Spain. This was not intended to interfere with the settlement or to intrude on it, but the probability that English ships would be using Chesapeake Bay and that continuing contact with England would be maintained in this way could have acted as a powerful encouragement to people who wanted to live their own life yet not lose all ties with their homeland except through occasional cargoes going and coming on a commercial basis.

John White was to be governor of the city of Ralegh. His emergence in this position often surprised earlier writers who could not believe that the painter would also have ambitions to be an entrepreneur. His drawings certainly reveal a man of considerable sensibility;

his cooperation with Harriot had brought him sophistication and knowledge of a wide range of skills. His feeling for the country and for the people he had drawn and lived among shines through all the materials, few as they are, he has left us. With him, and with some powers to control, as well as, we can assume, to advise, were twelve Assistants. One of them was Simon Fernandes, whose genuineness in support of the venture remains in doubt; another was his son-in-law Ananias Dare of whose capacities, beyond the fact that White had entrusted him with his daughter as his wife, we know little. Of the other ten it can truly be said we know nothing at all. Because in the list we have Roger Baylye's name appears next to White, he may well have been his most trusted associate. Christopher Cooper, John Sampson, Thomas Steevens, William Fullwood, Roger Pratt, Dyonise Harvey, John Nicholls, George Howe, and James Plat remain as blank to us as they have been ever since their names were first printed by Richard Hakluyt in his *Principall navigations* in 1589.

The document that we do have is a record of Ralegh's attempt to gain these men social status befitting the potential rulers of a new social unit—indeed, in prospect, a new society—in America.[13] This was to grant each of them a coat of arms, which, in English social custom, automatically made them gentlemen and endowed them with a lineage that would make them, as founders of families in the colony, a minor aristocracy. The Office of Arms, under William Dethick, "Garter Principal King of Arms and Chief Officer of Arms for the Most Noble Order of the Garter," was expected to issue grants of arms only to persons who were able or willing to assume arms, which involved the payment of fees and the endorsement of persons of rank. Dethick had made it an unscrupulous business, by which he sold grants of arms (and therefore certificates of gentility, for what they were worth) to anyone who paid for them, and would devise coats of arms as required. In this case Sir Walter Ralegh paid him to grant coats of arms both to the city and to the thirteen persons who were to govern the new City of Ralegh in Virginia. This was a publicity exercise, aimed at giving status to the enterprisers of what may well have seemed to cautious business interests in London a dubious and catchpenny venture. It has also considerable psychological value as an incentive. The colonists could be confident of being led by

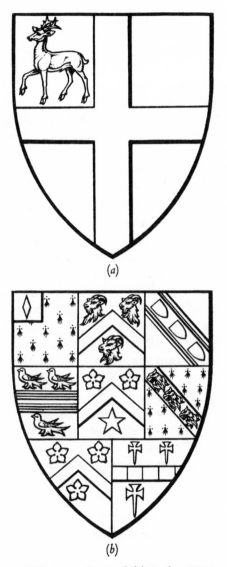

(a)

(b)

19. 7 January 1587, Arms Granted (a) to the "Cittie of Ralegh,"
and (b) to John White.
Drawn from Grant of Arms, College of Heralds, London, for D. B. Quinn,
The Roanoke Voyages, 1584–1590 (Cambridge: Hakluyt Society, 1955) vol. 2,
facing p. 509.

men who had received, if not necessarily earned, the right to be regarded as gentlemen and so could carry that status over into their leadership of the colony. First, the City of Ralegh was to have its arms—the red cross of St. George, symbolizing its continuity inside the English dominions of the Queen and, in the first quarter, the roebuck, the badge of Sir Walter Ralegh. This was an elegant and justifiable adjunct to the creation of a new urban enterprise such as this; in the end, it would be, or so it was hoped, a "City" in a wide sense, a colony-city of a new kind.

It was easy enough to grant John White arms because he undoubtedly had Cornish gentry among his forebears, but his coat of arms was a complex one of eight quarterings linking him not only with the Whites of Truro, which was probably correct, but with no less than seven other armigerous families, mainly of the southwest, which may or may not have been justified. A close analysis of the other coats by John A. Neville[14] suggests that several of them indicate links of some sort, more probably invented than real, between a few of the other Assistants and arms-bearing families in the southeast of England, but no satisfactory direct linkage has emerged, nor is it necessary that there should have been one. Coats of arms were granted to Simon Fernandes and to three of the other Assistants, John Sampson, Thomas Steevens, and James Plat, whose names were not even known to the person who compiled the official record of the grant. The whole thing was an elaborate showpiece designed to enlarge the status of the leaders, and it is not impossible that Ralegh, with his strong sense of theater, arranged that the arms be formally granted and the parchments setting them out presented to the recipients by an officer of the Office of Arms at Durham House or some place inside the city itself where the occasion could be used to publicize the colony. If so, we might conclude that the ceremony took place on 7 January 1587, the date of the grant—but all of this must remain conjecture.

We know astonishingly little about the preparations for the new colony. White and his associates had evidently received a sufficient number of promises from people willing to participate before the documents of 7 January were signed. Arrangements for their departure to North America would involve selling their established businesses or properties and turning the whole, or the greater part, of the proceeds into equipment for the journey. In many cases one would presume that they left some of their money with friends whom they could trust to safeguard it for them in case they needed further supplies from England or in the event of their return. In the majority of cases wives and children, we should assume, were left behind; they would be sent for in due course when the colony was established. John White would be able to inform the colonists about what kind of weather they could anticipate. However, because the winter of 1585–86 evidently had been exceptionally mild, he did not know how bitter even the Chesapeake Bay area could be in winter, or at least in the depth of some winters, and may not have advised them to bring enough warm clothes. We can be sure that he could offer very good advice about what they would need in the way of household equipment, cooking utensils and instruments, tools, weapons, fishing gear, and so on. It is not at all unlikely that he ordered a supply of tiles to be used to ballast the ships; later, in the colony, they would be used to secure the wooden houses as a neces-sary precaution against their casual destruction by fire. He would stress the need for a forge and handmills and saws as well, probably, as equipment to build water-driven mills for grinding corn if they could be contained in reasonably small bulk. Certainly quantities of bar iron were added to the ballast, as some was later found on Roanoke Island; lead, copper, and other durables would also be necessary. What he suggested should be brought for the Indian trade he undoubtedly hoped for we cannot say precisely, but his list probably included much copper (some of it cut to suit Indian desires for gorgets and decorations of various sorts), beads in quantity al-most certainly, trinkets like bells, fancy ribbons and pieces of colored cloth, and, perhaps, too, English dolls such as the one the little girl he drew at Secotan found so acceptable. Perhaps experience had suggested other things useful for exchange about which we do not know—for example, the casting counters the 1585–86 colony used, either for accounting or for gifts.

By now, it was also clear to White the range of craftsmen he would need. His own equipment of painting materials, paper, and so forth he would have chosen carefully. He had a collection of maps, includ-ing no doubt detailed versions of his own. He had framed drawings, his own and perhaps Le Moyne's, to decorate what would be the principal house in the settlement, that of the governor, where public business might also be transacted. And as the governor and a gentleman, he had his suit of armor, possibly as much for show as for protection, because stout buff coats would turn most Indian arrows. The choice of a smith or smiths and of one or more carpenters he would regard as crucial to the welfare of the colony. He would not worry about metallurgists or perhaps apothecaries (though a surgeon with some medical as well as surgical experience would be highly desirable). He would not need to have specialized traders because many of the people accompanying him would have had experience in commerce, though he would have to assign individuals to care for stores on the voyage and afterward. As he had women with him, he would need to provide them with means of replenishing their wardrobes and repairing and renewing those of the men. Bolts of both fancy and utilitarian cloth would appear to have been necessities.

White could not count on peaceful conditions—his armor and the cannon he provided were to be mute witnesses to this later—so that some of his men would be expected to have experience in fighting. He evidently did not want to be burdened with any of the soldiers of Lane's expedition—nor they with him. From among the colonists of 1586, only John Wright and James Lasie were to remain at his side. We do not know what specialty either man could offer, but we would expect that, just as White himself had learned some Algonquian, so these two also could make themselves understood by their new neighbors.

With children in tow he would need the equipment of learning: hornbooks, writing materials and paper, and books, elementary and advanced. Above all, whatever the precise religious affiliations of the would-be colonists, a number of Bibles (one per family of those who were literate, and most probably were) and prayer books would be required. Practical manuals would be more useful than imaginative or even theological literature. There is no suggestion that a clergyman was considered necessary, though most probably a chaplain sailed on one of the ships and returned on her.

It is reasonable to assume that White circulated some promotional literature, either in the form of a broadsheet setting out the advantages of the colony or a manuscript summary that could be passed from household to household, along with copies of a few of his drawings. It may not be carrying conjecture too far to suppose that he had induced Harriot to prepare a short summary statement of the advantages he saw in continued colonization, and we are sure Harriot was hard at work in the early weeks of 1587, if he had not begun before then, in writing what was to be *A briefe and true report of the new found land of Virginia*, a small book that would fully set out in print the advantages of the new land. But Harriot was always a perfectionist and, in this, his earliest treatise of which we know, a dilatory one as well: it was not finished and dated until February 1587. This was too late to be of any use for the colony of that year—internal evidence strongly supports this unorthodox view of its compilation and completion—and it was put to one side, although we can venture to suggest that a copy accompanied White on his outward voyage. The denunciation of the libelers of the first colony, as Harriot thought them, is too fresh and topical to have been written more than six months or so after their return and his statement that Ralegh was prepared to approve the grant of five hundred acres to any who went clearly applies to a term in the detailed agreement constituting the City of Ralegh of which we have no full record.

The determination to bring some 150 people and to make it a mixed body of men, women, and children was revolutionary, but very much in line with what was going on in Munster at the time, even though the distances and dangers were much greater in the American voyage than in the Irish one. The married women who elected to come were brave and clearly closely attached to their husbands; the unmarried ones may have been servants. Some had probably moved earlier in their life to London and could see moving again as part of a comparable process, but others would never have been uprooted except to marry and settle into homes of their own. When they brought children they were giving additional hostages to fortune, but we must remember it was an age when children, if they survived, had to grow up fast and learn quickly to contribute to the domestic economy, unless they were the minority whose tastes were centered on book learning. Too, the value of an individual child, however much she or he was loved by their parents, was less in ways we find it difficult to understand. Infant mortality was so high and the percentage of births that never reached maturity so large that a woman could risk her child or children perhaps more easily as she could reasonably expect to bear a string of others, more of whom she might hope would survive in the healthy and warm climate of America than in the smoke- and disease-laden atmosphere of London.

In the end, the response of assured and certain colonists was disappointing. Many of those who promised to participate in the venture evidently did not keep their promise, some for good and some for what we might think frivolous reasons. In addition, White and his associates found fewer women who were willing or able to come than would ensure an equally mixed colony, which, we think, was originally intended. It is likely that less than 100 people rather than the hoped for 150 actually left London.

Because our only authority for the colony's progress is John White's diary and he was writing it for Ralegh and other people like Richard Hakluyt, who were presumed to know about the details of the arrangements made before he left England, we know very little indeed about the shipping he employed. The flagship or "Admiral" was the Lion and on her White was to act as captain and Simon Fernandes as chief pilot. She was, by the standards of the time, a substantial vessel of 160 tons, and she was accompanied by a flyboat, a bulk-carrier designed to hold most of the supplies of the colonists. The name of the flyboat is unknown to us, but her master was Edward Spicer (to be drowned three years later in the waters of Pamlico Sound). The pinnace, evidently to be left with the colonists, was under the command of the experienced Captain Edward Stafford, who had been Lane's right-hand man and whom we consider likely to have been the "Colonel of the Chesepians" who had led the Chesapeake Bay party in 1585. If this was so, he would be the most appropriate person to place the colonists in their new home.

These ships were prepared in London, where supplies were laden and many of the colonists boarded. But it is probable that a number preferred to make their own way to Portsmouth to wait for the ships there because there may have been danger of their being detained by winds and weather in the Downs. In due course all three vessels reached Portsmouth, and took on, we may assume, the remaining colonists, possibly including a few who had come to prefer North America to Ireland. On 26 April White moved the ships into Cowes Roads and evidently had some contact with Sir George Carey at

Carisbrooke Castle on the Isle of Wight. There was clearly a link between Carey's interests in privateering and those of White, which will be examined later. The vessels sailed down the English Channel and made a final call at Plymouth, probably to take on supplies of fresh water and also perhaps to make contact with Sir Richard Grenville, before they finally set sail on 8 May.

The pace of preparation at the end of 1586 and the beginning of 1587 had been so rapid that the leisurely excursion down the channel is scarcely explicable, unless the ships had met with bad weather or problems regarding their seaworthiness. The sailing date of 8 May was far too late to set out to plant a settlement firmly before the autumn. Had the colonists left in March they might have had a chance of planting some seed in May or at least getting the benefit of summer fruits and berries, whereas the construction of suitable housing would be best done as soon as possible so there would be time for such refinements as making furnishings and finishing walls, which could be continued over winter. If we were to read backward what happened on the voyage we might even think that Simon Fernandes, for some obscure purposes of his own, was holding back the expedition to prevent a rapid crossing to North America.

White had with him, we must not forget, both Manteo and Towaye. The latter remains an unknown entity to us. It is not unlikely that he had come as a servant to Manteo. Manteo himself had become largely anglicized, at least in English religion and probably also in English letters. Ralegh had given White special instructions regarding him. Roanoke Island must be visited on the way out. From what White's journal says, it might appear Sir Richard Grenville's men would be left there to provide a military presence on which Grenville could build, but Roanoke Island and the surrounding land and water were to be placed in the hands of Manteo as lord and ruler thereof under Sir Walter Ralegh and the Queen. The area was to become, in modern terms, an English protectorate under a civilized Indian ruler and so would guard the rear of the new colony and assist it, as necessary, against any hostile neighbors they might encounter farther north. We can say no more about Manteo except that, so far as can be told, he remained in this position during the hard times that lay ahead.

Concentration on what we know about the preparations for John

White's colony and its apparent objectives should not lead us to
ignore the probability that other things were intended for North
America besides peaceful farming settlement in the interior (as will
be argued) south of Chesapeake Bay. The interest of Ralegh and Lane
in Chesapeake Bay was centered on the likelihood that here at last
was a deep water base that could be used for privateering purposes,
where after a Caribbean campaign ships could find water and fuel,
repair themselves, and put their prizes in order before returning
across the Atlantic. It is possible, too, that if such a program could be
initiated, the bay might do still more, namely provide a base from
which vessels might set out to attack Spain in the Caribbean and,
above all, assault her main fleet, the flota, as it sailed majestically
across the ocean from the New World to Spain each summer or early
autumn. By this time Ralegh knew very well, from Drake in particular, that the Spanish were well aware of the danger that an English
occupation of the Chesapeake Bay would present to them, and that it
was likely some attempt would be made to preempt the English and
settle a Spanish garrison there. This was one reason, it can be suggested, why it was planned to settle the new colony well inland, to
prevent its becoming vulnerable to Spanish reconnaissance patrols
(as indeed it remained concealed from such a patrol in 1588), at least
until a major English military and naval depot could be established in
one of the harbors in the bay itself.

It seems almost certain that some experiment in using the Chesapeake Bay for watering and refitting would be attempted by privateering groups during 1587. On 29 January, Sir George Carey received
authority to send out three privateers, which apparently were designed to test this strategy.[15] These were the ship Commander, of 200
tons, under Captain William Irish, the bark Swallow, of 70 tons, and
the pinnace Gabriel, of 30 tons, carrying 165 men, a formidable little
unit such as was becoming common in the fight against Spain, and
quite competent to overpower a group of merchant vessels or stragglers from the flota though not, of course, to challenge the fleet itself.
On their way home, one or more of these ships was to call in on the
area where the English were expected to be settled. White's visit to
Carey before he sailed suggests that there may have been a more
significant commitment, namely that one of the vessels would carry
some additional stores for White's colony and possibly even a hand-

ful of the laggard colonists who had not appeared at London or
Portsmouth at the time arranged. It would be very unwise to press
this latter suggestion too far, but the former one, the arranged call,
does indeed appear to have been settled.

Moreover, Sir Richard Grenville was by no means out of the running even though he had returned only in December 1586 from his
protracted tour of Atlantic waters. A few days after Carey received
permission to send out his privateering squadron, Grenville was
given a strictly comparable one.[16] Grenville himself was to command
the *Virgin God Save Her*, a mocking name given to his prize of 1585,
Santa Maria de San Vicente, or the Puerto Rico ship more recently taken
and converted for English privateering purposes. The *Roebuck* of Bideford—probably Grenville's own, for whose name he adopted Ralegh's crest as a symbol of their continued cooperation—was under
the command of Richard Willett. A pinnace under Alfred Stockambe
and just possibly another flyboat completed the squadron. This
sounds very much as if Grenville was going to the Caribbean and was
intending to make a call, comparable to that of Carey's ships, at the
English colony to test out Chesapeake Bay. If there was to be a fourth
vessel with him, a flyboat, the possibility that she was to carry further
supplies for White cannot be ruled out. As we have already indicated, Grenville was very much occupied in official duties in the
southwest of England and involved in Munster, and he may or may
not have allowed his ships to sail without him. It is unlikely that he
would fit them out and then not use them, but if they did sail they
have not so far appeared in any records of privateering spoils taken
in that year and it is almost certain that they did not touch at Roanoke Island.

In Florida the Spanish were very confident that an English colony
continued to exist somewhere to the north, in the vicinity of St.
Mary's Bay, our Chesapeake Bay and their Jacán. Pedro Menéndez
Marqués, Florida's governor, was determined to seek it out and
destroy it as soon as he had put St. Augustine on a firm footing after
Drake's destruction. Early in May 1587, while White was still not far
out into the Atlantic, a frigate arrived from Spain with orders to go
north and find out where the English were. With two smaller vessels
Menéndez Marqués set out almost immediately. He said afterward:[17]
"I coasted to latitude 37 degrees, very near Jacan, which is St. Mary's

Bay.... Along all the shore that I coasted there is no knowledge of any corsair." It is clear that he did not find any opening in the Outer Banks or any Indians who knew or would tell about English doings. A fierce storm from the northeast blew him southward from what may have been only a few miles from Cape Henry, and so he was forced to return to Havana and plan some further search at a later time.

In many respects 1587 was a crucial year for England and for Spain. In Spain itself a great fleet was being prepared which Philip II expected would be able to destroy England and place the United Provinces under his control. Only a few weeks before White reached Plymouth on his way to America a great concentration of armed vessels, the Queen's and those of private shipowners, had set sail to cripple Spanish preparations. While White was at sea Drake was attacking ships at Cadiz, occupying for a time an outpost in Portugal and eventually sailing out into the ocean to intercept and take back to England an enormously rich Portuguese prize. Such dramatic action overshadowed almost everything else in the early part of this year. It is likely that preparations of men and ships throughout England were beginning to override the activities of privateers, nor indeed can we be sure that Grenville's little squadron would have been allowed to sail, or, if it had, it had not been absorbed, as many privateers were, into Drake's fleet. With these great events in course, White's enterprise must have seemed, even to Ralegh, a puny one, marginal to events at sea and on land that threatened the whole future of England.

A Colony Created

When John White, after his unhappy return to Southampton on 8 November, completed his narrative of the 1587 voyage and of what befell the colony, he impressed on those who were to read it in private in the next two years and those who read it afterward when it was printed by Richard Hakluyt in 1589, that it was his personal impression of the voyage and its aftermath. Indeed, it is the only true and direct narrative we have of the events from 1584 onward, authentic in a way that the documents surviving on the voyages of 1584–86 are not, as they were trimmed and screened before publication. We, therefore, live with him and with his personal preoccupations in these months between April and November 1587 in a way that so far is unique in the history of the voyages. His tale is a piece of autobiography. As such it is not necessarily, and indeed for the most part is not, history. It tells what he experienced: it does not relate fully in any sense what happened. We do not know what occurred at many stages in that story because we have no corroborative evidence. But where the narratives of Arthur Barlowe and Ralph Lane, as we have them, are trimmed and reshaped, we can read between the lines sometimes to recreate what really happened. In the case of White's narrative it is more difficult to do this, probably impossible, because his vision is focused so closely on his own reactions to events and disregards so largely circumstances that did not affect him personally.

Where we have had little need to follow in detail the daily events of the voyages in 1584, 1585, and 1586, it is wise, perhaps, to follow White's 1587 narrative in this way because his personal reactions influenced the course of later events to such a considerable extent. The first example of this comes when he says:

The 16. Simon Ferdinando, master of our admiral [the Lion],
lewdly forsook our fly-boat, leaving her distressed in the Bay of
Portugal.

The use of "lewdly" here is equivalent to "maliciously." What was
wrong with the flyboat we cannot tell, but the parting of company
with her is attributed to malice on the part of the master of the
flagship. But while Fernandes, as master, was responsible for the day-
to-day sailing of the ship, the job of the captain was to command
her. Here White virtually admits that as early as the ninth day after
leaving Plymouth his command was only a fiction: the real commander was Fernandes. This sets the tone of the narrative throughout, though precisely how just or unjust it is to Fernandes and how
far it represents the consensus of the sailors who supported him
against White we cannot tell. And if Fernandes's behavior was so
"lewd" it is clear the flyboat did not suffer: she made her landfall at
Dominica only two days later than the Lion, and both had a good
crossing time for the voyage.

The problems of carrying a mixed complement were illustrated
when the ship's company (indeed, both ships' companies) went
ashore to rest at the island of St. Croix. Men, women, and children
ate the first fresh fruit that came to hand; it turned out to be poison-
ous and those who had eaten it became violently ill. Fortunately
none of them died and after twenty-four hours the sickness wore
away by itself. White, who had been this way before, was not concerned that no one had warned the colonists that care should be
taken in eating strange fruits in strange places. He was clearly above
such practical considerations. Moreover, the only standing water
proved to be contaminated and made some of those who drank it
very sick. The only benefit derived from the call for refreshment was
the few sea turtles that were caught. These, which were like the ones
White had drawn so well earlier, were evidently of value in providing
fresh meat, even if White is more concerned with their great size
than their food value. A more thorough search of the island the next
day produced the information that the island was indeed inhabited—some Indian pots were found early on and a party saw some
inhabitants in the distance. There were parrots and some lignum
vitae trees, valuable for their medicinal qualities, to be found and

also, after all, a spring at some distance, from which decent water could be had. Here White criticizes Fernandes for asserting the island was uninhabited. To blame him for the presence of a party of wandering Caribs seems excessive, just as it was to censure him for the Bay of Portugal episode.

The pinnace under Captain Edward Stafford, which was now with the other two vessels (she had probably kept station with the Lion throughout the voyage), was sent by Fernandes to Vieques Island, off the south coast of Puerto Rico; he said there were sheep there, but none were found. He then moved the fleet to Puerto Rico itself, to "Musketos" Bay, evidently Sir Richard Grenville's old Guayanilla Bay of 1585. There they took on fresh water, but White grumbled that they drank as much beer as the water they replenished. His carping attitude continues. At this point the loss of two Irishmen who deserted to the Spanish, Darby Glavin and Dennis Carroll, cannot have been felt as any great disaster even though they may have been servants indentured to some of the planters. The next stop was near Cape Rojo, where Fernandes promised salt would be found, but there was none. Here in 1585 it will be remembered, Grenville's men had removed some heaps of prepared salt as both White (who had made a drawing of the event) and Fernandes knew, but its absence on this occasion is again made the basis for a reproach against Fernandes. White then claims he knew that roots of oranges, pineapples, mammee apples, and plantains, which he wished to take to the colony (as had been done in 1585, but some of the plants were apparently spoiled when the Tiger struck), could be found at St. Germans Bay (Boqueron Bay) on the west coast of Puerto Rico, but that Fernandes would not let them land, insisting on going ahead to Hispaniola. Once again the master was in command of the captain. Then Fernandes took them along the north coast of Hispaniola, saying first he intended to make contact with a French merchant with whom he had had earlier dealings (in 1585?), but later excused himself for not going ashore because Ralegh had heard that this Frenchman had in fact been removed by the Spanish.

The voyage along the greater part of the coast was thus fruitless, in several senses of the word, Fernandes simply refusing, according to White, to bring the vessels in toward land. So, wrangling as they went, they turned northward toward the Florida Channel. On the

way they called at the Caicos Islands, where Fernandes again said
they would find salt but, of course, they did not. The islands did
produce some birds, especially swans, which fell to the colonists'
guns. And so, on 7 July, they turned toward the mainland coast of
North America.

How far can we accept White's story of Fernandes's actions? We
can be sure that the two men did not agree and that when it came to
a decision it was Fernandes who prevailed. But the accidents of
finding this and not finding that can scarcely be taken as evidence
that at this stage Fernandes was deliberately sabotaging the expedition, except for one interpretation of the conflict between them.
That is that Fernandes was determined, as in the past, to go after
prizes, and White, thinking of his colonists' safety, refused. Consequently, on some occasions Fernandes misled White in order to get
him to agree. This is not certain, but his cruise along the north coast
of Hispaniola without stopping to trade or to take on roots or water
makes little sense unless he was on the lookout for possible prizes
and failed to see any, and therefore did not wish to take the risk of
being caught on shore by Spanish land forces. On the other hand,
one can take White's view that Fernandes was a sabotaging villain,
and that all his mistakes were deliberate—which is somewhat hard
to accept. What we can say is that, despite apparently being unable to
pick up plants or livestock and despite a few casual illnesses caused
by bad fruit and water, the colonists were taken safely through the
Caribbean without encountering any Spanish opposition (which may
well have been chance) or without serious sickness or loss of life
(which was the result, one assumes, of good care by the officials in
charge).

It is unfortunate that White spent so much time complaining
about Fernandes and that he did not give us a more detailed portrait
of the colonists, about whom we know so little. His description of
the men, women, and children who ate the first fresh fruit they
found on the island of St. Croix presents a vivid picture of sea-
stricken landsmen who, when they experimented, were "fearfully
troubled with a sudden burning in their mouths and swelling of their
tongues so big, that some of them could not speak. Also a child by
sucking one of those women's breasts had at that instant his mouth
sent on such a burning that it was strange to see how the infant was

tormented for the time." If White could write like that he could have given us many similar vignettes of shipboard life that would have proved invaluable. Then, too, he showed briefly the enterprising nature of the colonists: splitting into parties they explored St. Croix and brought back news. Thus one company affirmed that "they had seen in a valley eleven savages and divers houses half a mile distant from the steep or top of the hill where they stayed. The other company had found running out of a high rock a very fair spring of water whereof they brought three bottles for the company." On East Caicos, too, many of the colonists "spent the latter part of that day in other parts of the island, some to seek the salt ponds, some fowling, some hunting swans, whereof we caught many." Clearly they were people with enterprise and spirit who were willing to experiment and learn in the new environments in which they found themselves.

The Fernandes of the narrative was even a bad pilot. As the ships at last approached the Outer Banks, only Captain Stafford's vigilance saved them from grounding on what White called Cape Fear but which was in fact Cape Lookout, "such was the carelessness and ignorance of our master." But eventually on 22 July the ship Lion and her pinnace, "arrived safe at 'Hatoraske.'" It is worth noting that neither now nor later was White willing to call the inlet Port Ferdinando, as it had been known from 1584 to 1586. Fernandes had wiped himself literally off the map—for White—and Port Ferdinando was replaced by Hatarask, or as White was to spell it on his map "Hatrask." The flyboat had broken company and rejoined the fleet only on the twenty-fifth, and once more White's malice toward Fernandes emerged:

Fernando grieved greatly at their safe coming, for he purposely left them in the Bay of Portugal and stole away from them in the night, hoping that the master thereof, whose name was Edward Spicer, for that he never had been in Virginia would hardly [scarcely] find the place, or else being left in so dangerous a place as that was, by means of many men-of-war [privateers] as at that time were abroad, they should surely be taken or slain, but God disappointed his wicked pretences.

Here White's attack on the master reaches the point of paranoia, because he was himself in command of the Lion and could have intervened at any time to make Fernandes carry out his instructions to continue to keep company with the other ship. From what he says, the parting would almost certainly appear to have been an accident: why should Fernandes wish to prevent the planters on the ship from reaching their destination? White almost forces us to conclude that either Fernandes had gone into the pay of Spain (which his later service against the Armada would seem to negate), or else White was determined to cover up his own weaknesses by blaming everything he could, or could imagine, on the Portuguese. It is possible that too much stress is being laid on this, but it is important to make clear how far White went in his account in order to explain his later actions.

Once White came to his accustomed landing place his narrative becomes specific and businesslike. He intended, he said, to go to Roanoke Island at once and to find the men left by Grenville. Apparently he did not plan to take them with him, as usually has been thought. If we are to read him literally his purpose was "to have conference" with them "concerning the state of the country and savages, meaning after he had so done to return to the fleet." Consequently, it would seem that these men were intended to sit it out on Roanoke Island until Grenville called in on his privateering voyage, which White evidently thought he would do, and made separate arrangements regarding the continued occupation, or otherwise, of Roanoke Island. This interpretation is not certain, but it appears to follow from what the narrative says.

White then planned to regain his ship and set out for his final destination "and pass along the coast to the Bay of 'Chesepiok' where we intended to make our seat and fort according to the charge given us among other directions in writing under the hand of Sir Walter Ralegh." There is every indication here that White had not only his own plans for the creation of the City of Ralegh but also very specific instructions from Ralegh as to precisely how this was to be done. "Fort" and "seat" are a little ambiguous. They could mean a fortified enclosure of a "town" such as had been created in 1585. Or they could mean the establishment on Chesapeake Bay of a fortified post at a suitable anchorage for future vessels, and then the establishment elsewhere of the civilian settlement that his colony was clearly designed to create. If this reading is correct—and either interpretation seems equally valid at this state of our knowledge—then the "fort" was intended to be visited by some later comers, some of Sir George Carey's ships perhaps, or by Grenville if he carried out his intended expedition.

The crux of the expedition arrived almost immediately. White was about to set out in Captain Stafford's pinnace, which was of sufficiently shallow draft to pass through Pamlico Sound, when he was suddenly confronted by an unnamed gentleman, one who had come on the voyage but did not intend to remain with the colony, with news that a whole new scenario had been written. Fernandes had determined, and the company of the Lion had evidently agreed, to alter all the arrangements. This man "called to the sailors in the pinnace, charging them not to bring any of the planters [those who had not disembarked at Hatarask] back again, but to leave them on the island except the governor [White] and two or three such as he approved, saying that the summer was far spent wherefore he would land all the planters in no other place." This order evidently staggered White but it was accepted by the sailors in both ship and pinnace (we do not hear that even Stafford protested); White weakly adds "wherefore it booted not the Governor to contend with them, but passed [on] to Roanoke."

This weakness on White's part is one of the great puzzles of his career. He was sent in command of an expedition to carry out a specific program and yet, when confronted with a totally opposite one, he weakly acquiesced. Why did he not try to assert his, evidently, very limited authority and at least make a fight to carry out the original plan? One reason could be caution: he did not wish to endanger the lives of the men, women, and children under his command. If he resisted, threats to their safety might well have followed. But did he half wish to follow out the program set by Fernandes? Roanoke had been, on the whole, a happy place for him. He knew the surrounding country very well indeed and, moreover, he knew many of the native inhabitants. In any event, Manteo and Towaye would be left on Roanoke Island and the whole area entrusted to Manteo's care as Queen Elizabeth's representative.

Clearly, White intended that in the end the colony would go to Chesapeake Bay, if that was what his people wished, but Roanoke Island would provide a means of fitting them for life in a still largely unexplored area to the north. There were clearings, there might be houses, there would be, he expected, the men left by Grenville who could provide some real continuity with the colony of 1585–86 and so link up with whatever plans Grenville may have had for the future use of the island. The colonists, too, may have felt that this was at least less of a break with the past than immediate removal to Chesapeake Bay. But for them such a halfway house could also cause, and almost certainly did cause, great material problems. Their gear would have to be unloaded and then reloaded and retransported. They would have to set up temporary households on Roanoke Island instead of permanent ones on Chesapeake Bay. Yet there is no hint of protest or resistance in White's narrative. And this is so even after White had made his preliminary visit to the island. Of this, he said:

> [we] went on land on the island, in the place where our fifteen men were left, but we found none of them nor any sign that they had been there, save only we found the bones of one of those fifteen which the savages had slain long before.

Although this melancholy introduction to his well-loved island was a shock, he did not attempt to change the orders given by Fernandes. He simply went ahead with his search:

> The 23 of July the governor, with divers of his companions, walked to the north end of the island, where Master Ralph Lane had his fort, with sundry necessary and decent dwelling houses made by his men about it the year before [this means two years before], where we hoped to find some signs, or certain knowledge, of our fifteen men. When we came thither we found the fort razed down, but all the houses standing unhurt, saving the nether [first floor] rooms of them, and also of the fort, were overgrown by melons [cucurbits] of divers sorts, and deer within them feeding on those melons.

This is a difficult passage to analyze correctly and only an attempt can be made to do so. The obvious meaning of the statement that the houses were "about" the fort suggests that they were located around the fort. This would go against everything that has hitherto been said and we must take "about" in this instance simply to mean "near." Once again he writes of the "fort" being "razed down," when all the archaeological evidence indicates that Fort Raleigh was not "razed down" at this time, and survived so long that we have a fairly complete record of it for over a century before the restoration of the 1950s. So the "fort" here clearly must mean the enclosure, and involve the leveling of at least some of the banking which it has been assumed must have surrounded the settlement. The statement that the "nether rooms of them [the houses], and also of the fort" were overgrown is also ambiguous. It does inform us that the houses of the settlement had an upper story, probably simply an attic, but if it is read carefully it does not mean that the house in the fort [Fort Raleigh as it has hitherto been taken] also had an upper story, or, indeed, that there was not more than one room in the fortifications in the enclosing ditch and strong points. This question, with others, must be left for archaeologists to establish or elucidate, if it can be done at all. It is quite obvious that fifteen men could not man or maintain an enclosure intended for over a hundred colonists. They could barely man a single strong point, if that. White was told that they were living, undefended, in some of the cottages, and had their stores and armor installed in another building, of which we only know that it had a thatched roof and was presumably one of the nonresidential structures inside the 1585 enclosure. However, this does not necessarily mean that they had not begun to build for themselves a new defensive structure, that excavated in part in 1965, which was appropriate to their numbers, but was never completed and remained unnoticed by White, though this cannot be established conclusively. Here White's simple prose leads us into unexpected difficulties, but this is not the only occasion where it does so.

Why indeed should Fernandes insist on depositing the colonists at Roanoke Island? Was it very largely spite and hatred engendered by his conflicts with White on the way over? Fernandes had behaved very badly on Fenton's voyage in 1582 and had won himself a great deal of enmity, yet it seems extravagant to believe that this was the primary reason for his actions. An opposite view is also possible. Fernandes had been with Philip Amadas in 1584 when (as we think) he had run into trouble in Chesapeake Bay,[1] and he may have thought the colonists would be safer at Roanoke than within reach of violently hostile Powhatan Indians, but that is to put a gloss on his character that is scarcely justified by other, less savory aspects of which we are well aware. The strangest thing is that he should have involved himself so deeply in the enterprise, become one of the Assistants to the City of Ralegh, and received a gentleman's status with Ralegh's assistance, and so had, one would imagine, every incentive to keep the colony on the track that had been agreed upon and that White was prepared to follow.

Of course, it can be argued that Fernandes convinced the sailors by saying that if they wished to get any prizes they had better not stay longer than could be helped in this area. They might succeed in capturing Spanish ships, which would give them an adequate, or rich, return for their labors, but in fact it was a late August starting point that had brought Grenville his capture in 1585. Further, the ships hung about long after their arrival at Hatarask; in that time they would have been able to take the colonists to Chesapeake Bay, or much farther, and still get on with their prize-taking if that was their primary objective. The ways and means of this episode seem in many respects inscrutable.

White, pragmatically, told the planters he had with him to repair the houses they found standing and to erect "other new cottages for such as should need." He was clear that the stay at Roanoke Island could not be a mere short transition. It would take care and thought before the island could be exchanged for another place, now one that offered some difficulties of access, even though the Chesapeake was no great distance to the north and the pinnace would be at their disposal. At the same time it seems clear he made no attempt to restore the defensive enclosure or strong point for defense.

The arrival of the flyboat under its master, Edward Spicer, on 25 July brought the remainder of the colonists, "to the great joy and comfort of the whole company." The crossing for both parties seems, apart from the storm off the Iberian peninsula, to have been a good one. Good spirits at rejoining their friends rapidly overcame any hostile reaction there might have been against the change of location.

Their first shock was the killing of George Howe, one of the Assistants, three days later. Indians had come over from the mainland, either to hunt deer or to spy on the new arrivals. They caught Howe, unarmed, catching crabs with a small forked stick two miles away from his companions. They brought him down with no less than sixteen arrows and then battered his head with their wooden clubs, before flying to the mainland.

This and the continuing threat of violence and danger that it imposed must have exercised a dampening effect on the whole settlement, and made some, at least, wonder whether they had done the right thing in agreeing to settle on Roanoke Island. It may well have speeded plans for relocation. Soon after Howe was killed, White began to mobilize his own forces. Probably at Manteo's urging he had Captain Stafford bring the pinnace, which was now plying inside the sounds, so that White, Manteo, and others could go across the water to Croatoan, where Manteo's mother headed his people. This was on the south side of the inlet just north of modern Cape Hatteras, and either the village or the inlet, or both, was known as Chacandepeco. As they reached the shore the villagers turned out as if to resist them but fled as the English advanced. Manteo called after them to identify himself and soon some returned "embracing and entertaining us very friendly, desiring us not to gather or spill any of their corn, for that they had but little." The memory of Ralph Lane's pressures on the mainland Indians to supply him with corn in the spring of 1586 may still have been fresh. This concern for corn may also suggest that the fertile area on the Outer Banks was limited and did not supply any large quantity of grain. White reassured them that they came only to renew old friendships. The Indians then brought them to their "town" and feasted them "after their manner." They wished the Englishmen to give them some badge or distinguishing mark so that they would not be mistaken for enemies, because the previous year Lane had encountered some of them on the mainland and had attacked them, thinking them to be Wingina's men, and at least one of them still had a wound to show for it. Unfortunately, this was not to be the last misunderstanding of this sort.

The English party then settled down to confer with the Croatoan people about the general situation on the sounds. What about the people of Secotan, Aquascogoc, and Pomeioc? Had there been any important changes in the balance of power between them? Would the Croatoans act as ambassadors on behalf of the English, offering them friendship and making known their desire that old frictions should be forgiven and forgotten? The detached position of this group probably made them well fitted for this task. White had to know roughly what to expect in case there should be any combination against him and his vulnerable band of settlers. This they, the village councillors (weroances), who assisted Manteo's mother in her rule, agreed to do. She herself appears in White's narrative only in passing. It was proposed to bring as many of the leading chiefs as possible from the tribal groups around Pamlico Sound to Roanoke Island for a conference or at least to get them to send a reply within a week. Dasemunkepeuc was different. It was inhabited by a remnant of Wingina's men, among whom Wanchese was prominent. They had been responsible for the killing of George Howe and would need to be neutralized. But now, too, White was able to hear the history of the end of Grenville's little party which has already been told. What was alarming was that the people of Secotan and Aquascogoc had joined the remnants of Wingina's men in the attack on and eventual dispersal of Grenville's men. Lane had left such a bad impression on the peoples of the sounds that those of the southern part of Pamlico Sound had combined with those of Dasemunkepeuc to attack and try to wipe out the little group, even though the majority of them had got away in their boat and had not been heard of since. Would they or would they not receive favorably the overtures now being made? Much might depend on this for the future safety of the colonists.

White now sailed back to Hatarask off which the ships were lying at anchor, no doubt gradually completing the transfer of the colonists' property to the island. We are told nothing of the stages by which this transition took place. Indeed, nothing further is heard from White until 8 August, when he says that no emissaries or messages had been received from any of the Indian groups within the time limits set at Croatoan. The prognosis then must have been that hostility was more likely than friendship. White thus had begun to think in terms of a preemptive strike against the village of Dasemunkepeuc, as Lane had in June of the previous year. On the night of the eighth, White took the pinnace under Captain Stafford, Manteo, and twenty-three men to attack and destroy the village. This is the first occasion in which White had been involved in violence against a native group: revenge for George Howe was one immediate motive, and the attack on Grenville's men, inspired and largely carried out by this group, was another.

The strike against Dasemunkepeuc was a very unfortunate affair. It turned out that the hostile group had taken fright after Howe's killing and fled from the village. The Croatoans, somehow learning of this, had come across to pillage the standing corn, pumpkins, and tobacco left open to the depredation of birds and deer. Knowing nothing of this, White and his men secretly went ashore in the darkness, crept through the woods, and got between the woods and Pamlico Sound so that they were able to invade the village from all sides. Without warning they burst in on a group of people sitting around a fire. Taken wholly by surprise, the Indians fled into the woods without resisting, but one was shot through the body and probably died. In one case a woman escaped because it could be seen that she was carrying a baby on her back. In another, a man recognized Captain Stafford and called out to him that they were friends. As soon as possible the mistake was rectified, but rather too late. The woman who, with her child, had barely escaped killing was the wife of Menatoan, one of the *weroances* of the Croatoan group. Manteo had not acted in time because he too had been deceived. There was evidently something of a crisis for him when he fully understood what had happened. White says: "although the mistaking of these savages somewhat grieved Manteo, yet he imputed their harm to their own folly, saying to them, that if their *weroances* had kept their promise in coming to see the governor at the day appointed they had not known that mischance." As it was, the mixed party, having gathered all the ripe corn, pumpkins, and tobacco, came over to Roanoke Island in the pinnace. Every effort was made to smooth out the regrettable incident, which, however much it may have been glossed over with the Croatoans and, no doubt, was accompanied by gift-giving in recompense, is likely to have caused fresh doubts about the Europeans to circulate among the remaining villages on the sounds, which are not known to have made any subsequent friendly approaches to White and, indeed, may have ignored what was happening on Roanoke Island. And of most of this we too are entirely ignorant, as we are of the settling in of the colonists—their protective measures (as surely they took some), their guard system, and the distribution of houses between family and non-family groups. All this is omitted entirely from White's narrative.

We then jump to 13 August when we are told "our savage, Manteo, by the commandment of Sir Walter Ralegh was christened in Roanoke, and called lord thereof and of Dasemunquepeuc, in reward of his faithfull service." Manteo had evidently received some instruction in the Christian religion, but had not been formally admitted to the Church of England. His christening was a voluntary event, but held back, we may surmise, until it was seen how he would behave in relation to the English settlers once they had reestablished themselves in the colony. The reward of the lordship of Roanoke and Dasemunkepeuc was a significant step. This placed Manteo in the position previously aspired to by Wingina, creating a link between these two villages, and the area of hunting ground they comprised, with the Croatoan territory on the Outer Banks. This could, in turn, pave the way for his recognition as their superior by the other villages on Pamlico Sound. Manteo was not required to turn his people into Englishmen or even Christians, but he was probably expected to teach them something of what he had learned of English ways during his protracted stays in England in both 1584–85 and 1586–87. Whether he did in fact communicate much in the way of English customs to the people he ruled, and whether his theoretical control of the island and of the mainland village site meant anything, we cannot tell. We do not even know whether there were enough Croatoans to engage in the colonization necessary to achieve such control. Manteo was not a passive figure. White had made this obvious. His installation, however, made one thing absolutely clear. The colonists regarded their stay on Roanoke Island as only temporary; after their departure, it was to be under the authority of a friendly and largely anglicized Indian ruler.

Five days later, on 18 August, an event took place that has seemed symbolic of the rooting of English people in North America. Elenor (Elenora) Dare, daughter of the governor and wife to one of the Assistants, Ananias Dare, gave birth to a daughter. It is significant of White's confidence, and that of his associates, that his four months' pregnant daughter was brought on the long voyage and survived her pregnancy, apparently her first, on board ship. At least one other married woman, as we have seen, had ventured across the ocean with her baby at her breast. The pioneers of 1587 were willing to risk their own lives and those of their children in order to achieve their aim of settling in a new land. It has proved easy for writers to sentimentalize about these facts. However, life was hard in sixteenth-century England and those who survived the perils of infancy in a large city like London were inured to danger and poor conditions. At the same time, the birth does point to the new character of the party of colonists: they were people who, for one reason or another—and we can scarcely guess what some of them were—had been willing to go as members of a family and take an active part, few as they were in numbers, in the creation of a new life in a wholly novel environment.

On Sunday, 24 August, the baby was christened and, White tells us, "because this child was the first Christian born in Virginia, she was named Virginia." Virginia Dare, therefore, was the first of the new blood of English stock to be born and brought into the Church of England on North American soil. She thus made good material for the legend of American beginnings. Long before, Spanish women had given birth to children in St. Augustine and Santa Elena (perhaps at San Miguel de Gualdape, too). But because the history of the invasion and settlement of North America was to be written mainly from an English perspective, which minimized Spanish and other European activities and influences, the birth of the first English child in America has seemed a particularly good starting point for the involvement of the English people, not merely in visiting North America, but in being born and dying there. Speculation has naturally turned on the person who baptized both Manteo and Virginia. There may well have been a ship's chaplain on board the Lion; just conceivably there may have been a clergyman among the colonists themselves, but, if so, he has remained successfully anonymous. John White, as commander of the colonizing squadron and as governor, was competent, by English tradition, to carry out the baptism according to the Book of Common Prayer and there is no particular reason to think he did not do so.

White gives us a glimpse of the activities that now took place. The "goods and victuals of the planters" were installed safely on shore without accident. The two ships, the Lion and the flyboat, were caulked and trimmed and supplied with fresh water and wood. The colonists had written their letters and sent on board little tokens of remembrance for their friends and families in England. By 21 August the ships were getting ready to leave, with White in command of the colony and the sailors now ready to set out on their privateering venture. This was precisely a month since Fernandes had decreed he could not sail the one or two days farther to Chesapeake Bay because the season for privateering was so far gone, and yet more than four weeks later he was only preparing to go. In the light of this delay, the ruse that set the colonists ashore at the wrong place becomes all the more inexplicable.

White, who had passed over in his journal the installation of the colony in the most laconic way, now becomes willing to go into considerable detail. Here he is concerned with justifying and explaining his actions. The first thing was that although the Lion was almost ready to sail on the twenty-first, many of her men were still on land, presumably at Hatarask, when a sudden storm blew up the next day. It was so severe that Fernandes had to cut his cables and run out to sea. If all his men had been on board he might well not have returned, but as it was he came back and reanchored off Hatarask on the twenty-seventh.

In the meantime a major controversy had developed among the settlers. They had submitted to being dumped on a shore and installed in a place where only two of them—James Lasie and John Wright—had been before. Evidently they had made themselves comfortable up to a point, even if evidence of Indian hostility clearly alarmed them and they could not feel safe enough to consider staying where they were for any length of time. They had two primary concerns: first, how much did their stores amount to? and second, when and how would they get more? With regard to the latter, there was a question of where these stores would be delivered, as it appeared likely that, although Grenville, if he did come, would probably come to Roanoke Island, he might go directly to Chesapeake Bay, whereas any help from Carey's ships would almost certainly go to Chesapeake Bay. These questions were so serious that it was decided among the remaining seven Assistants, who, in effect, made up the council of the colony, that two of them should go to England to make sure that supplies would be sent quickly and that they would, somehow, come to the right place.

After much debate, it was decided that only one, Christopher Cooper, who apparently did not have any female dependents in the colony, should go. But "the next day, through the persuasion of divers of his familiar friends," he changed his mind, perhaps also influenced by the attitude of the remaining six Assistants. What had been brewing in their minds was that only one man could be relied on to go and return with supplies at the earliest possible time, and only one man really knew from personal experience the area around Chesapeake Bay, the intended site of the colony. (Even though Lasie and Wright could have been with him there in 1585–86, their authority and memory were not likely to be sufficient.) The man, of course, was John White. He had, in the trite phrase, given hostages to fortune—in the shape of his daughter and granddaughter. If anyone would do all in his power to serve their needs it was White. Indeed, the Assistants may have decided that the colony's next steps, demanding a decisiveness he had not shown so far, could be best taken without him.

On 22 August "the whole company, both of the Assistants and planters, came to the Governor and with one voice requested him to return, himself, into England, for the better and sooner obtaining of supplies and other necessaries for them." Whether he had seen this coming or whether it was a shock to him, White tells us he refused. He set out in some detail his reasons: "one was that he could not so suddenly return back again, without his great discredit, leaving the action and so many whom he partly had procured through his persuasions to leave their native country and undertake that voyage." Here he admits that his own efforts had been largely influential in assembling the present group of colonists and that, in leaving, it would appear that he had deceived them and their dependents and relatives—and we must assume that many had left wives, parents, and children behind to embark on the enterprise. He had another reason, too. We have seen that Harriot had stressed in his little book the hostility of many of the returned settlers of 1585–86 to any further efforts at colonization. Some evidently had shown this hostility during the collection of the present group of colonists and may have influenced some not to go, as White had not been able to bring as many as he had expected. They "would not spare to slander falsely both him and the action by saying he went to Virginia but 'politikely' [with some crafty, underhand purpose] and to no other end but to lead so many into a country in which he never meant to stay himself, and there to leave them behind him." If there was genuine malice abroad this was not an unlikely charge to be made against him, however unreasonable it would appear to some of his backers such as Ralegh. These were his more general reasons and there is much to be said for them. He could not absolve himself from responsibility for bringing the colonists to America, and no doubt he felt he, himself, had the best knowledge and skill to make a success of the colony in the longer run.

From these general reasons he turned to the particular. All had not been sweetness and light in the settlement, nor were all of the planters awed by their governor, who had shown himself so weak in dealing with Fernandes. While he was away on his expedition against Wingina's men, some person or persons had plundered some of his personal belongings, packed in chests. His possessions were clearly not safe with at least a minority of the settlers.

It is here that he lets us, also as a side issue, into the vital decision that the Assistants had taken, and the planters had agreed to, that they would not remain on Roanoke Island for longer than they could help "seeing they intended to remove 50 miles farther up into the main [land] presently." In that case his remaining goods would not be safe. His own part in this decision to move to the site to which they had originally been directed—namely, we can have no doubt, to the Chesapeake Bay region—is not known, but he would certainly have approved it in theory. His comment stresses, however, not the project to move or details about it, but its impact on his possessions: "he being then absent, his stuff and goods might be both spoiled and most of them pilfered away in the carriage, so that at his return, he should be either forced to provide himself of all such things again or else at his coming back again to Virginia find himself utterly unfurnished."

We have here the unvarnished response of a man who had not been accustomed to possessions but who had accumulated whatever he could both to equip himself worthily as governor and to provide some comfort and decoration in his permanent dwelling in which, it may well have been, he intended to spend the rest of his life. His personal possessions loomed large in his mind at a point when we would have wished him to give more general considerations greater weight. But it is an honest reply. His decision on these grounds was that he could not and would not go.

On 23 August, however, a fresh deputation, both of Assistants and others, pleaded with him to change his mind. They considered him to be the best man to assure them of supplies and, moreover, they promised "to make him their bond under all their hands and seals for the preserving of all his goods for him at his return to Virginia, so that if any part thereof were spoiled or lost they would see it restored to him or to his assigns, whensoever the same should be missed and demanded." Some, at least, among them had experience in drawing up legal documents and they presented him on 25 August with a formal assurance that he went at their insistence and that he was best suited to supply their wants.

As this is the first (and last) formal document to emanate from the body of planters left on Roanoke Island in 1587, it is worth giving in full:

> May it please you, her Majesty's subjects of England, we your friends and countrymen, the planters in Virginia, do by these presents let you and every of you to understand that, for the present and speedy supply of certain of our known and apparent lacks and needs, most requisite and necessary, for the good and happy planting of us or any other in this land of Virginia, we all, of one mind and consent, have most earnestly entreated and incessantly requested John White, Governor of the Planters in Virginia, to pass into England for the better and most assured help and setting forward of the foresaid supplies. And knowing, assuredly, that he both can best and will labor and take pains in that behalf for us all, and he not once, but often, refusing it, for our sakes and for the honor and maintenance of the action, hath at last, though much against his will, through our importunacy, yielded to leave his government and all his goods among us and, himself, pass into England, of whose knowledge and fidelity in handling this matter, as all others, we do assure ourselves by these presents and will you to give all credit thereunto. The five and twentieth of August.

Signatures would have been added to the original and these probably comprised all the adult males and females in the colony. White, having accepted his role as rescuer of the colony from loss and starvation, had only half a day left to ready himself for the voyage. The flyboat had ridden out the storm and was able to come in toward the little harbor at Hatarask, while the Lion, which some had probably given up by this time, had reappeared and her men left behind on the island were able to board her. The flyboat had weighed anchor and was well outside the bar when White joined her about midnight on 27 August, leaving the colony for what he hoped would be a short time only, but which was to be forever.

In all his writing about whether or not he would go to England, he never took time to describe how the colony was to be led and administered in his absence. It would be natural to assume that Roger Baylye, whose name follows his on the list of Assistants, was to act as deputy governor and was to be counseled and advised by the remaining six Assistants, though it is not impossible that the planters selected a few other men to aid them in their deliberations. He says nothing of who was to command the pinnace when Edward Stafford left. It is tragic, too, that he does not identify the place where they had decided to go. This has given rise to many speculations over several hundred years, though in fact there is no real mystery about the general area, which was that south of Chesapeake Bay. But we would especially like to know whether the colonists had selected any particular location there and how they had proposed to transport themselves.

There is a certain preoccupation with self in all of White's journal. There is not even a word about the tender farewells that he must have had time for, even at the last long rush to reach the ship in time. It is interesting that he intended to go in the flyboat. Edward Spicer was a friend, Fernandes in the Lion an enemy. He could be sure that the flyboat would make the best speed she could to get him back to England, even though accident was to disappoint him. At long last the Lion was off to hunt prizes, not, we think, attempting to catch any ships off Bermuda, but heading directly for the Azores where most of the privateers gathered and where there was always a chance, though there was much competition, of capturing a Spanish ship of some sort.

White was out of luck. Stafford had gone in the Lion, perhaps nominally in command, even if Fernandes was in effective control. There were only fifteen seamen on the flyboat, besides Spicer, White, and the steward, and when they raised the anchor an accident occurred with almost tragic consequences. The great bars that ran through the capstan needed to be manned by the whole of this small complement. One of the bars broke and the two others spun around so rapidly that, before the men could fall back, the bars had hit and severely injured a number of them, some of whom, White says, never recovered. A second attempt was made, perhaps with the remaining two bars, but they also flew out of control, once more inflicting fresh injuries. There was nothing to do but cut the cable and follow the Lion. Regardless of her handicaps the flyboat kept station with the Lion more than halfway across the ocean, so she must have been a good sailer. This was in spite of twenty days' unfavorable weather, with winds slackening and water leaking from their barrels so that by the end they were almost without any. On 17 September they passed the two western islands of the Azores, Corvo and Flores. By this time there were only five able-bodied seamen able to work— though evidently others recovered to help later. The next day contact was made with the Lion and White learned she was pursuing her way to Terceira to await Spanish vessels. Accordingly, he arranged to have letters and messages for home taken from her, the expectation being that his ship would arrive ahead of the Lion. The flyboat set out again with her limited crew—Fernandes evidently did not attempt to spare a single man to assist her. After parting company with the Lion, a storm on 28 September was their next trial. This northeaster blew them off course for six days, and left them thirteen days to recover their position after it had died down. By then they were in a desperate condition. The remaining men were sick and two died. Spicer could not take a latitude sight for as much as four days at a time because neither sun nor star was visible.

The men in the flyboat were down to the last stinking dregs of water, beer, and wine, and almost famished, when they made a landfall on 16 October. They did not know where they were, but fortunately the port was Smerwick, on the coast of County Kerry in Ireland, and in its spacious waters there were two vessels, one from Dublin and the other from Southampton. Because they had even lost their boat, it was only when the Southampton pinnace sent hers to inquire who they were that White and the others learned their location. Their rescuers supplied them generously with water, wine, and fresh food. John White and Edward Spicer went ashore and hired horses to take them to Dingle, five miles across country, to try to get assistance from that busy little port. But when they arrived with help, they were too late. Three men died on board ship (one after White had left) and three others who were very ill were taken to Dingle to be cared for. Probably arrangements were made to salvage the ship. White had done all he could. On 1 November he and Spicer took passage in the *Monkey* of Southampton, which landed them at Marazion in Cornwall. From there they rode to Southampton, arriving on 8 November, to learn that the *Lion* had earlier put in at Portsmouth, prizeless, and that she too had suffered sickness and death among her crew, so much so that she was barely able to make the home port, and her men had to be helped ashore by a small Portsmouth vessel.

White ended his narrative abruptly with the names of three of the men who had died on the flyboat, all he could remember. He made no general comment on the implications of the long delay for his mission to supply and rescue his colony. If the voyage to America was one of frustration, the return to England was one of narrowly-escaped disaster, so that he had not had much joy in his maritime experiences. The greater burden that hung over him was the fate of over one hundred people for whom he was, to some considerable degree, responsible.

The Years of Frustration,
1587–1589

In 1587 a great ambition had been satisfied. John White and those
who agreed with him, and Sir Walter Ralegh who backed him, had
established a group of men, women, and children on North American soil who could form the nucleus for a new, nonaggressive community. That community, it was thought, would be capable of settling
alongside Native American communities without trying to displace
them. From the start, or almost so, it would be self-dependent in
production and should soon need no vital imports from England
unless to purchase luxuries with the products it could raise on
American soil. There was a degree of optimism in all this not so far
confirmed by any objective factors. The success of the venture would
depend on a number of unknowns and those who embarked on it
may, or may not, have appreciated the risks they were taking. At
stake was the survival of themselves, their wives, and their children.

John White's hopes were high when he set sail in May 1587, but
they were lessened by his friction with Simon Fernandes during the
voyage and by the landing of the colonists on Roanoke Island, instead of on the Chesapeake as planned. They were depressed further
by the discovery that the colony's stores might not be adequate
beyond the winter and would need to be replenished in the spring
before new crops could be harvested. This, perhaps, resulted mainly
from the failure to obtain supplies of food, plant stocks, and, above
all, livestock in the Caribbean. If the voyage over was comparatively
rapid (seventy days), it was also unproductive. The stores had been
depleted rather than augmented. Therefore, though the colonists
had adhered to the decision to make the journey to the Chesapeake

and were ready to go when White left, there was clearly left in his mind a feeling of incompleteness. Did they or did they not need his help? Could the plan he had begun to formulate, we think, over the winter of 1585–86 be implemented without his specialist knowledge of the terrain and the people of the Chesapeake tribe? The insistence of the colonists that he should be the one to go to England to assure them of springtime stores was both a compliment and an affront. It was a compliment in that it showed that the colonists trusted his integrity, as they could trust that of no one else, and that they believed, if Ralegh or their London friends could be persuaded to send help rapidly, he was the one person who could be relied on to do so. It was an affront in that, because the project was so very much his own, to be excluded from the vital stage of its actual establishment was not only painful but also suggested he had not proved himself a very effective leader, as, indeed, he does not appear to have been based on his own narrative of the outward voyage.

The colony also had other serious problems. There was the obvious imbalance between the sexes in the colony. The majority of colonists were men. Only a handful of women were available to add to the number of children already in the group. It is difficult to avoid the assumption that one of the firmest instructions White would have received from the Assistants when they insisted he should leave them and return to England would have been that he bring out wives and children and affianced women who had been left behind, as their menfolk did not wish them to undergo the initial pains and dangers of settlement. We may suspect that at the last moment a number of the intended colonists—male and especially female—had got cold feet and stayed behind, but might be willing to change their minds again if the prospects seemed good. Single, unaffianced men would need other women, too, if they could be enticed to come. Beyond that there was the question of whether the colony would be large enough, even supposing living conditions turned out to be as favorable as White had hoped, to provide a continuing community that could not only survive but grow. (We may recall that 150 was the number initially planned for.) White must be credited with recognizing that a settlement of, say, 500 or 600 persons, would disrupt any Indian society alongside which it was placed, but he must also have understood from his experience in 1585–86 that a group numbering only about 100 was not enough. The potential risks involved—a chance attack by enemies, an epidemic that could carry off as many as 50 people, a season in which more hands would be needed to ensure self-sufficiency—must have suggested that the original number of around 150 people would stand a better chance of meeting mischances and yet not be too numerous to alarm or infringe on the traditional culture of the inhabitants, especially if an approximate balance between the sexes could be achieved. The need to satisfy such requirements, besides the mere fact of bringing out more stores, must have laid a very heavy burden on White as he stepped ashore after his wretched voyage home, which he had only barely survived.

It would be a mistake to think that in 1587 White's colony was the sole English project afoot in North America. It is clear to us now that sooner or later a major effort would be made to establish a military-naval base on the shores of Chesapeake Bay to step up the western offensive against Spain. The objective here, as already suggested, would be to build a more or less self-contained supply depot, heavily defended, where ships could be based and revictualled for the continuing struggle in the Caribbean and against the Europe-bound Spanish fleets. The English probably intended the base to be located a considerable distance from the civilian colony—at Lynnhaven Bay, for example, it would be some thirty miles by water from a settlement fifteen miles up the Elizabeth River—and to be quite distinct from it. They also likely intended that it occupy no more land than was considered necessary for strategic purposes, though the Spanish in Florida had found it difficult to limit the orbit of their garrisons in this manner and, where they had tried to do so, the garrisons had proved vulnerable to Indian attack. Consequently, involvement of such a post in Indian politics was almost inevitable. In particular, it would almost certainly attract hostility from what we can call the Powhatan Confederacy (even if we are not certain that Powhatan had reached the top of that tree by 1587). This tribal group on the James and York rivers and Eastern Shore was already powerful. It had a record of opposition to Europeans from 1570 to 1572 and very probably would resist an English coastal garrison. Even if White's settlers were to be sheltered in the interior some miles away to the southwest, they would inevitably be involved in such controversy and, possibly, warfare. Such a post, too, would be a powerful magnet for Spanish reprisals. White did not know that, earlier in the summer of 1587, Pedro Menéndez Marqués had already attempted to reconnoiter Chesapeake Bay in search of the English settlers he thought he would find there and had been unsuccessful only because of adverse weather conditions, which had driven him away from the entrance. Once English ships were known to be operating from Chesapeake Bay, Spain would make a powerful thrust to destroy their base and replace it with a Spanish garrison. The reality of such a threat was no mere fantasy but a live issue. In such a case, White's settlers could not long be protected and could easily succumb to a Spanish attack.

Sir Richard Grenville had certainly planned to send out a privateering squadron in 1587, even though we have no evidence that it was intended to touch at any part of North America. Whether the squadron authorized to sail in February 1587 ever set out we do not know. So far no further record of their activities in that year has been found. And there is no reason to conclude that they were necessarily bound for Chesapeake Bay if they did so. The position with regard to Sir George Carey's little squadron, under the command of Captain William Irish, was rather different. The ships *Commander*, *Swallow*, and *Gabriel* did make for the Caribbean in 1587; that, coupled with White's delay of eight days in Cowes Roads and his evident contact with Carey at Carisbrooke Castle before he left England, strongly suggests some measure of cooperation between Carey and White, though what it amounted to we cannot say, unless fresh evidence emerges from some English source. What is not in doubt is that Irish agreed to make contact either with Roanoke Island (where, theoretically, Grenville's men would still be located) or with some designated place on Chesapeake Bay where White's men would have met him and given him enough information about the bay to enable him to evaluate it for Carey, and for Ralegh with whom he was closely associated, as a potential base for aggressive action against Spain. How such an arrangement could be made precise enough to ensure a meeting is beyond our ability to estimate.

Irish duly made a number of Spanish prizes in the Caribbean, and on his way homeward made a call at some point where he expected to make contact with either Grenville's or White's men. The unfortunate thing is that our evidence for this is both secondhand and imprecise. Our only source is a deposition taken from a Spanish seaman who was captured by Irish and sailed homeward with him; subsequently, he was released and made his way back to Spain.[1] Alonso Ruiz had been taken prisoner when a frigate captained by Francisco de Avalos was captured near Matanzas, on the north coast of Cuba, one of five prizes in all taken by Irish. According to his report, they made their way "along the Florida coast until they came to the Bahia de Santa Maria in 37 degrees. There they stayed to take in water and found traces of cattle and a stray dark-brown mule. . . . The sailor says they were three days in the Bay after which they set sail again with one of the Santo Domingo ships taken near Matanzas." This is infuriatingly imprecise. In Spanish parlance the Bahia de Santa Maria sometimes had been confused with Wococon, the inlet on the Outer Banks where the *Tiger* had gone aground, but by 1588, when the report was made, it is much more likely to have been Chesapeake Bay. How then could Irish have located a place where he expected to find White's colonists on Chesapeake Bay from mere verbal reports and perhaps a chart derived from White's cartographical activities in 1585–86? It seems impossible to say. If he had done so, how could he have found the stray mule and "traces" (what traces?) of cattle at any point along the southern shore of Chesapeake Bay? We cannot be sure that no cattle were carried from England on board White's ships, but it seems unlikely. It would be more probable that a mule would have come from the Caribbean (although White tells us he picked up no livestock there) than from England.

One solution might be that White had indicated the mouth of the Elizabeth River, the site of modern Norfolk, as a rendezvous, that he had sent some of the colonists around by sea to this point in the pinnace with any livestock they may have had, and that, while they were making their way to their inland objective (Irish perhaps being late), they accidentally lost one mule. If they were by this time settling in near Skicóac, they would not be easily accessible to Irish and his men. But this scenario, which depends almost entirely on guesswork, is not very plausible. All we can say with confidence is that Irish, after a successful privateering raid (he declared for customs duty at Bristol nearly £5,000 worth of prize goods, which might mean he took in fact twice as much), did make some attempt to link up with White's colonists but failed to do so, even though he just may have put in at Hatarask expecting to find Grenville's men in place. Much more plausibly, the mule could have been found there or on Roanoke Island.

In 1587 Ralegh had become captain of the Queen's Guard, a position of prestige rather than power but one that bound him to Elizabeth's side for much of the time. At the end of the year, he was probably preparing to leave for Ireland where his Munster planters were settling in and needed his personal attention. In addition, he had to look after his own dwellings, a house in Youghal and Lismore Castle, which he was having rebuilt. How much Ralegh could have done for White immediately, and how little his London associates could do because they may not have had the resources to do anything at all, we cannot tell. It is probable that White was totally frustrated in his earliest requests for a ship and supplies to be sent across the Atlantic, but that he was soon diverted to Bideford. There Grenville had indeed been gathering ships for a transatlantic voyage.

The struggle with Spain was reaching a critical point. War was by now official and Spain was preparing a vast fleet that would bring both England and the insurgent Netherlands to their knees. Sir Francis Drake had set off in 1587 and destroyed part of its resources, but Spain was too powerful for this to be more than a temporary setback. A diversionary attack across the Atlantic, such as Drake had conducted in 1585–86, now seemed a possible way of drawing off Spanish forces from England if the Queen and her more cautious councillors could be persuaded to agree with this strategy. Although on 9 October 1587, royal orders had prohibited all vessels from leaving English ports,[2] Ralegh had some latitude. Because he was virtually the Queen's principal representative in the southwest and concerned with mobilizing land and sea forces, he was prepared to let Grenville's squadron leave port.

Undoubtedly, Grenville meant to try out Chesapeake Bay as a base. White could either sail ahead on one of his supply ships for the more immediate relief of the colonists or wait to accompany Grenville when his fleet departed. It is almost certain that White urged the former course as strongly as he could on both Ralegh (who almost certainly was investing heavily in the expedition) and Grenville, but without success. They may not have had a suitable ship ready or they may have been reluctant to allow a vessel to risk crossing the Atlantic alone at a time of maximum hostility of English, French, and Dutch against Spain and Portugal and of Iberian ships against all interlopers. Or the weather may have ruled out a crossing. The prospects for taking a smallish vessel, which would be all that could be spared then, down the Bristol Channel and out into the Atlantic in late winter or early spring were not good. Even if a ship did get to sea, a voyage across the Bay of Biscay and thence westward to America may not have seemed possible. It is most probable that all White could do was to bring any additional colonists he could collect down to Bideford and hope that Grenville would put to sea early, so that the vessel in which he was carrying vital stores could sail ahead of the main squadron as soon as it was safe to do so. It is known that some men and women did go down to Bideford to await White's departure, but how many and with what resources we cannot tell.

By late March the omens seemed good. Grenville was ready. The *Galleon Dudley*, of 250 tons, was a fine armed merchantman that had come around from London. She was commanded by James Erisey. The *Virgin God Save Her*, of 200 tons, was now ready to sail. One of the two vessels named *Tiger*—possibly the one that had been with Drake in 1585–86 rather than Grenville's flagship in 1586—together with a *Golden Hind* (not Drake's), the *St. Leger*, named after a famous west-country family, and two or three smaller vessels, made up a formidable privateering squadron. It was not comparable to Drake's fleet in 1585, but sufficient to cause alarm and damage in western waters so that Spain might well divert ships to combat it. The vessel that would carry White, his associates, and their supplies would be detached as soon as possible, whereas the main squadron would almost certainly make for the Caribbean and create as much havoc there as possible, and only then head for Chesapeake Bay to reconnoiter a place for a base before taking some or all of the ships back to England. It is unfortunate that we do not have firmer indications of what the proposed strategy was to have been.

Whatever the precise plan was, it was soon frustrated.[3] Had the winds been favorable Grenville might have got away, but he was still held up by contrary winds when orders came for him to abandon the voyage. The Queen and her Privy Council were engaged in a desperate attempt to mobilize every effective ship and man to meet the Spanish threat. The Armada year, 1588, was, in their considered view, not one for adventures by a strong squadron in the western ocean when its guns and men were all needed for the defense of their homeland. On 31 March Grenville was sent firm orders to bring his ships as rapidly as possible to Plymouth to join the western fleet being assembled under the lord high admiral (Lord Howard of Effingham) and Sir Francis Drake. This was to be an effective force in the Armada campaign in the following July. The wind that had held Grenville back now changed to let all suitable ships in his squadron join Drake at Plymouth. Grenville himself was required for shore duties in North Devon and Cornwall. This was a severe blow to White: he could no longer be sure of effective escorts through what had become, in fact, a maritime battle zone. At the same time two of the "unsuitable" ships, which had not gone to Plymouth, were made available to him. The larger of these was the *Brave*, a bark, of 30 tons, whose captain, Arthur Facy, had commanded a ship in Grenville's 1586 expedition and so knew how to reach the North American coast by the most effective way, and whose pilot was the Spaniard Pedro Diaz, taken by Grenville in 1585. The other vessel was the *Roe*, of 25 tons, rated as a pinnace, whose master is not known. The plan was evidently to sail as directly across the ocean as possible, avoiding the Caribbean, perhaps in latitudes farther north than those attempted by Grenville in 1586, even though this might have brought them up against contrary winds, or even no winds at all. In normal circumstances these two small vessels would have had a good chance of making the crossing. A number of privateers of no greater tonnage had done well in the Caribbean, though this was certainly not a normal year. In eastern Atlantic waters they were highly vulnerable.

Thomas Harriot redated his *Briefe and true report* "this month of February, 1588" and it was at last sent to the press. It bore Ralegh's arms, and contained a foreword by Ralph Lane praising the author and his work:

> Thus much upon my credit I am to affirm that things universally are so truly set down in this treatise by the author thereof, an actor in the colony, and a man no less for his honesty than learning commendable, as that I dare boldly avouch it may very

well pass with the credit of truth even amongst the most true relations of this age.

Whether this was written early in 1587 or early in 1588 we cannot tell, but it does imply that Lane did not disagree with what Harriot said about the behavior of the first colonists both on Roanoke Island and after their return to England. Although it carried no printer's or publisher's name, it is known to have been printed by Robert Robinson.[4] But it cannot have appeared before the middle of March at the earliest and is unlikely to have had any value as propaganda for Grenville's venture, though it could well have circulated in manuscript earlier in 1588, as it may have done early in 1587. The inability of Harriot to get any writings rapidly into print probably explains why this, the best and fullest treatise on North America to be published before 1612, was of little or no use in raising colonists to take part in the ventures of either 1587 or 1588. At the same time, it was seen by discriminating authorities on North America, notably by the younger Richard Hakluyt, as an outstanding piece of work, and so was to have a long and important life after 1588. But so far as John White and his problems in 1588 were concerned, it unfortunately had no relevance whatever.

White's efforts in London, aided we would expect by the three Assistants left behind in 1587, and also possibly in Portsmouth, had led to the assembly at Bideford of an appreciable number of intending settlers and stores that were evidently thought adequate. How many people changed their minds when Grenville's expedition was cancelled we cannot tell. The intrepid few who were willing to sail on the *Brave* and the *Roe* almost certainly had relatives or husbands among the colonists left behind in 1587. There were seven men and four women on board the two vessels. With White, they made up a reinforcement of only twelve in all for those left behind in America, too small a number to make much difference to their prospects, but a clear indication that support for the settlement still existed and that the colonists had not been deserted by their friends and relatives.

When the two small vessels put out over Bideford Bar on 22 April 1588, they were carrying, besides the planters, stores of ship's biscuit, meal, vegetables, and no doubt other less basic commodities. They also bore letters from Sir Walter Ralegh "wherein among other matters he comforted them with promises that with all convenient speed he would prepare a good supply of shipping and men with sufficience of all things needfull which, he intended, God willing, should be with them the summer following." It is probable that he meant White's vessel to get away much earlier and that the "shipping" was Grenville's squadron and the "summer" that of 1588. But this is not certain, because White goes on to say that he was still at Bideford and ready to set out with Grenville when the countermanding order arrived. It is possible, therefore, that Ralegh was thinking of 1589 and of a reinforcement primarily intended to build up White's colony, and not the naval base which, it appears, Grenville hoped to establish, independently of the colony, in 1588, though even this is by no means certain.

Arthur Facy and Pedro Diaz alike, with their companions, had little or no consideration for White and his colonists.[5] From the very start they were primarily, we might say solely, concerned with robbery. As they emerged from the Bristol Channel, they chased and then boarded four vessels (their nationality is not known), taking three men to make up their complement of seamen. On 24 April they chased two vessels, one Breton, one Scottish, which they robbed of anything they fancied and then released. A Flemish vessel tried to fool them into thinking she was English, but when she found they were heavily armed, as they must have been, she avoided an action, for which they were thankful, "for it was a very tall ship and excellently well appointed and now ready to clap us aboard." The Roe pursued a large merchant vessel (a "hulk"), probably Flemish, on the twenty-ninth, stopping to borrow some men and equipment (boarding nets?) from the Brave before resuming the chase, but eventually broke it off. She was soon off after another vessel but again could not catch her. Meanwhile, the Brave, proving a very bad sailer, was effectively unable to take any part in these chases, so that the Roe was soon out of her sight and was not seen again at sea.

On 5 May, when the Brave was some thirty leagues from Madeira, she was overtaken by a Rochelle ship, which exchanged friendly signals with her; but, seeing she was well laden and such a bad sailer (as a pinnace or small bark could often put on enough speed to escape from a larger vessel), returned to her consort to take on additional men and then made after the Brave again. A fierce fight followed. A broadside from the *Brave* did some damage to her attacker and mortally wounded her master gunner, while at the same time her own master gunner was shot in the head. The French then attempted to board with thirty men but met with fierce resistance, White himself being in action. There were heavy casualties on both sides: no fewer than twenty-three were killed or badly wounded. White says "I myself was wounded twice in the head, once with a sword and another time with a pike, and hurt also in the side of the buttock with a shot." He says further, "three of our passengers were hurt also, whereof one had 10 or 12 wounds."

The French boarded the *Brave* and forced the English to surrender; then, says White, they "robbed us of all our victuals, powder, weapons and provision, saving a small quantity of biscuit to serve us scarce for England." The captain's offer to spare them if they surrendered was not agreeable to his men who had lost so many of their companions and did not wish to make any concessions. But during their haste to strip the *Brave* they overloaded their boats, sinking one and damaging another. In the end, the French ship sailed off and the *Brave* was left with cables and anchors, her ordnance, and "most part of our sails." This left her barely viable; otherwise, she would have been a helpless hulk. The men who could work set "to new rigging and mending our sails, tacklings and such things as were spilled in our fight." By these means, "God justly punishing our former thievery of our evil-disposed mariners," they were "constrained to break off our voyage intended for the relief of the colony left the year before in Virginia and the same night to set our course for England." By the time they were rerigged they were fifty leagues northeast of Madeira, that is, approximately in latitude thirty-five degrees north, ironically almost the same as that of Cape Hatteras but still nearly 2,000 miles away.

Pedro Diaz said that before the French ship departed they had begged her captain to let them have him as an expert pilot to take them safely home as all their skilled men were injured and they might perish in consequence; he was equally insistent that the French take him with them. As the latter, no doubt, could also do with an experienced pilot such as he was reputed to be, they accepted him on board their ship. They would not let him go as he requested when they landed at the Cape Verde Islands, but he tricked them and got away, eventually finding passage to Havana in a Spanish vessel, where he gave an interesting, and for us important, account of his adventures on the high seas and in England between 1585 and 1588, which he related to an official there on 11/21 March 1589. In the meantime, the *Brave* had gone ahead as well as she could, keeping to the north to avoid pirates. On 20 May she sighted the Irish coast and then slowly made her way up the Bristol Channel, putting into Bideford on 22 May.

White gives no account of the *Roe's* adventures after her parting with the *Brave*, but within a few weeks she returned to Cornwall. He concludes his weary but graphic recital by lamenting that both vessels had returned "without performing our intended voyage for the relief of the planters in Virginia," and adding, in a somewhat banal fashion, "which thereby were not a little distressed."

By late May 1588 all eyes, and most hands, were turned to the southwest coast where the Great Armada was expected daily. Thus, the return of the *Brave* and the *Roe* is unlikely to have caused any appreciable stir. Both Ralegh and Grenville were too busily engaged in preparing the land defenses against a Spanish landing and seeing that the fleet at Plymouth got all the supplies and support it needed to take any action on White's behalf. It would be surprising if any sound seamen left on the two little ships were not conscripted to serve on the fleet, while John White and the injured were left to recover as well as they could. How long this took and when White eventually made contact with Grenville and Ralegh is not known, the latter being particularly elusive, as after the dispersal of the Armada he made for Ireland and remained there for some time. We can assume that White, when he was sufficiently recovered from his three wounds (which appear to have healed completely), went to London to see whether anything could be somehow arranged, sooner or later, to get help to the settlers in America.

What was not known in England, nor was it to be known within the lifetime of any of the sponsors of the American ventures, was that if White had, in fact, got away in the *Brave* and *Roe* he might well have encountered a Spanish expedition which, at last, penetrated into the area where the English settlement was thought to be located.[6] Although Pedro Menéndez Marqués had failed in 1587 to

enter Chesapeake Bay, where he was confident the English had settled, he did not give up the attempt to do so, but in 1588 he could
not go himself. He acquired a bark (*uno barco luengo*), which was very
much like an English pinnace, though lighter, because oars could be
used to help its progress when sails did not serve. He placed in
command of the vessel a competent pilot, Captain Vicente González,
who had been in Chesapeake Bay in 1570, and under him his second
in command of his soldiers in the St. Augustine garrison, the ser-
geant-major Juan Menéndez Marqués, a relation of his own, together
with thirty seamen and soldiers. Their purpose was to "run along the
coast up to the bay of Madre de Dios del Jacán [as the Spanish had
now come to call the Chesapeake], in order to obtain knowledge of
and to reconnoitre the English settlement and fort," about which
they had had a number of reports, the latest probably from Darby
Glavin, the Irishman who had deserted from White in Puerto Rico in
1587. According to our source, an abbreviated version (all so far
known) of the final report, they noted the headlands of the Outer
Banks of North Carolina as they went north but did not investigate
the inlets. Setting out toward the end of May, they entered Chesapeake Bay without difficulty early in June. The bay was impressive:
"the mouth of this bay is about three leagues wide, without shoals or
reefs, and is more than eight fathoms deep at its entrance. It runs
northwest-southeast and forms a large circular gulf." A description of
the mouth of the James River follows in our source. They were
amazed at the size of the rivers, particularly of the Potomac, up
which they traveled for some distance, remarking on the apparent
fertility of the land near its banks. Eventually they entered the Sus-
quehanna River, but were checked by great rocks. They made several
landings but their report does not mention any contacts with Indians
and gives no indication that any trace of English activity in the area
was found. According to two subsequent statements made by Juan
Menéndez Marqués and Vicente González many years afterward,
they did see Indians with "gold" ornaments and also much copper.[7]
One of these Indians was brought back to St. Augustine, where he
filled the Spanish with tales of gold, copper, and diamonds; however,
his stories were not sufficiently credited to lead to other expeditions
following in the wake of that of 1588. But the exploration of the bay

from its mouth to its end was a notable achievement and we could very well do with a fuller version of the official report, though one has not yet been found.

On leaving the bay on the return voyage, the bark kept close to the shore going south from Cape Henry. The report states:

All that night they worked their way south with the aid of a strong west wind. The same was true of the next day until sunset. The wind then freshening so much they were forced to dismast the ship and bring her to the shore by means of oars. They entered on a bar of very little depth [Hatarask, the former Port Ferdinando], and inside found a large cove the southern part of which at low tide was almost dry. The view towards the north gave on to a great part of the bay [the entrance to Albemarle Sound] and revealed a large arm in the north-west curve which was heavily wooded [the northern part of Roanoke Island]. And along the shore towards the north there was another opening which appeared to be better than that by which they had entered, this part of the coast for about a league, between one bar and the other, being low and free of sand.[8]

The only other mention of this entry of the Spanish ship into Pamlico Sound is more specific:[9] "For landmarks there are three great sand-dunes on the shore which have two entrances." We must remain indecisive about whether they are speaking of the Port Lane or the Trinity Harbor of the 1585 expedition, or even of some movement in the inlets that had taken place over the previous three years, which seems unlikely.

The report then comes to the point that is of special interest in connection with the colony left in 1587:

And on the inside of the little bay they had entered there were signs of a slipway [*varadero*, usually a boatyard] for small vessels, and on land a number of wells made with English casks [*pozos hechos de pipas*], and other debris indicating that a considerable number of people had been here.

This is important evidence. It indicates that there was a small cove somewhere well to the north of Baum Point, which has long gone, and that this had been used by the colonists, probably almost continuously since 1585, for landing their boats and goods, and that barrel-lined wells had been dug nearby, as was done in later settlements. It cannot be certain that the evidence of many people having been there was the result of the departure of the 1587 colony for their northern home, but it strongly suggests that this was so. The debris could have partly accumulated earlier, in 1586 in particular, but it was evidently considerable and consequently probably new. Not a single Englishman was seen and evidently no Indians either. No landing was made on the island to see whether any English settlers were there. Probably González and Juan Menéndez Marqués were quite satisfied to have found where the English had settled, without risking their small force against any large group that might be hiding on the island. But their very casualness may suggest that they considered the island to have been deserted by this time. We are only told, laconically, "the next day they again departed." A precise date cannot be assigned to this visit, but it was probably at the end of June, as the Spaniards returned to St. Augustine in July. Had White completed his expedition, he could have arrived anytime from mid-June onward and could very easily have been caught by the Spanish, or have caught them. The possible implications of this Spanish visit can be considered later in connection with the Lost Colony. Pedro Menéndez Marqués was encouraged by the disclosures that the English were not located on Chesapeake Bay and, if any were still on Roanoke Island, which he might well doubt, they were there in no great strength. He devoted much of his energy to planning a great expedition that would plant three hundred Spanish soldiers on Chesapeake Bay and deny it forever to the English.

From May 1588 to March 1589 we have no further direct news of John White, but some indirect indications of his activities. Either before or after his abortive voyage he presented a copy of his drawing of the swallowtail butterfly to Thomas Penny, who noted "This White the Painter [Candidus Pictor] brought me from Virginia, 1587." Penny also referred to copies of drawings of fireflies that White had found both in Hispaniola and North America, the former clearly in 1585, as well as of a cicada (brought by White, "the not uncelebrated painter") and a gadfly from Roanoke.[10] This contact with a celebrated naturalist, who was compiling a book on insects illustrated with drawings of specimens, is perhaps an indication that after his return in 1587 White had been building up his contacts in London and continued to do so in 1588, again after his return from North America. He also contacted John Gerard, the herbalist, who had a celebrated garden in Holborn just inside London's walls, and gave him specimens of the milkweed and of the "salsaparilla" or smilax. The contact with Gerard was to have some significance, as this member of the Barber-Surgeons' company was one of the men White began to gather around him in 1588.

White was also in close contact with the younger Richard Hakluyt, who was now back in London from Paris, because Hakluyt obtained from him—probably before the end of the year—narratives of both the 1587 and 1588 voyages. It is not clear that White received any help from the three Assistants who had been left behind in 1587, and no doubt he had to rely for personal support by making several sets of finished drawings from his North American collection. One of these, through Hakluyt's means, was acquired by the Frankfurt publisher, Theodor de Bry, and probably brought him a substantial return. The bound volume that now forms the primary British Museum collection was probably made at this time for some great man at Court—Walsingham, Leicester (though he was to die on 20 September 1588), or Sir Christopher Hatton—for which he is also likely to have been well rewarded.[11] It is even more likely that he had another set made up for Ralegh, if White had not already presented him with an adequate one after his return in 1586. White's household in London possibly may have still existed, though the absence of any mention of his wife might suggest that she had died. His son John (if it is correct that he had a son of that name) may have been born to him later after a subsequent marriage.

In any event, little could be done in the latter part of 1588 to revive the project for relieving the 1587 colony. The dispersal of the Armada left the country disturbed and unsettled—if relieved and very proud at the outcome—for much of the rest of the year. The ban on the sailing of commercial vessels was retained in force, and Ralegh, after his active part in preparing forces to meet a Spanish landing, was anxious to get to Ireland. But we can be reasonably certain that White sought him out and met him in London within a few months of his return, after White had recovered from his wounds, and that they had long discussions about the possibilities for doing something as soon as the war fervor had died down and the prohibition on sailings had been removed. What is unlikely is that Ralegh did anything positive at this time to arrange for a further voyage to North America. Instead, it can be surmised, with reasonable probability, that he introduced White to his business manager in London, William Sanderson, and to the richest promoters of the day, the two Thomas Smiths (or Smythes), who were father and son. For the next thirty years, the younger Smith was to be the most active single figure in English overseas commercial enterprise, especially after he inherited the great fortune his father (d.1591) made as the "farmer" or contractor for the Queen's customs duties in the port of London. He had already had financial dealings with Ralegh.[12] It was apparently to these men that Ralegh left the development of some scheme for underwriting further ventures to aid the 1587 colony and for the future exploitation of his Virginia rights, though it took some time to work out an appropriate organizational form for this purpose.

The final solution was what, in modern terms, might be called a holding company. A body of men was assigned by Sir Walter Ralegh to join with the original Governor and Assistants of the City of Ralegh in order to assure them funds to support future ventures and, in particular, to relieve and reinforce the 1587 colony.[13] Each of these men, we might expect, would contribute, or guarantee, a certain sum, which could then be used as a capital fund for the relief of the colonists. William Sanderson and one of the Thomas Smiths (the younger is the more likely) were joined by a number of persons, several of whom we have already met—Richard Hakluyt and John Gerard. Of the others, the best-known figure was the pilot, navigation theorist, and protégé of the Smiths, Thomas Hood. We might suggest that Walter Baylye had some connection with Roger Baylye, who, it is thought, may well have remained at the head of the colony after White's departure, though this is not established. Similarly, Richard Wright, haberdasher of London, could have been related to John Wright who was in both the 1585–86 and 1587 colonies, though, again, this is a guess. William Gamage, ironmonger, was connected to the Sidney family by marriage and, through it, had links with Ralegh. Edmund Nevil, Thomas Harding, Walter Marler, clothworker or salter, Thomas Martin (perhaps a member of a family of goldsmiths later concerned with Virginia in the early seventeenth century), Gabriel Harris, William George, William Stone, clothworker, Henry Fleetwood, Robert Macklyn, Thomas Wade, and Edward Walden are still unidentified, though, because all are described as merchants of London, each can doubtless be associated with one or other of the London companies. Enough is known of the leading members of the group, however, for it to be clear that these men had enough capital to finance a relief expedition with little burden to themselves. With them were those who appeared on the revised list of Governor and Assistants of the City of Ralegh. Seven of them, again headed by Roger Baylye, were assumed to be still in White's colony. John White, with John Nichols, the only one of the three Assistants left in England in 1587 to appear—he could have been a connection of William Nicoles who was in the colony—and a newcomer, Humfray Dimmocke, made up a body of ten instead of the original thirteen Assistants, Fernandes being in disgrace and William Fullwood and James Plat either retired or dead.

The newcomers were to be "made free of the corporation, company and society lately made by the said Sir Walter Ralegh in the City of Ralegh." They undertook to "adventure divers and sundry sums of money, merchandises, shipping, munition, victual and other communities into the said foreign and remote country." In return they, and their assignees and factors or apprentices, were to have the right to trade freely with the City of Ralegh and with any other part of America in which Ralegh had any claim, because, as we have seen, his patent of 1584 gave him authority over any part of North America he could occupy—except Newfoundland—that was not already in the hands of Europeans. Thus, in the formal document at least, it appeared that Ralegh still intended to create further colonial settlements in North America, apart from the 1587 colony. Ralegh himself was prepared to make a free gift of £100 to the new corporation "for and in especial regard and zeal of planting the Christian religion in and amongst the said barbarous and heathen countries, and for the advancement and preferment of the same, and the common utility and profit of the inhabitants therein," as well as, it may be said, for "encouragement" of the new assignees to play their part in the venture. The missionary motive was perhaps inserted at the insistence of Richard Hakluyt, but the phrasing was little more than window dressing, because £100 was only a small fraction of what would be needed to perform the objectives of the syndicate, though we might guess that it represented the minimum sum that each of the new associates would be expected to contribute to the venture. Finally, Ralegh undertook to obtain a charter from the Queen to enable the new organization to obtain privileges for itself in the City of Ralegh territory such as Ralegh had been granted in 1584, and so assure it of permanence and, one might say, respectability as a chartered company under the Crown, whereas the assignment to the original grantees of 7 January 1587 was wholly abrogated. The date of this elaborate document, which proved in the end to have so little substance, was 7 March 1589.

One of the great unanswered questions is why this, we may assume, well-funded corporation did not send aid at once to the 1587 colonists. They had been seriously in need of it, they had maintained, in August 1587. John White had made a desperate attempt to bring them such assistance in 1588, and, if he failed, it was not through his own defects or failings. He had done all that one man could do. Why, now that more than eighteen months had passed and the need even more urgent, did no vessel leave England for North America in 1589? Plausible, perhaps compelling, reasons can be suggested. We cannot be entirely certain that no preparations were attempted. But because 7 March was already rather late for preparing a relief expedition, any such preparations may have failed to take effect through accident or delay until it appeared the sailing season, which made an approach to America feasible that year, was over. This, however, is only guesswork, with little or nothing to support it.

Less unlikely is the assumption that neither White nor his associates, new and old, were prepared to send out a small, vulnerable expedition, such as White had attempted in the *Brave* and *Roe*. Help would need to be sent by way of a substantial squadron capable of resisting assaults by other privateers or pirates, or even the Spanish, on the high seas. This virtually would require the associates to send out a major privateering expedition that could fight its way through the Caribbean and reach the colony intact and, if fortunate, with prizes as well. Such a venture involved obtaining the cooperation of a privateering syndicate already in being and ready to put to sea at short notice. Even though major London merchants were involved in the so-called holding company, no member of the major London syndicates, which by this time had made privateering a big business, was represented among the associates. To persuade such a syndicate to divert a substantial part of its activities during a privateering season to the needs of a handful of English people, who in any event might be difficult to locate, was virtually impossible.

The ban on private sailings was still in force in 1589 but exemptions appear to have been moderately easy to obtain, or else some vessels slipped away without asking for permission. Privateering expeditions to the South Seas, Brazil, and the Caribbean all got to sea and took prizes, but it is clear that none of these was amenable to the direction of the London associates. What was almost certainly the decisive factor was the Lisbon expedition that Sir Frances Drake and Sir John Norris were preparing at Plymouth.[14] The vast majority of the merchant fleet, virtually all heavily gunned for the Armada campaign, was being mobilized for a major assault against Spain by way of Portugal (which it was thought might revolt). No less than 143 privately-owned vessels were among the 150 ships that sailed from Plymouth in April, and a large part of the capital to float the expedition (and pay 18,000 soldiers) was raised in London. It was hopeless to try to compete with this mobilization of ships, men, and money. Thus, unfortunately for the colonists, the year 1589 was one of the worst, apart from 1588 itself, for raising any sort of expedition that could reach North America. So, if it is difficult to forgive the syndicate for not making an effort to relieve the colony—and indeed they may have tried to do so—the overriding reasons why they did not and could not are reasonably clear and decisive.

The end result of two years' effort was that neither John White, nor for that matter Ralegh himself, was able to relieve the colony. The organization, if it could be got to work, was now there, but the means and, perhaps, too, the will on the part of at least some of the merchants involved in the 1589 agreement were lacking. What White must have felt about this state of affairs we cannot tell precisely, but there is no doubt that his continuing intention of returning to North America, if and when he could, remained as strong as ever.

A Last Voyage

The year 1590 was the year of the privateers. The Lisbon expedition had provided more loss than gain to the nearly 150 armed merchantmen that had participated in it. The owners of many of them were willing, and often able, to equip their vessels with extra supplies of war materials, men, and food for six-month voyages preferably to the Caribbean, but many to lie off the Azores and other approaches to the Iberian lands. The Virginia syndicate now had its chance to show what it could do. But it seems to have been strangely reluctant to make a move. When Sir Walter Ralegh returned from Ireland early in the year, he must have been shocked that nothing was being done to get an expedition to sea. He found no preparations afoot to combine a voyage through the Caribbean, which would gain some prizes, with a relief expedition to the colonists.

Why this was so we cannot tell. Possibly, men like the younger Richard Hakluyt were too single-minded and wished to have a truly independent expedition, such as that of 1587, which would go as directly as possible to Roanoke Island and the Chesapeake without getting involved in the risks of fighting in the Caribbean if they could possibly be avoided. Perhaps the Thomas Smiths and their other London merchant associates were unable or unwilling to link up with the privateering firms, which were busy preparing all the ships they could for purely plundering expeditions and did not care to be burdened with supplies for a colony that would have to be searched for on the North American coast when the time might be spent more profitably in a privateering cruise alone. It is also likely that John White wished to bring men and women to North America, some of those perhaps who had been steadfast enough to attempt the 1588 voyage and had survived, and possibly others. This would make the prospect of looking for the rest of the colonists still less appealing because the intending settlers would get in the way of the fierce and often bloody combats in which privateering vessels engaged.

Ralegh, who was absorbed in Irish affairs and had commitments at Court that did not give him much room to maneuver,[1] was not himself in a position to equip ships in time for an American voyage. We can accept that he was wholly sympathetic to White's urging that something should be done as quickly as possible, even if he may have wondered whether relief might not now be too late. Richard Hakluyt had been deeply involved in seeing his more than 800-page book, *The principall navigations, voyages and discoveries of the English nation*, through the press in 1589 and was probably only able to show finished copies in the spring of 1590.[2] Thus his active aid counted for little, and in any case he did not have much money of his own. The one man on whom Ralegh could exert pressure was William Sanderson, whose finances were closely tied up with Ralegh's own and who was, therefore, not able to escape his obligations under the 1589 agreement. Sanderson was told to find a ship and a crew. He acquired a small ship of eighty tons called the *Mary Terlanye*, renamed her the *Moonlight*, and commenced to equip her for the voyage. In the rush of privateers to get to sea, it may not have been easy to find men and guns to fit her out. He was fortunately able to locate Edward Spicer, who, as master of the flyboat, had been a good friend to John White in 1587, and appointed him captain. The assembly of forty men, and possibly of seven serviceable cannon, appears to have been slow, as also may have been the collection of stores (we do not know what they amounted to or even whether any additional colonists were to go on the voyage).

There was also another problem. The *Moonlight* could not carry enough provisions for the total reequipment of the colonists. More room was needed. Moreover, she required protection. On her own she would be vulnerable as she passed through the Caribbean in this war-torn year. Evidently Ralegh was the only one who could make an arrangement for her to be convoyed safely to North America. He did so by inducing, or pressuring, John Watts who, with his partners, formed one of London's most powerful privateering syndicates. It appears from later Spanish reports that the flagship of his little squadron of privateers, the Hopewell, also known as the Harry and John, of some 150 tons, was to carry artillery in the hold for the fortification of a post on Chesapeake Bay. Her captain was the very experienced and intelligent Abraham Cocke and her master, Robert Hutton, her ship's company is variably estimated at from forty to eighty-four, the latter being the more likely, and her armament between sixteen and twenty-four guns. It was intended that she should carry White and other persons destined for the colony, though we would expect the Moonlight to have carried some others.

The Hopewell's consorts were the Little John of over 100 tons, with anything up to a hundred men and nineteen guns, and the pinnace, John Evangelist. The Little John was to have Christopher Newport as captain and Michael Geare as master, both to become well-known in later maritime operations; William Lane was to command the pinnace. In February the Queen made an attempt to hold up the sailing of some of the privateers, owing to rumors of further aggressive Spanish plans, though it was clearly ineffective. But this, John White says, enabled Ralegh to put pressure on Watts to agree to convoy both White and the supply ship Moonlight to North America if his ships were released without further delay. Sanderson claimed credit for making the final arrangements by which Watts posted a bond for £5,000 to carry out his obligations to the settlers, but in doing so he was merely acting as Ralegh's agent, though White was to claim that it was his own continued pressures that led to this action being taken.

When at the end of February White came down to where the ships were about to sail from the Thames, Abraham Cocke refused to accept the settlers and the equipment they brought with them. He would only give White himself passage on the Hopewell, which apparently had already stowed cannon and possibly other heavy equipment for the colony in its hold. White could not reach Ralegh and Sanderson in time and accepted Cocke's terms, evidently sending his intending settlers back to their homes. (We cannot tell whether any came in the Moonlight later, but most probably not.) The ships sailed from Plymouth on 20 March 1590. Watts may not have known of this denouement until it was too late for him to prevent it.

It is easy, in retrospect, to consider that Cocke ruined White's chance, his last chance as it happened, to reinforce the colony. Yet as

an experienced privateer he knew something of the discomfort a
heavily manned privateering vessel offered even to her own men.
Even more clearly he knew the dangers to passengers when an
engagement became necessary at sea, more particularly if some of
them were women. His men may well have flatly refused to sail if
passengers were carried. Two things are clear. First, White acquiesced
in the arrangement and Cocke was not unwilling to make it known
in the Caribbean that he was carrying with him the governor of an
English colony in North America that he intended to reinforce. And
second, Cocke had expected the Moonlight to join the other ships
before they left Plymouth, but she did not appear. Prior to leaving
the Thames, he had agreed to accept the Moonlight as a partner in the
privateering enterprise. This was almost certainly part of the deal
with Watts—and contingency plans had been made for the Moonlight,
if she could not keep company, to rendezvous with Cocke off Cape
Tiburon in Hispaniola by about the beginning of July.

The Moonlight duly sailed, probably early in May, but not alone.
Spicer was evidently afraid to make the passage unescorted, so he
had arranged to sail with the Conclude, a well-armed pinnace owned
by another major London privateering firm, Thomas Middleton and
Company. Her captain was Joseph Harris and her master, Hugh Har-
dinge. At the time, this was in some ways an unfortunate arrangement as the "consortship" agreement—to share captures—made between these two vessels was to cause controversy later when the
Conclude's owners claimed a share of the prizes taken under the
Hopewell's leadership after both the Moonlight and Conclude had joined
Cocke in the Caribbean. It is, however, fortunate in another sense,
because the disagreement about consortships led to a long case in
the High Court of Admiralty in 1590–91, which permits us to know
much more about the voyage than would otherwise have been possible. For example, White mentions nothing in his account about the
arrangement by which the Moonlight was to be fitted out by Sanderson
and used to assist the colony, and remains silent about a number of
other important incidents of the voyage.[3]

White's journal of the Hopewell's Atlantic crossing is laconic in the
extreme. Cocke's ships made a landing at a Moroccan port where
they acquired two boats to make up for the loss of two shallops on
the way south. They passed on to the Canaries, where Newport's

Little John took a large flyboat, carrying wine, cinnamon, and other goods, which was sent back with a prize crew to Dartmouth. They anchored off Dominica on 30 April and did some trading with the Island Caribs on the following day. Newport was left behind to try to pick up Spanish ships attempting the Dominica Passage, while the other two vessels sailed on along the inner fringe of the Leeward and Virgin Islands. After going ashore on an islet off the eastern end of Puerto Rico to kill seabirds, the two vessels divided once more, the pinnace sailing along the south coast of Puerto Rico and the *Hopewell* passing through the Virgin Passage to the north coast of the main island. Sailing close inshore, the *Hopewell* was sighted by the Spanish who lit fires to warn small ships at sea that pirates were present. In spite of this, after stopping to take in water at an uninhabited bay in eastern Puerto Rico, she took a small coaster laden with hides and sugar. There they lost a man, Pedro, a mulatto, who had been captured on some earlier venture and was probably being used to provide detailed information on the islands. He surrendered to the Spanish and gave them much detail about the English, including the information that the governor of a North American colony was on board the *Hopewell*, along with artillery for the colony.[4] He also told the tale that no less than seven privateers were going to a North American base to refresh their men before returning to the Caribbean, while a great fleet of privateers was proposing to do the same thing in 1591. Four ships, apparently all in 1590, would be carrying women for the colony.

It is very difficult to know precisely what to make of this. Certainly Captain William Irish, who had attempted to contact the colony in 1587, had gone out early in the year to the Caribbean in the *Bark Young*, owned by Sir George Carey and his associates, in company with the *Falcon's Flight*, owned by John Norris of Barnstaple.[5] Moreover, on entering the Caribbean, Irish was able to pick up a valuable prize and put a prize crew on board. He told the Spanish prisoners he released that he was putting into a North American port to pick up two hundred English people stranded there, or so they said when questioned. He did not succeed in taking further prizes. It seems very probable that, as in 1587, he made an attempt to find the colonists in Chesapeake Bay, but failed to do so because they were not located on the shore of the bay. His later fate was to call at

Newfoundland early in August for fish and water and to be set on by powerful French fishing vessels which relieved him of his prize and sent him home with little gain.

Although it would be unwise to say so with certainty, it would appear that there was some idea of reviving the 1587–88 plan of Sir Richard Grenville, with Ralegh's knowledge and approval if not necessarily his active participation, for establishing a shore base for privateers on Chesapeake Bay. Carey would appear quite likely to have asked Captain Irish to make a further search for a site for such a base and to attempt again to make contact with the colonists. Similarly, the presence of the Barnstaple ship might indicate that Grenville was cooperating with Carey in sending a ship in which he had an interest to assist in the search. The rumors that Pedro spread among the Spanish of English plans to send privateers and women settlers to a North American base in 1590, and a large fleet to the same area in 1591, may well represent conversations on board the *Hopewell* between Cocke and White about what they would like to have happen, rather than anything that had been planned in detail. The evidence, such as it is, suggests that Irish at least did make a further call in Chesapeake Bay in search of the colonists and of a site for a base, and was again unsuccessful in the former aim and not unduly impressed with the facilities to be found for the latter. Although it appears unlikely that Cocke was planning to go on to Chesapeake Bay after he had delivered White to Roanoke Island and had completed his search there, it is not impossible that this was the original plan, altered only by the circumstances of the actual visit to Roanoke Island in August.

John White's pacific tendencies had been well illustrated during the outward voyage in 1587, but he had brought armor with him to Roanoke Island and shown in 1588 that when roused to defend his helpless passengers he could fight as bravely as any. From this time on he was to be part of the fierce and often bloody struggles that privateering in the Caribbean often involved. Fortunately for the English ships, in 1590 Spain had not yet put into effect the numerous measures she devised for the protection of her fleets and of inter-island traffic once the lessons of the Armada struggle had been slowly translated into action. As the decade went on, Spain was to make it progressively more difficult for English privateers to make easy captures.

Captain Cocke's objective was to seize the squadron of merchant vessels leaving Santo Domingo for Havana in order to be incorporated in the *flota*, the combined convoyed fleet that left for Spain each year. As it might sail around either end of Hispaniola, Cocke divided his forces. The *Little John*, which had come up prizeless, was given the small Spanish pinnace just taken at Mona to watch the eastern end. But again she was unsuccessful in finding any prizes. The *Hopewell* made for Cape Tiburon, at the western end of Hispaniola. The *John Evangelist*, sailing some way behind her, attracted the attention of the solitary guardship, a galley, patrolling off Santo Domingo, but she was too fast for the galley; after exchanges of cannon fire, which did neither ship any appreciable damage, the Spaniard broke off and returned to port. The vessels concentrated for a short time off Cape Tiburon, where Cocke picked up a man who told him there was a ship at Yaguana, on the western side of Puerto Rico. The *John Evangelist* and one of the small prizes were sent to take her, which they did without difficulty. She was the *Trinidad*, of sixty tons, with a useful cargo of hides, cassava, ginger, and articles from Spain such as copper pans, as well as some slaves and passengers.

Cape Tiburon had been appointed for the rendezvous with the *Moonlight* if she failed to catch the main squadron at Plymouth. She and the *Conclude* had evidently had an easy voyage, though no details of it survive. They found Cocke at the rendezvous; the three prizes he had taken increased his squadron to six, so there were now eight vessels in all. On that very day the fourteen vessels of the Santo Domingo squadron came into view. Immediately Cocke sent all his ships after them. Their tactic, however, was to split up so as to divide the English forces and hope to make their way separately to Havana. Their speed was such that the English failed to catch any ships during the day-long chase along the south coast of Cuba during which they themselves became separated from each other. When darkness fell the *Hopewell* and the *Moonlight* were in company, along with the *Conclude*, the latter claiming to have been the first to sight a large Spanish vessel and bring her to the attention of the other ships. At the signal, the three English ships closed in on her. It was not until morning that they came within close range, some thirty miles offshore from Cape Tiburon. The *Hopewell* and *Moonlight* poured in what shot they could on the starboard side and the *Conclude* to port. The fight lasted for some hours. After a number of men had been

killed on the Spaniard, she surrendered and Cocke, as commander
of the squadron, went on board to receive the Spanish submission.
She was a fine prize, *El Buen Jesus* of Seville, of 300 tons or more, and
Cocke decided to take her with him.

It is likely that it was during 3 July, which was spent "rifling, rum-
maging and fitting the prize to be sailed with us," that White and
Edward Spicer of the *Moonlight* were able to make contact for the first
time, and perhaps have a few words about the Roanoke visit. In the
meantime there was no sign of the other Spanish vessels that had
been lost sight of in the chase. The *Moonlight* and the *Conclude* were
sent ahead of the *Hopewell*, which was sailing slowly, perhaps having
too much loot on board and too few men to man her effectively
after supplying a prize crew for the *Buen Jesus*. The two small vessels
reached Cape San Antonio at the southwest end of Cuba only to see,
to their chagrin, the great Spanish fleet of twenty-two large ships,
well-guarded by royal galleons, bearing the silver from Cartagena to
Havana, without being able to take any action against it. The *Hopewell*
came up and the three vessels then awaited the Mexican fleet, which
normally was not well-guarded, on its way to join the *flota* at Havana.
But they were becalmed for eleven days, and in that time found their
prisoners such a nuisance that they landed all but three on the south
coast of Cuba. Meanwhile, the remaining English ships had followed
other vessels of the Santo Domingo squadron. They were driven
down to the Jamaica coast, where the Spanish flagship, after exchanging gunfire with Captain Newport, took refuge in a harbor; two
others were driven ashore and one sank, but the other was pulled off
and made a prize.

The *Little John* and her companions now set about trailing the *flota*
from Mexico, the main part of which reached Havana unmolested.
Three stragglers, however, were seen and chased, one of which
turned back to Mexico. Newport and his small consorts had a desperate fight with the two remaining Spanish ships. After a time they
boarded the smaller vessel, with Newport leading the way. In the
engagement his right arm was severed though evidently he was not
put out of action. No fewer than twenty-four men were killed and
wounded. While this Spanish vessel was being looted, she proved to
be so badly holed that she sank, taking with her thirteen large casks
of silver that had not been unloaded. The larger vessel, the *Nuestra*

Señora del Rosario, had cast loose and made for Havana. But she too was badly holed and her crew had to run her aground. Two of the galleys of the guard from Havana came around and soon were busily engaged in keeping the English away from her, but she sank with a rich cargo. The vicissitudes of the privateering war could scarcely be better illustrated. Newport was expected to rendezvous with Cocke at Matanzas off the north coast of Cuba but he was so denuded of men, and so discouraged by his own mishaps, that the Little John and John Evangelist went directly back across the Atlantic to the Azores. Newport had already lost contact with the Trinidad and her prize crew and may not have had enough men left to bring the two small Spanish prizes back with him. He missed the chance of gaining his first sight of North America because of his wound, but the one-armed captain was thereafter to have a long and successful career in the Caribbean and in the founding of Virginia, 1606–8.

Meanwhile, Cocke with the Hopewell, Moonlight, Conclude, and the remanned Buen Jesus had no further good fortune either. Three small pinnaces from Mexico nearly ran into them, but took fright just in time and escaped under the guns of the great fortress of Havana. They, too, are likely to have been carrying silver. When he reached Matanzas, Cocke was well beyond the time arranged for the rendezvous with Newport, and no doubt White was pressing for the Roanoke visit to take place without delay. The Conclude was sent about her own business and the Buen Jesus was prepared for a direct passage to England under her prize crew. No other ships appeared, and on 27 July Cocke turned northward to the Florida Channel, which he entered the next day. At last White was on his way, he hoped, to relieve his colonists.

Unfortunately, the Hopewell and the Moonlight began to encounter hurricane weather as they worked their way up the Florida coast:

On the very first of August the wind scanted and from thence forward we had very fowl weather with much rain, thundering and great spouts, which fell round about us nigh unto our ships.

They sailed within sight of shore and managed to get a latitude reading of thirty-four degrees north on 3 August; "towards night we

were within three leagues of the low sandy islands west of Wococon"—that is, in the vicinity of Cape Lookout. But the bad weather
continued and forced them to remain at sea until 9 August, when a
calm enabled them to put in to a narrow, sandy island west of
Wococon. Thus in six days they had gained no distance. At least
those on board were able to get some water and catch fish. Here, the
Outer Banks were only about a mile from the mainland, or so they
thought; thus the latitude of thirty-five degrees White gives may be a
little high. They sailed on in the morning of the twelfth and were
soon finding a way through the long tongue of shoals that extends
outward from Cape Hatteras. This was a hazardous undertaking but
with careful sounding they came through and found themselves opposite the inlet to which the name Chacandepeco is attached at the
northern end of Croatoan. If some of the 1587 colonists were with
Manteo at this time, as seems highly probable, they may even have
seen the two ships slowly working their way through the shoals.
Toward evening on the fifteenth they were able to anchor about
three leagues off Hatarask, the former Port Ferdinando. At this distance columns of smoke could be seen rising from the general direction of Roanoke Island, which greatly encouraged White as a possible indication that the colonists were alive and active.

So far, Captain Cocke and Captain Spicer had behaved impecca-
bly once their commitment to prize-taking had been satisfied—and
there seems little doubt that the *Buen Jesus* was carrying prize goods
from her own and other cargoes. This would set at rest any fears that
they might not have made a profitable voyage for the owners (Watts
and Company at least). At the same time, the privateering crew of the
Hopewell would not wish to spend more time than they could help in
performing their special task on the coast of North Carolina.

The next morning, 16 August, White, with Captains Cocke and
Spicer, set out in the ships' boats belonging to the two vessels. They
intended to pass through the inlet at Hatarask and to sail up Roanoke
Sound to where they might locate some signs of the colonists. They
also arranged that, when they were well on their way, the *Hopewell*
would fire some of her heavy guns to alert any colonists who might
be on the island. On their way to the Outer Banks they could see a
long way along the island of Hatarask to the high dunes that White
called Kenricks Mounts, beyond which lay Cape Kenrick (already

submerged and named Wimble Shoals by the eighteenth century) and there, too, they saw a great plume of smoke ascending. This diverted them from their original plan. They landed and marched south to Kenricks Mounts, but could find nothing, not even fresh water which they now needed, the spontaneous brushwood fire having burned itself out. Trudging back, dead tired, to the inlet, they found the sailors had brought casks on shore at the inlet to get fresh water. White encouraged them to dig in the sand of the little island between Hatarask and Port Lane because it was possible to reach impermeable strata in the dunes, and soon they succeeded in tapping fresh water. When this was done White, with the two captains, returned to their ships, putting off the Roanoke Island search until the next morning.

By then the ships had moved to within two miles of the Outer Banks. The *Hopewell's* boat, carrying White, was about halfway to land before Captain Spicer set off in his and, encountering very rough water, was brought into shelter at the inlet with some difficulty, "saving only that our furniture, victuals, match and powder were much wet and spoiled." It was evident that the turbulence from the hurricane they experienced earlier had been replaced by a vigorous northeasterly that was to upset their plans drastically. White says "the wind blew at Northeast and direct into the harbor [at Hatarask] so great a gale that the sea broke extremely on the bar and the tide went very forcibly at the entrance." Situations like this are very familiar to those who sail in these waters in modern times. The *Hopewell's* boat was hauled on shore in the sheltered cove behind the inlet and their wet things spread out to dry.

Captain Spicer's boat was now making for the bar and had almost passed over it when tragedy overtook her crew. White blamed the steersman, Ralph Skinner, for bad tactics as "a very dangerous sea broke into their boat and overset them quite." Most of the men clung to the boat as she overturned and was soon stranded on the bar. Those who tried to wade ashore were swept away by the sea. Captain Spicer and the unfortunate Skinner hung onto the boat as long as they could, but she was turned over and over by the waves and soon they were lost under them. Only four of the men—the best swimmers—got into deeper water and could be saved. Captain Cocke and some other good swimmers from his boat rowed out to them and got them safely on shore, but seven of eleven were drowned—among them Captain Spicer, Hance the Surgeon (the Haunce Walters of 1585–86?), Edward Kelley, a 1585 colonist, and Robert Coleman, who may have been a relative of the Colmans of the 1587 settlement.

This was such an upset that the crew of Cocke's boat "were all of one mind not to go any further to seek the planters." Only Captain Cocke's persuasions and, perhaps White's, induced them to change their minds. White does not record his own feelings but it is evident from the emphasis he places on the incident in his narrative that it seemed to him a turning point in the success or failure of the whole enterprise. It revealed how little the privateer's crew cared about the settlers, whereas Spicer's men had been, it seems, solicitous about their welfare and anxious to look for them. And now most of Spicer's men were drowned. However, Cocke imposed his will on his own men, and the two boats, Spicer's being recovered from the beach, were duly manned with nineteen men in all. As they made their way up Roanoke Sound darkness fell and they overshot the cove beyond Baum Point, which had been used previously; thus they came around something like a quarter of a mile toward the north end of the island. There they could see a great fire burning in the woodland. They dropped their grapnel near the shore and "sounded with a trumpet a call and afterwards [sang] many familiar English tunes of songs and called to them friendly, but we had no answer." Again the fire was probably spontaneous combustion of undergrowth, fanned by the strong winds into a blaze, or even caused by lightning in the recent storm.

After spending the night in the boats, they landed at dawn and found "the grass and sundry rotten trees burning about the place." Then they walked through the woods to Croatan Sound, "directly over against Dasamonquepeuc," and after that worked backward "round about the north point of the island until we came to the place where I left our colony in the year 1586 [1587]." As they went, White could see tracks of Indian feet, the broad, splayed feet that he himself had drawn so often in the past, made, he thought, during the previous night. At last "we entered up the sandy bank upon a tree, in the very brow thereof were curiously carved these fair Roman letters CRO." This was on a forested dune a little to the north of the fort site. White evidently did not ask himself why the word carved on the tree was incomplete, which could have meant that the carver had been interrupted and had to flee. Instead, he says:

which letters presently [not immediately] we knew to signify the place where I should find the planters seated [namely Croatoan], according to a secret token agreed between them and me at my last departure from them, which was that in any ways they should not fail to write or carve on the trees or posts of the doors the name of the place where they should be seated.

At this point White is confused and continues to confuse later readers of his narrative because he goes on: "for at my coming away they were prepared to remove from Roanoke 50 miles into the main," namely, to the Chesapeake. Hence he does not take into account the possibility that they had split into two groups, one, the larger, going on to the Chesapeake, the other taking shelter with their Indian friends nearby to wait for White. However, he continues, in a famous passage:

Therefore at my departure from them in Anno 1587 I willed them that if they should happen to be distressed in any of these places that they should carve over the letters a cross in this form ✠, but we found no such sign of distress.

Again he is confusing himself, or us his readers, because "any of these places" could mean that he did not necessarily expect to find them all in one place. But the discovery gave him thought: it was "well considered"—suggestive if not conclusive. Then came the climax of his search:

We passed toward the place where they were left in sundry houses, but we found the houses taken down and the place [where the houses had been?] very strongly enclosed with a high palisado of great trees, with curtains and flankers very fortlike, and one of the chief trees or posts at the right side of the entrance had the bark taken off and 5 feet from the ground in fair capital letters was graven CROATOAN without any cross or sign of distress.

The removal of the houses might well indicate that they were stripped of anything that might be useful to them in rebuilding a new settlement. Sir Francis Drake had taken the doors, locks, and windows from St. Augustine to equip an enlarged Roanoke settlement, he hoped, in 1586. So we might see the settlers in 1587 stripping the houses not only of what they themselves had brought with them in the way of household equipment, but also of anything left since 1586—hinges, bolts, locks, and so forth, and possibly even tiles if any of the buildings were tiled—and then pulling up the posts and tumbling the thatched roofs, so that the houses were soon just small piles of rubble that could be burned or tidied away into the woods, most probably by those who were left behind.

The palisade (an unsolved puzzle which will be discussed later) evidently contained no newly erected buildings. Its precise location in relation to the "town" and "fort" of 1585 has not been determined. We have only White's description, accurate or not, of its nature. His next steps were to investigate inside the enclosure:

> we entered into the palisado where we found many bars of iron, 2 pigs of lead, 4 iron fowlers [light cannon], iron saker shot [for heavier guns] and such like heavy things thrown here and there, almost overgrown with grass and weeds.

Such heavy equipment could not easily be removed for the colonists' journey to the Chesapeake; they had evidently intended to return for it if they needed it. It is clear, from later information, that they took with them at least one mortar and firearms, and, by implication, their forge with at least some bar iron. In 1701 John Lawson saw something at the site that White had missed: "a brass gun, a powder horn, and one small quarter-deck gun, made of iron staves and hooped with the same metal." He tells us too that English coins had also been discovered; thus the long age of plunder was well on its way by the end of the seventeenth century.

White also looked for other things:

> We went along by the water side towards the point of the creek [apparently well to the northeast of the fort] to see if we could find any of their boats or pinnace, but we could perceive no sign of them, nor any of the last falcons [other light cannon] and small ordnance which were left with them at my departure from them.

It is clear, or almost so, that the slipway had been removed and the debris found by the Spanish cleared away (or taken by the Indians), whereas the wells by then would have been covered by vegetation.

Some of the sailors who had been left in the vicinity of the palisade now ran to meet White, reporting they "had found where divers chests had been hidden and long since digged up again and broken up, and much of the goods in them spoiled and scattered about but nothing left of such things as the savages knew any use of undefaced." Long before this White must have been very puzzled by what he had found and still more by what he had not found, but this news is bound to have alarmed him. Perhaps the colonists had indeed had to leave in a hurry if they buried things rather than taking them with them.

White and Captain Cocke made their way to this place as soon as they could and found that "an old trench made two years past by Captain Amadas [in 1585 surely, five years before]," and probably forming part of the original fortifications, had been used for the temporary storage of perishable articles—five chests—which the Indians had rooted up. To White's great chagrin:

> of the same chests three were my own, and about the place many of my things spoiled and broken, and my books torn from their covers, the frames of some of my pictures and maps rotten and spoiled with rain, and my armor almost eaten through with rust.

This must have angered him greatly as he had evidently set great store by the personal possessions he had brought with him and had strictly enjoined the colonists to take good care of them during his absence. More than anything else so far, this discovery must have made him feel that in three years much had happened to distance him and his possessions from the colonists' regard. If one might legitimately interpolate here it would be to suggest that if the colonists divided, the main party going off to the Chesapeake, the men left behind to wait for White would, when he failed to appear, have been much less concerned about his property. If they left in a hurry, they might even have abandoned their own property as other chests were also buried and looted besides White's. White considered,

probably rightly, that the damage was the work of Wingina's former
followers from Dasemunkepeuc "who had watched the departure of
our men to Croatoan, and as soon as they were departed digged up
every place where they suspected anything to be buried." He still
leaves us in doubt whether by "our men" he means the whole
colony, or a part of it left behind to await his return. A distinct
possibility is that he was totally confused about whether some or all
of the colonists had gone to Croatoan, even though he had expected
them to have gone, or most of them, to the Chesapeake. He appears
to have hoped they were all at Croatoan. In this narrative White wrote
more vividly than he had done elsewhere but, nonetheless, from
time to time he is ambiguous. He implies his search for other remains was thorough but he does not note that he found anything
else. There was now no more White could do.

Captain Cocke, with a John White who was half hopeful and half
apprehensive, returned to the inlet and ordered the boats' crews to
row out to the ships as rapidly as they could "for the weather began
to overcast and very likely that a foul and stormy night would ensue."
By the time they reached the ships, the wind and sea were rising so
fast that it was only with difficulty they got back safely on board.
Cables and anchors were soon straining, so much so that Cocke
evidently believed they might have to cast off and run out to sea. But
he had a problem. Six of his men were still on the little island
between Port Lane and Hatarask with the water barrels they had
been filling earlier. The captain sent a boat ashore to get them. It
succeeded in reaching and picking up the six men, but was unable to
load the casks on board and so they were left behind. However, all
survived the stormy night.

In the morning, when the wind had gone down somewhat, a plan
was worked out. The Hopewell and Moonlight, the latter now commanded by her master, John Bedford, would raise their anchors and
sail southward to Croatoan, where they would try to go ashore and
make contact with the colonists who, in White's view, were there
with Manteo. When they had done so and satisfied White's burning
and inevitable curiosity, they would come back for the casks left on
the little island as fresh water was badly needed on board ship. But
again there was a mishap. To begin with, the cable broke on the
Hopewell's capstan just as the anchor was almost aboard and so she

lost her second anchor (the first evidently had broken loose when the storm began). Thereupon the *Hopewell* was driven toward land, past the great dunes known to the search party as Kenricks Mounts, and down to Cape Kenrick. There she was very nearly cast ashore, saved only when a deep channel was found close to shore, enabling her to make out to sea again. The *Hopewell* was now left with only one anchor and cable, and had left behind her casks and fresh water because it seemed too risky to turn back toward the north again.

Captain Cocke was still anxious to be cooperative, or at least he contrived to give White that impression. He proposed going back to the Caribbean to look for water at Puerto Rico or some other island in the area, and White concurred. It was also tentatively agreed that, if they could pick up stores ("supply our wants of victuals and other necessities") at Hispaniola, Puerto Rico, Trinidad, or elsewhere, they would winter in the Caribbean and carry on their privateering cruise in the spring "with hope to make two rich voyages of one" and then, "at our return to visit our countrymen at Virginia." Captain Cocke and White himself had to plead hard with the *Hopewell's* crew to accept this plan, but accept they did in the end, White says. But Bedford in the *Moonlight* had lost so many men and the ship was in such a weak condition that he said he could not agree to continue. Finally, it was decided that the two ships would part company, the *Moonlight* going directly home and the *Hopewell* carrying on with the wintering plan. And so the *Moonlight* set sail for England with "their weak and leak ship."

The *Hopewell* continued southward for two days but the winds remained contrary and she had to sail under much reduced canvas. Finally, on 28 August it was decided that she should not try to make for Trinidad, the preferred choice of a winter base, but should sail to the Azores for water and then return to the Caribbean and thence to the North American coast. The voyage across the Atlantic was not without incident. The weather was very changeable and, as they reached the western Azores, became stormy. They could not make land at either Corvo or Flores. On 18 September they came up with a Spanish ship, which turned out to be the *Trinidad*, the prize taken by the *Little John* and *John Evangelist*, on her way to England with a prize crew. From her men they learned of the dramatic chases and fights of the two smaller vessels of Cocke's squadron and their bad luck in

losing the Spanish silver after already having had four men killed
and sixteen injured (including Captain Christopher Newport, whose
right arm was severed) in the fight off the coast of Cuba. The Trinidad
then set sail for England, though nothing is known of the value of
her cargo. When the Hopewell reached the roads off the north coast of
Flores, she came up with a number of privateers. One of them was
identified as the Moonlight. Bedford had not made directly for England after all, hoping perhaps to bring something home to show
William Sanderson as a result of the expedition and possibly having
recruited a few men at the Azores. But she avoided contact with the
Hopewell—maybe her memory of their association was too painful—
and sailed away to England.

Cocke, as an experienced privateer, was delighted to find, and
soon after join, a great fleet of the Queen's ships and many private
men-of-war under Sir John Hawkins. Roanoke and the colonists
were forgotten in the excitement of joining this fleet, which was
hoping to catch the Spanish treasure fleet as it reached the Azores.
But, learning that they had missed it, the English dispersed on 23
September for the coasts of the Iberian peninsula. The Hopewell, with
a flyboat which had joined her, remained behind for a few days.
Cocke planned to get water at São Jorge, but, failing to reach her
shores owing to unfavorable winds, finally ended all attempts to
prolong the voyage. White tells us nothing further except that on 1
October the Hopewell turned for England and at last, on 24 October,
"we came in safety, God be thanked," as he says, "to an anchor in
Plymouth." Cocke could claim that he had done all he could reasonably be expected to do for White and that his return without a
further search for the colonists was forced on him by circumstances.

White apparently did not disagree, nor did Ralegh make any attempt to forfeit the bond for £5,000 imposed on John Watts for the
safe conduct of White and his settlers to Roanoke and the supply of
the colony there. What White was to complain about was that the
first priority of his ships in the Caribbean had been prize-taking and
not the relief of the colony. He alleged that the agreement between
Ralegh and Watts was first broken when he was refused permission
to bring additional settlers and goods on board the Hopewell at her
departure, but by omitting to make clear that the Moonlight was Sanderson's supply ship, designed specially to carry stores, he gives a

very partial picture of the rescue plan. White continues to blame Cocke for spending so much time in the Caribbean:

> Thus both governors, masters and sailors, regarding very smally the good of their countrymen in Virginia, determined nothing less than to touch at those places, but wholly disposed themselves to seek after purchase and spoils, spending so much time therein that summer was spent before we arrived at Virginia. And when we were come thither the season was so unfit and the weather so foul that we were constrained to forsake that coast, having not seen any of our planters.

He goes on to stress the loss of Spicer and his men in the boat accident and the loss of anchors, cables, and water casks which drove them from the coast:

> which evils and unfortunate events (as well to their own loss as to the hindrance of the planters in Virginia) had not chanced if the order set down by Sir Walter Ralegh had been observed, or if my daily and continual petitions [which may have done more harm than good] for the performance of the same might have taken any place.

He does not, however, criticize Captain Cocke for returning as and when he did, having, we might think from his "God be thanked," had enough of the sea by the time of the *Hopewell*'s return. Yet in after years all he could say of his last voyage was that "seeing it is not my first crossed voyage I remain contented." A mood of regret, an attitude of acquiescence, marks the end of John White's memorable association with the Roanoke colonies.

John White was not involved in any way in the epic struggle in the High Court of Admiralty, which had begun even before the *Hopewell* reached England, about the sharing of the spoil of the *Buen Jesus* between Thomas Middleton for the *Conclude* and William Sanderson for the *Moonlight* against John Watts and his three ships. The plaintiffs sought to gain a share in the spoils by virtue of actual or implied consortship with Watts' ships and by asserting that both the *Conclude* and the *Moonlight* played an active part in the capture. The *Buen Jesus* had already been sequestered by the admiralty before Cocke reached Plymouth, but he was to be Watts's chief witness, along with his men and three Spaniards he had brought with him as original members of the crew of the *Buen Jesus*, that the Spanish ship had been taken by the action of the *Hopewell* and had surrendered to Cocke alone. The case, which tells us much about the Caribbean side of the voyage on which White is silent, ended in January 1591 in total victory for Watts. The appraisal put the value of her cargo, with nominal valuation only of the vessel herself, at £5,806 10s 4d, one of the richest prizes taken from Spain at the time. After the Queen's customs and the Lord Admiral's tenth (totaling £871 11s 0d), Watts and his company received, as shippers and victuallers, two-thirds of the value (about £3,289 7s 4d), the remainder (£1,644 13s 8d) to be divided, in shares according to rank, among the company of the *Hopewell*. The assumption is that the *Little John* and *John Evangelist* were compensated by the return on the *Trinidad*, the prize they had sent to Plymouth, the valuation of which is not known. The only direct relevance of the case to the Roanoke voyages is that Sanderson's failure to get any share of the spoils, in compensation for the expenditure of the 1589 syndicate on the equipment of the *Moonlight* and the undoubtedly poor condition in which she returned, effectively ended any participation of the syndicate in further attempts to help Ralegh and White to continue their North American venture. Then too, the profits to be made from privateering, when measured against the costs without return from colonization, made the continuance of the latter quite uneconomic. No capitalist would invest in colonization from this time until the end of the war in 1604 or later except under very special circumstances.

In 1589–90 Spain was taking very seriously the significance of the supposed English occupation of the Roanoke area. In 1588 White had failed to reach Roanoke Island, but a Spanish reconnaissance venture did. The reverse happened in 1590: White got to Roanoke Island, for all the good it did him or the settlers, whereas the great Spanish expedition projected for that year never got beyond the stage of paper planning. Pedro Menéndez Marqués, once he received the report of the 1588 voyage, was anxious to return to Spain to plan the installation of a Spanish force in the region after wiping out any English he might find there.[6] He was held up in Havana long enough to hear the report about William Irish's call at Santa Maria Bay in 1587 and, more important, the long report of Pedro Diaz given, as we saw, in March 1589 in Havana. This outlined the history of the English ventures of 1584–88 and expressed "the opinion that the people who remained on the settlement should have by this time, died of hunger or been exposed to great need and danger." Based on the 1588 report and that of Diaz in 1589, it did not appear that the Roanoke Island colony offered any great threat to anyone, though what use would be made of it in the future was another matter.

Pedro Menéndez Marqués, with Juan Menéndez Marqués who had been with González in 1588, arrived in Spain only in July 1589, full of demands for action against the English. He reported to the Council of the Indies, and to two of its members who were specially assigned to deal with the matter, which was considered urgent. The governor of Florida was at once ordered to prepare an expedition in Spain that would comprise four vessels with soldiers and supplies. These were to proceed to Florida and exchange some of their raw men for seasoned soldiers from Florida, and then proceed northward. They were to destroy whatever post existed on Roanoke Island (though they would have found no more than White) and then proceed to Chesapeake Bay, select a site for a fortress and garrison of three hundred men, and, when they were established, return to report what had been done. It was not easy to achieve such ends in Spain in 1589–90, but there is every reason to believe that this expedition was almost ready by the spring of 1590. But then there was a sudden change of policy. It could not be spared, and the plan had to be postponed. Pedro Menéndez Marqués was given the urgent task of bringing the New World silver safely to Spain through an attempted English blockade. This vital task he performed with speed and panache. He had designed light but strong and fast vessels, known as *galizabras*, in the Caribbean, and two of these were put at his disposal. Leaving Seville on 10/20 May 1590 he was back with the treasure safely on 4/14 September, thus making it impossible for Sir John Hawkins's fleet lying off the Azores to catch any treasure ships because there were none, the Spanish having hoodwinked the English. The Spanish equivalent of the settlement on Chesapeake Bay planned by Sir Richard Grenville in 1588 and frustrated by preparations to thwart the Spanish Armada was also discarded as a result of the maritime struggle and Spain's utter dependence on silver to keep

20. John White's General Map of Southeastern North America.
This represents John White's view of the relation of Spanish Florida
to Ralegh's Virginia.
British Museum, Department of Prints and Drawings, 1906-5-9-1 (2).

its economy afloat. It is a comment on its success—and the failure of England—that Spain got more silver from the Americas in the 1590s than it had ever obtained before.

An amusing tailpiece is that one of John Watts's ships picked up some letters written at San Juan de Puerto Rico on 22 August/1 September that reported to Spain the kind of "information" about English intentions and activities in the Roanoke area that Ralegh, White, and Abraham Cocke would have liked very much to have been able to bring home. According to these letters, an English ship had been actively taking prizes off Puerto Rico that summer. The translation states:

> The English ship was of 200 tons and had 26 pieces of iron ordnance (and them at the bottom of the ship) and 220 men. This ship [evidently the *Hopewell*] went to Florida [the Roanoke area here] to assist those people that already we have there with artillery, which was at the bottom of the ship, and they carried likewise a governor [John White] with them who was to be left there. . . . He said that our Englishmen do fortify there apace and that the same place doth serve us notably to take in fresh-water and to refresh our men. And if any of our ships happen to come late, they do winter there. . . . Therefore he doth advise the king [Philip II] very earnestly to prevent the fortifying and continuing of our men in Florida which he sayeth may be best done by sending some galleys thither.[7]

This is exactly the scenario that the English planners of the Roanoke voyages would themselves have wished to write, but it was, unfortunately for them, totally untrue. The English did not go back to Roanoke; the Spanish did not attempt to forestall them. So much the war achieved.

A Colony Is Lost:
New Explorations Continue

A Colony Is Lost and Found?

Almost everything that has been said up to now about lost colonies and lost colonists has tended to have an emotional content in North Carolina. This is understandable enough. At least since the 1840s, historians, publicists, novelists, and even poets in North Carolina have found several things to write about that have become part of the foundations of the state's self-consciousness and sense of history. The first, that the Roanoke colonies were the first English attempts to settle permanently in North America, has a solid foundation, even if the state, as now constituted, has no direct continuity with them. Throughout what has been written here, this fact has been kept in mind and is indeed the justification for writing still more about the colonies and for the celebration of North Carolina's four hundredth anniversary. Another is less easy to pin down. The colonies of 1585–87 ended in a birth and a mystery. Elenor Dare and her daughter Virginia Dare, the first Englishwoman known to have been born on North American soil, have become in a sense figures of myth and romance that stand at the beginning of North Carolina's history, literature, and fantasy.

The historical value of the myth is, of course, questionable if venial. But the position of the mother and daughter in North Carolina mythology is embedded in the greater mystery, the disappearance of the colonists of 1587, the Lost Colony, which has attracted writers, and dramatists especially, in the present century. How did these people, over a hundred of them, deserted by the chances of war and the uncertainties of sea passages in early modern times, survive or die? Surely they died, as they had begun to live, inside what is now North Carolina. Had they not, as seems most probable, somehow dispersed themselves among the Indian population? If this was so

341

did they leave traces that survive, hidden in the swamps and fields
and even in the ancestry of the people of North Carolina today?
The strength of these sentiments and questions has been strong and
has not been overcome by systematic historical research, which has
found no evidence, or certainly no clear evidence, for them. The
most that can be said with some degree of probability is that a
handful of them may have contributed some genes to the Hatteras
Indians, the last three or four of whom were known to be living near
Cape Hatteras in 1729,[1] but that is all.

The full and true story of all the colonists, lost, stolen, and strayed,
will probably never be known, but substantial steps can be taken in
exploring what happened to a major part of them, the main body of
the 1587 colony in effect, though archaeology must still be the only
hope of tracking down at some future date material remains of their
last enduring place of residence. In addition to the factual information we have about lost colonists, there are contemporary or near-
contemporary guesses and assumptions that must be sorted out and
analyzed along with the reasonably well established facts. But when
all is done, a considerable exercise of the historical imagination is
necessary to bring any coherence to the story, and, as with many
historical sequences for which only limited data survive, hypotheses
only remain good until they are superseded by better ones, those
which explain more in simpler ways, or until a single piece of data
emerges that is incontrovertible and that upsets existing sequences
of information or attempted syntheses. At the same time, the problems of lost colonists present a challenge to the historical writer, one
that he should attempt, however incompletely, to meet.

The Algonquian Indians of the North Carolina Outer Banks had
long memories and in 1584 they knew of no Europeans who had
remained on the coast between Cape Henry and Cape Fear. In the
1550s, it was told to the Englishmen in 1584, a Spanish ship had, in
fact, been wrecked on the Outer Banks and some of her men res-
cued by the Secotan Indians. The survivors had patched two boats
together from the wreck and set out southward, but shortly afterward the boats were found cast away along the shore and it was
presumed that all had drowned. They were the last and only Europeans of whom memory remained, even though a Spanish party had
landed farther north in 1566; but it saw no Indians and sailed away
again.

The 1584 expedition lost no men to the Indians of the Outer Banks, although when Philip Amadas (as we consider probable) entered Chesapeake Bay, a few of his men may have been killed or wounded by those later known as the Powhatans of southern Virginia. The Spanish story that some of the English were taken and eaten seems unlikely in the absence of any hint of it from English sources, though reports of a clash of some sort derives from two widely separated and distinct Spanish sources, and can be viewed as highly probable. But we have no evidence that any were left behind either in the Roanoke region or Virginia.

It was very different in 1586. Sir Francis Drake in his sweep through the West Indies had released from the galleys at Santo Domingo and Cartagena hundreds of slaves of many nationalities— French, blacks, a large number of subjects of the Turkish sultan, and members of other European countries. The Moors he promised he would bring to their homeland, and so too the other Europeans. Many of them may have helped out as seamen when his own men began to die off with fever and other diseases; others may have succumbed. Black slaves came to him at these ports and at St. Augustine asking to be freed. He promised them freedom if they sailed with him. After leaving Cartagena, he is said by the Spanish to have taken on board some three hundred South American Indians who had helped him at Cartagena and were at risk from the Spanish. We are certain that, at first, Drake's intention in visiting the Roanoke colonists was primarily to warn and rearm them in view of an intended Spanish attack and that his destruction of St. Augustine was intended to cripple the Spanish effort. His carrying of the contents and fittings of houses to Roanoke Island was also a means by which he hoped to place reinforcements with them. Having taken a number of black household slaves to whom he promised freedom, he proposed to give it to them at Roanoke. But if he had Indians with him as well, he is likely to have left them at St. Helena Sound. The hurricane that destroyed most of his smaller vessels and pinnaces, mostly taken from the Spanish, is likely to have drowned a good many of his intended reinforcements for Roanoke. Whether any of them got ashore on the Outer Banks and were deserted there when Drake sailed away we cannot say, but it is not unlikely that a few of them saved their lives in this way, though nothing has been heard of what became of any who may have done so. We know only that

Drake brought Europeans and Moors back to England and, perhaps, a handful of blacks but no considerable number.[2]

A few colonists were deserted, however, when Drake left as one of the journals of his voyage records that Drake's ships "brought thence all those men with us except three who had gone further into the country and the wind grew so that we could not stay for them."[3] These are the first genuinely lost colonists of whom we have definite evidence. The probable explanation is that they were sent to take back Ralph Lane's hostage Skiko to his father, Menatonon, and either returned to find their companions gone or were held captive by the Chawanoac chief, as his successor was apparently to do to some Lost Colony survivors some twenty years later. They might even have been left deliberately to prepare the way for a future search for copper sources. The colonists of Sir Richard Grenville must not, however, be forgotten. The thirteen men who survived the Indian attack, which John White learned of in 1587, reached their boat, which may well have been a shallop, somewhat larger than the ordinary long boat, "and landed on a little island on the right hand of our entrance into the harbor of Hatorask where they remained a while, but afterwards departed, whither, as yet, we know not." Were they indeed lost at sea or did they come ashore elsewhere on the Outer Banks either north or south of Roanoke Island? If they had landed to the south, Manteo's people are likely to have heard of them by the time White questioned them. They, too, disappeared and were lost either at sea or, less probably, on land.

It has already been suggested that, when White left the colony in 1587 to obtain supplies in England, he was told that the colonists would divide and that a party would await him at Roanoke Island to direct him and his ships to the final location of the main body of settlers. His confusion in 1590, when he at last did come, might suggest, alternatively, that the arrangement was somewhat less definite than that, namely, that he had been told that *someone* would still be on Roanoke Island to meet him when he returned. His confusion in 1590 could therefore have arisen because, although he knew the main body had indeed decided to make the fifty-mile journey to its chosen area of settlement with the Chesapeake Indians, he could not be certain that it had done so, as he was not present when it actually went. His satisfaction at receiving the messages on the deserted Roanoke Island that all or some were with Manteo at Croatoan made him wonder, it would appear, whether the main body had changed its plan and *all* of the colonists had gone to Croatoan in spite of their careful planning. His judgment on this was clouded by sentiment if he did so, because he well knew that the land at Croatoan, even more so than that at Roanoke, was unsuitable for an agricultural colony such as that proposed for the region near Chesapeake Bay. Because there was no positive evidence that the colonists had gone north, and none surfaced until after 1600, as will be argued, then a natural assumption of subsequent writers and actors in the affair, like Ralegh himself, was to accept for a long time that Croatoan was the probable location of the whole colony. If, as it seemed from White's evidence, some had gone there, why not all? Ralegh, it will be suggested, had come to disbelieve this by the autumn of 1602, but it was still considered probable in Plymouth in 1604, and it was not until Jamestown had been established for a year and a half that clear evidence emerged that the main body of the colonists had indeed joined the Chesapeake Indians as early as 1587 and had lived and perished with them. The material that makes up the story of rumors and assumptions, and the gradual emergence of firm evidence of the long survival and eventual destruction of the colonists and their hosts, is difficult to piece together and needs a few further scraps of evidence to tie it firmly into a unity for the whole period between 1587 and 1606, but in essence it appears to be reasonably sound and satisfactory.[4]

White left behind on Roanoke Island 85 men, 17 women, and 11 children (10 male and 1 female), making 114 in all. If, hypothetically, 20 to 25 remained on the island with their pinnace and at least one boat (they would surely be more than the vulnerable 1586 group), at least 60 men and 28 women and children went to the new Chesapeake settlement. They would have had with them very substantial baggage. If White had left three chests of personal goods and the others had left spare chests of belongings (which White found in 1590), then we would have to allow at the rate of two chests for each of the seven Assistants and one for each of the remaining men and women, which would give something on the order of 110 to 120 chests (allowing a few for the boys who had crossed the ocean and who were intending settlers, not just children of tender years). As a very rough estimate, a seaman's chest would weigh about 100 pounds, and this could be taken as a base. This would make a lading (taken with them) of up to 12,000 pounds, that is, between 5 and 6 tons. They would have several tons of tools and implements, and a forge, together with as much bar iron as it seemed possible to carry. They also had light artillery, including a mortar (a gun with a wide bore capable of throwing wildfire or stone shot on a high trajectory, but relatively light to carry), and at least two falcons, guns firing a 2½-pound shot and weighing about 1,100 pounds each, with their shot and possible carriages, making up another ton. They might just possibly have had a saker (as White found some shot for it in 1590) which would add 3,500 pounds plus shot and a possible carriage, which would make another two tons. The rest of the "small ordnance" White said he left could have included 400-pound serpentines and 300-pound robinets, so perhaps still another ton should be added for one of each and their appurtenances. This would add up to a minimum of some 11 tons for their essential gear, but in fact they are likely to have had more, because they were going for an indefinite stay. Figures of 15 tons for gear and 25 tons or more for foodstuffs would appear to be minimal allowances. For the human cargo, at a body weight for adults averaging 130 pounds, and making some allowance for the children, we would estimate between 13,000 and 14,000 pounds, another 6 tons.

The purpose of these guesses about weights is to permit us to make a rough estimate of how many excursions the pinnace would have to take to bring the whole expedition out from Hatarask or Trinity Harbor along the coast to Cape Henry and then some fifteen miles up the Elizabeth River. The pinnace is unlikely to have had a capacity of more than twenty tons (measured in capacity of the largest wine barrels, tuns or tons), so it might be that two ladings would be sufficient to carry everything that has been estimated. But this is very much a minimum, and it cannot be concluded that the settlers had no livestock with them. They might, for example, have managed to bring in the flyboat a few superior milch cows from England together with a bull and some smaller creatures like fowl; they would also have had a number of dogs—at least a few mastiffs for defense. They could also possibly have rounded up a few odd animals, cattle and mules, for example, from Roanoke Island and the

Outer Banks where they had been left by the 1586 expeditions, though they would have had to survive Indian attacks in the meantime. The stray mule and traces of cattle found by Captain William Irish, perhaps near the mouth of the Elizabeth River if he was well primed about the probable destination of the colony, could represent the landing of a small but significant number of animals by the pinnace. In that case it might be better to assume that the whole removal took three sailings rather than two, provided that the pinnace was able to reach Skicóac. Otherwise, more complex procedures would have been necessary.

It is not essential that all the movement should have taken place by sea. Although White noted on his map that Currituck Sound was difficult to traverse and Lane reinforced this view in words, theoretically it was possible for boats or canoes to work their way up what is now North Landing River and to leave them within a dozen miles from Skicóac, not more than a day's march. Naturally, not enough is known of local conditions at that time to determine whether this was feasible but, if it was, parties of men could have made their way northward overland from where the boats could take them and join up with the colonists brought by sea at Skicóac. Such a move could have simplified the removal of the remainder by water.

The moving of the colonists northward in September 1587 would make sense, as they would wish to be established before winter. They could throw up pole and frame houses quickly and thatch them for shelter, making do with temporary mat sidings until the spring. Unless the winter was harsh they would not suffer too much from cold, as English houses were not very adequately heated at the time and the climate there was appreciably colder than in the twentieth century. A great deal would depend on what kind of welcome they received from the Chesapeake Indians at Skicóac. There would need to have been messengers sent, probably overland, to warn them of the approach of the colony, and one or two men must have spoken enough of their language to be able to communicate effectively with them, with, perhaps, the guidance of one of Manteo's Indians. The ground allocated to them for their village would probably have been land already used in the past for Indian fields and its clearance hampered by no more than secondary growth, though there appears to have been naturally open ground in this area. But

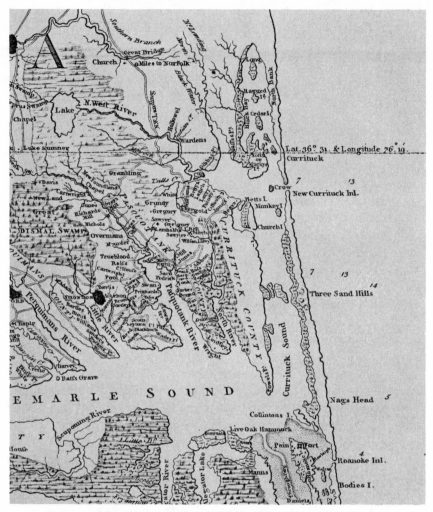

21. Extract from John Collet, *A Compleat Map of North Carolina from an Actual Survey* (London, 1770).
This map shows the Southern Branch of the Elizabeth River before modification of the Great Dismal Swamp. It also marks the track from the N. W. River (now North West Landing River) across land which was firm before 1770 and may well have been so in 1587.
Raleigh, Division of Archives and History.

they may have managed to live, or some of them at least, in a few Indian houses set apart for them by the settlement, as was the case in 1634–35 in Maryland, where it now appears that the first settlers at St. Mary's City lived for a time in Indian houses and even shared the village site with them for some months. As has already been suggested, the presence of women and children and the generally non-aggressive attitude of the settlers would have greatly facilitated their reception. If their dealings with the party of 1585–86, of which Harriot and White were members, were as friendly and cooperative as is indicated by the limited references we have, the ground would have been well prepared for their friendly association with the people of Skicóac.

The first winter and the first growing season would be crucial. It may be that a permanent village site was carved out in 1588 at some little distance from the main Chesapeake town to allow the settlers to develop their own community life. If they proved to be reliant in hunting over the winter and skillful in growing crops in the spring, while at the same time exploiting seafood effectively, then there should not have been friction of a major sort. Helping them over the winter with some limited amount of corn and perhaps much more game would not have been too difficult a burden for the Indians in this region, which was more fertile and at the same time much more accessible to game than the coastal fringe of North Carolina. These settlers had come, it should always be remembered, determined to work for themselves, to be self-reliant, and to be confident of their own efficiency in domestic, horticultural, and agricultural tasks. If they survived, as they did, they must have fully proved their quality in these respects.

The settlers would have been buoyed up with hope that sometime in 1588 White would appear with wives and children who had been left behind and with additional married couples and single men and women to add to their strength and increase the size of the colony to the planned 150, or even to an appreciably higher figure. He would also bring supplies and additional equipment for their new life. When White did not appear, it is certain that the group would have been depressed but would have been thrown increasingly into association with their Indian neighbors. They might well have kept themselves separate as a community during 1589, but when he did not come then they must, in effect, have given up hope of his coming at all, and this would have led them gradually toward a measure of integration with their hosts. Some of the men would almost certainly have found partners among the Indian women if indigenous custom did not set its face against such mingling. Although this may not have happened for some little time, the later authority on their ultimate fate indicated that intermingling did take place and this is not likely to have been delayed more than two or three years at the most. It may be assumed that the pinnace did not return to maintain contact between Roanoke Island and Skicóac after 1587. We can suggest, however, that it most probably remained available to the party left on Roanoke Island through the season 1587–88, though we cannot rely on its having survived after that. If Roanoke Island was as deserted looking as White found it in August 1590, it seems unlikely that the pinnace and her complement had come north from Chacandepeco that season at all, or if it did come it can only have made a cursory visit because no traces of recent English activity there were found. It might be safer to assume that the pinnace ceased to be viable after 1588 or 1589. In that case the men were more closely tied to the Outer Banks except for longish journeys across the sounds by canoe, or by a boat if they still had one. It is, in fact, simpler to assume that by 1590 they still hoped White would come and it was up to him to find them with the aid of their signs, and not they him. At Croatoan they were a long way from the main body near Skicóac and there is no reason to assume they made, or even attempted to make, any further contact with the colony. The two groups were divided by a substantial stretch of land and water and were, it seems necessary to assume, being gradually integrated into the respective Indian communities in which, or alongside which, they were living.

All contact with the Lost Colonists, proper, the main body which we can assume with some confidence to have settled in what is now Norfolk County, Virginia, is lacking from 1587 to at least 1603. In those fifteen years, Virginia Dare, if she survived, would have been more than fifteen years of age, and so be of marriageable age by both English and Indian standards. This will give us some measure of what time would have done to the remainder of the settlers. Those who had been in their twenties were in, or approaching, their forties; those who were forty were, by the standards of the time, old men or women of fifty-five or more. If they lived a healthy life, and barring a conflict with Indian neighbors, the chances are that they did so, the eighteen females might be presumed to have given birth to at least two children each and, at a conservative estimate, to have reared one of them. If the deaths among the original number of men, women, and children were not more than eighteen, a little more than one a year, then the community of 80 to 100 persons would have remained about the same size as it had been in the first settlement. Under very favorable conditions it could have been larger; under less favorable, smaller. This does not say very much except to put the possible scale of the survivors into some perspective. But if there were about 70 males (including the boys who would have reached the age of puberty) and only 18 females, then more than 50 of the former would have had to take up with Indian women or remain without partners. We might reasonably expect at least half of them to have found Indian women with whom they could live and bear mixed-breed children. We might then assume that the total number of English or part-English could have reached the 150 level or even gone somewhat higher.

It seems logical that, to begin with, the colonists would have erected a village based on pole and frame houses, with wattle and daub filling as they became established. Conceivably, they could have made brick for hearths and even chimneys. We would also expect them to have built a defensive paling of stout poles joined by riven planks such as Ivor Noël Hume has found at Martin's Hundred.[5] As they settled more firmly, they are likely to have constructed a communal structure to use as a church and for community activities, as was done in Jamestown at a very early stage. There would have been wells and outhouses and enclosures for breeding rabbits and perhaps other livestock. They are likely, at least for a year or two until they had developed full confidence in their hosts, to have raised some stronger defensive works (watchtowers, for example) to protect their village and deployed there the ordnance that had evidently been removed from Roanoke Island. In time such defenses may have been superfluous though they could well have maintained them to ward off attacks on the Chesapeakes by the Nansemonds or even, conceivably, the Powhatans. There would have been a store-house for their harvest produce. There would also have been garden plots, possibly small fields like those used by the Indians, probably mainly for Indian crops, though they could have had English seeds that survived the winter of 1587–88.

The small segment of a village recently excavated on the west side of Broad Bay and linked with Lynnhaven Bay and near Virginia Beach is likely to have been a Chesapeake community of some size. It is farther west than White's Chesepiuc, but it might have been it all the same (though I am not inclined to think so). However, what re-mained of the site when professional excavation became possible in 1981–82 "revealed," as E. Randolph Turner of the Virginia Research Center for Archaeology informed me,[6] "part of a palisaded village with two longhouse structures inside . . . the first in coastal Virginia to be clearly identified archaeologically." This is very valuable infor-mation. Another site is also known, which could have been the Apasus added in the engraved version of White's map. But Skicóac was a good way to the west of these sites, namely, fifteen to twenty miles and inland. The Chesapeake settlements in general appear to have been very similar to those of the Indians of the North Carolina Sounds, which White's pictures show.

With our very limited knowledge of the Chesapeakes we cannot estimate how large the tribal group may have been. If Skicóac was in fact a very large village, and if there were more than two other villages (that of Broad Bay may have been another), we might guess that, being able to remain independent of Powhatan for so long, they numbered at least 1,000 people, but this is at present pure guess-work. If assimilation occurred, the settlers could well have adopted Indian ways of living to a considerable extent, perhaps transforming their village into an Indian-style one or even amalgamating with Skicóac or another community. Such a community, no doubt sepa-rately organized at first, with the opportunities for hunting, fishing, and agriculture that the area afforded, could enjoy a good living, given the absence of war, internal dissension, and epidemic disease, any or all of which of course we cannot eliminate. Because the only statement we have on their association is that they lived together peaceably, losses by war can perhaps be ruled out, and we are also told that they had intermingled with the Indians, which would certainly mean that mixed-breed alliances would have produced children neither wholly English nor wholly Indian.

All else is purely conjecture, but we can assume a considerable degree of cultural assimilation, with the interpenetration of customs and techniques and with, more than possibly, a Christian tinge over it all, even if there was no direct conversion of the Indian tribe to Protestant Christianity, as the colonists are least likely to have surrendered their faith and religious practices. After twenty years, however, their Englishness would be wearing thin, and they would be approaching virtual assimilation. If this was so, we may not be correct in thinking of them—before the end came—as wholly English or vitally concerned about renewing contact with their countrymen. The balance of their concerns could have gone either way, but if intermixture had proceeded as far as has been suggested, they were very different in almost every way from the people who set out from Roanoke Island in 1587 and their children were perhaps wholly so. Whether a site on which they lived will ever be found we cannot tell, but if one were found, it would contain at least some European artifacts, though Powhatan looted their settlement as well as had them killed. At the very least pottery fragments would be found and possibly other things as well, lost or thrown away or still existing after the killings and the almost certain clearance of the site. But there should still be remains substantial enough for identification if a settlement were ever to be located.

Until 1603 the Lost Colonists, as the inheritors of Ralegh's 1584 grant, remained alive in English legal fiction. His interest in them was intermittent but did not die, even if for some years he made no attempt to find them. In his Guiana enterprise of 1595 the Lost Colony emerged from oblivion: he told the Spanish that he had come to Trinidad only on the way to the place where his colony was situated, though this was an obvious bluff. Nonetheless, in his own small book, *The discoverie of the large rich, and bewtiful empyre of Guiana* (1596), he insisted that he would have performed this duty, as he felt it, "if extremity of weather had not forced me from the said coast," which may just conceivably be true. And in the fragment of his long poem "The Twenty First and Last Book of the Ocean to Cynthia" there are lines that point to his continual feeling of loss at the breach in continuity in his searches and his sense of the colonists' plight. In their original form they read:

> to seeke for moysture in th'arabian sande
> is butt a losse of labor, and of rest
> the lincks which time did break of harty bands

> words cannot knytt, or waylings make a new,
> seeke not the Soon in cloudes, when it is sett . . .

> On highest mountaynes wher those Sedars grew
> agaynst whose bancks, the trobled ocean bett

> and weare the markes to find thy hoped port
> into a soyle farr of them sealves remove
>
> (Book 11, lines 478–86)[7]

The "Cedars" are reminiscences of Barlowe's report of the 1584 voyage and "into a soil far off themselves remove" his recognition of the breach with the colonists who have passed out of his vision. Then, about 1599, he began sending small expeditions to collect medicinal roots—sassafras and china root and gums thought to have medicinal properties—along the shores near which they might be. It was natural that he would have focused this search on Croatoan since this was a precise location to which some were known in 1590 to have gone. If, as White also believed, the main body had moved fifty miles away, his men stood less chance of locating it inland from Chesapeake Bay. Before 1603 none of his ships made any contacts which gave clear indications of the whereabouts of any white person living along the shores of what is modern North Carolina, but there may have been hints, if coastal Indians were met with, of such persons living well to the north of the Carolina Outer Banks. There had been a rumor as early as 1592, circulated no doubt to put Spanish agents off the scent since they reported it, that Richard Hawkins, who was preparing to set out in that year, was bound for Virginia and not for the South Sea. This, of course, was a diversion, except that it represented a continuing Spanish belief that there was an English colony still living there. In 1600–1602 this was still maintained in Spanish Florida, and in 1603 and again in 1606 the Constable of Spain stated it was his opinion that the English had for a long time been occupying the coast.

John Gerard, the herbalist, took it for granted in 1597 that in "Virginia . . . are dwelling at this present Englishmen," unless disease had wiped them out. It is true that the law took a different view and in 1594 applied the rule that seven years' loss of contact implied the death of the person concerned, so that the administration of the estate of Ananias Dare, White's son-in-law, showing he had left some property in London, was based on the assumption that he was deceased. In 1600 the Reverend George Abbot expressed in print the probability that all contact had been lost and the country left to its old inhabitants, but the younger Richard Hakluyt, his fellow clergyman, was more cautious in the third volume of *Principal navigations, voyages, traffiques and discoveries of the English nation*, the second edition, which he published in 1600. He printed White's 1593 (or 1594) letter implying the colonists were still alive and in another passage noted that some plans were afoot to revive colonization, though he did not commit himself in any way to the survival of the earlier colony up to the time of publication. It is clear that the one reconnaissance we know a little about, that of Samuel Mace in 1602, did not get farther north than modern Cape Hatteras, if that far.[8] If he encountered any Indians, and we do not know that he did, he could have picked up some hint that there were white settlers still living far to the north which he did not follow up. Ralegh's actions in 1603 might indicate that Mace did bring home some suggestions that Chesapeake Bay should again be explored.

The years 1603 to 1605 present us with more substantial but yet circumstantial indications. It does seem very likely, though it remains to be proved by precise evidence, that news at second hand reached England of the survival of the settlement in the vicinity of Chesapeake Bay, and that this was publicized in ways about which we know nothing certain so far. We do know that in 1603 Ralegh engaged Bartholomew Gilbert and Samuel Mace to go with two ships to Chesapeake Bay to look for the colony, having presumably reviewed his former efforts and considered they had probably been misdirected. The voyage of Bartholomew Gilbert in the *Elizabeth* of London (50 tons) was a disastrous one: he repeatedly failed to find the entrance to Chesapeake Bay, went ashore somewhat either north or south of the entrance to Delaware Bay, and was killed, with several of his men, by an Indian war party on which they stumbled. The master of the ship, Henry Shute, brought the ship home with a crew of only eleven men and boys, reaching the Thames toward the end of September.

On Mace's voyage we have no direct information whatsoever, so that what follows must remain circumstantial, though it all appears to point in a single direction. One distinct possibility is that he made his way into Chesapeake Bay and sailed up the York River, there encountering a number of Indians belonging to Powhatan's tribe, of whom he induced several to come on board and then kidnapped them. We know men were apprehended by someone, as Powhatan complained in 1607 that "two or three years before" (but it could well have been four years) some of his men were seized and brought away by a white man. Indians had been taken to England from the Roanoke Island area both in 1584 and 1586 (and this was to be done again in 1605 from Maine) so that language and local conditions could be learned from them before a colonizing expedition was sent out. If it was Mace's ship that carried these men from Chesapeake Bay, it must have arrived in London at the very end of August 1603. On 2 or 3 September a Thames wherry towed an Indian canoe and carried some Indians up the Thames to the landing place leading to Lord Cecil's house in the Strand.[9] In subsequent days they gave displays of canoe-handling for Sir Walter Cope (an enthusiast for American colonization) and others, in the absence of Sir Walter Ralegh (a prisoner since July in the Tower of London, accused of treason), and of Lord Cecil, who was attending the King in Hampshire because the Court had moved out of plague-stricken London.

Ralegh's monopoly of American colonization had reverted to the King, and there was now no one to take responsibility for the Indians except Cope, who may have continued to do so if they were not killed by the plague. But if they had been taken to England by Mace, and if they had come from York River, Thomas Harriot, at least, could have spoken to them in their own language and learned that white settlers were still living in association with the Chesapeake Indians to the south of the bay. He could even have taken them to Syon House, where he was in the Earl of Northumberland's service. Harriot, however, was lying low as his long association with Ralegh made him suspect, though he had given some help in preparing

Mace's expedition in 1602. Although the suggestions made here are far from being certain, word seems to have got around that settlers still survived in North America.

Twice in 1604 George Waymouth (a member of a seagoing and shipbuilding family) presented versions of a treatise called "The Jewell of Artes" to James I, which suggested various projects for helping navigators and voyagers.[10] Among them, he set down no less than six rather fanciful plans for towns, as well as for a number of castles, to be built by and for colonists in America. He urged the erection of fortified towns and castles "in the land of Florida [which could cover almost the whole east coast of North America] in those parts thereof which long have been in possession of our English nation . . . as but weakly planted with the English and they more weakly defended from the invasions of the heathen, amongst whom they dwell [are] subject to manifold perils and dangers. Whereas it being so fruitful a soil, so abounding with woods [and] so goodly rivers . . . those parts . . . might easily be fortified and well planted with the English." He thus took for granted that the Lost Colonists were no longer unlocated, but that they survived and ought to be reinforced and strengthened. Indeed, it would appear that he assumed King James to be already familiar with the information that something had been heard of the Lost Colony at last, or his observations would not be easily intelligible to him. King James, we might conclude, was being reminded that he had subjects living in America for whom he was now directly responsible. It may have led him to put Waymouth forward as the leader of an expedition to North America in 1605, though, by accident or design, it was directed well to the north of Ralegh's Virginia.

It is also likely, though no scrap of direct evidence has yet appeared to establish it, that a ballad or broadsheet was circulating in London with some puffed up and exaggerated material about the Lost Colonists in it. The play *Eastward Hoe*, an entertaining romp in which three distinguished playwrights—George Chapman, Ben Jonson, and John Marston—had a hand, was produced in London in 1605. This contained a well-known gibe about settlers in America making their fortune: "A whole Country of English is there man, bred of those that were left there in 79 [sic]. They have married with the

Indians and make them bring forth as beautiful faces as any have in England, and therefore the Indians are so in love with them that all the treasure they have they lay at their feet." This reference could make no sense to a London theater audience, eighteen years after the colony had been left behind in America, if there had not been some popular publication to which it alluded. Just such a ballad or broadsheet would have stressed the survival of the colony by inter-marriage with the Indians and the supposed resulting golden tribute derived from such mingling.

This network of references would seem to make it feasible to conclude that something, whatever precisely it was, about the sur-vival of the Lost Colony reached London between 1603 and 1605. It may also be worth noting that Captain Christopher Newport, who was to be chosen in the following year to command the first English expedition to the Chesapeake, which founded Jamestown, had an audience with King James after a Caribbean voyage in 1605.[11] At this audience he presented the King with an alligator or crocodile, per-haps from Hispaniola but conceivably picked up on the southeastern shores of North America; if so, he may also have reconnoitered the route to Chesapeake Bay which he was to pioneer in 1606, but it appears unlikely, if he did so, that he entered Chesapeake Bay him-self. His unerring voyage into the mouth of the bay in 1607 could, however, suggest that he had already made some reconnaissance of it during his frequent voyages returning from privateering in the Indies. It is also worth remembering that on bringing the "second supply" to Jamestown in 1608 he was specifically instructed to search for the Lost Colonists.

One of the most unexpected pieces of evidence that the Lost Colonists were believed to be alive and still living at Croatoan in 1604 comes from the interrogation of prisoners at St. Augustine who were captured by a Spanish force in St. Helena Sound with the ship *Castor and Pollux* and her consort.[12] This expedition sailed under a French license, but in English ships with an English captain, John Jerome of Plymouth, who may well have known about the Roanoke voyages from persons who had taken part in them. The mission of this Anglo-French venture was purely commercial. It was to make its way through the Caribbean and then sail along the coast of North America from Florida to the Bay of Fundy, trading where it was possible to do so. Unfortunately, it had only got as far as making some exchanges with the Cusabo Indians of modern South Carolina, at St. Helena Sound, when it was overwhelmed by a Spanish naval squadron in March 1605.

Instructions for the voyage, compiled in England in May 1604, directed Jerome's party to call at Croatoan, where there were Englishmen settled, and to trade with them for the herb "Oyssan" or "Bissanque." The cape merchant of the expedition (in command after Captain Jerome was killed), a Frenchman, Bertrand Rocque, when interrogated about Croatoan, in which the Spanish naturally had a great interest, answered:

> he does not know where the said place is, but he understands that its latitude is thirty-six and a half degrees, and they were to go in search of it along the coast, and that he does not know how many Englishmen are settled there, but he believes that they came to settle fifteen years ago, and he does not know with what authority except that they were sent by an Englishman called "Guater Rale" [Walter Ralegh], who himself brought them and left them the first time [showing that the myth of Ralegh's personal establishment of the first colony was already current] and now they had to go in search of them.

He was then asked what herb "Oyssan" or "Bissanque" was:

> he says that he has not seen it, but he knows that when the Englishman 'Guatarrale' came to settle some Englishmen, they took some of the said grass to England and announced that the Indians spun it to make cloth, and they worked it in England and saw that it was silk, like that from China, and for that reason he was to seek it along this coast and take back what he could, and he believes that it is to be found where the English are settled.

This may combine the notion that the seed pods and stems of the *wisakon* or milkweed could be used to make silk, and the notion of making of samples of cloth (grosgrain) from the yucca in Thomas Harriot's *Briefe and true report* in 1588. John Gerard had mentioned the milkweed (both as a medicinal plant and as a source of silk) and illustrated it in his *Herball* in 1597. The capture of the *Castor and Pollux* and her smaller consort and the interrogation of members of her complement led the Spanish to send Ferdinand de Écija to search for the colony later in 1605 but he did not even get as far as Cape Fear before returning without news of any English settlement.

The Anglo-French expedition of 1604–5 indicated that some people in England believed that there was still in 1604 a viable English trading colony living with Manteo's tribe at Croatoan and that the expedition could exchange some of the many utensils, tools, and weapons it carried for milkweed, yucca, and other products of the colony. Unfortunately, they were frustrated and we shall never know what, if anything, they would have found on Croatoan had they reached it. Clearly, not all hopes of the survival of at least some of the Lost Colonists were centered on Chesapeake Bay.

The personality, authority, and actions of Powhatan now become crucial. For several decades before 1600 he had been building up his authority in the Virginia Tidewater, subjugating by diplomacy or war, or both, tribe after tribe along the James and York rivers and on the Virginia Eastern Shore.[13] Not all the tribes on the south bank of the James or the southern shore of Chesapeake Bay were prepared to acknowledge his authority, or at least to do so on a permanent basis, and at least one tribe on the north bank of the James, the Chickahominy, perhaps because of their military skill, retained substantial autonomy. Among the tribes that evidently did not pay him tribute were the Chesapeakes. Moreover (if our assumptions are correct), they were harboring and making marriage alliances with a group of white refugees who had appeared many years before but had, apparently, not played any part in the politics or warfare of the area and so had not been molested. But the entry of a Spanish ship in 1588 into the Chesapeake Bay must have given Powhatan some grounds for alarm, though this vessel had not made any contacts whatever with the white settlers or, indeed effectively, with any of his own dependent tribes. After 1588, however, no European ship had entered the bay, so far as we know, until 1603 at the earliest. If an English ship did so in 1603 (under Samuel Mace) and took away several of Powhatan's men by force, his fears of European intervention would be aroused. It is likely that he kept a continuous outlook for further intruders. In addition, it is not unlikely that he put pressure on the Chesa-

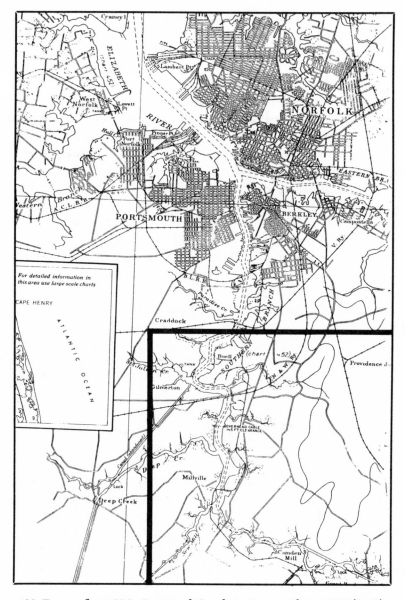

22. Extract from U.S. Coast and Geodetic Survey Chart 1227 (1937),
revised 21 July 1947.
The area squared off is likely to include the area in which the majority of
the Lost Colonists were located between 1587 and, perhaps, 1606.

peake Indians to submit to his authority and perhaps demanded they should hand over to him the assimilated white associates, if our discussion of their status and survival is correct.

If we are to take literally William Strachey's later statement,[14] to be discussed in detail below, that the Lost Colonists (and the Chesapeakes with them as well, because they were intermixed) were slaughtered "at what time" Newport's ships entered the Chesapeake Bay, then the massacre took place at breakneck speed between 24 and 27 April 1607, and the evidence of their killing was covered up, at least to some extent, within that space of time. This assumption, which places Powhatan in a position to take punitive action on a large scale at a moment's notice, is not easy to reconcile with our general understanding of Indian resources, but it is not impossible. Otherwise, the massacre must have taken place shortly before this time and on the strength of prophecies by Powhatan's priests that white men would soon come to deprive him of his kingdom, as indeed the English were to assert was the immediate cause of his actions. But he would most probably take the opportunity of posting lookouts to watch for ships that might enter the bay. If his lookouts were posted on Cape Henry before 24 April, or thereabouts, then it would tend to put the killings appreciably earlier than the actual sighting of the *Susan Constant, Godspeed,* and *Discovery.* The Virginia Company, chartered in April 1606, had at last got an expedition to sea under Captain Christopher Newport which had sufficient resources, it was believed, to establish a permanent English colony on Chesapeake Bay.

There is, however, a complex story to unravel on what happened after the three ships sighted the entrance to Chesapeake Bay and made their way into its mouth. It is by no means certain that our evidence is sufficient to set the record straight, though from that point on we do have some specific evidence. Once around Cape Henry, Captain Newport's party landed a little to the west of the cape on 26 April and found its first sight of the country favorable. At night, its camp was attacked by a group of Indians coming from "the mountain" (which can only be an uneroded Cape Henry); the Indians wounded several of the English and were dispersed by gunfire in the direction from which they came. Later, they were made out to be members of the Chesapeake tribe but there are very serious doubts if they could have been. The explorers then moved to Lynnhaven Bay, where they assembled their knocked-down pinnace, and on the twenty-seventh explored it, seeing only a small party of Indians who retreated to "the mountain." They followed a stream into Lynnhaven Bay on 28 April and "saw a plain plot of ground where," George Percy, who recorded these events, said: "we went on land and found the place five miles in compass without either bush or tree."[15] But there was no Indian settlement to be seen, even if in White's day there had been at least two villages in the vicinity. By implication, we might suggest that all evidence of occupation had been cleared from the area by Powhatan's force.

The men then proceeded some miles farther, apparently to the west, where all they saw before reaching the forest was a "great smoke of fire," which they believed had been set by the Indians (Powhatans?) to a large expanse of grass. We might think that this, too, was a coverup of a clearance of Indian or Indian-white settlement in the area. Passing through the burnt-off area, Gabriel Archer tells us they passed "through excellent ground full of flowers . . . and as goodly trees as I have seen." He went on to say: "Going a little farther we came to a little plot of ground full of fine and beautiful strawberries," but in "all this march we could neither see savage nor town." The existence of so much open ground, exceptional in the region, may have explanations in the surface geology of the district, but this does not mean that there would not have been visible, in normal circumstances, real evidence of Indian, or even of Lost Colony, occupation.

Although the explorers went back to their pinnace and moved over to the north shore without reaching the Elizabeth River on the south bank, it is very difficult to believe that the Chesapeake Indians, even if not the surviving Lost Colonists, could have been in any part of the area they had explored without showing signs of their existence and of their dwellings and fields. The assumption that the hostile bowmen first encountered were Powhatan's men appears to make it highly probable that the principal inhabitants had been killed or removed. At the same time, there is every indication that Powhatan and his subordinates were determined to keep alive the idea that the attackers were Chesapeakes and that the English would do well to steer clear of them.

If this interpretation is correct, what we had when Newport's party reached the falls of the James River (below modern Richmond), after Jamestown had been chosen as the settlement site and a party had gone ahead to explore the river to the west, was an elaborate charade. Rarahunt, one of Powhatan's sons (Tanx Powhatan), pretended to be the great man himself and solemnly declared that all the tribes of the region acknowledged him as their overlord except the "Chessipians" alone, whom, Archer reported, "we perceived to be an enemy generally to all these kingdoms,"[16] Because it was they who were said to have attacked the settlers at their first landing, Archer replied, he reported, "I took occasion to signify our displeasure with them also, making it known that we refused to plant in their country." This was precisely what Powhatan would have wished to happen so that his destruction of the Chesapeake tribe and the killing of the colonists should remain unknown to the English.

The area was not left wholly uninhabited for long. William Strachey reported that (by 1610–11) "such new inhabitants that now inhabit 'Chessapeak' again (the old extinguished as you have heard . . .) are now at peace with him [Powhatan]." Captain John Smith, from what he had heard, estimated the fighting strength of the Chesapeakes, as he thought them, in 1612 at some one hundred warriors,[17] but he may well have obtained the figure from Powhatan sources. It was not, however, until he published his *Generall historie of Virginia* in 1624 that he gave any account of his penetration into this area at the end of his final expedition up Chesapeake Bay, when he entered what was evidently the Elizabeth River at the beginning of September 1608.[18] He wrote:

> because we had only but heard of the "Chisapeacks" and the "Nandsamunds," we thought it as fit to know all our neighbors near home, as so many nations abroad. So setting sail for the southern shore, we sailed up a narrow river up the country of "Chisapeack." It hath a good channel, but many shoals about the entrance. By that we had sailed six or seven miles. We saw two or three little garden plots with their houses, the shores overgrown with the greatest fir trees we ever saw in the country. But not seeing nor hearing any people, and the river very narrow, we returned to the great river.

There Smith soon encountered the Nansemond Indians who submitted only after a fight. The "new inhabitants" of the shores of the Elizabeth River, of whom Strachey was to speak several years later, kept wholly out of sight, presumably because if they were encountered it would become clear that they were not the original Chesapeakes at all. Thereafter, until well after 1622, we have no record of any Englishman setting foot in this territory, so that its secrets never came to light.

So far as we can reconstruct the story of how the massacre of the Lost Colonists became known, we must begin with the unguarded statements of Powhatan to Captain John Smith at his last meeting with that ruler in December 1608. Smith made no mention of this conversation in any of his published writings, probably, in part, because it might reflect on him if the Virginia Company suspected that he had withheld from it information which was apparently first sent confidentially direct to King James so as to obtain his reactions to the disclosures. These indeed came in the form of instructions that were issued in May 1609 by the Royal Council for Virginia, not the Virginia Company itself, to deal with Powhatan for his crime. Yet in 1623 Samuel Purchas could write in his tract, "Virginia's Verger", published only in 1625, that "Powhatan confessed to Captain Smith that he had been at their slaughter and had divers utensils to show."[19] Moreover, Purchas added a note to his large compilation *Hakluytus Posthumus, or Purchas his Pilgrimes*, published in 1625, saying that "Powhatan confessed that he had been at the murder of that colony and showed to Captain Smith a musket barrel and a bronze mortar and certain pieces of iron which had been theirs."[20] There is no doubt that Purchas got this information from Smith himself, who had been cooperating with him closely in collecting material for the *Pilgrimes* for some time before it appeared, and that it was true.

Our other main authority is William Strachey, appointed secretary to the Jamestown colony in 1609, but shipwrecked on Bermuda so that he was unable to take up his post until 1610. He remained in Virginia for over a year, putting its records in order and compiling his own account of what had happened since 1607. He tells us in his *Historie of Travell into Virginia Britania*, "how that his Majesty hath been acquainted that the men, women and children of the first plantation at Roanoke were by practice and commandment of Powhatan (he himself persuaded there unto by his priests) miserably slaughtered without any offence given him." We would suggest that this letter, which has not survived, was dispatched toward the end of 1608 and reached England in the spring of 1609. The Royal Council for Virginia, at the King's command, gave instructions in May 1609 to Sir Thomas Gates,[21] who was coming to Virginia as lieutenant governor (but whose *Sea Venture* grounded on Bermuda). Those instructions contained two significant passages, though it was only later in the document that it was made clear that the reason for them was Powhatan's killing of the Lost Colonists. The second of these reads:

> For Powhatan and his *weroances* it is clear even to reason beside our experience that he loved not our neighbourhood, and therefore you may in no way trust him, but if you find it not best to make him your prisoner, yet you must make him your tributary and all other his *weroances* first to acknowledge no other lord but King James and so we shall free them all from the tyranny of Powhatan.

The first passage expresses the following view of the council:

> we think it reasonable you first remove from them their *iniocasockes* or priests by a surprise of them all and detaining them prisoners. . . . And in case of necessity or convenience, we pronounce it not cruelty nor breach of charity to deal more sharply with them and proceed even to death with these murderers of souls and sacrificers of God's images to the Devil.

These instructions would have been in Strachey's charge while he was stranded in Bermuda and would have been brought by him to Jamestown when Gates eventually arrived there as lieutenant governor in improvised vessels in 1610. It may be noted also that they were reissued to Lord De La Warr when he came out as governor in 1611.

Strachey in his *Historie of Travell into Virginia Britania*, completed in 1612 but written mainly in Jamestown during 1610–11, makes clearer what these instructions implied. The massacre had been reported to King James, Strachey said, and:

> because his Majesty is of all the world the most just and most mercifull prince, he hath given order that Powhatan himself, with his *weroances*, shall be spared and revenge only taken upon

his *quiyoughquisocks* [his priests, spelled otherwise above], by whose advice and persuasions was exercised that bloody cruelty, and only now that Powhatan, himself, and the *weroances*, must depend on his Majesty, both acknowledging him for their superior lord.

He goes on to say that the subordinate tribal leaders (*weroances*) would be amenable to detaching themselves from Powhatan and establishing a direct attachment to and dependence on the English because it would offer them great advantages and relieve them of many burdens imposed by Powhatan. We can see, however, that this would involve splitting up the Powhatan Confederacy into its constituent parts, which the English never felt strong enough to attempt while Powhatan was alive. Moreover, it is clear that the killing of the Lost Colonists was known in England early in 1609 and that formal arrangements were made to punish Powhatan and his dependents in the same year. Yet, by the failure of the instructions to arrive and the desperate straits of the colony in 1610, with its continuing weakness even into 1612, these measures, which Strachey considered to be very limited in any case, were never put into effect. There can be no doubt, however, that Powhatan was recognized to have been responsible for the violent and bloody end of the Lost Colony.

Strachey alone indicates when the Lost Colonists were killed, saying that for "twenty and odd years [they] had peaceably lived and intermixed with those savages [the Chesapeakes] and were off his [Powhatan's] territory." Granted that Strachey might not know precisely to the month when the Lost Colonists arrived in the Chesapeake territory, this would put their killing as recently as early in 1607. His statement that they lived peacefully with the Indians and intermingled with them is the source of earlier suggestions on this subject. Elsewhere, he spoke of "the slaughter at 'Roanoke' at which time this our colony (under the conduct of Captain Newport) landed within the 'Chesapeack Bay,'" which would place it toward the end of April 1607, a possibility we have already taken into account, with the assumption that "at 'Roanoak'" and elsewhere "of Roanoak" means, not Roanoke Island, but the settlers of the Roanoke colony who had moved to the Chesapeake area.

The massacre of the Chesapeake tribe is dealt with by Strachey in a separate section of his *Historie* concerned with Indian wars. Proph-

ecies by the priests, lay, he said, behind many of Powhatan's violent
actions. He continued:

> Not long since it was that his priests told him how that from
> the "Chesapeack" Bay a nation should arise which should dis-
> solve and give end to his empire, for which not many years
> since [we wish he had said how many] (perplexed with this
> devilish oracle), according to the ancient and gentile custom,
> he destroyed and put to sword all such as might lie under any
> doubtful construction of the said prophecy, as all the inhabi-
> tants, the *weroances* and his subjects of the province, and so
> remain all the "Chessiopeians" at this day, and for this cause,
> extinct.

It has already been indicated that if the Lost Colonists were living
among the Chesapeakes, and were indeed intermingled with them,
the killing of the Lost Colonists and of the Chesapeake tribe must,
of necessity, have taken place at the same time, but we have also
indicated that, although it might have taken place toward the end
of April 1607, it could, more probably, have happened earlier. In
this case we might wonder (with no evidence at all to back it up)
whether, indeed, the priests could prophesy the impending arrival of
the English colony. Or were they not farsighted politicians who had
argued from the appearance of a foreign vessel in the Chesapeake
Bay a few years before that the time to strike a potential enemy close
at hand, namely the Chesapeakes and the Lost Colonists, was before
any such intruders reappeared? In that case it was coincidence that
led to the killings in 1607, whether or not they occurred at the
precise time when Newport's ships appeared on the horizon. This
we will never be able to tell.

Once the Virginia Company was established and began to prepare
to settle both North and South Virginia, the latter being Chesapeake
Bay and the area to the north and south of it, the location of the Lost
Colonists would clearly become a high priority. It would be a matter
of national pride to link up again with English people who had been
lost for twenty years. They could be of the greatest value to the new
colonists in providing them with information both on the nature
and condition—not to mention the languages—of Indian society and

on how to establish themselves successfully, grow crops, and prospect for minerals, as well as assisting in innumerable other ways. Although the "Instructions by way of advice" of 1606 did not impose any requirement on the colonists to find the Lost Colonists[22]—indeed, they provided only rather general prescriptions for settling—it is almost certain that finding the colonists ranked among their practical aims. It may well be that Newport had enough hints from what was already known or surmised in England about the location of the colonists to induce him to make some discreet inquiries about their continuing survival, but we do not know how far he did so.

One problem that confronts us is that we do not know how much of the language of the Powhatan territory the English could understand or speak. Thomas Harriot had helped Samuel Mace in 1602 by providing him with some sort of vocabulary, and we now know that he had devised a system for pronouncing the Algonquian tongue as he had heard it in the colony of 1585–86 and compiled a word list of the language. The phonetic system has survived but the vocabulary, or dictionary, appears to have been destroyed in the Great Fire of London in 1666. Harriot knew George Percy, a brother of the Earl of Northumberland, who had been living at Syon House where Harriot also resided, and may have taught him a little of the language as Percy, in the narrative he wrote about the first contacts of the colonists in 1607, suggests he was not wholly ignorant of what was being said and may even have been able to speak a little. Gabriel Archer had been in contact with Indians who spoke several of the New England dialects in 1602 and may have been sufficiently interested in language to have taken lessons from Harriot on the Algonquian of the Virginia Indians before he set sail for Virginia. It is Archer who gives us the first coherent accounts of conversations with Indians during the early stages of the exploration of the James River and we might presume he did not invent what he reports, though he may have exaggerated his understanding in order to give his report continuity and meaning. Captain Christopher Newport certainly was anxious to pick up Algonquian words as he went up the river, but we need not suggest that he had studied the language before he set sail or picked up more than a few words, perhaps, from Percy and Archer on the voyage. Unless we consider this question of language we shall not be in a position to judge what these early observers learned, or heard, about the Chesapeake Indians and, perhaps, even about the Lost Colonists, though they tell us nothing about the latter. Although we lack good authority for the southern colony, there is direct evidence for the North Virginia venture—the Sagadahoc colony of 1607—that James Rosier provided the settlers with an Abenaki vocabulary compiled with the help of the five Indians captured on the coast of Maine in 1605.

Captain John Smith, as an experienced traveler, had certainly developed a technique for acquiring rapidly a small working vocabulary from new peoples with whom he was in contact, but he too had other things to do rather than attempt to interrogate the local Indians for information on the Lost Colonists. It was not until the end of 1607, when he was captured by Opechancanough and brought to Powhatan's chief town at Weromacomico on the York River, that he had any chance to use the vocabulary he had by then acquired to make inquiries about the Lost Colonists. He did indeed do so, but beyond telling him that some members of their community had been seized a few years before by a white man and that it was thought, to begin with, that Smith was the man, but having examined him they found he was not, they told him nothing about the real fate of the Lost Colonists at their hands. Instead, separately, Openchancanough and Powhatan, concealing all knowledge of the Lost Colonists as such, fobbed Smith off with a vague account that clothed (white) men still lived well to the south, at a place called Ocanahonan,[23] which we might think was a mere tale (even though it was to be supported by later investigations), and that another group lived far to the north (the latter being, genuinely enough, the French). Indeed, in his published writings of 1608, 1612, and 1624, Smith said nothing about hearing news of the Lost Colonists during his long expeditions around Chesapeake Bay and up to its rivers during 1607–8.

Smith did, however, probably following instructions brought by Newport in January 1608, make some effort to search for them to the south of the James River. He enlisted the services of Wowinchopunk,[24] the chief of the Paspahegh Indians, who previously had been hostile but now, wishing to win Smith's approval, agreed to go with two of the settlers to search well to the south for the village of Ocanahonan, which may have existed either on the Chowan or Roanoke rivers. The two Englishmen and the chief did go very much farther south. It is clear from inscriptions on a map, now in Spain (the so-called Zúñiga map which Smith had something to do with),[25] that they had entered the Roanoke River and were told of deposits of copper at a place called Ritanoe (probably in the later Virgilina district through which the river cuts, where natural copper was to be identified, as has already been suggested). They explored still farther either inland or to the south and heard that, at a village called Pakerikanick, "here remain the four men clothed that came from 'Roonock' to 'Okanahowan.'" This apparently meant they were persons who had escaped from the Chesapeake massacre and were not men who had been with Manteo. They were said to remain there still, though the searchers did not succeed in reaching them. There is some confusion in the inscriptions on the map. Pakerikanick is shown on a river well to the south (Neuse?), while Ocanahowan is on what is clearly the Roanoke River. As will shortly be evident, four men (the same four?) were said to have remained with the Chawanoac tribe further north again.

A report on this expedition, which has not survived, was sent to London and was the basis for further entries in the orders given by the Royal Council for Virginia in May 1609, which we have already mentioned, and which told Sir Thomas Gates to have a further settlement made farther south, in modern North Carolina, where "two of the best rivers [the Roanoke and Chowan rivers] will supply you. Besides you are near to rich copper mines at Ritanoe and may pass there by one branch of this river, and by another Peccarecomicke." "Peccarecomicke" may be the Pakerikanick that we have already encountered, but we cannot expect London officials, in the absence of adequate maps, to have understood the topography of the Carolina Sounds. However, they added something further, saying that at the latter place "you will find four of the English alive, left by Sir Walter 'Rawley', which escaped from the slaughter of Powhatan of Roanoke upon the first arrival of our colony." The four men are therefore to be identified (as they or another party were later) as survivors of the massacre of 1607. Gates was told "they live under the protection of a *weroance* called Gepanocon [who was presumably a successor to Menatonon, head of the Chawanoac tribe], by whose consent you will never recover them." It may be recalled that the three colonists deserted by Lane in 1586 may well have been detained by, or returned to, Menatonon and remained in the Chawanoac tribe. There may thus be a link between the men of 1586 and the survivors of

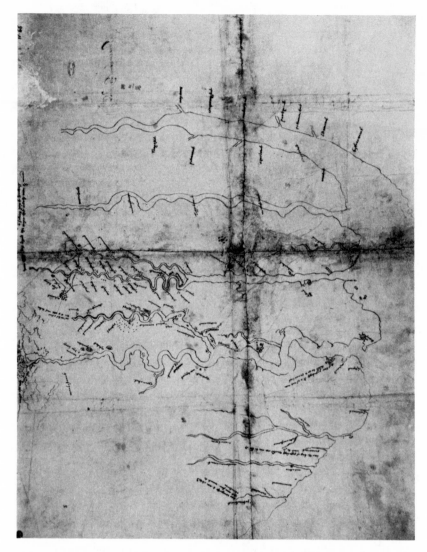

23. Extract from the Zuñiga Map, circa June 1608.
Simancas, Archivo General, M.P. D.IV.66-XIX-163, after P. L. Barbour, *The Jamestown Voyages under the First Charter, 1606–1609.* The relevant captions, which are not legible on this scale, are [a] "here paspahegh and 2 of our men landed to go to panawick"; [b] "nansamund"; [c] "chisiapiack"; [d] "imhamoack"; [e] "Roanock"; [f] "Chawanoac"; [g] "Vttamuscawone"; [h] "here the king of paspageh reported one man to be"; [i] "panawick"; [j] "ocanahowan"; [k] "morottico"; [l] "muchamonchocock"; [m] "aumocawpunt"; [n] "rawcotock"; [o] "here rema[n]eth 4 men clothed that came from roonock to ihanowan"; "pakeranik".

1606–7. We might surmise that the men who were refugees from the Chesapeake were retained at least partly because they had some knowledge of how to employ the natural copper which Menatonon had coveted and of which his successors had now acquired a quantity or even the source. The London instructions do indicate, which Smith never made clear, that the men sent to look for the Lost Colonists in 1608 had in fact brought back a coherent story both about the massacre and the survival of a few members of the Chesapeake colony in what we may understand, provisionally, to have been the territory of the Chawanoac tribe even though apparently they did not make direct contact with the survivors, who were kept out of sight.

The Virginia Company took note of the 1608 report only in 1610 when its official pamphlet, *A true and sincere declaration . . . of the plantation begun in Virginia* (London, 1610) reported that "intelligence by some of our nation planted by Sir Walter Ralegh, yet alive, within fifty miles of our fort . . . can open the womb and bowels of this country, as is testified by two of our colony sent out to seek them, who, though denied by the savages speech with them, found crosses and letters, the characters and assured testimonies of Christians cut in the barks of trees," reminiscent of the signs left for White in 1590. But that was all. Contact was not maintained. The survivors were never seen again.

A further strand of a story on these lines was derived by William Strachey from a friendly Indian, Machumps, who, in 1610–11, told him that at "Peccarecanicke" and "Ochanahoen" the people had built houses with stone walls and one story above another, "so taught them by those English who escaped the slaughter at 'Roanoak' at what time our colony . . . landed within the 'Chesapeack' Bay." The tale that houses built of stone were inspired by English survivors sounds unlikely, though they could, conceivably, have taught them how to construct two-story houses made of poles and timbers. The Indian went on to say, or so Strachey reports, that "at Ritanoe the *weroance* 'Eyanoco' [the Gepanocon above?] preserved seven of the English alive, four men, two boys and one young maid, who escaped and fled up the river of 'Choanoke' [Chowan?] to beat his copper, of which he had certain mines at the said Ritanoe." It might appear from this statement that the Chawanoac tribe had by this time acquired substantial supplies of natural copper, perhaps originating

in the Virgilina district (though Ritanoe has not been located and
could have been a nearer source). These were most probably obtained by trade with Ralph Lane's Mangoaks, the Tuscarora, or some
other inland tribe, and so they did not mine the copper themselves,
though they may have used it to extend their power and influence.
The employment of refugees from the Lost Colony to "beat" copper
for them would make sense if they had the skills to harden copper
for use as weapons by techniques of hammering or even annealing.

The first search made for the Lost Colonists has been followed
into 1609, but it was not the only one made in 1608. Newport came
out in October 1608, and among his orders was one to bring back
"one of the lost company sent out by Sir Walter Ralegh," though
Smith mentions this in a sneering way and does not indicate that
Newport made any attempt to look for survivors. But Smith himself
did something. In December 1608 he sent out two search parties.[26]
The one under Michael Sicklemore ventured as far as the Chowan
River and returned with some news about the country into which
the colonists of 1585–86 had penetrated "but found little hope and
less certainty of them [that] were left by Sir Walter Ralegh." The
second search party, led by Nathanial Powell and Anas Todkill, was
conducted by an Indian tribe living south of the James into the
territory of the "Mangoages," the Iroquoian Tuscarora, and the cop-
per-owning Mangoaks Lane was looking for up the Roanoke River in
1586. The search was thus temporarily diverted to the interior in the
southwest. The expedition was without result, Smith saying after its
return "but nothing could we learn but they were all dead." Later,
Smith gave some description of the country they passed through,
and mentioned that the language of the Indians was different from
that of Virginia, pointing to their being from the Iroquoian language group and making their identity with the Tuscarora certain.
For North Carolinians the knowledge that a considerable part of
eastern North Carolina was explored as a result of the search is
of considerable interest, as is the proposal, which was not implemented, for creating a settlement on the Roanoke River.

However, after Newport had left in December 1608, Smith learned
from Powhatan of his part in the killing of the Lost Colonists. One
possible reason for his silence in his published works has already
been suggested, though he did charge Powhatan with other killings.
A point of difficulty in publishing his confession in full was that

Powhatan had earlier in 1608 been given insignia sent out to confirm him as a dependent of King James and it would be unwise for Smith to declare publicly that he must now be treated as an open enemy without having the King's permission. It is even possible that he had learned that the ceremony in 1607, when he believed he was being prepared for execution and was saved only by the intervention of the young Pocahontas, really meant that he was being received into Powhatan's circle as a *weroance* and so had become, formally at least, a vassal of a murderous ruler who later brazenly admitted the slaughter of the Lost Colonists. Smith was a proud man, a social climber too, and he would not wish his part in the earlier dealings with Powhatan to become known, though he could report confidentially to King James what he had learned in December 1608 of Powhatan's direct responsibility for the killings. It was only in conversation with Samuel Purchas some fourteen years after his return from Virginia that he admitted he had had specific admissions from Powhatan that he had killed the Lost Colonists.

It is a strange thing that even though it was known by 1609 and confirmed in 1610 or 1611 that survivors of the Lost Colony were apparently living at no great distance from the James River, and were employed in copper working by the man we have understood to be the chief of the Chawanoac tribe, no concerted attempt was made to recover them. Whether a military operation was possible is not clear—the colony remained in a tenuous state for some time and an adventure of this sort might have been thought too risky. But it was not out of the question to send emissaries with sufficient bribes to the Chawanoac chieftain that he could scarcely refuse. At the same time, the value of survivors to the new colonists decreased as the colonists themselves became familiar with the country and needed less help from possible old inhabitants of the 1587 colony. After 1611 it may have seemed mere sentimentality to expend any great effort to recover a handful of individuals. Under the spartan regime of Sir Thomas Dale, from 1611 to 1616, this seems plausible. But we are left entirely in the dark. The survivors were deserted completely, so far as we know, for twelve or thirteen years, and so all chance of making the earlier much-desired linkage was lost. All this time we hear nothing of attempts to search the Outer Banks for colonists who had remained with Manteo. They are never even mentioned and pass into oblivion for the rest of the seventeenth century. We are forced to accept as a fact that they became Indian themselves, and their children and grandchildren wholly so, as the century went on.

When John Pory went to Virginia as secretary to the colony in 1619, it may have been love of exploration or even a touch of sentiment (as he had helped Richard Hakluyt compile the second edition of the *Principal navigations* and had been steeped in the story of the Lost Colony) that led him to renew the search. He was the first, in all this long period, whom we know to have made his way southward from the James to the area where survivors of the massacre of 1607 were supposed to have taken refuge. George Sandys wrote, from Jamestown on 3 March 1622, of his expedition as far as the Chowan River and described the country there as combining great forests with excellent corn-growing country. We do not have Pory's own narrative, which has been lost, but John Smith reported his lack of success in finding out anything about the Lost Colonists. And so we have Smith's epilogue that, after thirty-five years, "we left seeking our Colony, that was never any of them found, nor seen to this day in 1622."[27] The handful of fugitives had been allowed to vanish without further trace. In any event, if even one of them was alive in 1622, he or she would have been so thoroughly Indian in outlook and culture that the past in a white community near the Chesapeake Bay, let alone in England before 1587, would long have faded, become dim, or died. So indeed, the last little group of which we have any tenuous knowledge fades finally into oblivion.

There were Indians on Roanoke Island when Francis Yardley went there in quest of land in 1653. They were friendly and willing to cooperate with the Englishmen, but they had nothing to say of how the earlier colonists had met their end except to point out to him the remains of the "old fort." Nearly half a century later, John Lawson visited not only the fort site but also Croatoan Island, by then known as Hatteras Island.[28] The Indians there may have been descendents of Manteo's band, as Lawson described them as differing from the other Indians of the area, though many changes of population may have taken place in the meantime. Lawson says:

> These tell us that several of their ancestors were white people and could talk in a book [read] as we do, the truth of which is confirmed by gray eyes being found frequently amongst these Indians and no others. They value themselves extremely for

their affinity to the English, and are ready to do them all friendly offices. It is probable that this settlement miscarried for want of timely supplies from England or through the treachery of the natives, for we may reasonably suppose that the English were forced to cohabit with them for relief and conversation and that in the process of time they conformed themselves to the manners of their Indian relations.

Here we may see, if we wish, in the handful of Hatteras Indians of 1701 the last record of those who, expecting John White but not waiting long enough for his arrival, had gone to Croatoan and, more than a century later, revealed themselves by their features and their traditions and mixed ancestry. Edward Moseley's six or eight surviving Indians, about 1729, were noted on his map of North Carolina published in 1733, and nothing more is known even of them. But the time span was too long for certainty. Other groups may have been wrecked on the Hatteras shoals and found refuge with and assimilated to the native society in which they found themselves, or deserters from the Virginia colony could have gone there. But if we wish to have a sustaining myth of continuity from Lost Colonists to the white settlement of modern North Carolina we have it here. It may be a myth but it is not wholly without historical foundation, even if it is far from being fully established. Excavation in sites occupied by the Chawanoac Indians, especially Chawanoac itself, could conceivably bring to light some slight traces of the survivors of the Lost Colonists from the Chesapeake.

Although it can be said that the "mystery" of the Lost Colonists, or at least the fate of the majority of those who had survived for nearly twenty years and their progeny, has been clarified with reasonable certainty, the long gap in our knowledge of what occurred during their residence among the Chesapeake Indians has not been filled. There remains the tantalizing question of whether there was indeed an English element left from some of them in the Outer Banks and, finally, whether survivors of the Powhatan massacre contributed in any way to the life of the Chawanoac Indians or were simply absorbed by them without a trace. The dramatic and romantic elements in the story survive, alongside what now appears to be a measure of solid history.[29]

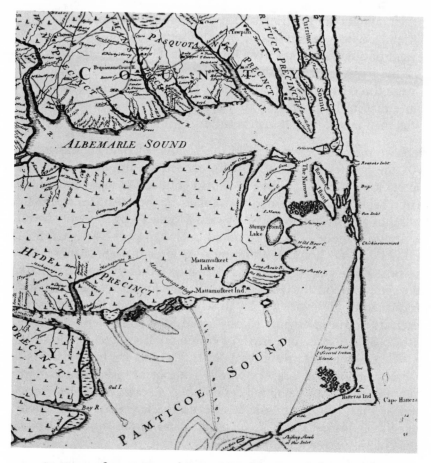

24. Extract from *A New and Correct Map of the Province of North Carolina.*
By Edward Moseley, late Surveyor General of the Said Province, 1733.
This map was published in London. Copy in East Carolina University
Library; photocopy in Division of Archives and History, Raleigh.

·◦[C H A P T E R 2 0]◦·

An Archaeological Resurrection?

The archaeology of the Roanoke settlements is a most interesting and important topic, but so far it is not one that can answer many of the questions that the surviving documents leave obscure, though it can assist in understanding at least a few of them. Archaeology and history, for the period when documents exist, have always been potential allies and capable of complementing each other, but practitioners in history and archaeology (which, in the United States, has long been a branch of anthropology) have in the past normally worked in isolation from one another. In more recent years, however, they have been coming together, each making use of the methodology and the results of the other, so that a novel subject has been developing and establishing itself as a reputable academic discipline, Historical Archaeology. In the development of this subject, which is still to some extent an experimental one, the Roanoke Island settlements have played an important part, largely through the work of the National Park Service there and, in particular, through the expertise and forethought of the leading archaeologist in the National Park Service between 1935 and the sixties, Jean Carl Harrington, who has continued to write on the subject since his retirement. It was he who made possible considerable advances in both the understanding of the Roanoke settlements and in the integration of the historical evidence on the site.

In the 1980s new sensing and other scientific equipment, which have been introduced by the Southeast Archeological Center, promise to give answers to the question of what, if any, further evidence is to be found on the settlement site. But the character of the island and its surroundings have altered. The Outer Banks have lost from between a half-mile to a mile in width, while inlets in them have opened and closed intermittently over four hundred years. Roanoke Island's surface has not been too greatly altered (except by man-made construction) in its central area. On the other hand, there has been major erosion at the northern end of the island. The site of the Indian village of 1584 has long been removed by erosion and an area of marsh has been eliminated. Some estimates suggest that the total erosion of the north shore was as much as 2,000 feet,[1] though this is considered excessive by others. The erosion of the western shoreline as a result of the deepening of Croatan Sound is generally regarded as of relatively recent origin. On the other hand, Roanoke Sound has tended to become shallower and perhaps somewhat narrower, though there has been some erosion at the northeast end.

Generally, the noneroded parts of the island have appeared to sink slowly through the centuries, while sea level has risen. The general consensus appears to be that, in the area where the settlement enclosure was located, levels have not changed substantially. However, in the area to the east of the site, Bruce S. Cheeseman concluded in 1982 that "the marshy area now extending along the northern shore of Shallowbag Bay from Dough's Creek to Baum Point was indeed much firmer land in the eighteenth century, perhaps even suitable for settlement and perhaps, more so, it might be concluded in the sixteenth."[2] At the waist of the island, where it narrows in the middle, and at the southern end there are and have been marshy areas that are not suitable for cultivation though some have now been filled. On the other hand the loamy sands of the central area, both to the north and the south of the waist, have become fertile and able to support agriculture, and to produce in nature "a dense tree covering of pine, oak, gum, cedar, bay, persimmon, dogwood, holly, sassafras, maple and other related species. The understory of these trees consists of several kinds of huckleberries or relatives, muscadine vines, dwarf sumac, wax-myrtle, yaupon and a variety of herbs and small shrubs." It is not believed that this vegetation in the fertile area where the fort and "town" were established has altered basically, except where the forest cover has been removed by man or killed by the action of hurricanes. Blown sand has tended to cover the humus layer, which then has taken a considerable period to consolidate and again support heavy vegetation, or, for that matter, agriculture.

The reconstruction suggested in the narrative of the 1585–86 colony was largely imaginative, but, in considering the archaeology of the Roanoke settlements, it should be understood that the theory behind that verbal reconstruction was that the word fort does not necessarily refer to Fort Raleigh alone (though it may in the end turn out that this was the only proper "fort"), but to a palisaded settlement ranging much beyond Fort Raleigh, and including it as only part of the defenses. Fort Raleigh may have been only a bastion in a more complex system of protection for the settlement, even though possibly the most important strong point in that system. Definitive knowledge of the layout and detailed articulation of the settlement area may take some years for archaeologists to complete, and it is so far only possible to make certain assumptions, which may turn out to be mistaken. The work that was done in 1982 and 1983 was admirably performed; it was simply incomplete. But as it so happened that the outline of Fort Raleigh survived above ground and the rest of the settlement disappeared, it was inevitable that attention should center on it.

John White was the first to record archaeological evidence for the settlement site. In 1590 he found, besides the palisade, which will be discussed later, "many bars of iron" (we might think anywhere from 10 to 20), 2 pigs of lead (defined as oblong mouldings of the smaller size, the larger being "sows"), 4 iron fowlers (guns weighing about 450 pounds each without their carriages), iron saker shot (not enumerated, but perhaps anywhere from 3 to 5 in number, about 5½ pounds each), and some other "heavy things" not enumerated. His men also found "divers chests" buried in a ditch and excavated by Indians. Because three were his own, this would suggest that three was a minimum allowance for the governor—they would be heavy wooden sea chests perhaps bound with metal. Only two of the others found are here specified, but we might interpret "divers" as anywhere from 5 to 10. These artifacts, except for two cannon, are not known to have been ever seen again.

In 1654 Francis Yardley reported that traders with whom he was associated had been shown by the local Indians "Sir Walter Ralegh's fort, from which I received a sure token of their being there."[3] The island was occupied by English settlers from 1670 onward, though

perhaps for a few years they merely grazed stock there. They and
their successors fortunately never plowed the area in which the later
Fort Raleigh was situated, but they may well have cleared and
plowed areas to the east and southeast of it which are now considered potentially important.

John Lawson's discovery of artifacts has already been noted. He
found them "where the ruins of a fort can be seen at this day,"
though his successor as surveyor general, Edward Moseley, did not
mark the site on his published map of 1733, but John Collet did so
on his map of 1770. We hear of President James Monroe being taken
on 7 April 1819 "to view the remains of the fort, the traces of which
are still distinctly visible, which is said to have been erected by the
first colony of Sir Walter Raleigh." The site attracted the attention of
early holidaymakers to the Outer Banks and was well picked over.
George Higby Throop, visiting it about 1849, reported seeing "the
remains of the fort, glass globes, containing quicksilver, and hermeti-
cally sealed [part of the equipment of Joachim Ganz?] and other
relics occasionally discovered." In 1850 B. J. Lossing reported seeing
"slight traces of the fort." Charles H. Johnson, sketching the island
during the early stages of the Civil War, made the first known sketch
of the surviving earthworks which shows they were at least two to
three feet high in places in 1862. Sometime before this Frederic
Kidder "visited the site of Lane's fort, the present remains of which
are very slight being merely the wreck of an embankment. This has
at times been excavated by parties who hoped to find some deposit
which would repay the trouble, a vial of quicksilver [Throop's?] being
the only relic said to have been found." So much for the early
references, which are mainly valuable for providing something of a
continuous record, and one which helps to explain why the discovery of artifacts on the site by modern scientific methods thus far
has been so slight.

Edward C. Bruce provided the first detailed description of what
then remained of "Master Ralph Layne's stronghold and the City of
Ralegh with its intrenchments." According to Bruce (who visited the
site before 1860):

The trench is clearly traceable in a square of about forty yards
each way. Midway of one side, that crossing the foreground of

our sketch [unfortunately replaced by an irrelevant woodcut] another trench, perhaps flanking the gateway, runs in some fifteen or twenty feet. This is shown. And on the right of the same face of the inclosure, the corner is apparently thrown out in the form of a small bastion. The ditch is generally two feet

25. Charles Johnson's Drawing of "Earthworks Built by
Sir Walter Raleigh's Colony," 1862.
Charles Johnson, *The Long Roll*. New York: East Aurora, 1911. Facing p. 129.
Print courtesy North Carolina Collection, University of North Carolina at
Chapel Hill.

deep, though in many places scarcely perceptible. The whole site is overgrown. . . . A fragment or two of stone or brick may be discovered in the grass.

This seems to be the first mention of a bastion and the only mention of a trench independent of the ditch. The loss of the sketch Bruce made is unfortunate, but what he says is valuable as it gives some idea of what was to be seen before the Civil War. The Civil War garrison troops are said to have dug pits inside the ditch but to have been restrained from their activities by a local landowner. Indications of these pits were found in the excavations of the 1947–53 period. They may have done further damage to the area to the southeast.

The work of Talcott Williams between 1887 and 1895 was the first significant attempt at education and led to the formation of the Roanoke Colony Memorial Association and the purchase by it of the land on which the remains were seen to be located so that these remains received thereafter a measure of protection. Williams himself excavated Indian sites on the island and then, in cooperation with the association, turned his attention to the site. He reported in 1895 that he "was careful to avoid any disturbance of the embankment and its slope, the surface disturbed was carefully plotted and fixed by bearings and measurements, and a minute record kept and deposited with the association" though it is not now in the possession of the association's successor, the Roanoke Island Historical Society. He says:

In all 13 trenches, most of them 5 x 3 feet, were opened and carried from 4 to 9 feet deep . . . Wherever trenches were sunk and, it is fair to conclude, over the entire area, there was found a thin and undisturbed layer of sandy humus of 6 inches to a foot, then a layer of black ashy earth, containing many fragments of charcoal and frequent fire pits. This layer rested directly on undisturbed sand, often penetrated by fire pits . . . Toward the base of the black, ashy layer were found small pieces of iron, a corroded nail, a chipped piece of quartzite, and some small fragments of Indian pottery, networked. No one could reasonably expect to find any objects of importance on a site ransacked as this must have been, but I confess my surprise at the absence of small fragments, particularly of pottery. For a site occupied as it was the place proved singularly barren of debris.

He details where the trenches were dug and also where the embankment was sounded with an iron rod, while trial excavations were also made in the ditch and at various points in the woods "showing there an undisturbed surface and no remains of a layer of coal and ashes beneath the surface." In 1896 Williams assisted the Roanoke Colony Memorial Association in defining the perimeter of the surviving embankment by the placing of granite markers. On the whole these proved, after 1947, to have been well situated, though in themselves they reflected some damage to the embankment. Williams donated a collection of Indian artifacts (pottery shards) to the Smithsonian Institution, but there is no record that he contributed any English artifacts that may have been found on the site.

This amateur but, for the time, careful probing of the visible remains at the site was the basic archaeological record before the National Park Service took over the site in 1941. The outlines of the surviving defenses and ditch were from that time on known with reasonable certainty and were protected to some extent by a rail fence erected in 1896. Between 1895 and 1936 various horrors were perpetrated on the site, destructive of archaeological remains rather than in any way progressive. A large memorial commemorating Virginia Dare, located in the center, damaged the site both when being erected and being removed. When a film was made there in 1921, a deep trench was dug all around one side of the remains (it was traced and distinguished from the older workings only in 1950). The Fort Raleigh property was transferred to the state of North Carolina in 1934. Between 1934 and 1936 the Roanoke Island Historical Society and the North Carolina Historical Commission arranged for the "reconstruction" of Fort Raleigh and its adjacent "town." Under various relief programs the federal government provided labor and money for this work. A palisade of logs was built to surround the whole area; then log cabins and a chapel, guardhouses at the gate, and finally a major log building inside the old earthworks were constructed, according to the views of a self-styled "expert," Frank Stick. This did much damage to the natural and artificial features of the site, both on the surface and beneath ground. By the time the site was transferred to the federal government to be administered by the National Park Service in 1940, it was known that log cabins were not used by the early English settlers and the whole fake village and fort became suspect. It was, however, only after the war was over and the National Park Service was fully prepared for archaeological work in 1947 that this travesty of a reconstruction could be gradually unshipped and finally eliminated.

Nothing need be said here about the many celebrations and presentations that were held at the site between 1895 and 1947; these do not appear to have had major adverse effects on the surface remains. The most important innovations involved the creation of a theater by the waterside, which since 1937 has presented each summer Paul Green's The Lost Colony, and the construction of an Elizabethan Garden by the Garden Club of North Carolina. These have been fully dealt with in William S. Powell's Paradise Preserved (1965).[4] Although some care was taken to see that no major intrusions indicating earlier human occupancy were disturbed during these extensive operations, it cannot be said with any confidence that no damage was done to the sites adjacent to the fort. Modern archaeological techniques employed in these areas before construction was begun could well have told another story.

The National Park Service had to start afresh, clearing as they went the debris of past piety and vandalism and trying to circumvent the major damage that had been done in so many ways to the site and its immediate surroundings. Fortunately, they were able to put the excavations in the charge of the pioneer archaeologist of the Jamestown excavations, J. C. Harrington. Under his direction, during the years 1947 to 1953, the area was explored and transformed. The exploration involved numerous frustrations but many of them were surmounted by ingenuity and skill. Harrington, in his Search for the Cittie of Ralegh (1962) and An Outwork at Fort Raleigh (1966), and his most recent pamphlet, Archaeology and the Enigma of Fort Raleigh (1984), as well as in numerous periodical articles, has told all that had been discovered down to 1982. He not only has made it possible to understand how far archaeology can help the historian but also has helped to impress on him the limitations which excavation entails, especially where wooden structures used for only a short time are concerned. This does not mean that his work is definitive on the question of the nature of the settlement enclosure and the place of Fort Raleigh in it. Indeed, in his latest pamphlet he states: "At Fort Raleigh, archaeology failed to answer the most important question of all: Where was the settlement located?"[5]

One approach an historian can take to the archaeological materials on North Carolina's Outer Banks and Roanoke Island is to consider where the colonists are likely to have left remains of their visit and to build upon that where there is anything to build on. At Lane's Port Ferdinando (the later Hatarask) of 1585 there was a twelve-foot entry on the bar at high water, which would permit the reasonably safe entry of vessels drawing nine or ten feet at the most. The Outer Banks at this point were much wider than they are today and the total width of the land bordering the south side of the entry would have been well over a mile. It is clear that on that side of the channel there was a cove which vessels of some seventy tons could enter and where they could get shelter. It was here that vessels of that size were first unladen—the two barks of 1584, the two small vessels, *Elizabeth* and *Dorothy*, of 1585, probably some of Grenville's vessels in 1586, and the pinnace only of 1587. Neither of the ships of 1590 could enter. Otherwise, shallops or ship's boats were used for transshipment from vessels riding at anchor off the shore. For those that could enter, as well as for the boats, it is probable that either a landing stage or a slip (an inclined plane suitable for unlading) was constructed so that the vessels larger than the pinnaces and smaller than ships of over seventy tons could land their cargo, which could then be reshipped to the island. It seems reasonable to assume that something of this sort, to facilitate the landing of men and stores, existed between 1585 and 1587, though it was not noted by Vicente González in 1588. Lane in 1585 contemplated building a sconce or small fort to protect the entry but was evidently dissuaded because it would help Spanish vessels working along the coast to locate the site of the colony, just as the Spanish lookout post helped to guide Sir Francis Drake through the channel to St. Augustine in 1586. This would have rotted away rapidly and have been destroyed by storms and, as the forms of the Outer Banks altered its site, would probably soon be removed or deeply buried in sand.

The second place where the colonists left traces of their presence was clearly the cove near the main settlement, to which the pinnaces (of thirty tons and under) could make their way along Roanoke Sound and, with boats accompanying them, land supplies and men. As has been indicated, this cove has not yet been located, though Edward Moseley's map, published in 1733, shows a deep entry into the northeastern shore of Roanoke, quite distinct from Shallowbag Bay on the east, which may be the "creek" referred to by White in 1590. It is known that there has been a movement of sand northward along the eastern side of the island and that it is being deposited near the northeast shore of the island. In June 1588, as has already been stated, González reported that he had found there a *varadero*. This was the Spanish word for a shipyard; the contemporary English word was "slip." This could have been either an artificial slope of solid material made beside a navigable water to serve as a landing place, or an inclined plane of timber, sloping gradually down to the water, on which ships and other vessels were built or repaired. It will be clear that the Spanish description could cover either of the closely related uses of a slip (or, as it became known in the nineteenth century, slipway). On this sloping construction of wood goods could be, and no doubt were, landed both in 1585 and 1587. In June 1588 there was a considerable amount of debris around it, which might suggest either attempts to build boats (not impossible in 1587–88) or, more probably, the surplus packaging and other remnants of the hurried departure of the colonists in June 1586 or the less frantic departure of the bulk of the 1587 colony in that year after John White had left for England. That the colonists used the area around the slip for more than casual visits and that they repaired or built boats there might be indicated from the discovery that large English barrels were sunk in the ground to line wells. This assumes that the wells were found adjacent to the slip, as it is difficult to suggest that they could have been seen elsewhere. This does not exclude the possibility that there were similar wells elsewhere nearer to the settlement site.

Early in 1982, Phillip Evans, in charge of the historical interpretation of the Fort Raleigh site, located remains of two wooden barrels in the tidal zone southeast of Fort Raleigh. One barrel had been made of stays with wooden hoops; the other, from a hollowed-out tree. Carbon dating suggests that both of these could well date from the period of the settlement, so that it becomes a strong probability that the two wooden features were associated with the 1585 colony and were representative of the barrel wells located by the Spanish near the landing place.[6]

It seems unlikely that any remains of the slip, or the creek which White's reference might suggest ran inland from it, will be found. When White landed at the cove in 1590, he found the tree on which were carved the letters CRO on a high dune adjacent to the cove, where the slip may be presumed to have been in 1588. Erosion has so altered this area that, unless artifacts are displaced and come to light on the shore, nothing more is likely to be found.

The trial excavations of the surviving ditch and parapet, which go to make up Fort Raleigh, and the complete excavation of 1950, together with the subsequent restoration of the ditch and parapet, provided a good picture of the enclosure constructed in 1585. In his 1962 report, J. C. Harrington states:

> The ditch profile varied somewhat, averaging 2 to 3 feet wide at the bottom, 3 to 4 feet deep, with both inner and outer slopes ("scarp" and "counterscarp") at an angle of about 45 degrees. The nature of the fill revealed quite clearly that the initial filling of the ditch occurred very soon after the fort was constructed, since the bottom few inches was clean sand ... Higher in the ditch, however, irregular accumulations of humus were encountered, indicating a gradual filling over the years, but with an occasional rapid deposit, presumably from erosion of the parapet ... In most of the cross sections through the fort traces of some remnant of the original parapet was found, usually no more than a few inches in thickness ... The layer of gray sandy humus encountered under the remnants of the fort parapet was first thought to be a foreign material deposited intentionally when the fort was built. Later evidence, however, showed it to be the remains of the original topsoil, peculiar to certain areas in this vicinity and not confined to the fort site. It is very likely the "layer of black, ashy earth" reported by Talcott Williams. In every instance, this peculiar soil stratum terminated a few feet from the top of the original ditch slope, and eventually was shown to mark the approximate extent of the fort's para-

pet. . . . The first step in building the fort was to dig the ditch,
piling up the earth to form the rough parapet. Then, either to
lower the grade within the fort or to secure more material for
the embankment, or both, the earth was removed inside the
fort to a depth of about 6 inches.[7]

Harrington shows that this new level forming a firm surface can be
described as the "parade," and that it marks the original interior
dimensions of the feature. It was inside this that a guard house was
erected, within an area of fifty feet square.

To return to the main feature, Harrington says: "No evidence of
a palisade was found, either in the bottom of the ditch or in the
scarp or counterscarp." There was too little evidence for a palisade
("fraises") to be discerned on the parapet slope. It will be necessary
to return to this question at a later stage.

The 1950 season's work involved the complete excavation of the
ditch and the restoration of the fill down to the undisturbed layer,
and its reerection into a parapet, using only the original material. "In
retrospect," Harrington said in 1984, "building the fort still seems
fully justified. The precise amount of earth necessary for reconstruct-
ing the parapet was known. . . . The width of the parapet was known
quite precisely from archaeological evidence."[8] This brilliant achievement, which enables us to see at least the greater part of the ditch
and parapet as they were originally constructed, with only minimal
construction details derived from contemporary plans of fortifications, was the crowning achievement of the restoration.

The form of the feature that emerged from the excavations was
redrawn by Harrington in 1962 and appears to represent his final
view of the enclosure of 1585.[9]

The disturbance of the ground on the "parade" inside the enclosure was such that no postholes or other firm indications of the
guard house were found, except that there was, in two parts, an
"intrusion over 30 feet long and from 7 to 11 feet wide, extending
some 12 inches into the soil," which was "possibly the depressed
floor of a structure in the center of the fort." But, if this was so, "a
rectangular building oriented at right angles to the main fort entrance could not be longer than the overall length of the two early
intrusions, or roughly 36 feet. Using this length the width would
have to be limited to provide passage space at the corners." He

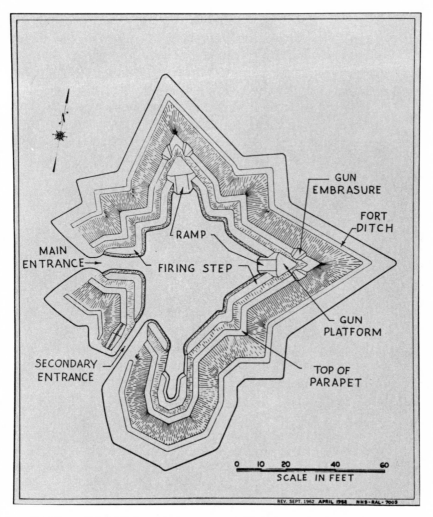

26. Plan of the Earthworks at Fort Raleigh, by J. C. Harrington, 1962.
J. C. Harrington, *Search for the Cittie of Ralegh* (1962), p. 30.
This shows the details of the reconstruction of the ditch and parapet,
undertaken by J. C. Harrington for the National Park Service between 1950
and 1953.

considered that "one long, narrow structure, would probably be better suited to the varied requirements than a shorter wider one. . . . Also that a single long building would be more economical of space than several isolated ones."[10] Such a building, especially if it was tiled rather than thatched, would have provided adequate quarters for a guard of six to ten men, which might be changed on a rota of six, eight, or twelve hours as the sergeant major might lay down. With so little archaeological evidence to go on, Harrington's decision not to attempt any reconstruction of the guard house (corps de gard) was a wise one.

The basic form of the feature followed the European fortification convention which applied either to the triangular, rectangular, or pentangular forts themselves or to the major bastions that projected from their angles. As has been shown and illustrated (fig. 5), the upper bastion in what has been termed the "practice fort" near Cape Rojo in Puerto Rico, follows precisely the pattern of Harrington's model, the four-pointed star, inside which a rectangle has been inserted, thus providing for four major and four minor projections in the parapet. The Puerto Rico example leaves one side open to link up with the main enclosure. The main projections, embrasures, were places where gun platforms would normally be inserted, while the minor projections would enable guards, mounting the firing step, or walking along it, to use them as lookout points. The Fort Raleigh plan follows the Puerto Rico example very closely indeed for the northern and eastern embrasures, which would, we may assume, hold the main armament of the feature. Since saker shot was found by White in 1590, we are probably entitled to assume that gun platforms were constructed for both of these and that the saker, a cannon of only moderate size and weight but all that could be usefully employed in such a fortification, would be mounted probably on a ship carriage. The saker, a gun nine feet long, weighed some 3,500 pounds and used a ball of some five to six pounds. These would be fixed cannon and we would expect that the forest was cleared in front of them to give them an adequate field of fire. The other guns mounted would be mobile on their field carriages; iron fowlers of some 450 pounds weight, probably swivel guns, throwing a ball of only one-pound weight, would be adequate for most circumstances. White found four of them, unused, in 1587.

The ditch and parapet did not follow the Puerto Rico example precisely. The southern projection was both longer and narrower than the model would have prescribed and had a pentangular external outline. Its precise function proved difficult to explain. Possibly it was intended to overlook and protect the "town" or, we might perhaps now say, play some part in a more complex and extended pattern of defenses. The western projection too, most affected by earlier intrusions, also presented problems in interpretation. Harrington's solution seemed the right one at the time he adopted it, namely a substantial bank and ditch in the middle, broken by two entrances, one larger and one very small, on either side.[11] If Fort Raleigh was the only strong point, as was assumed throughout until 1983, then this made sense. If the feature was only one of several strong points, then it is possible that the bank was all that remained of a cavalier, a tall platform, with boarded sides, which would carry a cannon at a level higher than the parapet and so "command the field," as the 1585 suggested plan for the settlement and fortification suggested. But this is wholly theoretical, and for the time being Harrington's solution stands.

Extensive trenching by Harrington in 1950 to the west of Fort Raleigh produced no evidence of habitation sites, and scarcely anything in the way of artifacts, those found being in the ditch fill or inside the enclosure. Parts of the "town" must certainly have been there, much disturbed earlier by the collecting activities of Indians and white visitors between 1586 and 1947. It seems likely that the lack of sensitive testing instruments led him astray into regarding faint traces in the sandy subsoil as tree roots when they may well have been the vestigial remains of postholes of buildings, some of which can now be discerned by remote sensing instruments, even if only minimal signs of disturbance remain. A single trench only was made to the east of the Fort Raleigh area (then privately owned) and the results were negative, so this line of inquiry was not pursued. Yet it has been shown from the documents that the thatched cottages "for the better sort" and "sundry necessary and decent dwelling houses," as well, probably, as barracks, stores, warehouses, a jail, and other erections, were built, as well as a work area set aside for the smith, the metallurgists, and carpenters which would appear to have been essential. Even though the articulation of such a settlement can

be hypothesized to have been present in 1585–86 and we know that
the dwelling houses were extended in number in 1587, nothing
emerged from Harrington's work between 1947 and 1953 to clarify
their location.[12]

Lane seemed to set another problem about the layout of the defenses and the settlement area when he said that in June 1586 Wingina proposed to have set fire to the buildings "as well for them of
the fort, as for us at the town." Did this imply a division between the
fortified and the unfortified areas? It has seemed hitherto to imply
that Fort Raleigh was the fort and the cottages, et cetera, were the
town. It certainly makes it difficult to think of the fort and town as
being comprised within a single enclosing perimeter. But if Fort
Raleigh was not the sole element in the fortification scheme, as now
seems likely, then the possibility must be considered that there was
an enclosed, fortified area and another lightly enclosed residential
zone. Or did Lane mean by his division that those in the fort were
the men on guard duty only?

The fifteen (or possibly eighteen) men left by Sir Richard Grenville
in 1586 to form an interim colony could have possibly found a guard
house or houses sufficient for their needs, as Lane's colonists had no
time to dismantle anything, nor would they have wished to do so if
they had had. Although they had four fowlers, swivel guns weighing
some 450 pounds and throwing a one-pound ball, they would find it
difficult to man the parapet, and it might appear that the early erosion into the ditch, noted by Harrington, began as soon as Lane had
sailed away. To man four guns, or even three with one in reserve,
would require guard duty for most of the men for most of the time.
The slight evidence we have is that to begin with they may well
have abandoned the fort area altogether, and lived in the houses in
the "town." White mentions "the houses where our men carelessly
lived," which indicates that they did not take any systematic precautions against Indian action. When a party of thirty Indians appeared,
they treacherously killed one of the leading Englishmen; once this
was observed "the other Englishmen" fled to the aid of the other
man, but were chased by the intruders so "that the Englishmen were
forced to take [to] the house wherein all their victual and weapons
were," which the Indians promptly set on fire and drove them out.
This is interesting as one of the individual cottages would not have

held the provisions, weapons, and so on for fifteen or eighteen men. Consequently, it is probable that for these purposes, they were using a building corresponding to one of the barrack-like constructions that have been suggested. Occupation of one such major building as a headquarters, and dispersion among the houses for individual residence, appears to be a not unlikely explanation for their way of living so soon and so fatally disrupted by the Indians, though in the event at least thirteen got away. The evidence just quoted is not direct. White got it from Manteo who got it from his own Indian informants, so it is rather tenuous to use with any precision.

White's direct evidence of what he found in 1587 is not unambiguous. He says, "We found the fort razed down" (that is, leveled to the ground), but Harrington found that the parapet of Fort Raleigh had not been destroyed at this time. Only a small amount of fill had entered the ditch by this time, and the rest was to accumulate by slow attrition over the next three centuries or so. If, however, the "fort" was not just Fort Raleigh but a larger fortified area of which it is the only surviving part, then his description becomes intelligible: the defenses—a curtain wall perhaps—had been breached and, in part, flattened. He sets us another problem too when he says they "found all the houses standing unhurt saving the lower rooms of them and also of the fort . . . overgrown with melons of divers sorts." This certainly implies that the cottages and other buildings of the town had more than one story (an attic would be sufficient for the second) and that the sidings had decayed sufficiently to let in enough light to permit squashes to establish themselves on what were evidently earthen floors. But when he is speaking of the fort, his meaning is not at all clear. Is he talking of a single building or of an area? The simple explanation is that he was referring to a single building and that this is the guard room of Fort Raleigh, which had also more than one story, but he can very well have meant "and also of the fort [area]."

There is a possible explanation of why Grenville's men were so unprepared for an attack and that is that they were busy constructing a smaller defensive area for themselves and that it was unfinished, and not even a single cannon mounted in it (as White found all four fowlers abandoned), when the attack came. A modest enclosure of this type at no appreciable distance to the west of Fort Raleigh was first suspected in 1959 and was excavated by Harrington in 1965, who described it in his work *An Outwork at Fort Raleigh* (1966).[13] This consisted of a small strong point, very different from that of Fort Raleigh itself, namely a rectangular structure built of logs laid horizontally on one another. It was about 9 feet wide by 10 feet long and had a base some 1½ feet below the natural level. The logs that formed the defenses walled it in on all four sides and were laid on the ground, revetted on the outside by earth raised from a shallow ditch about 2 feet in depth, the logs being wedged against trees which, in effect, formed posts for their support. Harrington thought of it as a firing pit, but it now appears more probable that it was the base of a flanker, a projection from a different type of fortification than the star fort, one distinguished by rectangular projections, made of timbers laid horizontally rather than vertically and depending on the stoutness of the timbers rather than on the ditch and parapet of the star fort. Such fortifications have been identified in Virginia for the early seventeenth century, though constructed with planked fences rather than logs. When complete, such a fortification could be either a defensive work on which a small cannon could be mounted or a watch tower. From this rectangular feature (now known as Feature 65) an irregular enclosure evidently was being built, but only part of the area could be excavated in 1965 and it may never have been completed, though a further extension was examined in 1983. But the size and nature of this enclosure would suit a small garrison such as that of 1586 rather than the larger fort of 1585. It could, indeed, have gone unnoticed by White in 1587 if it had been stopped at an early stage in construction by the Indian raid. This is only one possible explanation for this feature, which has proved puzzling to all those who have examined the surviving evidence, and it may not be correct, but it seems the best that is so far available.

As noted above, White's own description of ruins of the fort is open to interpretation. He appears to say that both the dwelling houses and also the guard house (or houses) of the bastion (or bastions) were all intact, even though they had lost enough of the mat, light sheathing, wattle and daub, planking, or whatever was used for their sidings to let in enough light to permit squash to grow. We can accept that part of his statement which refers to the dwelling houses and use it as evidence that they had an attic floor. But it is difficult to accept if for the "fort," since the guard room (or rooms) must have been more soundly constructed than to allow of their deterioration in such a short time. He *may* refer to other buildings inside a fort enclosure, the possibility of the existence of which will be discussed in some detail below.

White appears to have done little during his short stay on Roanoke Island in 1587. He makes no more mention of the enclosure or its main defenses in any way. He merely says that because Lane's "sundry necessary and decent dwelling houses" were intact, that "the same day order was given that every man should be employed for the repairing of those houses which we found standing, and also to make new "Cottages" [the first time the word is used] for such as should need." Thus we have the town being rehabilitated and extended. We cannot tell, unless and until the pattern of settlement laid down in 1585 is uncovered, how the new "cottages" were laid out in relation to the older "houses." We can assume legitimately that the family groups would have been allotted a house each and that many of the other dwellings would be occupied by one or more men, or unattached women and children, but again the problem of the scale of accommodation to be provided arises. There were nearly 120 people to fit in. At even four people to a house this meant about 25 houses, or perhaps a few more than that if they were in pairs, and it is very doubtful whether there were that many. And four to a house measuring 16 feet by 12 feet in plan, with an attic, would mean some severe overcrowding, which not all the colonists would have been used to, or prepared to tolerate for long, even if they could have slept in the open from August to September or October (mosquitoes permitting). We are left then with the probability that some larger buildings were intact, that is, one or two of the barrack-type buildings that have been proposed. If forty to eighty of the men could have been thus accommodated, then the building of many new cottages would not have been necessary. The only other thing that can be said is that no livestock had been acquired in the Caribbean unless White is misleading us about the voyage. This does not, as has already been suggested, entirely eliminate the possibility that some livestock had been brought from England. Failure to acquire sufficient livestock in the Caribbean, which White blamed on Simon Fernandes, could have imposed severe handicaps on the group of families who were to make up the colony.

John White's final contribution to the historical archaeology of the site was his well-known and already cited description of 1590: "we found the houses taken down and the place very strongly enclosed with a high 'palisado' of great trees, with curtains and flankers very fort-like." The bark was stripped from "one of the chief trees or posts at the right side of the entrance" and the letters CROATOAN carved on it. Inside the palisade they found the iron, fowlers, saker shot, and other heavy debris and, later, "in the end of an old trench made two [five?] years since by Amadas" they found the chests which the colonists had buried there until they were rooted out by the Indians.

The removal of the houses would be natural if a party was to stay on the island temporarily after the main body had departed. They would know that the houses had been a death trap for Grenville's men and their removal would have reduced the number of places from which Indians could infiltrate, and would give them a clear field of fire. We might also suggest again that before the main body left the island they would take from the houses any doors, hinges, locks, window frames, and suchlike that were portable and that would be useful on their new site.

There was evidently no sign that the enclosure had been recently occupied or that the guns found were mounted—the implication is that they were not and were simply lying with the heavy debris. Indeed the absence of the remains of any dwellings—if they were there, he certainly would have remarked on them—is itself a puzzle. One possible suggestion is that after the Spanish appeared in 1588, the remaining colonists dismantled whatever houses were being used and kept the enclosure merely as a shelter-zone for occasional visits to the island from Croatoan.

The enclosure found by White remains a mystery. Clearly the indication which stated that a party of colonists was at Croatoan was inscribed on a vertical post formed by a tree trunk, from which a part of the bark had been scraped off. His description of the palisade as "high" clearly suggests that the posts were vertical, not horizontal, his "curtains" were the walls or ramparts connecting up a system of bastions, while his "flankers" were projecting features (of which "bastions" is usually a synonym) in that system, the whole making up a complete fortification comparable with Fort Raleigh, but, one would assume from his description, a larger one. Phillip Evans has suggested that the "outwork" (Feature 65), already described, could have been White's enclosure.[14] Its small size seems to preclude this possibility, unless White is giving a wholly exaggerated description of its nature, while the apparently unfinished character of the other feature would seem to operate against this assumption. It cannot be entirely ruled out that the smaller enclosure has lost part of its defenses in the course of time, but its spatial relationship to Fort Raleigh would appear to rule out any possibility that it was much larger than the area so far excavated indicates. We must admit too that White may indeed have exaggerated, while the method of construction—horizontal log walling instead of vertical posts—is not necessarily wholly at variance with White's description, though it is not the most likely one. But it must be stressed that, in all probability, White's enclosure has not been found, nor do we know where it was located, near, perhaps, but not on the old settlement site.

The excavations of 1947–1953 and 1965 have to be taken into account in any general treatment of the history of the Roanoke colonies such as this. They are, however, part of a continuing process of investigation and discovery which may in the end add much more than they have done so far as our knowledge and understanding of the structures created in the relevant years increase. New documents could conceivably be found, but the chances of this occurring appear slight. The opportunities for further discoveries by archaeological exploration are much brighter and have given encouraging signs of what they may in the end reveal. In any event, the story of the colonies is a continuing process of discovery and interpretation, to which an end is not in sight.

Objects used by colonists on other sites have added much to the understanding of their way of life, but in the case of the Roanoke colonies the aid they provide is limited. Artifacts have been found within the fort and settlement area, but they are relatively few in number and kind considering that 108 men lived there in 1585–86 for ten months, fifteen or eighteen more for several months in 1586, and well over 100 persons in 1587 for an indefinite period (but probably only a short time for most of them, though a few may have remained longer and later have paid brief visits). White's brief search for survivors in 1590 would not have left any artifacts to speak of.

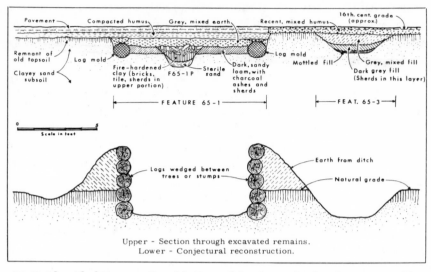

27. Unidentified Feature, Possibly Part of the Original Palisade, Excavated by
J. C. Harrington in 1965.
From An Outwork at Fort Raleigh (1966; used with permission of the author and
Eastern National Park and Monument Association).

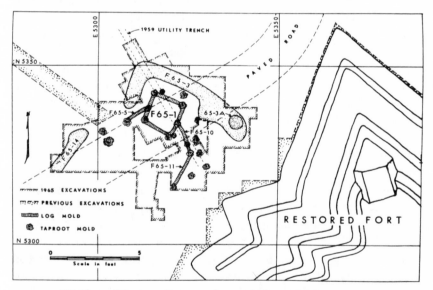

28. Plan of Feature Excavated in 1965 by J. C. Harrington.
From An Outwork at Fort Raleigh (1966; used with permission of the author and
Eastern National Park and Monument Association).

The most helpful way to categorize the more interesting of the artifacts that have been found would appear to be by function. Only a selection of the more easily identifiable objects need be covered, as some materials—in particular, fragments of iron—cannot be usefully assigned to any category, whereas too detailed a list of fragmentary objects would be tedious. As far as function is concerned, the most important objects were made of brick and tile. When the ditch fill was excavated, "one brick fragment and one small piece of flat roofing tile" were discovered. It was only when the strong point and enclosure were found in 1959 and excavated in 1965 that bricks and tile were observed in any quantity. Inside it, after it was recognized as a feature forming part of a contemporary construction, was found an Indian fire pit, in which brick and tile fragments were evidently salvaged from the site to support the pointed Indian cooking vessels and jumbled together. To quote Harrington's 1966 report:[15]

> Four whole bricks were recovered and pieces from two or three others that were whole when placed in the firepit, but, at the time of restoration too badly broken to be restored. There were enough isolated pieces to have made another full dozen or so bricks.... In addition there were about twenty that had been altered in shape prior to having been placed in the firepit. These ... had been ground down or abraded on one or more surfaces.

This was a major discovery. What was also important, and unexpected, was that the soft, friable bricks had been made by hand in sanded wooden molds, but not all were symmetrical or complete. A careful analysis revealed that they had been made on the island from local sand and clay, neither of which was very suitable, and this was reflected in their poor quality and finish. They provided clear evidence that one activity of the colonists, almost certainly of the 1585–86 group, was brickmaking. Unless a great many more are found, it can only be concluded that they were not manufactured in large quantity. But nineteenth century reports, as noted already, indicate that brick fragments were lying around to be picked up on the surface before any excavation had taken place. They could have been used as bases for interior fireplaces: there is likely to have been one inside each guard house and others in some of the houses. They also would have been needed in outdoor cookhouses. The Indians' sub-

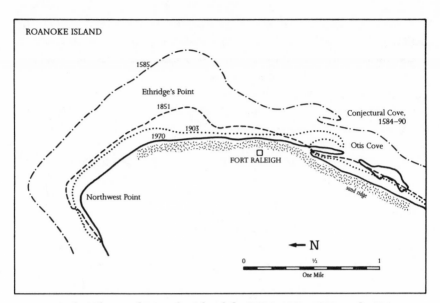

29. Shorelines of Roanoke Island for 1585, 1851, 1903, and 1970.
After R. Dolan and K. Bosserman, "Shoreline Erosion and the Lost Colony,"
Annals of the Association of American Geographers 62 (September 1972): 425.
Erosion may not have been so drastic as is depicted here.

sequent use of the bricks prevented the observation of any evidence of their earlier use in association with fire. It is unlikely that they were used for chimneys, except perhaps as bases for wood and clay chimney structures, if such were present. No mortar could be identified on the bricks found; thus, it is not easy to conclude that these particular bricks were cemented together at any stage (for a hearth they need not have been, but for a chimney breast they would need to have been held together by mortar). The abraded bricks had evidently been used in a cookhouse or armory to sharpen metal blades.

Equally, or more, significant was the presence in the pit of roofing tiles.[16] Only two fragments had previously been found, one at the bottom of the fort ditch: now "Enough fragments were recovered to account for about three whole tiles, but undoubtedly more than that number are represented." Although a few tiles do not make a roof covering they are very suggestive that some structure had a tiled roof.

If a guess is legitimate, it would be likely to be the guard house, but this is still beyond the bounds of probability. The tiles were made of "hard and dense" material, of uniform texture, of different clay, "and with much greater skill." Harrington has been unwilling to comment on their possible origin, but their transport from England, where they could be used—as bricks often were—for ballast, seems not unlikely. However, many habitation sites would need to be found before any realistic estimate of quantities could be made.

Other construction materials included a group of wrought iron spikes discovered inside the parapet of Fort Raleigh "mostly in a limited area, suggesting that they had been left there in a pile or in a container."[17] It seems likely that some workman put them down and forgot them. This group of nine in all, together with isolated specimens found elsewhere and some fragments of nails, point to the construction of the guard house. Other remnants of iron objects may also have been associated with construction as, undoubtedly, were the fragment of a hinge and an iron bar about one foot long. Found in the bottom of the fort ditch was a rusted carpenter's auger, which would have been used in preparing timber for construction. A hand ax, picked up many years before and retained in a single family for a long period (it is now in the North Carolina Collection), is regarded as authentic and is the best iron object so far associated with the site.

Domestic articles did not offer a very wide range. The most significant were numerous fragments of Spanish olive jars, "used for transporting and storing liquids, such as wine and oil, although very possibly [in the absence of a well] they were used at the fort as water containers"; one large shard indicated a diameter of over one foot.[18] Two fragments of majolica ware, probably forming small parts of a single apothecary jar, were recovered. A surprising feature was the absence of identifiable pieces of English-made pottery, the most frequent artifacts found on all colonial sites. Apparently, what debris that lay about the Fort Raleigh area was gradually removed by visitors, but there still remains in nearby areas a substantial scatter of this material and even major concentrations. However, in the strong point, substantial fragments—enough to make a partial restoration possible—were recovered of a ceramic bottle or costrel, originally having a wickerwork cover and used, like the olive jars, to store and transport liquids. This appears to have been French in origin.

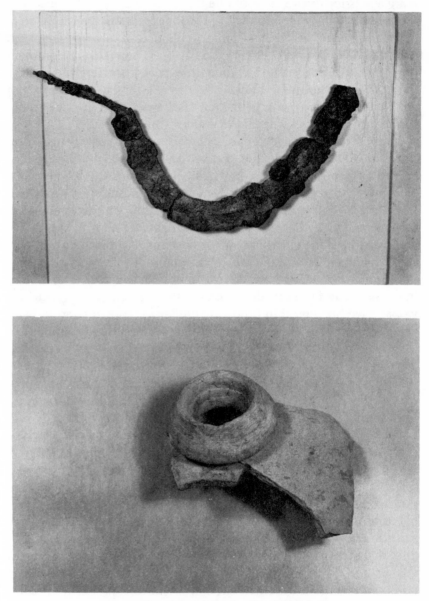

30. Artifacts Found on the Fort Raleigh Site.
(a) Wrought Iron Sickle; (b) Fragment of Spanish Olive Jar.
J. C. Harrington, *Search for the Cittie of Ralegh* (1962), pp. 18, 22.

Substantial evidence of agricultural activity rests so far on only one wrought-iron sickle, originally twenty-two inches long. It was lost early, as it was found near the bottom of the fort ditch, the fragments of which have been reintegrated into a substantially complete specimen. Other iron fragments at the bottom of the ditch may have been part of another sickle.

The trade objects found were very few but interesting. The most important were three casting counters, made by Hans Schultes in Nurnberg between 1550 and 1575 from a cheap alloy known as latten. These little disks were used for manual reckoning, but as they are pierced they were evidently threaded on strings as ornaments for the Indians (they are known from other early colonial sites and one was even found at an Indian site near Cape Hatteras). A single glass bead, apparently from the ditch fill, would appear to represent another constituent in the trade with the Indians in "trifles," on which Harriot remarks. But much more would need to be discovered before any conclusions about commerce could be drawn.

The most interesting group of objects is associable with the scientific, principally metallurgical, work carried on at the settlement. A single balance weight indicates that small objects or small quantities were weighed. These were normally used by apothecaries but may have been involved in the work of either Thomas Harriot or the metallurgist Joachim Ganz. Tiny fragments of a crucible, unused, show that experiments in metallurgy were conducted.[19] The discovery of a used crucible would make more clear what metals were being tested. One of these was clearly copper, "two chunks of surface-pitted copper ... pure copper, of a rough spongy appearance," weighing, respectively, 21½ and 12 ounces. Enough information emerged from a preliminary test to show that the metal had been smelted. Unfortunately the specimens were lost by a federal agency before detailed analysis had been done to distinguish whether they were European or Native American. However, there seems little doubt that they were smelted on Roanoke Island and that Ganz had a furnace capable of reaching the almost 2,000 degrees Fahrenheit necessary to melt copper. It is likely that they were of native origin as the settlers made every effort to locate copper in Indian hands and to search (unsuccessfully) for it in the field. An isolated pit, containing unused charcoal, may have been associated with the furnace.

Before 1983 the total number of identifiable objects excavated from the site was disappointingly small. The discovery in that year, in the vicinity of the 1965 feature, of thirty-eight ceramic fragments, which have still to be fitted into a general analysis, has begun to alter this situation. They include English earthenware, Rhenish stoneware, and Spanish majolica (John E. Ehrenhard, Gregory L. Komara, *Archaeological Investigations at Fort Raleigh National Historic Site, Season 2, 1983* [Southeast Archaeological Center, National Park Service, Tallahassee, Fla., Feb. 1984], pp. 15–21). They suggest strongly that future archaeological exploration can add substantially to what is known about the conditions of living on Roanoke Island between 1584 and 1587.

The relationship of the Indian village site which Barlowe saw in 1584, and which subsequently appeared in the 1590 engraving of the arrival of the Englishmen, has been difficult to determine on account of the substantial erosion of the northern shores of Roanoke Island. When the National Park Service took over the Fort Raleigh National Historic Site, initial surveys revealed fragments of Indian pottery on the eroded foreshore of Northwest Point, and it has hitherto been assumed that these were all that remained of the otherwise completely eroded village of 1584. Recent investigations by Professor David S. Phelps for America's Four Hundreth Anniversary Committee[20] have revealed that traces of Indian occupation at Northwest Point can still be found, but belong to a much earlier phase of occupation than the sixteenth century. This makes it probable that the site of the village abandoned by Wingina in 1586 still lies buried within the National Park Service area. In 1965 Harrington investigated a "couple of skeletons" from the eroded bank near the Dough family cemetery some way to the east (just west of the Elizabethan Gardens), and these were sent to the Smithsonian Institution. Phelps's researches show that these were the remains of an ossuary, or mass burial, of the type that is typical of the Carolinian Algonquians of the time (pp. 190–93), and point to the probable existence of the village site nearby. He has thus been able to indicate approximately the position of the village in relation to the English settlement of 1585 (which he places at .57 mile from the ossuary to Fort Raleigh). This is most valuable new information. It indicates that the settlers in the early days of the colony were physically very close to the Indians and, while relations remained good, must have been able to mix freely with them, thus, among other things, facilitating the work of Harriot and White in their survey. This being so, it is not surprising that, when relations became strained in the spring of 1586, Wingina should have removed his people from this village to the nearby mainland.

Anything that can be said about the new series of sensings and excavations which began in 1982 must remain entirely tentative and subject to revision. Since it may take a decade to investigate the site and surroundings of Fort Raleigh fully, it seems worthwhile to give some tentative results. There is available the final report of the 1982 work, namely the work by Ehrenhard, Athens, and Komara cited above. This demonstrates how remote sensing devices were used—together with small test excavations—in the area to the west and southwest of Fort Raleigh. This time, as distinct from the experiences of 1950, some positive indications of the settlement site were obtained, though no colonial artifacts were found, and the indications of possible building sites were sufficiently faint and imprecise as to make deductions from the findings very provisional. However, sufficient indications of a group of house sites (or what are considered to be house sites) were discovered.

The report stated that

A pattern of six anomalies occurred in two parallels of three anomalies each oriented north and south due west of the fort entrance. They are all approximately 4 by 9 meters in dimension and are spaced approximately 17 meters apart. An interesting and somewhat subtle linear pattern bisects the 6 features into two groups. This arrangement would be representative of up to six structures occurring in two parallel lines with a "road" leading to them from the fort entrance. Such a design would be consistent with contemporary town plans.[21]

To translate this scientific and cautious description into terms of part of the historic settlement is not only difficult but risky. However, it could appear that this discovery is of one part of the "town" making up six structures of some 13 feet by 29 feet each (which would fit in with the suggested size of the double "houses" of the basic type suggested on p. 80 above). This would give us a maximum of 12 cottages, laid out on an avenue leading directly toward the entrance to Fort Raleigh. At most, 12 of the smallest cottages would not go far in providing accommodation for 108 men, or perhaps only 6 cottages of the "better sort," but it marks a notable beginning in the placing and identification of the 1585 settlement and begins the process of establishing its articulation. In the 1983 excavations a substantial "non-defensive" structure, 16 feet by 32 feet, was identified, within a palisaded enclosure, but without artifacts. This could well have been the location of one of the utility buildings (barracks, stores, warehouses, and so forth), which it has been proposed were essential to the establishment of the 1585 colony, but it may well prove to be other when it has been fully examined.

The 1983 season was carried out in two stages, one to the west and southwest of Fort Raleigh and the second in the unexplored area to the east and southeast. This last established that there were many "anomalies" to be explored in this area, and very tentatively indicated that the settlement might have extended into it. The discovery by William P. Athens of "a major anomaly" (*Resistivity Investigations at Fort Raleigh National Historic Site* [Florida: Southeastern Archaeological Center, Tallahassee, 1984]) some 360 feet southeast of Fort Raleigh revealed the outlines of a feature comparable in size, and possibly in nature, to Fort Raleigh. The series of seven features disclosed could represent the bastion wall (though the surrounding ditch would have silted up) in a form very similar to that of Fort Raleigh. Two further outlines could represent buildings beside what could be the main entrance to a bastion. Conclusions on the nature of this feature must inevitably be very tentative, but it now appears that existing views about the nature of the 1585 settlement may have to be substantially revised.

There now appear to be three possible but differing layouts for the 1585 settlement and its defenses.

The first (fig. 31) is the conventional one, with Fort Raleigh as the sole major defensive work, but with the "town" laid out to the west of it. This view has been strengthened by the work of the 1982 season, when indications of some buildings were discovered near Fort Raleigh and in places where they had long been expected but never found. Had the excavations continued only within the area to the west of Fort Raleigh, that explanation would appear to have been

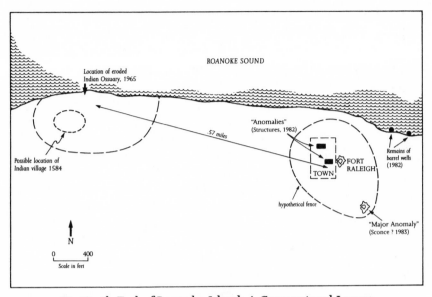

31. North End of Roanoke Island: A Conventional Layout
with New Additions.
Compiled by D. B. Quinn, with information from David S. Phelps
and Phillip Evans.

consolidated. The supposition that some fence or light enclosure surrounded the "town" is still a legitimate one, but it is not very likely that evidence will be found to establish or deny this proposal. But if this remains the standard picture, it cannot account for indications of further structures found to the east and southeast of Fort Raleigh in 1983, though the "major anomaly" could prove to be an outlying sconce, which, as we have seen, Lane considered useful, or, alternatively, a detached magazine.

The second alternative (fig. 32A) is that the whole settlement was enclosed by a multiangular fortification of which Fort Raleigh is one bastion and the new "major anomaly" of 1983 is another. The distance between these is some 625 feet and this could provide a measure of the other sides of the fort. It may be suggested that this could have been a pentangle. It may be remembered that in the 1585 plan for a fort the author stated: "I would have it a pentangle in this

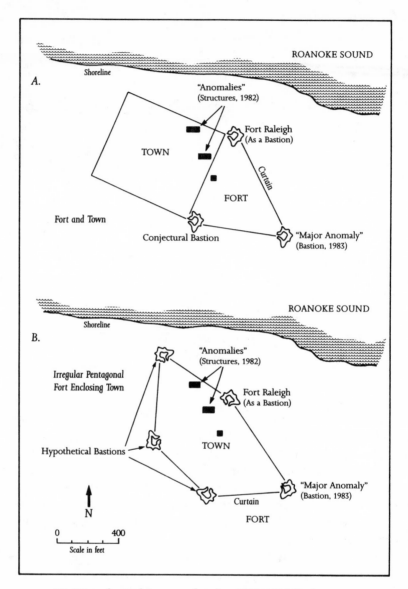

32. Hypothetical Layouts for the 1585–1586 Settlement.
Compiled by D. B. Quinn. (a) shows the possible combination of a
triangular Fort and enclosed Town; (b) shows the whole settlement
enclosed in an irregular pentagonal Fort.

manner, with five large bulwarks, the casemates of the bulwarks large and open, with a way out of the bulwarke and another into the street." This would demand very drastic changes in the whole conception of the fort, but the indications about the bulwark would fit what is known of Fort Raleigh. However, the layout of the structures to the west of Fort Raleigh would tend to make it irregular in shape, and an irregular pentangle has been suggested as the possible layout. While this would be a wholly unexpected conclusion, the possibility seems just worthwhile suggesting. It would solve a number of problems about the settlement, even if it would create many more.

The third alternative (fig. 32B) is that the fort was a triangular one, with three sides, 360 feet a side, of which Fort Raleigh is the bastion at the northwest, and the new "major anomaly" that to the southeast, with a hitherto undiscovered third bastion somewhat to the southwest of Fort Raleigh. This would provide an enclosed fortified area, not too large to defend, but one in which all the utility buildings could be accommodated safely. On the west the town would have been laid out in a systematic way. While a rectangular surrounding fence has been suggested, this might have taken any shape, but it would need to be elaborate or primarily for defense. The people from the cottages and houses could quickly take shelter in the fort and the guns from two of the bastions would cover the town in the event of a major attack. The advantage of this suggested plan is that it clearly meets the distinction that Lane made between the "fort" and the "town" and that it provides shelter for the whole colony in time of need, which Fort Raleigh could not do. If there is to be major change in what we have hitherto known of the 1585–86 settlement, this seems the least unlikely alternative. But it remains a purely hypothetical one in 1984.

It would be unfortunate to end a book which is intended to bring to life, or as nearly as an historian can bring to life, the men and women who first came to North Carolina in the years 1585 to 1587, with a somewhat arid series of speculations about where and under what conditions these people lived. The people were, as always in history, more important than the material surroundings in which they found themselves. We do, fortunately, know something about a few of those people, though far less than we would like to know, but it is they who give the attempted settlements their enduring value. It is their initiative and courage, their merits and defects, their successes and mistakes, which make the story worth telling, and which make the whole series of episodes one which is an enduring part of American—and British—history.

The Past and the Future

The aspect of novelty is what the reader carries away from the story of the Roanoke voyages. For England and Englishmen they were the first attempt to carry out overseas settlement across the Atlantic. A small number of intelligent, farsighted, and grasping persons had planned such colonies on paper over the decade before they were attempted. Over the previous two centuries, England's colonial activity had been confined to Europe. The half-century's colonization of Normandy in the fifteenth century had been followed by plans to recolonize Ireland from about 1520 onward, but tentative efforts to put those plans into effect after 1550 had met with little success.

North America was different. Fisheries in Newfoundland were summer affairs, not involving the permanent location of people overseas. Few English ships had systematically traversed the eastern shores of North America. Pirates had followed the route through the Caribbean by way of the Canaries current. They had come home on the Gulf Stream, scarcely sighting North American shores. But for transporting colonists this was the route to follow, even if it involved a diversion to coastwise sailing. Ships for effective colonization were laden with supplies and colonists. Their passengers were landsmen (and women) who had to be given luxuries and rest in the unoccupied islands of the Caribbean. The combination of piracy (legitimized from 1585 as privateering) with the conveyance of colonists, especially women, was not satisfactory, even if privateering provided the spice of conquest and the return of spoil which made colonizing voyages more attractive to investors than they might otherwise have been. At the least, it helped to ruin the chances of the very promising expedition of 1587.

In short term, the Roanoke colonies were primarily a matter for men and women in England. Initiatives came from there as well as the money to mount expeditions and maintain them. So did the supply of colonists, paid servants of the promoters or volunteers. The paper empire that men like the Richard Hakluyts built in North America had to be tested by experience and shown to be largely, but not wholly, impracticable. Yet once experiment began and experience had been gained—even if there had been more failures than successes—the process could go forward. The basic pressures, the sense of overpopulation, for example, persisted even after population growth had virtually ceased by 1630. The sense that exotic southern products could be grown by Englishmen for profit was not dispelled by the failures of the Roanoke colonists to establish that they could; the Jamestown colonists had to experiment for over a decade before they discovered one, the unlikely tobacco, which did prove a saver. The sending of hired men was taken from 1585 to the 1607–16 experiments in Virginia. The concept that free men and women could make an autonomous future for themselves in North America was first demonstrated by John White in 1587, not by the Pilgrims of 1620. What White's colony had too, and the Pilgrims did not, was the sense that the self-perpetuating community could fit into and alongside the Native American polity rather than displace it. Nor did this have a place in the Virginia Company's exploits in Virginia.

The experience of the Roanoke voyages did reveal significant weaknesses in the English command of the Atlantic. For each successful voyage there was one or more that faltered or failed. The long-term failure of the colonies is clearly shown to have been due more to the ineffectiveness of the organization and conduct of the expeditions than to the breakdown of the colonies themselves. Even the 1585 voyage was robbed of much of its effectiveness by weather, insubordination, and inefficient navigation. The failures of the supply ship and of Sir Richard Grenville in 1586 to keep to anything like an agreed timetable had more to do with the ending of the colony than did any divisions among the colonists themselves or between them and the Indians. Had Sir Francis Drake been able to anchor in a secure harbor, as no doubt he expected to be able to do, much of the effect of the storm that damaged his fleet would have been mitigated. The tale of ineffectiveness at sea extends right through the voyage of 1587, the attempted voyage of 1588, and the 1590 visit. Not that natural forces could be eliminated but they could be manipulated by care and, it should be admitted, luck. A combination of great skill and considerable good fortune made Christopher Newport's three voyages between 1606 and 1608 models of planning and performance. In the twenty years after White's failure, the mastery of the Atlantic had gone on apace even if it was always far from complete.

The Roanoke colonists and their planners were unable to achieve the ends they set for themselves. Although a small party could coast the southern part of Chesapeake Bay and penetrate the interior to the south of it in 1585–86, successive attempts to return there by sea were frustrated by inefficiency. The Lost Colonists were left to disappear without any effective attempt to find them for nearly twenty years. This fact (combined with Sir Walter Ralegh's self-interest) demonstrated that neither the will nor the means to explore further were present until prestige factors came into play after the Spanish war ended. The Roanoke experiments, however, did provide at least some inkling of the necessity for long-term and substantial deployment of capital resources if colonization was to be effectively attempted, but it should not have taken twenty years for this to sink in.

War, it is true, frustrated expeditions by both England and Spain that would have made the Chesapeake a wartime base for one power or the other. But after 1590, down to the Treaty of London in 1604, either side should have been able to carry out some part of its plans without affecting its war effort significantly, even if in the years before 1590 the exploitation of North America for naval purposes was not feasible. Lassitude overtook Spanish plans. English attention was diverted by Dutch successes in the East, and they moved to emulate them there rather than intervene before 1607 in North America.

There were positive results, too, from the Roanoke voyages. The maintenance of more than a hundred men for over ten months on Roanoke Island in 1585–86 indicated that Englishmen could live in North America, even if the experience of the early Jamestown colonists suggested the contrary. The introduction of European epidemic diseases by the same Roanoke colonists was not regarded as significant. If it was regarded at all it would have been thought to have been a good thing, a means of clearing the original occupants from soil it was thought they did not effectively exploit. There was little

awareness of the complications of introducing a progressive intrusive
series of colonies into a closed Native American society, every inch
of whose soil was part of the ideological property of its inhabitants.
Indians, if they would not move, might have to be removed. Or they
might, in Thomas Harriot's view, be introduced to the benefits of
European civilization and religion and remain in substantial parts of
their own territory, even if full assimilation was rarely contemplated.
The Roanoke voyages initiated for the English the intrusion that in
the relatively short run was to remove most of the eastern Indians by
death or their relegation to scarcely viable reservations inside their
former territories. There were cultural exchanges both in 1584–87
and after 1607. The Indians were to master the use of metal tools and
weapons; the English were to learn how to cultivate corn and other
Indian horticultural novelties. But neither exchanged enough of each
other's cultural heritage to make the exchange a radical, or, from the
Indian perspective, a fair one. The idealistic view, as it may be regarded, of John White was scarcely to be implemented.

The most enduring influence of the Roanoke voyages was the
literature they left behind. Richard Hakluyt felt so keenly that colonization in North America was the most appropriate and important
role for England that he recorded the voyages in print even before
White had made his tragic last crossing in 1590. The first edition of
the great collection of voyages and travels which he made, The principall navigations of the English nation, published at the end of 1589 or early
in 1590, contained Arthur Barlowe's narrative of 1584 and the accounts of the journal writer of the Tiger for the 1585 voyage, with a
letter from Ralph Lane recording the arrival at Port Ferdinando and
his first impression of the new land. For the colony of 1585–86
Hakluyt gave us Lane's brief description of the land and his long
explanation and apology for his actions. To these Hakluyt was able to
add the first important small book on North America written in
English—Harriot's Briefe and true report—which had already, by its publication in 1588, provided much valuable material on what was done
in the colony, but which reached a wider public when it was combined with the other materials in 1589. He could not find a full
account of Grenville's voyage in 1586 and so had to make up a rather
sketchy one himself, as he had been in Paris at the time when
Grenville returned and somehow failed to pin him or anyone else

down to give him details of what had happened, though he got the outline well enough. For 1587 he already had White's long and, in parts, very eloquent journal of the voyage outward with the second colony and of his own enforced return. To this he added the tragic story of the attempted voyage of 1588, when something of the fury of the war at sea was transmitted to his readers. He could add, last of all, the formal document by which Hakluyt showed himself to be a member of the supporting syndicate, but he does not tell why no expedition sailed to the rescue of the colonists in the year 1589 when he was completing his collection. This body of materials threw a brilliant but flickering and incomplete light for us on the Roanoke colonies but gave hundreds of people at the time the opportunity to read about them in some detail—we may estimate that the edition of 1589 numbered about 1,000 copies, whereas not more than 200 to 300 copies of Harriot's 1588 book would have been issued.

The opportunity for a still wider circulation of the materials on the Roanoke colony came when Theodor de Bry visited London in 1587 and Hakluyt was able to show him Harriot's little book, then, we think, in manuscript, and some examples of John White's drawings. De Bry, who was developing his engraving and printing business in Frankfurt am Main, was greatly attracted by this material and later, probably late in 1588, on a subsequent visit, returned to Germany with four items. These were a copy of *A briefe and true report*, at least twenty-four drawings by John White, probably enlarged versions of the sketches he had made in America and that he was now trans-forming into finished drawings, Harriot's notes on these drawings in Latin (the learned language into which he knew his little book was to be translated), and, finally, Hakluyt's own English translations of these notes. Out of these, and with the assistance of several learned translators, Theodor de Bry was able to issue the first part of *America* at Frankfurt in 1590. His desire to give the widest possible circulation to the events of 1585–86 in the first colony led him to make the very unusual experiment of issuing the text in four languages, Harriot in the original English and Hakluyt's translations of his notes on the engravings but with the engravings strikingly reproduced for all edu-cated Europeans to see. The edition in Latin had a fine translation of Harriot's book together with his own Latin notes. The French and German editions were provided with good translations of both Harriot's text and his notes. This fourfold publication had four different impressions of copperplate engravings of White's drawings to go with them.

These slim and elegant folio volumes brought the Roanoke voyages, or at least the work of Harriot and White on the first colony, into the homes and libraries of educated men throughout Europe even before White had failed to find his colony in 1590. It is thought that the Latin edition was the most successful of the four printings, as de Bry, and after him his sons, continued to produce reissues of it well into the seventeenth century. The German edition also seems to have done well and was reissued. On the other hand, it is thought that much smaller editions in English and French were produced because the potential market was more limited, but London booksellers would have had them to sell by the end of 1590 or 1591 at the latest, and apparently disposed of a certain number of copies at a time when it would be competing with Hakluyt's more general, if unillustrated, collection of English voyages and travels. In this way the story of the colony of 1585–86 became one of the best-known travel books of the period throughout western Europe. It was known, it is true, not so much for the deeds of Englishmen, as for the information it conveyed about North America. Harriot's little book was the first treatise that was at all scientific and comprehensive, but even more it became known for the lively and dramatic pictures of the Indians derived from White's drawings. If, to our eyes, these Indians look Europeanized, this did not detract from their value until they were subjected to critical scrutiny in the twentieth century. For generations engravers seeking illustrations for travel books about America, North or even South, lazily went to de Bry and copied and modified for their own purposes the engravings that came in the first place from Roanoke Island and its surrounding area. In this way England, and the first colony, contributed a vitally important chapter to Europe's knowledge of North America.

Richard Hakluyt did not forget the Roanoke voyages during the dark decade between 1590 and 1600. He revised and enlarged his collection and, in the prefaces to his second edition in three volumes which appeared between 1598 and 1600, he urged Sir Robert Cecil to resume the colonizing ventures that had begun so excitingly but ended so obscurely in the years 1584–90. The third volume of his *Principal navigations, voyages, traffiques and discoveries of the English nation,* in 1600 reprinted the basic narratives of the 1589 edition, lacking only the abortive voyage of 1588 and the equally abortive agreement of 1589 by which he and others had agreed to assist in the relief of White's colonists. He was able to obtain from White in February 1593 (or 1594) a letter from his residence in Ireland in which White expressed, as has been shown, his regret that he had to desert the colonists after all his efforts, but enclosing his narrative of the 1590 voyage with its poignant passage on the final empty search for the colony on Roanoke Island in 1590. He also expressed his belief that the colony remained with Manteo at Croatoan, though, as it has been shown, Hakluyt was cautious about expressing a firm opinion on whether it still existed in 1600.

Although *The principal navigations* in this edition was a book in three large folio volumes, and not one for poor men or men who did not set considerable store by books, there is good reason to believe that, when some adjustments were made to the first and second volumes in 1599, extra copies were printed over and above the standard printing of 1,000 copies so that there may possibly have been as many as 1,500 sets circulating in England during the reign of James I. Many of these were getting dusty in library cupboards and chests but others were being read and used. The "Book of Voyages" was taken on expeditions to many parts of the world including North America. Most important of all, it was the basis on which men began to build their expectations and hopes for new colonies in the early years of the seventeenth century, and it played an important part in guiding or suggesting the lines of settlement for the two divisions of the Virginia Company: that of London for South Virginia (essentially the Chesapeake, the objective of the years 1586–90) and of Plymouth for North Virginia, Sir Humphrey Gilbert's Norumbega. The beliefs that Mediterranean produce could be grown in Virginia and that the interior contained extensive mineral resources were carried over from the earlier ventures, but these were not to produce very happy results until tobacco, after many preliminary setbacks and failures, was found to provide a salable and profitable crop. The Roanoke voyages thus form the essential background for the activities of the London division of the company, the Virginia Company after the failure of the Plymouth division by 1609 to establish a colony in what was soon to be known as New England.

The influence of the accounts of the Roanoke colonies did not end here. Captain John Smith, when he was making his adventurous and informative explorations of Chesapeake Bay in 1608, consciously took his cues from Harriot and White. Not that he could draw, or did draw, Indians, their occupations, or their villages, but the way he collected information and assembled a conspectus of knowledge as he proceeded on his travels was based on Harriot and White, especially in the de Bry edition, though he probably had *The principal navigations* to refer to as well at his Jamestown base. His collection of materials on the Indian peoples, and his surveys of natural resources—animal and vegetable as well as mineral—owed much to Harriot's example. In many respects Smith was the more complete (though, of course, we have only Harriot's brief 1588 summary of his much more extensive collections), and he was practical and specific, if not as scientific in his approach. In his map, too, he was influenced by the published version of the White-Harriot map; by giving a great deal of additional information on the area he had explored and the territories beyond, of which he had heard from the Indians, it is clear he was attempting to outdo White's map. This acceptance of so much from the reports on the first colony of 1585–86 indicates that the influence of the first Roanoke survey was substantial. Smith even revived, with a new nomenclature, "Old Virginia" as a memorial to the colonies in his *Generall historie of Virginia* in 1624.

William Strachey, commissioned, as it is believed, to compile a full history of the early attempts to settle Virginia from 1607 onward, was almost certainly supplied with a copy of an early version of Smith's report. He departed from it to make his own descriptions and analyses of Indian life and did so in a rather more sophisticated, if less practical, way than Smith. When it came to using Smith's observations on fish, birds, animals, plants, and so on he contented himself with adding his own subsidiary observations to a number of Smith's items, though in many places virtually copying Smith's version word for word. Strachey, owing to the shipwreck on Bermuda in 1609 and to the many problems that beset him during his term (just over a year) as secretary of the colony in 1610–11, was hampered in his work. If Smith gave parts of it to the Virginia Company to justify his achievement, the company had no intention of publishing his report even if it was complete, as they did not wish too much to be known about their early efforts, which resulted in so many failures. Smith evaded their controls by publishing his *Map of Virginia* and *Description* at Oxford in 1612. So much of this was inevitably so near to what Strachey had written that, seek a patron as he would, he could never obtain support for its publication, more particularly because he did not have the heart to complete it. He might have done better to have gone on collecting and writing up a more coherent and fuller volume that would rival Smith's, which he could perhaps have found some publisher or patron to back in the course of time, but he was discouraged by Smith's success and, it must be admitted, by his convincing detailed narratives, based on personal experience, which he could not emulate. The three surviving manuscripts of Strachey's "Historie of Travell into Virginia Britania" bear witness to the continuing influence of Harriot on him, as well as that of Smith, as Harriot's pattern is apparent in them throughout. In one copy, in the British Library, he even cut out and added to his text the engravings by White from a copy of de Bry. But Smith was to plagiarize Hakluyt's narrative of the Roanoke voyages in his *Generall historie* in 1624: Strachey, had he had the will to do so, could have anticipated him.

The enduring influence of the materials on the Roanoke voyages is also illustrated by Robert Beverley, the Virginia historian who, writing his *History and Present State of Virginia* (1705) at the opening of the eighteenth century, followed the formula set down by Harriot and White and in a number of respects merely brought de Bry up to date. He even had the White engravings recut so that they could be used once more, well after a century had passed, to illustrate the life and character of Virginia Indians in the same way that White and Harriot, between them, had described the area behind Cape Henry to Cape Lookout on the basis of their experiences and work in the colony of 1585–86.

The men of 1585–86, directly, and the men, women, and children of the 1587 colony, indirectly, thus established themselves indelibly in early American history. They refused to be forgotten, in large part because the materials that survived about them were so graphic and their experiences so telling. Today, they still have not lost their importance or their appeal.

For Americans the Roanoke voyages have retained the implication that they pointed forward to later colonizing ventures that were, after initial crises in many cases, to lay down firm roots from which a unique set of communities could grow. After an interval, the Virginia Company of 1607–24 appeared to emerge directly out of the Roanoke ventures. New forces and new sources of capital were appearing in early Stuart England. The movement to settle in North America was, at the initial stage between 1607 and 1609, primarily a commercial venture, or, if the North Virginia colony on the Kennebec River in 1607–8 is taken into account, a pair of commercial ventures. There was, it is true, a strong exploring bent. In the southern colony during the years 1607–8, whole new segments were added to the map of eastern North America as the rivers of the Chesapeake basin and the territories between them were touched or examined, so that the overlap with the Harriot-White reconnaissance of the southern shore of Chesapeake Bay was continued and elaborated by Captain John Smith. Tentative explorations and plans for expansion into what is now North Carolina were considered from time to time, but soon forgotten in the struggle to master the James River basin. But the emphasis was on developing a viable commerce based on the James River, a colony manned by hired labor, the counterpart in a sense of Lane's soldiers of 1585–86, but designated to produce rather than merely to stand guard to protect exploring parties.

The strategic purpose of manning an outpost for aggressive war against Spain had retreated by 1607, though Spain could still offer a potential challenge. But Lane had shown that even if his men made Indians sick and die, he could keep his own men healthy. The Jamestown colonists did not learn how to do this and for a long time Jamestown remained a death trap. King James and his advisers, notably Robert Cecil, earl of Salisbury, decided that national prestige was at stake and thus in 1609, enlarged the scope of the Virginia Company and gave it a measure of royal and national support (so that its standing council became the Royal Council of Virginia as well as the directing body of a commercial venture). Had they not done so, the Jamestown colony might have gone the way of the unsuccessful colonies of the 1580s.

Queen Elizabeth could and would grant only nominal aid for the Roanoke colonies, though had Spain attacked them she might well have reacted more positively toward them. James I, in spite of his desire to stand well with Spain, was forced—if he did not wish to surrender all of North America to the Spanish king—to grant the new measure of support for and recognition of English colonial enterprise in North America from which he and his successors were never to retreat. Before the end of his reign, he was forced by circumstances to go further and take direct royal responsibility for the government of Virginia. Something very similar could have happened had the Roanoke colonies survived into his reign. He had not by this time fully come to grips with the colonial ventures farther north, but the Council of New England, created in 1620, was a first step toward doing so. His successive grants to developers of Newfoundland were another. The claim of English hegemony, which Sir Humphrey Gilbert and Sir Walter Ralegh had assumed under their paper charters, had become a reality. The whole area between the Carolinas and Newfoundland, with minor exceptions for the Dutch and Swedes and the recognition of French Canada, was to become an English sphere of interest and ultimately of colonization. The Roanoke colonies were undoubtedly the first link, if a broken one, in that long and important chain of events.

In the later twentieth century colonization, however, bears a dubious face. Did the Roanoke colonies not destroy, or begin the destruction of, the Native American society that had endured so long untouched by non-American influences? The Eastern Woodland culture, encountered by the Elizabethans and Jacobeans, had existed with some considerable degree of stability since roughly the time of the Norman conquest of England. Within fifty years after 1585 it had begun to be shattered by English intrusions, by English diseases, by English arms. The Roanoke colonies can be seen as striking the first blow at this culture in eastern North America.

For North Carolinians in the nineteenth and twentieth centuries the fact that the Roanoke colonies did, in the sense that has been described, represent the beginnings of a British empire in North America has been a source of pride, just as modern Virginians have been proud of the establishment of the first permanent English colony on their soil and New Englanders, even more, of the Pilgrims as the beginning. But North Carolina, for all that it took a long time for the colony to establish itself as a separate colonial entity, could also regard the Roanoke ventures as peculiarly its own. The selection, under Ralegh's auspices, of the island of Roanoke for the first settlement of Englishmen in North America provided a starting point for the colony and for the modern state and is an integral part of the state's historical mythology. The naming of the eventual capital of the state after Sir Walter gives a permanent basis for stressing that continuity. For North Carolina, the location of the site of the first English colonies, however temporarily, within its present boundaries, has aroused a special pride in being the earliest to celebrate the first four hundredth anniversary of English colonization in North America. The legend of the colonies as lying at the beginning of the history of the state has proved more powerful and enduring than ever the colonies were themselves, or, given the limited resources available to the Elizabethan state, could ever have been.

·◦[A P P E N D I X]◦··

An Archaeologist's View
of Indian Society

Author's note: At the time of this writing no technical summary of the findings of the current series of archaeological investigations of the Carolina Algonquians was available. Professor David Phelps of East Carolina University who is carrying out the excavations, has now given a summary of the prehistory of the area with which the English were in contact. This was published as "Archaeology of the North Carolina Coast and Coastal Plain: Problems and Hypotheses" in Mark A. Mathis and Jeffrey J. Crow, eds., *The Prehistory of North Carolina: An Archaeological Symposium* (Raleigh: North Carolina Division of Archives and History, Department of Cultural Resources, 1983), 1–51. His account of the Late Woodland period, into which the Indian culture of the period of the explorations falls, is here excerpted briefly, with the more technical references removed. Professor Phelps has stressed throughout how tentative conclusions must be about this phase of prehistory and early contact period history until much more archaeological work has been done. I have taken the liberty of adding a few footnotes of explanation and comment, but the words below are those of Professor Phelps himself. The author, editors, and publishers have graciously given their permission to reprint this material, and it is greatly appreciated. It will make clearer much of what has been said about the pioneer ethnohistorical work of John White and Thomas Harriot.

The Carolina Algonkians[1] were the southernmost representatives of a linguistic family distributed from North Carolina to Canada.

425

They were exclusively adapted to the Tidewater environment in the middle and southern ranges of that distribution.

The archaeological assemblage of the Colington phase (A.D. 800–1650),[2] as it is presently and incompletely known, includes the Colington ceramic series, a shell-tempered ware divided into types on the basis of surface finishing techniques.... A second ceramic series is found as a trade ware in the Colington phase sites.... The "grit" or pebble-tempered ware is more at home on the Inner Coastal Plain ... and its presence in the Colington phase sites apparently resulted from extensive trade between the two cultures.[3]

Projectile points are the small variety of the Roanoke triangular type[4] ... bifacial blades of various shapes, polished stone celts, gorgets, sandstone abraders, and milling stones are part of the lithic assemblage. Busycon shell hoes or picks, ladles, columella beads of tubular shape, and *Marginella* shell beads are known, as are freshwater pearls ... and a copper disc bead.... Bone artifacts include antler flakes, fish hooks, awls, and punches of various shapes, bone pins (sometimes incised) and a panther mask. Ceramic pipes with bowls attached either horizontally or at an angle are well known....

The territorial range of the Colington phase correlates with distribution of Carolina Algonkian societies as they are known from ethnohistoric sources.... Comparisons of data with Virginia researchers indicate that the southeastern corner of that state is archaeologically more similar to the North Carolina Coastal Plain than it is to the area north of Hampton Roads.[5] The southern boundary is presently conceived as a line drawn from New Bern to Cape Lookout, including the Neuse River estuary and north Carteret County....

Within this territory ... were a number of social units organized as chiefdoms, although it is tempting to speculate that there were embryonic state systems because of the presence of a formal religion and priesthood. The settlement pattern was relatively dispersed ... with site locations concentrated along the sounds, estuaries, major rivers, and their tributaries. Site types should include capital villages,[6] villages,[7] seasonal villages,[8] and camps for specialized activities. Also suggested is the farmstead, probably occupied by members of an extended family.... Villages of both regular internal organization with palisades and less formally structural open types were observed by the English explorers,[9] but insufficient work has been done to elucidate this intrasite variability.

Except for the camps, which appear to be directly related to seasonal gathering of shellfish, fishing, and perhaps collecting, all seasonal and larger villages are located where agriculture, hunting, gathering, and fishing could all be accomplished within the site catchment area. The summer seasonal village at Roanoke Island visited . . . in 1584 is an example.[10] Gardens were planted here, and fishing was a major activity while the corn-crop was maturing at the mainland capital village across Croatan Sound. Only one of the chiefdoms was located on the Outer Banks on Hatteras Island . . . some evidence remains in the Hatteras Village site. Hatteras is one of the few barrier islands with sufficient area at its present south end to support the subsistence needs of a large population.[11] Most of the large and small villages on the mainland are situated adjacent to streams or other bodies of water on high banks and ridges of sandy loams, the latter preferred for swidden agriculture. Oak-hickory forests interspersed with second-growth pine in previously cleared areas on the uplands, American beech forests, swamp forests, marshes, streams, and sounds provided ample resources. Subsistence data reclaimed from Colington phase sites include evidence of maize, hickory nuts, faunal remains of bears, deer, and a wide variety of small animals; alligators, terrapins, and turtles; fish and both marine and riverine cultigens (squash, sunflower, beans) and wild plants that were collected for food. . . .

·∋[NOTES]ɕ··

Chapter 1

1. D. B. Quinn and N. M. Cheshire, *The New Found Land of Stephen Parmenius* (Toronto: Toronto University Press, 1972), pp. 205–6.

2. See D. B. Quinn, *Raleigh and the British Empire*, rev. ed. (New York: Collier, 1962).

3. D. B. Quinn, ed., *The Voyages and Colonising Enterprises of Sir Humphrey Gilbert*, 2 vols. (London: Hakluyt Society, 1940). The introduction to volume 1 contains a biography of Gilbert.

4. D. B. Quinn, Alison M. Quinn, and Susan Hillier, eds., *New American World: A Documentary History of North America to 1612*, 5 vols. (New York: Arno Press and Hector Bye, Inc., 1979), 3:204–9.

5. D. B. Quinn, *Richard Hakluyt, Editor: with facsimiles of Richard Hakluyt, Divers Voyages Touching the Discoverie of America* (1582), and *A Journal of Several Voyages into New France* (1580), 2 vols. (Amsterdam: Theatrum Orbis Terrarum, 1967).

6. Reprinted and translated by Quinn and Cheshire in *New Found Land of Stephen Parmenius*, pp. 74–138.

7. Reprinted from second edition in Quinn et al., *New American World*, 3:27–34.

8. Reprinted Quinn et al., *New American World*, 3:34–60.

9. D. B. Quinn, ed., *The Roanoke Voyages, 1584–1590*, 2 vols. (Cambridge: Hakluyt Society, 1955), 1:82–89.

10. A brief survey will be found in D. B. Quinn and A. N. Ryan, *England's Sea Empire*. (Boston: Allen and Unwin, 1983).

11. See D. B. Quinn, *England and the Discovery of America, 1481–1620* (New York: Knopf, 1974).

Chapter 2

1. John W. Shirley, *Thomas Harriot* (Oxford: Oxford University Press, 1983), p. 87.

2. D. B. Quinn, "Thomas Harriot and the New World," in John W. Shirley, ed., *Thomas Harriot, Renaissance Scientist* (Oxford: Oxford University Press, 1974), pp. 36–53.

3. D. B. Quinn, ed., *The Roanoke Voyages, 1584–1590*, 2 vols. (Cambridge: Hakluyt Society, 1955), 1:139–44.

4. D. B. Quinn, *England and the Discovery of America, 1481–1620* (New York: Knopf, 1974), pp. 346–63.

5. L. A. Vigneras, "A Spanish Discovery of North Carolina in 1566," *North Carolina Historical Review* 46 (1969): 398–415.

6. Paul Hulton and D. B. Quinn, eds., *The American Drawings of John White*, 2 vols. (London and Chapel Hill: British Museum and University of North Carolina Press, 1964), 1:12–13.

7. William S. Powell, "Roanoke Colonists and Explorers: An Attempt at Identification," *North Carolina Historical Review* 34 (1957): 202–26.

8. D. B. Quinn, Alison M. Quinn, and Susan Hillier, eds., *New American World: A Documentary History of North America to 1612*, 5 vols. (New York: Arno Press and Hector Bye, Inc., 1979), 3:329–30.

9. Ibid., 3:204–6.

Chapter 3

1. There has been some unnecessary confusion about the landing place. The "twenty leagues" given as the length of the island on which they landed is clearly an attempt to estimate the length of the island in the Outer Banks of North Carolina north of Cape Hatteras, which is "Hatrask" and "Paquiac" on White's map (fig. 9). Hakluyt confused subsequent commentators by changing his 1589 figure to "six miles" in 1600. Six miles represented the width of the Outer Banks at certain places at that time. This interpretation is confirmed by the later statement that the place where they landed was seven leagues to the northwest tip of Roanoke Island, which is approximately correct. On his map (fig. 9) White names the northern part of the island "Hatrask" and the southern "Paquiac" but he does not use the latter name in the narratives.

2. D. B. Quinn, ed., *The Roanoke Voyages, 1584–1590*, 2 vols. (Cambridge: Hakluyt Society, 1955), 1:81.

3. D. B. Quinn, Alison M. Quinn, and Susan Hillier, eds., *New American World: A Documentary History of North America to 1612*, 5 vols. (New York: Arno Press and Hector Bye, Inc., 1979), 3:330.

Chapter 4

1. D. B. Quinn, ed., *The Roanoke Voyages, 1584–1590*, 2 vols. (Cambridge: Hakluyt Society, 1955), 1:126–29.

2. Ibid., 1:130–39.

3. Oxford: Bodleian Library, MS Tanner 169, folios 69v–70r (Commonplace Book of Sir Stephen Powle), published by F. P. Wilson, "An Ironicall Letter," *Modern Language Review* 15 (1920): 79–82.

4. D. B. Quinn, Alison M. Quinn, and Susan Hillier, eds., *New American World: A Documentary History of North America to 1612*, 5 vols. (New York: Arno Press and Hector Bye, Inc., 1979), 3:239–45, pl. 111a, and below pp. 102–3.

5. Ibid., 3:62.

6. Ibid., 3:65.

7. Ibid., 3:121–23.

8. Quinn, *Roanoke Voyages*, 1:147.

9. Compare Quinn, *Roanoke Voyages*, 1:178–79; Tom Glasgow, "H.M.S. Tyger" (*North Carolina Historical Review* 43 [1966]: 115–21); Mary F. Keeler, ed., *Sir Francis Drake's West Indian Voyage, 1585–86* (London, Hakluyt Society, 1981), p. 284. She was probably not the *Sea Dragon* renamed, as Glasgow proposes.

10. Quinn et al., *New American World*, 3:330.

Chapter 5

1. D. B. Quinn, "Sailors and the Sea in Elizabethan England," in *England and the Discovery of America, 1481–1620* (New York: Knopf, 1974), pp. 213–14 (and references cited); Helen Hill Miller, *Passage to America: Ralegh's Colonists Take Ship for Roanoke* (Raleigh: Department of Cultural Resources, 1983).

2. Tallaboa Bay in D. B. Quinn, ed., *The Roanoke Voyages, 1584–1590*, 2 vols. (Cam-

bridge: Hakluyt Society, 1955), 1:160–80, 403, but Samuel Eliot Morison, *The European Discovery of America: The Northern Voyages* (New York: Oxford University Press, 1971), pp. 633–34, established that it was the nearby Guayanilla Bay.

3. The John White drawing of the fort enclosure on Puerto Rico (Paul Hulton and D. B. Quinn, eds., *The American Drawings of John White*, 2 vols. [London and Chapel Hill: British Museum and University of North Carolina Press, 1964], no. 3, pl. 2.)

4. Irene A. Wright, ed., *Further English Voyages to Spanish America, 1583–1584* (London: Hakluyt Society, 1951), pp. 174–76; Quinn, *Roanoke Voyages*, 1:164–65.

5. Quinn, *Roanoke Voyages*, 1:184, 2:734–35, 740–43; Wright, *Further English Voyages*, pp. 9–10, 16.

6. Hulton and Quinn, *American Drawings of John White*, no. 4, pl. 3.

7. Ibid., nos. 11–14, pls. 10–13.

8. Quinn, *Roanoke Voyages*, 2:744–51.

9. Ibid., 1:201.

10. D. B. Quinn, Alison M. Quinn, and Susan Hillier, eds., *New American World: A Documentary History of North America to 1612*, 5 vols. (New York: Arno Press and Hector Bye, Inc., 1979), 3:330.

11. Hulton and Quinn, *American Drawings of John White*, nos. 16–32, pls. 15–30, 91b.

12. Quinn, *Roanoke Voyages* 1:210–12, 228–29.

Chapter 6

1. D. B. Quinn, ed., *The Roanoke Voyages, 1584–1590* (Cambridge: Hakluyt Society, 1955), 1:234–42.

2. Paul Hulton and D. B. Quinn, eds., *The American Drawings of John White*, 2 vols. (London and Chapel Hill: British Mu-

seum and University of North Carolina Press, 1964), no. 34, pl. 33.

3. Ibid., no. 37, pls. 32, 126a.

4. Ibid., no. 35, pls. 33, 126b.

5. Ibid., no. 34, pls. 81, 134.

6. Ibid., no. 38, pls. 35, 135.

7. Ibid., no. 39, pls. 36, 124a.

8. D. B. Quinn, Alison M. Quinn, and Susan Hillier, eds., *New American World: A Documentary History of North America to 1612*, 5 vols. (New York: Arno Press and Hector Bye, Inc., 1979), 3:330.

9. Quinn, *Roanoke Voyages*, 1:199–200, 207–9, 212–13 (and fig. 3), 215–17.

10. Chapter 20, p. 392.

11. Quinn, *Roanoke Voyages*, 1:210, 214.

12. Ibid., 1:177–78, 219–20, 226, 786–87.

13. Ibid., 1:210–13.

14. Fig. 7; details in Quinn, *Roanoke Voyages*, 1:215–17.

15. Fig. 2; Theodor de Bry, *America*, part 1 (Frankfurt am Main, 1590), pl. 2.

16. Quinn, *Roanoke Voyages*, 1:241.

17. See note 12 above.

Chapter 7

1. D. B. Quinn, ed., *The Roanoke Voyages, 1584–1590*, 2 vols. (Cambridge: Hakluyt Society, 1955), 1:228.

2. Ibid., 1:232–34.

3. D. B. Quinn, Alison M. Quinn, and Susan Hillier, eds., *New American World: A Documentary History of North America to 1612*, 5 vols. (New York: Arno Press and Hector Bye, Inc., 1979), 3:206.

4. William S. Powell, "Roanoke Colonists and Explorers: An Attempt at Identification," *North Carolina Historical Review* 34 (1957): 202–26.

5. Quinn, *Roanoke Voyages*, 2:834–38.

6. Ibid., p. 790.

7. Powell, "Roanoke Colonists," p. 214.

8. Ibid., p. 216.

9. Bruce S. Cheeseman, "Historical Research Report: Four Centuries and Roanoke Island—A Legacy of Geographical Change" (Unpublished report for Cape Hatteras National Seashore, National Park Service, September 1982), pp. 6–7.

10. Quinn, Roanoke Voyages, 1:196.

11. D. B. Quinn, ed., The Voyages and Colonising Enterprises of Sir Humphrey Gilbert, 2 vols. (London: Hakluyt Society, 1940), 11:408, 414, 417.

12. V. Bellis, M. O'Connor, and S. Riggs, Estuarine Shoreline Erosion in the Albemarle-Pamlico Region of North Carolina, UNC Sea Grant Publication SG-75-29 (Sea Grant Program, North Carolina State University, Raleigh, December 1975), p. 15.

13. John W. Shirley, Thomas Harriot (Oxford: Oxford University Press, 1983), pp. 462–64.

14. As John Twyt. Powell, "Roanoke Colonists," p. 217.

15. Though it is tempting to accept Powell, "Roanoke Colonists," pp. 215–16, in identifying Luddington as the Oxford don, it appears unlikely, because he was admitted M.A. only in July 1585 and would not have (normally) been allowed to do so in absentia. The Thomas Luddington who was a cousin of Thomas Lodge the dramatist and novelist may have been a different person and an alternative candidate (N. B. Paradise, Thomas Lodge [New Haven: Yale University Press, 1931], pp. 37, 135).

16. Quinn et al., New American World, 3:121–23.

Chapter 8

1. Paul Hulton and D. B. Quinn, eds., The American Drawings of John White, 2 vols., (London and Chapel Hill: British Mu-

seum and University of North Carolina Press, 1964), 1:136–37, pl. 59.

2. This site has been searched for extensively. I am indebted to Cheryl Claasen, Department of Anthropology, Harvard University, for the report on "The Secotan Project" (1982) in which she described her extensive fieldwork. No definite site emerged from her researches. The most likely was the extensive site at the southern entry to Durham Creek on the south side of the Pamlico River (her site Bf58), which was of appropriate size and date but which has not produced any contact material. If White's only visit was the July 1585 one, which seems likely, it would not be entirely surprising, as the Secotan tribe apparently remained hostile to Wingina for most of the relevant period.

3. D. B. Quinn, ed., The Roanoke Voyages, 1584–1590, 2 vols. (Cambridge: Hakluyt Society, 1955), 1:232–34.

4. See below, Chap. 20.

5. On his general map of eastern North America (Hulton and Quinn, American Drawings of John White, no. 57, pl. 58), White showed the Verrazzanian Sea cutting into the continent, almost dividing it in two by way of the Royal Sound. Thus, from the Roanoke River, access to the Pacific would not appear too difficult.

6. The standard work on these deposits is Francis B. Laney, The Geology and Ore Deposits of the Virgilina District of Virginia and North Carolina, issued as North Carolina Geological and Economic Survey, Bulletin no. 36, and as Virginia Geological Survey, Bulletin no. 14, Lynchburg, Va., 1917. He gives frequent references to small deposits of natural copper, but nothing of value, on the cutting through of the ridge by the Roanoke River. Nor does the most recent survey, Palmer C. Sweet, "Abandoned Copper Mines and Pros-

pects in the Virgilina District," (*Virginia Minerals* 32 [1976]:24–34). Surface material excavated from the basin of Kerr Lake when the cut-through of the Roanoke River was made, does not now exist, so that the source of the Mangoak copper cannot be verified.

Chapter 10

1. Typhus brought to Court by his captive Portuguese seamen killed him and many others in April 1586. Diary of Philip Wyot, in John Roberts Chandler, *Sketches of the Literary History of Barnstaple* (Barnstaple: E. J. Arnold, 1866), p. 91.

2. D. B. Quinn, ed., *The Roanoke Voyages, 1584–1590*, 2 vols. (Cambridge: Hakluyt Society, 1955), 2:756.

3. Drake's fleet is fully described in Mary F. Keeler, ed., *Sir Francis Drake's West Indian Voyage, 1585–86* (London: Hakluyt Society, 1981).

4. D. B. Quinn, Alison M. Quinn, and Susan Hillier, eds., *New American World: A Documentary History of North America to 1612*, 5 vols. (New York: Arno Press and Hector Bye, Inc., 1979), 3:309–10.

5. Lane's account is supplemented by Drake's sources, Quinn, *Roanoke Voyages* 1:299–302, 307–8, 310, 312, with comparable material in Keeler, op. cit.

6. Quinn et al., *New American World*, 3:156–72.

7. Historical Manuscripts Commission, *Manuscripts of the Marquess of Bath* (London: Her Majesty's Stationery Office, 1980), 5:72; Keeler, *Drake's Voyage*, p. 309.

8. Keeler, op. cit., pp. 317–18 and passim. We have his (unsigned) painting of the attack on Santiago (British Library, Egerton MS 2579; reproduced in Keeler, between pp. 124 and 125). The late Miss Jeanette Black found an early copy of his painting of Cartagena in the Massachusetts Historical Society, which has the copied signature of Baptista Boazio.

9. See Paul Hulton and D. B. Quinn, eds., *The American Drawings of John White*, 2 vols. (London and Chapel Hill: British Museum and University of North Carolina Press, 1964), nos. 9, 27, 31, 103, pl. 155.

10. Quinn et al., *New American World*, 3:309–10. A less favorable comment was made by Thomas Bayley to his master the earl of Shrewsbury on 27 July saying "we brought away such forlorn countrymen of ours as at Sir Richard Grenefield's departure thence were left behind to small purpose." (Historical Manuscripts Commission, *Manuscripts of the Marquess of Bath*, 5:71–72).

11. John Smith was to say: ". . . and it is near as much trouble, but much more danger, to sail from London to Plimoth, than from Plimoth to New England, so that half the voyage would thus be saved." *The generall historie of Virginia* (London: I. D. and I. H. for M. Sparkes, 1624), p. 221.

12. Quinn, *Roanoke Voyages*, 1:474.

13. Ibid., 2:787–92.

14. Ibid., 1:475–76.

15. Ibid., 1:480–87.

16. Ibid., 1:495.

17. Ibid., 1:494.

18. Ibid., 2:770–71.

19. D. B. Quinn, *Raleigh and the British Empire*, rev. ed. (New York: Collier, 1962), pp. 111–32. D. B. Quinn, "The Munster Plantation: Problems and Opportunities," *Journal of the Cork Historical and Archaeological Society* 71 (1966): 19–40, will provide the Munster context adequately.

20. Quinn, *Roanoke Voyages*, 1:339–40, 347, notes.

Chapter 11

1. D. B. Quinn, ed., *The Roanoke Voyages, 1584–90*, 2 vols. (Cambridge: Hakluyt Society, 1955), 2:790–91.

2. See below, p. 281.

Chapter 12

1. All the relevant drawings extant, and engravings from them, were published in Paul Hulton and D. B. Quinn, eds., *The American Drawings of John White*, 2 vols. (London and Chapel Hill: British Museum and University of North Carolina Press, 1964), the commentary and notes in the first volume and the reproductions in the second. Paul Hulton, *America 1585: The Complete Drawings of John White* (Chapel Hill: University of North Carolina Press, 1984) makes them more available in a less elaborate format. The list and notes in D. B. Quinn, ed., *The Roanoke Voyages, 1584–1590*, 2 vols. (Cambridge: Hakluyt Society, 1955), 1:390–464, may also be useful for quick reference.

2. The text of the 1588 edition of Thomas Harriot's *A briefe and true report of the new found land of Virginia* (London: [Robert Robinson], 1588) is fully annotated in Quinn, *Roanoke Voyages*, 1:314–89. The second edition, that published by Richard Hakluyt, *The principall navigations, voyages and discoveries of the English nation* (London: G. Bishop and R. Newberie, deputies to C. Barker, 1589) is included, with notes, in D. B. and Alison M. Quinn, eds., *The First Colonists: Documents on the Planting of the First English Settlements in North America, 1584–1590* (Raleigh: North Carolina Department of Cultural Resources, Division of Archives and History, 1982), pp. 46–76, 150–57. The third edition in Theodor de Bry's *America*, part 1 (Theodor de Bry: Frankfurt-am-Main, 1590) is reproduced in Thomas Harriot, *A Briefe and True Report of the New Found Land of Virginia*, with an introduction by Paul Hulton (New York: Dover Books, 1972). The fourth edition, published by Hakluyt in the second edition of *The principal navigations, voyages, traffiques & discoveries of the English nation*, 3 vols. (London: G. Bishop, R. Newberie, and R. Barker, 1598–1600), is in D. B. Quinn, Alison M. Quinn, and Susan Hillier, eds., *New American World: A Documentary History of North America to 1612*, 5 vols. (New York: Arno Press and Hector Bye, Inc., 1979), 3:139–55, without annotation.

3. A succinct account of the humoral theory in Rhys Isaac, *The Transformation of Virginia, 1740–1790* (Chapel Hill: University of North Carolina Press, 1982), p. 47, can scarcely be bettered:

people of European culture lived . . . with a stock of basic concepts derived from a cosmology that posited a direct nexus between the microcosm of the human body and the macrocosm of the physical universe that contained it. The interpenetration of these systems was formulated theoretically in the notion that the functioning of the body and its temperament were governed by four humors, each corresponding to one of the elements that composed the cosmos. There was blood, corresponding to air and tending toward heat and moisture; phlegm, corresponding to water and tending toward wet and cold; yellow or green bile (choler), corresponding to fire and tending to heat and dryness; and black bile (whence the word "melancholy"), corresponding to earth and tending toward cold and dryness. The health of the body depended upon a maintenance of balance between these humors. An excess of blood could make the body feverish and a temperament too sanguine, while too much phlegm could lead to coldness and dullness; and so on with bilious and melancholic disorders.

4. John Smith, *A map of Virginia* (Oxford, 1612), in Philip L. Barbour, ed., *The Jamestown Voyages, 1606–1609*, 2 vols. (Cambridge: Hakluyt Society, 1969), 2:321–74; William Strachey, *The Historie of Travell into Virginia Britania*, ed. Louis B. Wright and Virginia Freund (London: Hakluyt Society, 1953.)

5. See p. 93 above and Quinn, *Roanoke Voyages* (Cambridge: Hakluyt Society, 1955), 1:327-28. A detailed analysis of the constituents of the Suffolk Scarp could throw some light on his supposed identifications.

6. Ibid., 1:219.

Chapter 13

1. What is known of White is set out in Paul Hulton and D. B. Quinn, eds., *The American Drawings of John White*, 2 vols. (London and Chapel Hill: British Museum and University of North Carolina Press, 1964), 1:8–24. Paul Hulton's *The Watercolor Drawings of John White from the British Museum* (Washington: National Gallery of Art, 1965), and "John White, Artist," *Bulletin of the North Carolina Museum of Art 5* (Spring–Summer, 1965): 3-43, add further details. Paul Hulton, *The Work of Jacques Le Moyne de Morgues*, 2 vols. (London: British Museum, 1977), treats incidentally the relationship between White and Le Moyne.

2. Hulton and Quinn, *American Drawings of John White*, 2:43–47, nos. 114–18,

pls. 62-3, 84b, 85b, 147a.

3. Ibid., pls. 35, 135. The first plate is the original drawing, the second is De Bry's engraving.

4. See ibid., 1:100-101.

5. Ibid., no. 34, pls. 33, 81, 134.

6. Ibid., no. 46, pls. 42, 129.

7. Ibid., no. 41, pls. 37, 137. Communal graves were eventually used for the final disposal of these remains. Several of these ossuaries, in the coastal area, have been excavated by Professor David Phelps, who has kindly shown me his reports.

8. Ibid., no. 44, pls. 40, 141.

9. Ibid., no. 43, pls. 39, 132.

10. Ibid., no. 42, pls. 38, 133.

11. Ibid., no. 43, pl. 128 (engraving only).

12. Ibid., no. 49, pls. 44, 130a.

13. Ibid., no. 48, pls. 43, 130b.

14. Ibid., no. 36, pls. 33, 126b.

15. Ibid., no. 35, pls. 32, 126a.

16. Ibid., no. 37, pls. 34, 127a. White associates her with Pomeioc, but is probably mistaken.

17. Ibid., no. 39, pls. 36, 124a.

18. Ibid., no. 45, pls. 41, 124b.

19. Ibid., no. 53, pls. 48, 127b.

20. Ibid., no. 50, pls. 45, 125b. Harriot uses *weroance* loosely for both chiefs and elders but principally for the latter. However, in Virginia the word is confined to chiefs only and perhaps should be also in the Roanoke area. In that case this man may be a chief rather than an elder.

21. Ibid., no. 52, pls. 47, 123b.

22. Ibid., no. 54, pl. 138a (engraving only).

Chapter 14

1. The literature in this field is too extensive to specify here. Bibliographical studies will be found in James Axtell, "The Ethnohistory of Early America," *William and Mary Quarterly*, 3d ser., 35 (1978): 110-44, and his "A Moral History of Indian-White Relations Revisited," *History Teacher* 16 (February 1983): 169-90; Harry C. Porter, "Reflections on the Ethnohistory of Early Colonial America," *Journal of American Studies* 16 (August 1982):243-54. Neal Salisbury, *Manitou and Providence, 1500-1643* (New York: Oxford University Press, 1982), is especially useful on Indian religion.

2. D. B. Quinn, *The Elizabethans and the Irish* (Ithaca: Cornell University Press, 1966).

3. Again the literature is too extensive to cite in detail. Lewis Hanke, *Aristotle and the American Indian* (London: Hollis and Carter, 1959); Charles Gibson, *The Aztecs under Spanish Rule* (Stanford: Stanford University Press, 1964); and Carl O. Sauer, *The Early Spanish Main* (Berkeley: University of California Press, 1966), may perhaps be taken as representative.

4. *The Spanish colonie* (London: T. Dawson for W. Brome, 1583).

5. D. B. Quinn, Alison M. Quinn, and Susan Hillier, eds., *New American World: A Documentary History of North America to 1612*, 5 vols. (New York: Arno Press and Hector Bye, Inc., 1979), 3:43-8.

6. Ibid., 3:61–69.

7. Ibid., 3:70–123.

8. Salisbury, *Manitou and Providence*, pp. 34-39, is helpful on this subject, even though his examples are from New England.

9. Francis Jennings, *The Invasion of America* (Chapel Hill: University of North Carolina Press, 1975), chap. 2, especially p. 23.

10. D. B. Quinn, "Turks, Moors and Others in Drake's West Indian Voyage," *Terrae Incognitae* 14 (1982): 93-100.

11. D. B. Quinn, ed., *The Roanoke Voyages, 1584–1590*, 2 vols. (Cambridge: Hakluyt Society, 1955), 1:495.

Chapter 15

1. D. B. Quinn, ed., *The Roanoke Voyages, 1584–1590*, 2 vols. (Cambridge: Hakluyt Society, 1955), 1:474–75, 480-88.

2. Ibid., 1:232–34.

3. D. B. Quinn, Alison M. Quinn, and Susan Hillier, eds., *New American World: A Documentary History of North America to 1612*, 5 vols. (New York: Arno Press and Hector Bye, Inc., 1979), 3:330.

4. Philip L. Barbour, ed., *The Jamestown Voyages, 1606–1609*, 2 vols. (Cambridge: Hakluyt Society, 1969), 1:134–35.

5. John Smith, *The generall historie of Virginia* (London: I. D. and I. H. for M. Sparkes, 1624), p. 64.

6. Quinn, *Roanoke Voyages*, 2:549–50.

7. Ibid., 1:493–94.

8. The pervasive influence of Verrazzano's concept (1524) that the South Sea lay near the Carolina Sounds over a narrow isthmus, played a part in White's general map of eastern North America, which instead shows a channel to the Pacific from Port Royal Sound (see p. 113). The classic discussion is in Lawrence C. Wroth, *The Voyages of Giovanni da Verrazzano* (New Haven: Yale University Press, 1970).

9. Paul J. Kirk, Jr., ed., *The Great Dismal Swamp* (Charlottesville: University Press of Virginia, 1979), contains much about the swamp through the ages, although nothing on the Indians who inhabited its fringes in the late sixteenth century.

10. A careful genealogical chart, prepared for Paul Hulton in 1964, gives John White a son John, and may well be cor-

rect. It is now in the North Carolina Collection, University of North Carolina, Chapel Hill.

11. D. B. Quinn and N. M. Cheshire, *New Found Land of Stephen Parmenius* (Toronto: Toronto University Press, 1972), pp. 38–41, 69–61.

12. Professor Powell very kindly lent me his notes on published London sources, which are summarized in his paper, "Roanoke Colonists and Explorers: An Attempt at Identification" *North Carolina Historical Review* 34 (1957): 202–26. His specific identifications in the latter are often open to question but are always suggestive. His pioneer work on the background of the colonists, and of the Lost Colonists in particular, is beyond praise. The further information on Ananias Dare, printed in Paul Hulton and D. B. Quinn, eds., *The American Drawings of John White*, 2 vols. (London and Chapel Hill: British Museum and University of North Carolina Press, 1964), 1:16, note 5, also derives from him. What follows on Essex is based on his work at the Essex County Record Office, Chelmsford.

13. Grant of Arms, 7 January 1587. Quinn, *Roanoke Voyages*, 2:506–12.

14. In an unpublished study of the grant, which he has kindly allowed me to see.

15. Quinn, *Roanoke Voyages*, 2:512.

16. Ibid., 2:499.

17. Ibid., 2:779–80, 803.

Chapter 16

1. See above pp. 42–43.

Chapter 17

1. D. B. Quinn, ed., *The Roanoke Voyages, 1584–1590*, 2 vols. (Cambridge: Hakluyt

Society, 1955), 2:782–83.

2. Ibid., 2:544.

3. Ibid., 2:554, 559–62.

4. Ibid., 1:318.

5. Ibid., 2:793–95.

6. Ibid., 2:804–11. See p. 308–9 below.

7. Ibid., 2:816–25.

8. Ibid., 2:810–11. There the implication is that the landing was made on the Outer Banks at the Hatarask (or Port Ferdinando) inlet. New consideration makes it clear that the landing was near the northeast end of Roanoke Island.

9. C. M. Lewis and A. J. Loomie, *The Spanish Jesuit Mission to Virginia, 1570–1572* (Chapel Hill: University of North Carolina Press, 1953), p. 200.

10. Paul Hulton and D. B. Quinn, *The American Drawings of John White*, 2 vols. (London and Chapel Hill: British Museum and University of North Carolina Press, 1964), no. 108(b), pl. 76a.

11. Ibid., 1:24–29.

12. Quinn, *Roanoke Voyages*, 2:544.

13. Ibid., 2:557–59, 569–76.

14. See R. B. Wernham, *The Making of Elizabethan Foreign Policy, 1558–1603* (Berkeley: University of California Press, 1981), pp. 64–70.

Chapter 18

1. Ralegh was mayor of Youghal 1589–90. He made at least one visit to England, but was acting in person at Youghal on 6 June 1590. Samuel Hayman, *Notes and Records of the Ancient Religious Foundations at Youghal* (Youghal, Co. Cork: privately printed, 1855), p. 23.

2. Richard Hakluyt, *The Principall Navigations* (1589), with an introduction by D. B. Quinn and R. A. Skelton and a modern index by Alison M. Quinn, 2 vols. (Cambridge: Hakluyt Society, 1965). Questions on its composition and probable publi-

cation date are discussed in detail in the introduction.

3. White never mentions Sanderson's contribution of the *Moonlight* in his narrative, and his account of the privateering venture is unsatisfactory and incomplete. Materials on the High Court of Admiralty (Public Record Office, London) enable a much fuller and more accurate picture to be given. See D. B. Quinn, ed., *The Roanoke Voyages, 1584–1590*, 2 vols. (Cambridge: Hakluyt Society, 1955), 2:579–712.

4. Ibid., 2:587, 601, 799.

5. Ibid., 2:580–81, 587.

6. D. B. Quinn, *England and the Discovery of America, 1481–1620* (New York: Knopf, 1974), pp. 278–79.

7. Quinn, *Roanoke Voyages*, 2:799–800.

Chapter 19

1. Edward Moseley's map of North Carolina, published in London in 1733 but probably compiled in 1729, has the note: "Indians, none now inhabiting the See Coast, but about 6. or 8. at Hatteras, who dwell among the English."

2. D. B. Quinn, "Turks, Moors and Others in Drake's West Indian Voyage," *Terrae Incognitae* 14 (1982): 93–100.

3. D. B. Quinn, ed., *The Roanoke Voyages, 1584–1590*, 2 vols. (Cambridge: Hakluyt Society, 1955) 1:307.

4. A detailed study in D. B. Quinn, *England and the Discovery of America, 1481–1620* (New York: Knopf, 1974) pp. 432–81, includes much of the material in this chapter. References to material noted there have not been repeated unless the interpretation in the document has been modified. Subsequent information has been recorded in the notes.

5. Ivor Noël-Hume, *Martin's Hundred* (New York: Knopf, 1982).

6. In a personal communication.

7. *The Poems of Sir Walter Ralegh*, ed. A. M. C. Latham (Cambridge: Harvard University Press, 1929), p. 93. These lines were probably written between 1592 and 1594.

8. Quinn, *England and the Discovery of America*, pp. 405–18.

9. Ibid., pp., 419–31.

10. First published in D. B. Quinn and Alison M. Quinn, eds., *The English New England Voyages, 1602–1608* (London: Hakluyt Society, 1983), figs. 9–14, pp. 232–34.

11. K. R. Andrews, "Christopher Newport of Limehouse, Mariner," *William and Mary Quarterly*, 3rd ser., 11 (1954): 40.

12. D. B. Quinn, "An Anglo-French 'Voyage of Discovery' to North America in 1604–5, and Its Sequel," *Miscellanea offerts à Charles Verlinden à l'Occasion de ses Trente Ans de Professorat*, 2 vols. (Ghent: Ghent University Press, 1975), 2:513–34; D. B. Quinn, Alison M. Quinn, and Susan Hillier, eds., *New American World: A Documentary History of North America to 1612*, 5 vols. (New York: Arno Press and Hector Bye, Inc., 1979), 5:108–27.

13. J. Frederick Fausz, "The Powhatan Rising of 1622" (Ph.D. dissertation, College of William and Mary, 1977), contains the best survey of the growth of the Powhatan confederacy.

14. The William Strachey references, which are crucial to the later story, are to be found in *The Historie of Travell into Virginia Britania*, ed. Louis B. Wright and Virginia Freund (London: Hakluyt Society, 1953), pp. 15, 44, 59, 91, 104–5, 108, 125, 150.

15. Philip L. Barbour, ed., *The Jamestown Voyages, 1606–1609*, 2 vols. (Cambridge: Hakluyt Society, 1969), 1:133–35.

16. Ibid., 1:85.

17. Ibid., 2:340.

18. *The generall historie of Virginia* (London: I. D. and I. H. for M. Sparkes, 1624), p. 64.

19. Samuel Purchas, *Hakluytus Posthumus*,

or *Purchas his pilgrimes*, 4 vols. (London: W. Stansby for H. Fetherstone, 1625), 4:1813.

20. Ibid., 4:1728.

21. Susan M. Kingsbury, ed., *Records of the Virginia Company of London*, 4 vols. (Washington, D.C.: Library of Congress, 1905–35), 3:12–24.

22. Barbour, *Jamestown Voyages*, 1:49–54.

23. Ibid., 1:186.

24. Ibid., 1:190.

25. Reproduced in Barbour, *Jamestown Voyages*, 2:238–40. Smith had said Wowinchopunk returned within a few days, but the map makes it clear that he accompanied the two men to the end of their journey. The map itself is thought to have been a draft of Smith's own, sent to England in 1608 and somehow intercepted by a Spanish agent there. Its geography is hard to interpret and it might appear that the searchers did not go as far south as the inscriptions on the map indicated.

26. Barbour, *Jamestown Voyages*, 2:423, 449. See Quinn, *England and the Discovery of America*, p. 477.

27. Smith, *Generall historie of Virginia*, p. 331.

28. John Lawson, *A New Voyage to Carolina*, ed. Hugh T. Lefler (Chapel Hill: University of North Carolina Press, 1967), p. 69.

29. D. B. Quinn, *The Lost Colonists: Their Fortune and Probable Fate* (Raleigh: Department of Cultural Resources, 1984), closely parallels this chapter but is not identical with it.

Chapter 20

1. R. Dolan and K. Bosserman, "Shoreline Erosion and the Lost Colony," *Annals of the Association of American Geographers* 62 (September 1972): 424–26.

2. Bruce S. Cheeseman, "Historical Research Report: Four Centuries and Roanoke Island—A Legacy of Geographical Change" (unpublished report for Cape Hatteras National Seashore, National Park Service, September 1982).

3. The early sources are fully discussed in William S. Powell, *A Paradise Preserved: History of the Roanoke Island Historical Association* (Chapel Hill: University of North Carolina Press, 1965), pp. 15–16, 19, 23–24, 26–30, 33–35, supplemented by Charles H. Johnson, *The Long Roll* (New York: East Aurora, 1911), p. 194; and Talcott Williams, "The Surroundings and Site of Raleigh's Colony," in *Annual Report of the American Historical Association for 1895* (Washington, D.C.: 1896), pp. 47–61.

4. See Powell, *Paradise Preserved*, pp. 37, 80–82, 115–23, 141–45.

5. J. C. Harrington, *Archaeology and the Enigma of Fort Raleigh* (Raleigh: America's Four Hundredth Anniversary Committee, 1984), p. 3.

6. John E. Ehrenhard, William P. Athens, and Gregory L. Komara, *Remote Sensing Investigations at Fort Raleigh National Historic Site, North Carolina* (Tallahassee: Southeast Archaeological Center, 1983), pp. 53–54; Personal Communication from Mr. Phillip Evans, and see D. B. Quinn, ed., *The Roanoke Voyages, 1584–1590*, 2 vols. (Cambridge: Hakluyt Society, 1955), 2:811.

7. J. C. Harrington, *Search for the Cittie of Ralegh: Archaeological Excavations at Fort Raleigh National Historical Site, North Carolina*, Archaeological Research Series, no. 6 (Washington, D.C.: Department of the Interior, National Park Service, 1962), pp. 9–12.

8. Harrington, *Archaeology and the Enigma of Fort Raleigh*, p. 14.

9. Harrington, *Search for the Cittie of Ralegh*, p. 30, fig. 25. This is in a simplified form repeated in *Archaeology and the*

Enigma of Fort Raleigh, p. 8.

10. Harrington, Search for the Cittie of Ralegh, pp. 16–17, 32.

11. Full accounts of the reconstruction appear in Harrington, Search for the Cittie of Ralegh, pp. 27–33, and Archaeology and the Enigma of Fort Raleigh, pp. 6–15.

12. His retrospective of this failure in Archaeology and the Enigma of Fort Raleigh, pp. 16–22, is headed "The Elusive Settlement Site" and gives his latest view of that problem.

13. J. C. Harrington, An Outwork at Fort Raleigh: Further Archaeological Excavations at Fort Raleigh National Historical Site, North Carolina (Philadelphia: Eastern Parks and Monuments Association, 1966); Harrington, Archaeology and the Enigma of Fort Raleigh, pp. 23–27; Ehrenhard, Athens, and Komara, Remote Sensing Investigations at Fort Raleigh, pp. 19–23, where some novel suggestions of its nature and significance are put forward by Phillip Evans.

14. Ehrenhard, Athens, and Komara, Remote Sensing Investigations at Fort Raleigh, pp. 10–23, and in personal communications.

15. Harrington, An Outwork at Fort Raleigh, p. 5.

16. Ibid., pp. 30–31.

17. The artifacts, as a whole, are discussed in Harrington, Search for the Cittie of Ralegh, pp. 62–66.

18. Ivor Noël-Hume, Here Lies Virginia (New York: Knopf, 1983), pp. 30, 32–33, has described this piece in detail. He found that Drake was carrying olive jars as water containers when he reached Roanoke Island in June 1586 and suggested this may have been left by him. As it was located with other fragments in an area that had been in use by the colonists since August 1585, this seems unlikely, especially as Grenville had several captured Spanish prizes, which would al-

most certainly have carried such jars, when he reached the Outer Banks in July 1585.

19. Ivor Noël-Hume, Here Lies Virginia, p. 33, when discussing this find, suggests that it was unused because no metals or metallic ores were found to justify its employment, but he does not take into account two pieces of copper which had been melted, and indicate positive metallurgical activity on Roanoke Island.

20. David Sutton Phelps, Archaeology of the Native Americans: The Carolina Algonkians, Summary of Research, May 15–December 31, 1983 (Project Sponsored by America's Four Hundredth Anniversary Committee). Phelps kindly supplied me with a copy of this report and also explained his findings in detail in personal communications.

21. Ehrenhard, Athens, and Komara, Remote Sensing Investigations at Fort Raleigh, p. 65; I am also greatly indebted to personal communications from Phillip Evans for information on the progress of the investigations, as well as from personal contact with John E. Ehrenhard on site in June 1983.

Appendix

1. W. C. Sturtevant, ed., Handbook of North American Indians (in progress) accepts "Algonquian" as the official spelling of both the cultural and linguistic name, although many scholars prefer to distinguish the cultural group as "Algonkian" and the linguistic as "Algonquian." This has certain advantages. But "Algonquian" is invariably used in this book.

2. This is the type site, excavated by Professor Phelps, to which the Later Woodland of the Coastal Carolina Algonquian culture is now being referred. The

extraordinarily long period of its endurance makes critical assessments (with present-day limitations in dating such artifacts as are found within it) difficult. Its length shows that this was not an area where cultural change was taking place at any appreciable rate. It may not appear quite so static a society as archaeological expertise and activity increases, but it is the most remarkable feature of this culture group, as of most others in the East.

3. That of the Tuscarora of the Inner Coastal Plain being the other.

4. Roanoke points are a type of triangular pointed arrowheads carried over from the pre-850 A.D. period.

5. The Chesapeake tribe, of which much is said in the text, would thus fall within the North Carolina Coastal group from the archaeological standpoint.

6. Chawanóac (certainly, from Professor Phelps's continuing work there), Skikóac, from the descriptions we have of it in the 1584–7 documents. Weapemeoc would probably qualify. Professor Phelps would also place Pomeioc as one, but was this, or was Dasemunkepeuc, Wingina's only village on the mainland, and Pomeioc the chief village of another small hegemony?

7. There is still some contention as to whether a thin coastal fringe of Algonquian occupation did not extend down into the Cape Fear area. At present Pro-

fessor Phelps's views are more generally accepted.

8. Roanoke, Secotan (or was it a capital village?), with all but one of the sites on the north side of Albemarle Sound.

9. As drawn by White.

10. This seems doubtful because cornfields were maintained around the Roanoke village according to the De Bry engraving of the lost White drawing. The fact is also indicated in Lane's references. If corn was grown it was not just a "summer seasonal village" even if Wingina decided to evacuate it in 1586 for political reasons.

11. The Hatteras Indians, Manteo's family's chiefdom, on Croatoan (Hatteras) Island, at Chacandepeco and other sites, not recorded by White, lacked much corn-growing land (and requested White's men in 1587 to respect what little they had on which corn was growing; the robbery of the Dasemunkepeuc cornfield also indicates that corn was short on the island). In this case, in the years 1584–87, even if the Outer Banks were up to a mile wider, a substantial population dependent partly on agriculture could not have been maintained. In earlier times when the Banks were wider still this may well not have been the case. In 1984 Professor Phelps located an Indian site which could prove to be that of Manteo's village.

A full bibliography down to the end of 1953 will be found in D. B. Quinn, ed., *The Roanoke Voyages, 1584–1590*, 2 vols. (Cambridge: Hakluyt Society, 1955), 2:918–46, and is not repeated here. Valuable additions to this may be found in D. B. Quinn, ed., *The Hakluyt Handbook*, 2 vols., 1974. Writings by D. B. Quinn, 1931–76, are listed in K. R. Andrews, N. P. Canny, and P. E. H. Hair, eds., *The Westward Enterprise: English Activities in Ireland, the Atlantic, and America, 1480–1650* (Detroit: Wayne State University Press, 1978), pp. 303–9.

Basic Sources

These are those preserved by Richard Hakluyt, the younger (1552–1616). *The principall navigations, voyages and discoveries of the English nation* (London: G. Bishop and R. Newberie, deputies to C. Barker, 1589) contains all the basic Roanoke voyages material down to the end of 1588. A facsimile, with an introduction by D. B. Quinn and R. A. Skelton and a modern index by Alison M. Quinn, *The Principall Navigations* (1589) (2 vols., Cambridge: Hakluty Society, 1965), made it generally available. The second edition, *The principal navigations, voyages, traffiques & discoveries of the English nation* (3 vols., London: G. Bishop, R. Newberie, and R. Barker, 1598–1600), added material that became available after 1589, but deleted two earlier documents. The standard edition is *The Principal Navigations* (12 vols., Glasgow: J. MacLehose, 1903–5, and Hakluyt Society, extra series 1–12, 1903–5). D. B. and Alison M. Quinn, eds., *Virginia Voyages from Hakluyt* (London: Oxford University Press, 1973), reissued with an additional preface, as *The First Colonists: Documents on the Planting of the First English Settlements in North America, 1584–1590* (Raleigh: North Carolina Department of Cultural Resources, Division of Archives and History, 1982), contains all the documents Hakluyt published.

The documents on the Roanoke ventures, including the basic sources cited above, were collected and published with notes in D. B. Quinn, ed., *The Roanoke Voyages, 1584–1590* (2 vols., Cambridge: Hakluyt Society, 1955). This was reprinted by H. P. Kraus in one volume (Nendeln, Leichtenstein, 1967). To it it has been possible to add a number of documents in D. B. Quinn, Alison M. Quinn, and Susan Hillier, eds., *New American World: A Documentary History of North America to 1612* (5 vols., New York: Arno Press and Hector Bye, Inc., 1979). The documents on the Roanoke voyages and their background are in volume 3. The graphic records, which are an essential addition to the documentary material, were made by John White, and are complete in Paul Hulton and D. B. Quinn, eds., *The American Drawings of John White* (2 vols., London and Chapel Hill: British Museum and University of North Carolina Press, 1964) and Paul Hulton, *America 1585: The Complete Drawings of John White* (Chapel Hill: University of North Carolina Press, 1984). Theodor de Bry, ed., *America*, part 1 (Theodor de Bry: Frankfurt-am-Main, 1590), in Latin, English, German, and French, published a number of engravings from John White's drawings. They are all included in Hulton and Quinn, above. A facsimile edition of the edition in English, with the title Thomas Harriot, *A Briefe and True Report of the New Found Land of Virginia*, with an introduction by Paul Hulton (New York: Dover, 1972), provides a useful substitute for the original. Thomas Harriot's *A briefe and true report of the new found land of Virginia* (London: [Robert Robinson], 1588), the first edition, is included in D. B. Quinn, ed., *The Roanoke Voyages*, above. Edmund S. Morgan, "John White and the Sarsaparilla" (*William and Mary Quarterly*, 3rd ser., 14 [1957]: 414–17), prints an item from John Gerard, *Herball* (London: J. Norton, 1597), overlooked in *The Roanoke Voyages*. Irene A. Wright, ed., *Further English Voyages to Spanish America, 1583–1594* (London: Hakluyt Society, 1951), has much Spanish material on Sir Francis Drake's West Indian voyage of 1585–86, which is fully documented from the English side in Mary F. Keeler, ed., *Sir Francis Drake's West Indian Voyage, 1585–86* (London: Hakluyt Society, 1981). To it can be added Historical Manuscripts Commission, *Manuscripts of the Marquess of Bath*, vol. 5 (London: Her Majesty's Stationery Office, 1980).

Archaeology of the Roanoke Settlements

The publications of J. C. Harrington are the sole source for what was done between 1947 and 1966 on the Roanoke Island site: "Archaeological Explorations at Fort Raleigh National Historic Site" (*North Carolina Review* 26 [1949]: 127–49); "Historic Record Found" (*The Iron Worker* [Lynchburg, Va.] 15, no. 3, pp. 12–15); "Historic Site Archeology in the United States," in James B. Griffen, ed., *Eastern United States Archeology* (Chicago: University of Chicago Press, 1952); "Evidence of Manual Reckoning in the Cittie of Ralegh" (*North Carolina Historical Review* 33 [1956]: 1–11); *Search for the Cittie of Ralegh: Archaeological Excavations at Fort Raleigh National Historic Site, North Carolina* (Archaeological Research Series, no. 6, (Washington, D. C.: Department of the Interior, National Park Service, 1962); *An Outwork at Fort Raleigh: Further Archeological Excavations at Fort Raleigh National Historic Site North Carolina* (Philadelphia: Eastern Parks and Monuments Association, 1966); "The Manufacture and Use of Bricks at the Raleigh Settlement on Roanoke Island" (*North Carolina Historical Review* 44 [1967]: 1–17); *The Enigma of Fort Raleigh* (Raleigh: Department of Cultural Resources, 1984). The program of excavation begun by the Southeast Archaeological Center of the National Park Service at Tallahassee, Florida, in November 1982 will in due course add to this interpretation. The Center has produced the following reports on new archaeological work: John E. Ehrenhard, William P. Athens, and Gregory L. Komara, *Remote Sensing Investigations at Fort Raleigh National Historic Site* (1983); John E. Ehrenhard and Gregory L. Komara, *Archaeological Investigations at Fort Raleigh National Historic Site. Season 2, 1983* (1984); and William P. Athens, *Resistivity Investigations at Fort Raleigh National Historic Site* (1984).

Indian Archaeology and Ethnology

Bruce Trigger, ed., *The Northeast: Handbook of the Indians of North America* (general editor, William C. Sturtevant, Washington: Smithsonian Institution, in progress), vol. 15 (1978), contains authoritative summaries of the culture of the Coastal Algonquian Indians, notably that by C. F. Feest, "North Carolina Algonquians," pp. 271–81. Two preliminary studies of the Indian archaeology of the area are William G. Haag, *The Archaeology of Coastal North Carolina* (Louisiana State University Coastal Studies Series, no. 2, 1958); and Stanley South, *An Archaeological Survey of Southeastern Coastal North Carolina* (Institute of Archaeology and Anthropology Notebook no. 8, University of South Carolina, 1976). The detailed studies and reports of excavations by David S. Phelps represent an ongoing program for the area with which the settlers were in contact. They have been published by the Archaeological Laboratory, Department of Sociology and Anthropology, East Carolina University, Greenville, which has also a number of unpublished reports on file. The published papers include *Archaeological Salvage of an Ossuary at the Baum Site* (October 1980); *The Archaeology of Colington Island* (Archaeological Research Report no. 3, 1981); *Archaeology of the Chowan River Basin: A Preliminary Study* (Archaeological Research Report no. 4, 1982); *A Summary of Colington Phase Sites in the Tidewater Zone of North Carolina* (June 1982); *Archaeology of the Native Americans. Final Report, May 1, 1983–April 30, 1984* (May 1984). Mark A. Mathis and Jeffrey Crow, eds., *The Prehistory of North Carolina: An Archaeological Symposium* (Raleigh: North Carolina Department of Cultural Resources, Division of Archives and History, 1983) is valuable.

The Physical and Natural Environment

For geology the following provide basic information: Horace G. Richards, *Geology of the Coastal Plain of North Carolina* (American Philosophical Transactions 40, no. 1 [Philadelphia, 1950]); and P. M. Brown, *The Geology of Northeastern North Carolina* (Raleigh: Department of Conservation and Development, 1963). The historical geography has been well covered in Gary S. Dunbar, *Geographical History of the Carolina Banks* (Coastal Studies Institute, Louisiana State University, Technical Report no. 8, 1956); and Bruce S. Cheeseman, "Historical Research Report: Four Centuries and Roanoke Island—A Legacy of Geographical Change" (prepared for Cape Hatteras National Seashore, National Park Service, September 1982 [unpublished]). Erosion has complicated the picture of development on the North Carolina coast. A few of the many papers on the subject are P. Dolan and R. Glassen, "Oregon Inlet, N.C.: A History of Coastal Change" (*Southeastern Geographer* 12 [1973]: 41–53); V. Bellis, M. O'Connor, and S. Riggs, *Estuarine Shoreline Erosion in the Albemarle-Pamlico Region of North Carolina* (U.N.C. Sea Grant Program Publication SG-75-29, 1975); R. Dolan and K. Bosserman, "Shoreline Erosion and the Lost Colony" (*Annals of the Association of American Geographers* 62 [1972]: 424–26). William P. Cumming, *North Carolina in Maps* (Raleigh: Department of Archives and History, 1966), provides the basic topographic evidence on the historical cartography of the coastal region, earlier discussed in his *Southeast in Early Maps* (Princeton: Princeton University Press, 1958). David Stick, *The Outer Banks* (Chapel Hill: University of North Carolina Press, 1958), gives an indication of the transformation of the region.

The basic text for the flora is A. E. Radford, H. E. Ahles, and C. R. Bell, *Manual of the Vascular Flora of the Carolinas* (Chapel Hill: University of North Carolina Press, 1968), which is particularly valuable for its distribution maps. A useful introduction to wild-flowers is the Dunes of Dare Garden Club, *Wildflowers of the Outer Banks* (Chapel Hill: University of North Carolina Press, 1980). For birds, John Bull and J. Farrand, *The Audubon Society Guide to Birds of the Eastern Region* (New York: Knopf, 1977); and Roger T. Peterson, *Field Guide to the Birds: Eastern and Central North America* (5th ed., Boston: Houghton Mifflin, 1984), are adequate. E. R. Hall, *Mammals of North America* (2 vols., New York: Wiley-Interscience, 1981); Frank Schwarts and Jim Tyler, *Marine Fishes Common to North Carolina* (Raleigh: North Carolina Department of Natural and Economic Resources, Division of Commercial and Sports Fisheries, 1970); and B. S. Martof, W. H. Palmer, J. R. Bailey, and Julian R. Harrison III, *Amphibians and Reptiles of the Carolinas and Virginia* (Chapel Hill: University of North Carolina Press, 1980), are comprehensive.

Secondary Works

William S. Powell, "Roanoke Colonists and Explorers: An Attempt at Identification" (*North Carolina Historical Review* 34 [1957]: 202–26), is a valuable pioneer attempt, which should be carried further. His *Paradise Preserved: A History of the Roanoke Island Historical Association* (Chapel Hill: University of North Carolina Press, 1965), recounts the history of the historic site and the various activities that have surrounded it. R. A. Skelton, "Ralegh as a Geographer" (*Virginia Magazine of History and Biography* 71 [1961]: 130–49); L. A. Vigneras, "A Spanish Discovery of North Carolina in 1566" (*North Carolina Historical Review* 46 [1969]: 398–414); and K. R. Andrews, *Elizabethan Privateering* (Cambridge: Cambridge University Press, 1964), are of considerable peripheral interest. David B. Durant, *Ralegh's Lost Colony: The Story of the First English Settlements in America* (New York: Atheneum, 1981), David Stick, *Roanoke Island: The Beginnings of English America* (Chapel Hill: University of North Carolina Press, 1983), and Karen O. Kupperman, *Roanoke: A Colony Abandoned* (Totowa, N.J.: Rowman and Allenheld, 1984) are good brief accounts of the Roanoke voyages. John W. Shirley, *Thomas Harriot* (New York: Oxford University Press, 1983) is important, and his *Sir Walter Raleigh and the New World* (Raleigh: Department of Cultural Resources, 1984) is valuable. Robert D. Arner, *The Roanoke Voyages in Literature* (Raleigh: Department of Cultural Resources, 1984) is also of interest.

Papers and books by D. B. Quinn comprise "The Failure of Raleigh's American Colonies," in *Essays in British and Irish History in Honour of J. E. Todd*, edited by H. A. Cronne, T. W. Moody, and D. B. Quinn (London: Muller, 1949); "Preparations for the 1585 Virginia Voyage" (*William and Mary Quarterly* 6 [1949]: 208–36); "Spanish Reactions to English Colonial Enterprises" (*Transactions of the Royal Historical Society*, 5th ser., 1 [1951]: 1–23); "Christopher Newport in 1590" (*North Carolina Historical Review* 29 [1952]: 305–16); "Simão Fernandes, a Portuguese pilot in the English Service, circa 1573–1588" (*Actas, Congresso internacional de história dos Descobrimentos* 3 [Lisbon, 1961]: 277–85); (with Paul H. Hulton) "John White and the English Naturalists" (*History Today* 13 [1962]: 310–20); "Elizabethan Birdman" (*Times Literary Supplement*, 1 April 1965, p. 250); "The Road to Jamestown," in Louis B. Wright, ed., *Shakespeare Celebrated* (Ithaca: Cornell University

Press for Folger Library, 1966), pp. 31–60; (with John W. Shirley) "A Contemporary List of Hariot References" (*Renaissance Quarterly* 22 [1969]: 9–26); "'Virginians' on the Thames in 1603" (*Terrae Incognitae* 2 [1970]: 7–14); "Thomas Hariot and the Virginia Voyages of 1602" (*William and Mary Quarterly*, 3rd ser., 27 [1970]: 268–81); "Thomas Harriot and the New World," in John W. Shirley, ed., *Thomas Harriot: Renaissance Scientist* (Oxford: Oxford University Press, 1974), pp. 36–53; *England and the Discovery of America, 1481–1620* (New York: Knopf, 1974); (with Selma Barkham) "Privateering: The North American Dimension (to 1625)," in M. Mollat, ed., *Course et piraterie* (2 vols., Paris: Commission internationale de l'histoire maritime, 1975); *North America from Earliest Discovery to First Settlements* (New York: Harper and Row, 1977); "Turks, Moors and Others in Drake's West India Voyage" (*Terrae Incognitae* 14 [1982]: 93–100); *The Lost Colonists: Their Fortune and Probable Fate* (Raleigh: Department of Cultural Resources, 1984).

Paul Hulton, *The Watercolor Drawings of John White from the British Museum* (Washington: National Gallery of Art, 1965); "John White, Artist" (*Bulletin of the North Carolina Museum of Art* 5 [Spring–Summer, 1965]: 3–43); *The Work of Jacques Le Moyne de Morgues* (2 vols., London: British Museum, 1977); "Images of the New World: Jacques Le Moyne de Morgues and John White," in K. R. Andrews, N. P. Canny, and P. E. H. Hair, eds. *The Westward Enterprise* (Detroit: Wayne State University Press, 1979), pp. 195–214, are all contributions of value on the graphic record.

The publication program of America's Four Hundredth Anniversary Committee of the North Carolina Department of Cultural Resources includes (besides volumes and pamphlets already published) a monograph by David S. Phelps on the Algonquian Indians of North Carolina and a bibliography of Sir Walter Raleigh, as well as pamphlets by Joyce Youings on the Raleigh country, John Humber on preparations for the voyages, William P. Cumming on the cartography of coastal Carolina, Paul E. Hoffman on Spain and the Raleigh colonies, and William S. and Virginia W. Powell on poetry about Virginia Dare and related subjects.

Miscellaneous Citations in the Notes

Andrews, K. R. "Christopher Newport of Limehouse, Mariner." *William and Mary Quarterly*, 3rd ser., 11 (1954): 3–27.

Axtell, James. "The Ethnohistory of Early America." *William and Mary Quarterly*, 3rd ser., 35 (1978): 110–44.

———. "A Moral History of Indian-White Relations Revisited." *History Teacher* 16 (February 1983): 169–90.

Barbour, Philip L., ed. *The Jamestown Voyages, 1606–1609*. 2 vols. Cambridge: Hakluyt Society, 1969.

Casas, Bartolomé de las. *The Spanish Colonie*. Translated by M. M. S. London: T. Dawson and W. Brome, 1583.

Crosby, Alfred W. "Virgin Soil Epidemics as a Factor in the Aboriginal Depopulation of America." *William and Mary Quarterly*, 3rd ser., 33 (1976): 289–99.

Gibson, Charles. *The Aztecs under Spanish Rule*. Stanford: Stanford University Press, 1964.

Hanke, Lewis. *Aristotle and the American Indian*. London: Hollis and Carter, 1959.

Hayman, Samuel. *Notes and Records of the Ancient Religious Foundations at Youghal*. Youghal, Co. Cork: privately printed, 1855.

Isaac, Rhys. *The Transformation of Virginia, 1740–1790*. Chapel Hill: University of North Carolina Press, 1982.

Kingsbury, Susan M., ed. *Records of the Virginia Company of London*. 4 vols. Washington, D.C.: Library of Congress, 1905–35.

Johnson, Charles H. *The Long Roll*. New York: East Aurora, 1911.

Kirk, Paul J., Jr., ed. *The Great Dismal Swamp*. Charlottesville: University Press of Virginia, 1979.

Laney, Francis B. *The Geology and Ore Deposits of the Virgilina District of Virginia and North Carolina*. Issued as North Carolina Geological and Economic Survey, Bulletin no. 36, and as Virginia Geological Survey, Bulletin no. 14. Lynchburg, Va., 1917.

Lawson, John. *A New Voyage to Carolina*. Edited by Hugh T. Lefler. Chapel Hill: University of North Carolina Press, 1967.

Lewis, C. M., and Loomie, A. J. *The Spanish Jesuit Mission in Virginia, 1570–1572*. Chapel Hill: University of North Carolina Press, 1953.

Lodge, Thomas, and Greene, Robert. *A looking glass for London*. London: B. Alsop, 1596.

Miller, Helen Hill. *Passage to America: Ralegh's Colonists Take Ship for Roanoke*. Raleigh: Department of Cultural Resources, 1983.

Morison, Samuel Eliot. *The European Discovery of America: The Northern Voyages*. New York: Oxford University Press, 1971.

Paradise, N. B. *Thomas Lodge*. New Haven: Yale University Press, 1931.

Porter, Harry C. "Reflections on the Ethnohistory of Early Colonial America." *Journal of American Studies* 16 (1982): 243–54.

Purchas, Samuel. *Hakluytus Posthumus, or Purchas his pilgrimes*. 4 vols. London: W. Stansby for H. Fetherstone, 1625.

Quinn, D. B. "An Anglo-French 'Voyage of Discovery' to North America in 1604–5, and Its Sequel," *Miscellanea offerts à Charles Verlinden à l'Occasion de ses Trente Ans de Professorat*. 2 vols. Ghent: Ghent University Press, 1975. 2:513–34.

————. *The Elizabethans and the Irish*. Ithaca: Cornell University Press, 1966.

————. "The Munster Plantation: Problems and Opportunities." *Journal of the Cork Historical and Archaeological Society* 71 (1966): 19–40.

————, ed. *Richard Hakluyt, Editor: with facsimiles of Richard Hakluyt, Divers Voyages Touching the Discoverie of America (1582), and A Journal of Several Voyages into New France (1580)*. 2 vols. Amsterdam: Theatrum Orbis Terrarum, 1967.

————, ed. *The Voyages and Colonising Enterprises of Sir Humphrey Gilbert*. 2 vols. London: Hakluyt Society, 1940.

————, and Cheshire, N. M. *The New Found Land of Stephen Parmenius*. Toronto: Toronto University Press, 1972.

————, and Quinn, Alison, M., eds. *The English New England Voyages, 1602–1608*. London: Hakluyt Society, 1983.

————, and Ryan, A. N. *England's Sea Empire*. Boston: Allen and Unwin, 1983.

Ralegh, Sir Walter. *The discoveries of the . . . bewtiful empyre of Guiana*. London: R. Robinson, 1596.

_____. *The Poems of Sir Walter Ralegh*. Edited by A. M. C. Latham. Cambridge: Harvard University Press, 1929; revised edition, 1951.

Salisbury, Neal. *Manitou and Providence, 1500–1643*. New York: Oxford University Press, 1982.

Sauer, Carl O. *The Early Spanish Main*. Berkeley: University of California Press, 1966.

Smith, John. *The generall historie of Virginia*. London: I. D. and I. H. for M. Sparkes, 1624.

Strachey, William. *The Historie of Travell into Virginia Britania*. Edited by Louis B. Wright and Virginia Freund. London: Hakluyt Society, 1953.

Sweet, Palmer C. "Abandoned Copper Mines and Prospects in the Virgilina District," *Virginia Minerals* 32 (1976): 35–44.

Wernham, R. B. *The Making of Elizabethan Foreign Policy, 1558–1603*. Berkeley: University of California Press, 1981.

Williams, Talcott. "The Surroundings and Site of Raleigh's Colony." In *Annual Report of the American Historical Association for 1895*. Washington, D.C.: 1896.

Wroth, Lawrence C. *The Voyages of Giovanni da Verrazzano*. New Haven: Yale University Press, 1970.